CHINESE
POLITICAL
CULTURE

Studies on Contemporary China

Titles in this series are concerned with China in the second half of the twentieth century, but may also reach back to the roots of the communist movement from the 1920s on.

For a complete listing of titles in this series, see the back of the book.

Erratum

The following figure should appear in place of the one shown on page 253 of Chinese Political Culture, 1989-2000, *edited by Shiping Hua (Armonk, NY: M.E. Sharpe, Inc. 2001):*

Figure 9.3 **Provincial Gazette Publications in Qing and PRC** (titles; percentage in national total)

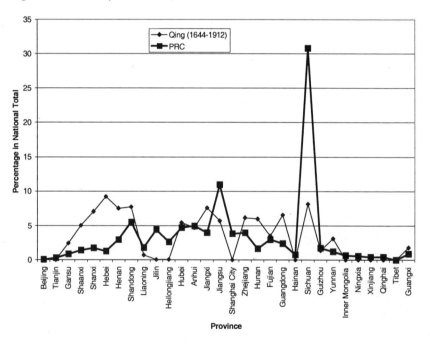

Source: Chu Shih-chia, "Compilations of Chinese Local Gazettes," *Shih-hsueh nien-pao*, 1 (June 30, 1932); *Zhongguo xinfangzhi mulu* (Beijing: Shumu wenxian chubanshe, 1993).

Studies on Contemporary China

CHINESE POLITICAL CULTURE
— 1989-2000 —

SHIPING HUA, EDITOR

Roger Ames
Yu-tzung Chang
Godwin Chu
Yun-han Chu
Edward Friedman
Huixin Ke
Cheng Li

Alan P.L. Liu
Kam Louie
Kalpana Misra
Peter Moody, Jr.
Chih-yu Shih
Wenfang Tang
Jonathan J.H. Zhu

Foreword by Andrew J. Nathan

AN EAST GATE BOOK

M.E.Sharpe
Armonk, New York
London, England

An East Gate Book

Copyright © 2001 by M. E. Sharpe, Inc.

Library of Congress Cataloging-in-Publication Data

Chinese political culture, 1989–2000 / edited by Shiping Hua.
   p. cm.
"An east gate book."
Includes bibliographical references and index.
ISBN 0-7656-0565-1 (alk. paper) — ISBN 0-7656-0566-X (pbk. : alk. paper)
   1. Political culture—China. I. Hua, Shiping, 1956–

JQ1516.C4528 2001   2001020049
306.2´0951—dc21   CIP

Printed in the United States of America

The paper used in this publication meets the minimum requirements of
American National Standard for Information Sciences
Permanence of Paper for Printed Library Materials,
ANSI Z 39.48-1984.

BM (c) 10   9   8   7   6   5   4   3   2   1
BM (p) 10   9   8   7   6   5   4   3   2   1

For my parents: Hua Jingwen and He Suxia

Contents

viii

List of Tables and Figures

Tables

Figures

Foreword

Andrew J. Nathan

An important part of American identity is, to adapt the words of our national poet Walt Whitman, that we "contain multitudes." But this is perhaps even more true of China, a nation that Americans often quite wrongly imagine as homogeneous. China is a land where identity matters intensely, but also a land of contending and layered identity options of unending complexity. A person can be both Chinese and not-Chinese (a Chinese citizen but a member of an ethnic minority), or can be Chinese simultaneously at many positions along a hierarchy of nested regional loyalties—Toisanese, Cantonese, Guangdongese, southern Chinese, overseas Chinese. The notion of "Chinese" can be political, ethnic, or cultural. Indeed, the neo-Confucian scholar Tu Wei-ming once proposed that anyone who values Chinese civilization can be considered Chinese.

In relating to Chinese culture, a person may position him- or herself as traditional-minded, neo-traditionalist, modern, postmodern, or at other places along a multidimensional spectrum of relationships to tradition. Nor is this tradition itself a single, fixed thing. It is diversely conceived and richly imagined and re-imagined. For a Chinese who thinks of him- or herself as traditional, for example, that identity might refer to the Confucian tradition or the Buddhist one, or to ancestor worship, Mazu worship, or simply to certain ideas about gender relations. Today, a traditionalist could even be someone who believes in the ideals Mao stood for, although these constitute an ideal that has never been practiced.

It is often said that the Chinese are collectivists, but we will find among them the most radical individualists, both today and in the philosophical tradition. It is said that they are authoritarians, but they are also strong democrats. They are nationalists—but also national skeptics. They are secularists, but also highly religious; peace-lovers, yet also willing to shed blood in conflict.

Scholars have argued for a long time about what makes Chinese culture distinctive. If culture as it is discussed in this book is in the first instance identity, identity always implies ideologies and values, attitudes and beliefs, perceptions and cognitions. Culture in such a broadly-defined sense cannot be captured by survey research, but surveys can certainly tell us something about it. It cannot be succinctly characterized as either one thing or another, and it tends to elude comparison because it involves so many registers of thought and emotion.

As the initial invocation of Whitman suggests, there is a sense in which Chinese and American cultures are similar—their diversity. One could also identify many specific values and beliefs held in common by many Chinese and Americans—or for that matter, Russians and Britons. In the end, however, one thing that all Chinese have that others lack is the conviction of their own Chineseness. Chinese know who they are.

This identity as a Chinese is as powerful a self-marker as the substance of Chineseness is multiform. But the identity is held in common not because of what the Chinese have in common but because of their common participation in a series of debates, choices, dilemmas, and disagreements. Difference brings them together.

This book attempts to make sense of this embarrassment of riches through a series of deeply informed essays on contemporary experiences of being Chinese. The structure of the book implies not only the diversity of Chinese political culture (Part III), but also the historical (Part I) and the contemporary (Part II) factors that contributed to this culture. In Part I, Kam Louie explores the multiple, and very modern, meanings that have been projected onto a traditional icon, Confucius. Centering on the traditional Chinese concept of *zhong* (loyalty), Godwin Chu analyzes a new individualistic assertiveness which is emerging under the shadow of the ruling Party's authoritarianism. Roger Ames explores recent reconsiderations of Confucianism which attempt to preserve this ancient philosophy by putting it into conversation with ideas from the modern West.

The essays in Part II suggest the range of options available today to ideologically engaged Chinese. Even while trying to shake off the iron shoes of Marxist orthodoxy, Chinese have found a remarkable range of ideas to believe in. Edward Friedman excavates levels of the complex syndrome of patriotism. Kalpana Misra provides insight into new-wave ideas of neo-Maoism and neo-conservatism which seem so retrograde to observers in the West, but which make sense as responses to China's contemporary dilemmas when understood in historical context. Peter Moody shows that to reject politics is to know that politics dominates Chinese life, as it has for decades. Jonathan Zhu and Huixin Ke show us how much, or how little, different parts of China know about an area that is culturally and politically Chinese, yet separate and different, Hong Kong.

Diverse identities and their linking threads are the subject of Part III—how Chinese people variously locate themselves in relationship to geographic space and historical time, in relationship to the political sphere, to the contemporary world of work, and hence in relationship to one another. For Cheng Li, to forge new roles as entrepreneurs requires seeking legitimations in terms of existing values. Alan P.L. Liu suggests that to reject overarching Chineseness in favor of a regional identity is still to accept a Chinese identity, since the regions are parts of China. Chih-yu Shih shows that to practice the competitive art of elections is to reaffirm the importance of the community within which that election takes place. Wenfang Tang introduces us to the wide range of religious attitudes in the Chinese world and the diverse ways in which religious belief interacts with political and economic attitudes. Yun-han Chu and Yu-tzung Chang explore the range of attitudes toward democratic legitimacy in four different political regions of larger cultural China—Hong Kong, Taiwan, mainland China, and the urban sub-population of the mainland. In short, each of these chapters in its own way illustrates how Chinese culture is a diversity within unity, a pattern of choices within a common matrix.

In each of these essays Chinese thinking appears paradoxical, but makes sense when its internal logic is deeply understood. Those of us who were lucky enough early in our lives to be steered into careers that centered on getting to know China have found our quest to be toward an ever-receding horizon. But this has been so in a rewarding rather than in a frustrating sense. As we see in this book, getting to know China increasingly means getting to know the Chinese in all their remarkable diversity of commitment and belief. In that sense this book represents a new generation of studies, one which puts us closer to the disparate world of Chinese culture as it is really lived.

Acknowledgments

I am grateful to Dr. Lucian W. Pye, whose works in Chinese political culture have inspired me since my college years. His encouragement and support for the current book were important. I am indebted to Dr. Lloyd W. Chapin, Vice President and Dean of Faculty at Eckerd College, who provided faculty development funds for this book. Dr. Tom Oberhofer, Chairman of Behavioral Science Collegium at Eckerd College, also provided some financial support. I am grateful to Linda O'Bryant, the secretary of the Collegium of Behavioral Sciences, Helen Gold, the librarian at Eckerd College, and Anna Engholm, my student work scholar, for their clerical support. Many friends and colleagues have either read parts of the book or shared their ideas with me regarding it. Finally, I am indebted to my wife Jia Qin, who has shared with me my joys and sorrows since I came to the United States in December 1987. Her spiritual support and practical advice have always been important for what I have done in my career, especially for this book.

S.H.

CHINESE POLITICAL CULTURE

Introduction: Some Paradigmatic Issues in the Study of Chinese Political Culture

Shiping Hua

Culture has played an extremely important role in Chinese social transformations in modern times. The "culture" here mainly refers to the political aspects of culture, not its non-political dimensions, such as diet, sports, or architecture.[1] In the Chinese context, the transformation of culture, or political culture, is often considered to be the key to the transformation of society. This situation was demonstrated clearly in China's three major social transformations in recent history.

The first took place from 1898, when Kang Youwei and Liang Qichao led the 100–Day Reform, to 1927, when the First Civil War broke out. In the half century between the 1840 Opium War and 1898, the Chinese ruling elites attempted no serious social reform. The so-called "Chinese studies as substance, Western studies for practical use" or *zhong ti xi yong*, effectively prevented profound social transformations of any kind.[2] The 100–Day Reform was a product of the failure of this policy of introducing Western technology without changing society fundamentally. The attempts at reforming China's political system failed with the collapse of the Qing Dynasty in 1911 and the elites' inability to establish a workable republic shortly afterwards.

These failures in reforming the political system finally led to the New Culture Movement (*xin wenhua yundong*), which was heralded by the

May Fourth Movement in 1919, with the new understanding that political reform couldn't be achieved without a transformation of people's political consciousness. This cultural transformation was characterized by a strong renunciation of China's cultural tradition and by an embracement of Western values, whether liberalism led by Hu Shi or communism led by Chen Duxiu. This transformation of culture was again a failure, partly due to the several decades of domestic turmoil brought about by two civil wars and the war against the Japanese.

The second major social transformation was the communist one led by Mao Zedong from 1949, when the mainland of China was united again, to 1976, when Mao died. The Mao regime struggled constantly to reform the Chinese society through various campaigns: the Hundred Flowers Movement in 1956–57, the Collectivization Movement in 1956–57, and the Great Leap Forward in 1958. Again, the epitome of Mao's communist social transformation was a cultural event: the Great Proletarian Cultural Revolution (1966–76). The so-called "Four Olds" (*si jiu*)—old ideas, old culture, old customs, and old habits—had to be eliminated. The "Four Olds" referred to not only China's Confucian tradition but also the Western influences which came after China's opening up to the outside world in the mid nineteenth century. The Cultural Revolution failed with the death of Mao.

The third transformation was the capitalism-oriented reform started by Deng Xiaoping in 1978. As was the case with the first two social transformations, Deng's reform started with non-cultural things such as technology and economics. But as the reform progressed, culture was on the top of the agenda again. The so-called "Cultural Fever" (*wenhua re*) and "The Great Debate on Culture" (*wenhua da taolun*) in the 1980s were demonstrations of this situation. This cultural fever was interrupted by the 1989 government crackdown on Tiananmen.

Thereafter, it was widely believed among China watchers that the 1990s were a period of real pragmatism. However, as the decade approached its end, the world was again in shock to discover another huge cultural event: in merely seven years, millions of Chinese were converted to the so called Falun Gong, a Qigong and quasi religion started by Li Hongzhi.[3] Hardly has any religion in human history succeeded in converting so many followers in such a short period of time. Culture has played such an important role in contemporary Chinese politics that the philosopher and historian Tu Wei-ming commented that although economics is the driving force of reform, culture determines the direction.[4]

The importance of political culture in social transformation is acknowl-edged even by economy-determinist orthodox Marxism, which views people's consciousness as having a powerful counter-effect on their economic activities. Sometimes, it was said, this counter-effect can be decisive.[5]

In spite of its importance, Western studies about Chinese political culture have been inadequate. The existing Western literature on the subject all deals with some specific aspects of the Chinese political cul-ture. For instance, we have book titles like *Cosmology and Political Culture in Early China, Popular Protest and Political Culture in Mod-ern China, Anarchism and Chinese Political Culture*, and so on. No com-prehensive study of Chinese political culture in the 1990s exists in the English-language sources. The present volume fills that vacuum. The authors of this book include scholars from a variety of origins: some from the West, others originally from China but now, having received their education in the West, teaching in American universities, and still others educated in the West but currently based in mainland China, Tai-wan, and Hong Kong. This mixture provides the readers with some uniquely different perspectives. In terms of disciplines, most of the contributers come from political science, although some are from phi-losophy, Asian Studies, and mass communication. Knowledge is inter-disciplinary, especially in the field of China studies.

This book addresses some important questions regarding the Chinese political culture. What is political culture conceptually? What are the characteristics that distinguish political culture in China from its coun-terparts in other societies? Is there one Chinese political culture or many? What are the factors that have an impact on the remolding of it, and how can we study it methodologically?

What Is Political Culture?

The term *political culture* is hard to define. First used by Gabriel Al-mond in 1956 (Almond 1956, 391–409), there has been no consensus as to what it really means. Generally speaking, one group of scholars tends to define political culture in a broader way. For instance, Almond be-lieves that political culture consists of the set of subjective orientations to politics among people. It includes knowledge and beliefs about po-litical reality, feelings with respect to politics, and commitments to po-litical values (Almond 1990, 144).

For Lucian W. Pye, political culture is the set of attitudes, beliefs, and sentiments which give order and meaning to a political process and provide the underlying assumptions and rules that govern behavior in the political system. It encompasses both the political ideals and the operating norms of a polity. These areas are "public opinion, political ideology, national ethos and the basic consensus, values, and constitutional integrating sentiments of a people" (Pye 1972, 287). It is the manifestation in aggregate form of the psychological and subjective dimensions of politics (Pye 1961, 218).

Another group of scholars tends to define the term in a narrower way. Lowell Dittmer believes that the key to understanding political culture lies in the determination of which empirical variables should be analyzed. This requires that political culture be separated both from political structure and from political psychology (Dittmer 1977, 552–553). Apparently, Dittmer's definition excludes the psychological dimension inherent to Pye's view, but then Pye's studies may be questioned on account of their being "tainted with Freudian insights" (Pye 1992, x). Another scholar, Stephen Chilton, lays out nine criteria for defining political culture, with the key criterion being "objective testability" (Chilton 1988, 419–445). This strong emphasis on objective testing may exclude political ideology from political culture, because it is hard to study through objective testing. Chilton's definition is also a departure from that of Richard Wilson, who views political culture as consisting essentially of political ideology (Nathan 1993, 931).

This lack of consensus on just what constitutes political culture has caused some methodological problems: If we don't know what it is, how can we study it methodologically? The disagreement over definitions centers on the scientific nature of political culture studies.[6] The viewpoint which defines political culture in a narrower way is in accordance with the fact that political culture study in the West after World War II has "moved in the direction of making [the concept of political culture] clearer and more usable as a focus for empirical hypothesis testing." It was said that any attempt at scientific development, including efforts primarily involved in the task of promoting conceptual development, should involve some kind of empirical referent (Stern, Dobson and Scioli 1973, 493–499).

Apparently, the narrower definition calls for a positivist approach while the broader definition is more methodologically inclusive. Either approach has its inherent advantages as well as its problems. The narrower, if applied properly, has the advantage of being scientifically rigorous. The disadvantage is that some important areas of the study may be left out because they are not easy to study scientifically. The narrower approach gained favor under the Behavioral Revolution, which has brought about many changes in social science research: in terms of research approach, it is more micro than macro; in terms of research target, public opinion towards politics was given more attention, often at the expense of in-depth analysis; in terms of the criteria for research, quantitative methods were stressed more, often at the expense of qualitative ones (Isaak 1985).

Survey research, which is the most frequently used positivist method in the study of political culture in the West, has the advantage of being empirical and quantifiable, but it also has its inherent deficiencies. Survey research can't go back in time, for instance, and suffers as well both from an intrinsic inability to identify attributes which are or might be culturally unique, except in a trivial sense, and a tendency to overly simplify those attributes which can be defined (Nathan and Shi 1993, 97). Clifford Geertz calls this kind of analysis "thin description," in contrast to hermeneutic methods, which he labels "thick description" (Chilton 1988, 423). The broader approach has the advantage of being flexible in terms of methodology so that important areas will be covered. The disadvantage is that some methods, such as the interpretative method, are sometimes hard to separate from speculation.

While the narrower definition of political culture largely refers to public opinion, the broader definition refers to various dimensions of political consciousness. Almond, for instance, divides political culture into the three dimensions of cognition, affection, and evaluation (Almond 1990, 144). Political scientists want to know whether people understand the political system or not, whether people love or hate the system, and how they evaluate the system. Such an approach can be viewed as an attempt to cut the "pie" of political culture horizontally.

In addition, political culture can also be divided vertically from bottom up into the three levels of the subconscious, the conscious-unsystematic, and the conscious-systematic (Hua 1999, 23–41). At the deepest level of political consciousness, people can have political attitudes without realizing them. A Chinese peasant can behave like a Confucianist without reading a single word by Confucius. This is close to political psychology. At the conscious-unsystematic level, people can have unorganized, sometimes inconsistent political attitudes. People can prefer to have comprehensive welfare for everybody but also be against any attempt to raise taxes. Political culture at this level is close to public opinion. At the top level, i.e., the conscious-systematic level, people can have a very systematic understanding of the political system. It is conscious because people are keenly aware of it; it is systematic because it is highly consistent. This dimension of Chinese political consciousness is often called political ideology.

If political culture can be viewed in a broader perspective like this, the research methods that can be used will be more inclusive. In addition to the positivist method, we can also resort to an interpretative method, hermeneutics, and ideological analysis.[7] In addition, these methods can be applied to the study of political culture correspondingly at different levels. At the subconscious level of political culture, the interpretative-hermeneutics method is a better choice. At the conscious-unsystematic level, positivist methods, especially surveys, are preferable, because public opinion is more straightforward. At the top level of people's political consciousness, the interpretative-hermeneutics, even ideological models, can be used.

With this picture in mind, which methodological approach should be adopted in the study of Chinese political culture? Such study in the post–World War II West differed from both the narrower and the broader approach, although it tilts towards the latter. This is the result of both historical factors and academic ones. Chinese political culture has unique characteristics that call for a different methodological approach, and post-war studies of it therefore evolved differently from studies of other societies. That this is true, however, does not mean that Chinese political culture needs to be studied with some magic methods which are uniquely Chinese. Rather, it is necessary to adopt methods eclectically in accordance with historical situations.

From a historical perspective, the Western methodological approaches to Chinese political culture studies can be put into the two general categories of positivism and hermeneutics. In a departure from the study of political culture in other societies, especially Western societies, interpretative-hermeneutics methods until quite recently were the main approach while the positivist method was on the margin (Nathan 1993, 925). This situation is related to at least two factors. Firstly, China until two decades ago was closed to the outside world. It was impossible for Western scholars to do *civic culture* type surveys in China. Internally, the Chinese government relied on reports by the Party apparatus to know the mentality of the Chinese people. Secondly, China lacked the resources as well as the technology to do massive public opinion surveys. This situation implies that it was appropriate for Western researchers to rely mainly on hermeneutic-interpretative methods before China's opening up to the outside world in 1978.

Because of Deng Xiaoping's reform in the last two decades, however, Chinese society is a lot more open, and it is now possible for Western scholars to do public opinion surveys on a regular basis. In addition, the weakened Party apparatus makes it hard for the CCP center to rely on internal reports. China's more abundant resources now also enable those scholars based in China to do similar studies. Therefore, more and more Chinese political culture studies have adopted positivist methods in recent years.

If there are historical reasons for Chinese political culture studies to be methodologically inclusive, academic reasons also exist. In particular, the unique attributes of Chinese political culture make it necessary to adopt an eclectic methodology.

What Are the Characteristics of Chinese Political Culture?

It is very difficult to characterize Chinese political culture. In terms of time, there are at least three major divisions: traditional Confucian political culture, Maoist communist political culture, and the reform political culture of the last two decades. The continuities as well as the changes between these periods are discussed in parts one and two of this book. In terms of social strata, there are at least two political cultures, that of the ruling elites and that of the masses. This is discussed in Cheng Li's chapter in part three. In terms of geography, China has about half a dozen areas with each having its own unique political culture. This is reflected clearly in part three.

Given its diversity, Chinese political culture tends to defy generalization. However, some distinct characteristics exist. We will examine briefly China's contemporary political culture in accordance with the two divisions of political culture: the horizontal division of the cognitive, the affective, and the evaluative, and the vertical division of the subconscious, the conscious-unsystematic, and the conscious-systematic. Since it is impossible to characterize the Chinese political culture in the small space available here, my main focus is on methodology: Why do we study the Chinese political culture the way we do?

First of all, Chinese cognition about political systems has always been difficult to measure. In Maoist China, people were required to spend a lot more time studying national politics than were Westerners. Nevertheless, only certain kinds of information were revealed to the people. More time spent in political studies does not equal more political knowledge. That was why during the 1990s, insiders' published stories about court politics and the private lives of Chinese leaders during the Mao regime were best sellers: such information had not been available to the masses previously.[8] The situation was a lot better during the Deng period, but still, people's information about national politics was influenced very much by the officially controlled media.

The evaluative dimension of political culture in China is also hard to measure. In the West, dissatisfaction with the government is reflected through demonstrations, the media, and elections, and researchers can rely on such tools as surveys to measure the level of popular satisfaction/dissatisfaction. During the Mao era, everybody in China seemed to have a positive evaluation of the regime on the surface, but this can be very far from the truth. Again, the situation in the reform era was a lot better, but open criticism of the regime remained difficult. That's why social critics sometimes resorted to indirect means to criticize national politics. For instance, the Oscar-nominated film *Farewell, My Concubine* conveyed a very critical political message through the story plot: the CCP is not as good as the KMT, and the KMT is not as good as the Japanese during the occupation period (Hua 1998).

Chinese affection for politics is in a similar situation. In the West, people's disgust with politics is reflected in lower voter turn-out, demonstrations, and media criticism. In China, official media are unlikely to carry negative viewpoints. Therefore, people resort to indirect ways. In the 1990s, anti-politics literature, represented by Wang Shuo's works, which reflected people's disgust with national politics, was very popular among the people. Peter Moody's chapter discusses this. Although mainstream political culture research methods from the West, such as public opinion surveys, have become more and more possible in China, they are sometimes less helpful than interpretative and hermeneutics-based approaches.

In addition to analysis along the horizontal dimension, political culture can be divided vertically from bottom up into the subconscious, the conscious-unsystematic, and the conscious-systematic. First of all, people don't have to be aware of their consciousness. Even if they are, the consciousness does not have to be real. During the Cultural Revolution, the

Red Guards, who were supposed to be the least traditional and the most communistic of comrades, displayed a loyalty towards Mao very similar to that which loyal subjects displayed towards the Emperor in imperial times. During the 1989 Beijing Spring, the student demonstrators who were supposed to be the most radically pro-West displayed some traditional traits too. In contrast to the behavior of the protesters in other former communist countries such as Romania, where demonstrators confronted the dictator in direct ways, three Chinese student representatives presented their petition by kneeling down for forty minutes in front of the Great Hall of the People while the leaders were holding a meeting (Wu 1989, 29). Most of the time, these Chinese youths were not aware of their traditional Chinese consciousness. Thus, survey questionnaires may be less helpful than hermeneutics methods in understanding this dimension of people's consciousness.

Because of China's rich cultural tradition, hermeneutics is especially useful as a tool to understand the subconscious dimension of Chinese political culture. Through analyzing such Chinese classics as *Shui Hu Zhuan* (The water margin) and *Xi You Ji* (The story of the monkey), Lucian Pye and Nathan Leites discuss the unique Chinese notion of "bungling," meaning that the Chinese believe that power lies external to the self (Pye and Leites 1982, 1150–1151).

Literature is not only a reflection of people's mentality but also an agent for remolding people's consciousness through indoctrination (*jiao hua*). Traditionally, China does not have a dominant religion. Indoctrination has to rely on an official ideology, the family, and literature. For this reason, literature is more important for the Chinese than for citizens of any other country (Bai 1992, 42). This situation makes literature an even more important vehicle for hermeneutics studies about people's deep political consciousness. In the West, where the Christian church traditionally is the main agent for remolding people's consciousness, ideological indoctrination through arts and literature is not as strong as in China.

Literature has played a crucial role in all of the three major social transformation periods in China. During the first, one of the most noted leaders was Lu Xun, whose stories such as *A Q Zheng Zhuan* (The true story of Ah Q) and *Kuang Ren Ri Ji* (The diary of a madman) served as social criticisms. During the second transformation period, i.e., the communist social transformation, the *Eight Revolutionary Model Operas* by Jiang Qing served as the artistic representation of communist ideology.

During the third period, i.e., the reform era, we had *He Shang* (Yellow River elegy) and *Ke Wang* (Yearning), which represent the ideological orientations towards the West and the Chinese cultural tradition, respectively (Hua 1991).

The study of public opinion, or the so-called conscious-unsystematic level of political culture, also has some unique characteristics. In recent years, many fruitful studies have been done using positivist methods. For instance, from 1979 to 1991, scholars in China conducted at least 181 surveys concerning political attitudes (Nathan and Shi 1993). In spite of the similarities, survey research in China differs significantly from that of the West. While it is common to ask a citizen from a Western country questions like "Have you taken part in any political protests or demonstrations?" researchers cannot do so in China's mainland, for political reasons. Some unique phenomena in mainland China, for instance, *tanpai*, or extra legal taxation, require specially designed questionnaires. Foreign researchers conducting surveys need the cooperation of Chinese who are very liberal-minded on the one hand, and take some risk with the government on the other hand. Due to political reasons, it is sometimes hard to do probability sampling in China (Manion 1994, 746).

The study of the conscious-systematic dimension of Chinese political culture, or official ideology, also requires special consideration. Students of China in the West often start their research with a study of Chinese official ideology. Compared with ideologies of other non-Western societies, Confucianism has received the most attention by Western scholars (Pye 1992, 14; 31). This is not accidental. An understanding of Chinese ideology is often the key to understanding Chinese politics. This strong emphasis on an official ideology continues to the present and is reflected in the three major social transformations in China's modern history. For the first social transformation, one needs only to open up the newspapers and magazines of the 1920s: the pages are full of debates between "isms": Marxism, liberalism, anarchism, socialism, communism, scientism, and so on. These are all ideological debates. The Maoist social transformation was a constant fight between socialism, communism, and capitalism. The Dengist social transformation started with seeking truth: practice is the sole criterion of truth. Questions concerning "truths" are often ideological ones.

This situation is different from the studies not only of Western developed countries but also of such countries as Japan or Mexico. In the

West, the political system is supposed to be separate from political ideologies. It is a forum wherein political groups with different ideological tendencies might contend. In the cases of Japan and Mexico, neither the Liberal Democratic Party (LDP) nor the Institutional Revolutionary Party (PRI) is an ideological party. Yet, both have been the dominant parties during most of the time after World War II.

In the case of Mexico, the PRI adopted drastically different policies before and after the early 1980s in response to domestic and international pressures—first import substitution and then structural adjustment. In the case of Japan, for many years after World War II, the most distinct policy difference that separates the LDP from other parties is a foreign policy one—the American occupation of Japan (Hauss 2000, 190–225; 468–502). In contrast, both the CCP and the KMT are ideological parties, although one can argue that China during the reform era does not have a stable official ideology either. But while Japan and Mexico can tolerate the lack of an official ideology, China can't. The Falun Gong case is a demonstration of this.

The Chinese political ideologies are so developed that their structures can be more easily seen than those of other societies. Sometimes ideological models can be constructed. All ideologies have the philosophical starting points of either the subjective or the objective; all ideologies have the political starting points of either left or right. At the center of these is man himself (Hua 1999; Almond 1990).

Summary of the Book

Diverse in terms of not only methodological orientations, but also of political persuasions, this book is divided into three parts. The first part deals with China's tradition and how this tradition has influenced contemporary Chinese political culture. For so many years, the maxim in the China field was "China is China is China," meaning China is different from any other country in the world. Apparently, the uniqueness largely lies with China's tradition.

Kam Louie argues that Confucianism has embodied different things during different time periods. In China's ancient past, the image of Confucius was that of a sage and a teacher. During the reform period, however, an ideal Confucian man could very well be a businessman. Godwin Chu traces the development of the concept of *zhong* from ancient China to the present day. The loyalty demonstrated among the people in China's ancient times and that during the Mao era are similar.

During the reform period, however, most Chinese have finally given up blind loyalty to the state. In line with the discussions of Louie and Chu, Roger Ames discusses the philosophical roots in Confucianism that makes this adaptability possible. Ames argues that Confucianism is very different from Greek philosophy in the sense that it is not analytical but biographical.

The second part of the book deals with the socialization process. In addition to China's cultural tradition, socialization plays an important role in the remolding of people's political consciousness. The important agents in this socialization include family, schools, government, church, and the media. For our purposes, we have chosen three papers that deal with the Chinese socialization process from the perspectives of the official ideologies, literature, and the media.

Edward Friedman and Kalpana Misra deal with the official ideologies of nationalism, Neo-Maoism, and Neo-Conservatism in contemporary China. Friedman argues that nationalism as an official ideology was used by not only the Mao regime but also the post-Mao regimes for the purpose of nation-building. This strategy could have very serious negative results. Misra argues that with the government's crackdown on Tiananmen and the collapse of Soviet and Eastern European communism, two official trends have emerged from the ruling elites: Neo-Maoism and Neo-Conservatism. The neo-Maoists picked up those old Maoist slogans such as "class struggle" and the "guard against the restoration of capitalism in China," while the Neo-Conservatism group agreed with the reform but was opposed to democratization.

Peter Moody deals with the role played by literature in the remolding of Chinese political culture. Instead of looking at the Chinese political culture from the official perspective as Friedman and Misra do, Moody looks at it from the un-official perspective, that of the counter-culture. Analyzing the literary works by Wang Shuo and Wang Meng, Moody points out that the antipolitical tendencies embodied in their works were a response to the politicization of the Cultural Revolution.

Based on a public opinion survey in Beijing, Shanghai, Guangzhou, and Shenzhen in 1995, Jonathan Jian-Hua Zhu and Huixin Ke found that exposure to Hong Kong television leads to an increase in factually based knowledge about Hong Kong, while exposure to the Chinese media induces subjective knowledge.

The third part of the book comprises comparative political culture studies: that between the elites and the masses and that between different areas. Cheng Li discusses the formation as well as the behavioral traits of the Chinese new entrepreneurs. He divides these entrepreneurs into several groups: "self-made entrepreneurs," "bureaucratic entrepreneurs," and "technical entrepreneurs." Not only do the Chinese entrepreneurs behave differently from the masses, they also manifest various behavior patterns within themselves.

The rest of the chapters in this part are comparative political culture studies in terms of areas.

Alan Liu puts the political cultures in China's different provinces into the four categories of modernism, traditionalism, parochialism, and separatism. The modernist identity is largely demonstrated in the southeastern provinces; the traditionalist political culture is shown in the North and Northeast; the parochial political culture is largely demonstrated in Shaanxi, Gansu, Guizhou, and Guangxi; the separatist political culture is demonstrated in Inner Mongolia, Ningxia, Xinjiang, and Tibet. Liu argues that dependency, not disintegration, is the real problem for the post-Mao regime. Except for regions like Tibet, most of the provinces have very weak provincial identities and so are highly dependent on the central government for support.

Chih-yu Shih's paper is based on interviews in three minority areas in China and one in Taiwan. He found that electoral competition is of value in none of these four minority areas—integration and unity are the major concerns. This is drastically different from the situation in the West. Based on some recent surveys in the mainland and Taiwan, Wenfang Tang has found that the Chinese government's efforts to reduce religiosity was effective in the sense that China's mainland is much less religious than Taiwan. Within the mainland, however, the South is more religious than the North. This means that local tradition can also have an impact on people's religiosity. Yun-han Chu and Yu-tzung Chang's paper is a comparative study of the political cultures in the mainland, Taiwan, and Hong Kong. Based on a survey conducted in the 1990s, the authors found that people in the mainland have a stronger affinity with the state than do the Chinese in Hong Kong and Taiwan.

Notes

1. Of course, people can make the argument that these things can be political, too. Nevertheless, these things apply to politics in a remote sense, and in extreme cases.

2. This policy was initiated by Zhang Zhidong, a governor in the late Qing era.

3. According to figures from the Falun Gong, over 100 million people were converted. The Chinese government's estimate is several million (Hua and Xia 1999).

4. Cited in Cheng Li's chapter.

5. There are many schools of Marxist thought. Here, I am referring to the version that probably has origins with Engels and then was developed by the Marxists in the former Soviet Union. One major feature of this school of Marxism is its strong emphasis on economics. That is, the economic base has a decisive impact on the superstructure (Engels 1970).

6. For a discussion of the limitations of positivist methods, see Kuhn (1962, 2–4).

7. The terms *interpretative* and *hermeneutics* sometimes are used interchangeably. But the latter may have the connotation of textual analysis. We can also use models to explain well developed ideologies. See Hua (1999).

8. Good examples are Quan Yanchi's books on Mao, Zhou, etc.

References

Almond, Gabriel. 1956. "Comparative Political System." *Journal of Politics* 18, no. 3 (August): 391–409.

———.1990. *A Discipline Divided: Schools and Sects in Political Science.* Newbury Park, CA: Sage Publications.

Almond, Gabriel, and Sidney Verba. 1963. *The Civic Culture: Political Attitudes and Democracy in Five Nations.* Princeton: Princeton University Press.

Bai, Hua. 1992. "China's Contemporary Literature." In H. Martin, ed. *Modern Chinese Writers: Self-portryals.* Armonk, NY: M.E. Sharpe.

Chilton, Stephen. 1988. "Defining Political Culture." *The Western Political Quarterly* 41, no.3 (September).

Dittmer, Lowell. 1977. "Political Culture and Political Symbolism: Toward a Theoretical Synthesis." *World Politics* 29, no. 4 (July).

Engels, Frederick. 1970. *Ludwig Feuerbach and the Outcome of Classical German Philosophy.* New York: International Publishers.

Harding, Harry. 1984. "The Study of Chinese Politics: Toward a Third Generation of Scholarship." *World Politics* 36, no. 1 (January).

Hauss, Charles. 2000. *Comparative Politics: Domestic Responses to Global Challenges.* 3rd edition. Belmont, CA: Wadsworth.

Hua, Shiping. 1991. "In Search of Chineseness: A Tale of Two TV Shows." *East West Center Views* 1, no. 4 (November–December).

———. 1998. "The Politics of Gender in the Chinese New Cinema" (Zhongguo xindianying zhong de zhengzhi), *Hong Kong Journal of Social Sciences* (Xianggang shehui kexue xuebao), no. 12 (Autumn 1998): 53–65.

———. 1999. "Definition and Methodology of Political Culture Theory: A Case Study of Sinology." *Asian Thought and Society* 24, no. 70 (January–April): 23–41.

Hua, Shiping, and Xia Ming. 1999. "The Battle Between the Chinese Government and the Falun Gong," *Chinese Law and Government* 32, no. 6 (September–October).

———. "Falun Gong: Qigong, Code of Ethics and Religion." *Chinese Law and Government* 32, no. 7 (November–December).

Huang, Philip C.C. 1991. "The Paradigmatic Crisis in Chinese Studies." *Modern China* 17, no.3 (July).

Isaak, Alan C. 1985. *Scope and Methods of Political Science.* Belmont, CA: Wadsworth Publishing Company.

Johnson, Chalmers. 1992. "What's Wrong with Chinese Political Studies." *Asian Survey* 22, no. 10 (October).

Kuhn, Thomas. 1962. *The Structure of Scientific Revolutions.* Chicago: The University of Chicago Press.

Lu, Xun. 1977. *Selected Stories of Lu Hsun.* New York: W.W. Norton & Company.

Manion, Melanie. 1994. "Survey Research in the Study of Contemporary China: Learning from Local Samples." *The China Quarterly,* no.139 (September).

Moody, Peter. 1994. "Trends in the Study of Chinese Political Culture." *The China Quarterly,* no. 139 (September).

Nathan, Andrew J. 1993. "Is Chinese Culture Distinctive?" *The Journal of Asian Studies* 52, no. 4 (November).

Nathan, Andrew J., and Tianjian Shi. 1993. "Cultural Requisites for Democracy in China: Findings from a Survey." *Daedalus* 122, no.2 (Spring).

Pye, Lucian W. 1961. *International Encyclopedia of the Social Sciences 12.* New York: Macmillan Co. and The Free Press.

———. 1972. "Culture and Political Science: Problems in the Evaluation of the Concept of Political Culture." *Social Science Quarterly* 53, no.4 (September).

———. 1992. *The Spirit of Chinese Politics- New Edition.* Cambridge: Harvard University Press.

Pye, Lucian W., and Nathan Leites. 1982. "Nuances in Chinese Political Culture." *Asian Survey* 22, no. 12 (December).

Quan, Yanchi. 1998. *Zouxia shentan de Mao Zedong* (The Mao who stepped down from the shrine of God). In *QuanYanchi wenji* (Anthology by Quan Yanchi). 9 Volumes. Huhehaote: Neimenggu renmin chubanshe.

Stern, Larry N., L. Douglas Dobson, and Frank P. Scioli. 1973. "On the Dimensions of Political Culture: A New Perspective." *Comparative Political Studies* 4, no. 4 (January).

Su, Xiaokang. 1988. *He Shang* (River elegy). Beijing: Dongfang chubanshe.

Wang, Aihe. 2000. *Cosmology and Political Culture in Early China.* New York: Cambridge University Press.

Wasserstrom, Jeffrey N., and Elizabeth J. Perry. 1994. *Popular Protest and Political Culture in Modern China.* Boulder, CO: Westview Press.

Wiarda, Howard J, ed. 1985. *New Directions in Comparative Politics.* Boulder, CO: Westview.

Wu, Mouren, Peihua Ni, Qingjia Wang, Jiaqi Yan, and Wuer Kaixi, eds. 1989. *Bajiu Zhongguo Min Yun Jishi* (Records of the Chinese democracy movement in 1989). Vol. 1. New York: n.p.

Zarrow, Peter. 1990. *Anarchism and Chinese Political Culture.* New York: Columbia University Press.

Part I

The Chinese Cultural Tradition and Its Modern Face

1

Sage, Teacher, Businessman: Confucius as a Model Male

Kam Louie

This chapter examines the constructions of Chinese male identity in the modern world. In particular, it looks at perceptions of Chinese masculinity as embodied in the scholar-intellectual (*wenren*, or man of letters) ideal exemplified by the *wen* god Confucius. My previous work has shown that in configurations of Chinese masculinity, the ideal man demonstrates both civil and military (*wen-wu*) accomplishments. The term *wen-wu* has no English equivalent, although approximate renderings are "literary-martial" or "mental-physical." In this chapter I focus on the *wen* half of this dyad. After first establishing the significance of the *wen* god Confucius in the framework of Chinese masculinity and then examining its significance to both sexes, I outline how Communist scholars in the 1990s constructed Confucius as a progressive educationalist whose "modern fate" is not a terminal one. In the final part of the chapter, I examine the iconic status of Confucius in the last two decades of this millennium to show that in the 1980s and 1990s *wen* ideals were fundamentally transformed so as to encompass commercial expertise alongside its traditional tenets.

Indeed, Confucius as capitalist entrepreneur definitely turns the orthodox understanding of *wen* as an exclusively moral and political force on its head. If this thesis is correct, constructions of Chinese masculinity have undergone a revolution the implications of which are truly cataclysmic. The "real man" in China today need not possess *wen-wu* attributes as they are traditionally understood—he may in fact be neither politically nor morally motivated—but he will acquire and flaunt such trappings of economic prowess as the latest and most powerful in mobile phones and laptop computers. The Chinese male ideal is therefore moving closer to the image of young executives found in in-flight magazines read by the international jet-set.

Confucius and the Framework of Chinese Masculinity

The theoretical basis of this paper derives from my research on the subject of Chinese masculinity. I have already demonstrated elsewhere that although *yin-yang* philosophy is the most commonly invoked paradigm in discussions of Chinese sexuality, this philosophy cannot be used to define masculinity precisely, because *yin* and *yang* are characterized as elements of femininity as well as of masculinity. I therefore proposed an alternative conception of masculinity in China by characterizing it as an expression of the dyad *wen-wu* (Louie and Edwards 1994). Unlike *yin* and *yang*, the *wen-wu* paradigm is exclusively male, invoking both the mental and the physical as essential. Of course, as a cultural construct, *wen-wu* is constantly evolving, and at times of social upheaval, such as the twentieth century, it is likely to undergo drastic transformations. As the social critic Zhang Kebiao caustically observed, the men of letters had by the early part of the twentieth century become dilettantes, trying to lead the privileged lives traditionally accorded them, yet at the same time imbibing superficial Western fads and tastes (cited in Lee 1973, 39–40). Nonetheless, no matter how the paradigms change, Chinese men continue to construe the more ostensibly refined features of *wen* as ingredients of manhood equally important as those of *wu*.

The operation of this dichotomy is summarized in the Confucian *Analects* in the admonition that "superior men may possess more and inferior men may possess less, but all men have something of the way of *wen* and *wu* in them" (Yang Bojun 1958, 211). The ideal man necessarily embodied the separate essences of *wen* and *wu* as well as an optimal balance of both, although at certain times only one or the other was expected. Importantly, *either* was considered to be acceptably manly. Nonetheless, *wen* has long taken precedence over *wu* as the ultimate masculine ideal, and the expression *wen-wu* always has *wen* preceding *wu*, never the other way around. This pre-eminence of *wen* is hardly surprising, as success in civil service examinations has always been the key to power and privilege.

That *wen-wu* is intricately tied to class considerations is best illustrated by the two icons which represent the separate parts of the dyad. In temples throughout China and the communities of the Chinese diaspora, Confucius is worshipped as the *wen* god and Guan Yu as the *wu* god. Thus, Confucius is known as the '*wen* sage' (*wensheng*) and Guan Yu the '*wu* sage' (*wusheng*), and Confucian temples are also appropriately known as '*wen* temples' (*wenmiao*). While Guan Yu is more popular in temples, comics, operas, and other forms of mass culture (Hodge and Louie 1998, 119–142), Confucius is much more highly revered by the elite, and until the twentieth century his teachings formed the basis of formal education in China. While these two icons represent the dual ideals of Chinese masculinity, therefore, Confucius is the one we must deconstruct if we are to understand the kind of manhood sought by those men who operate mainly with their minds, which is to say those who have inherited the functions of the traditional scholar-gentry class.

Of course, the proposition that both academic attainment and controlled physical prowess are necessary ingredients of manhood may also be true of other cultures. As Andrew Nathan has convincingly shown, we have a long way to go before we can prove empirically that Chinese culture is unique (Nathan 1997, 136–151), and I certainly do not want to imply that Chinese masculinity is an exception and somehow distinctive. The objective of this chapter lies elsewhere: while Confucius and Confucianism have for centuries been seen to embody the very essence of Chinese-ness, recent interpretations of the philosophy and its founder have moved closer to a universalistic than to a particularistic position. While the figure of Confucius has frequently been invoked for nationalistic purposes, the traditional strategy of equating him with Chineseness may, in the computer age, quickly become outdated. In this latter context, the Confucian icon will be unreadable even by the latest applications and platforms.

Traditionally, Confucius was regarded as a sage (*shengren*). Such status, although the ultimate goal of the neo-Confucians, was understood to be beyond the capabilities of the average man. For the last two millennia, therefore, most Chinese men have aspired instead to the Confucian ideal of the *junzi*. The word *junzi* appears in the *Analects* 106 times. Roughly translated as "gentleman," "refined man," or "virtuous man," it is for our discussion best rendered as "exemplary person" (Hall and

Ames 1987, 182–192). The close relationship between the *junzi* and *wen* is reiterated several times in the *Analects*, but the *junzi* is rarely associated with the *wu* aspect of masculinity. One of the best-known expressions linking *junzi* and *wen* occurs in Verse 27, Book VI, of the *Analects*, where Confucius says "the *junzi* is well-versed in *wen*" (Yang Bojun 1958, 68). A more elaborate description occurs in Verse 18, in which the Master explains that "when a man has more *zhi* than *wen*, he will be vulgar. If he has more *wen* than *zhi*, he will be a pedant. If he has a well-balanced mixture of these two qualities, he is then a *junzi*" (Yang Bojun 1958, 65). Most commentators agree that *zhi* is a relatively straightforward concept that refers to the basic or innate substance of a man (see for example Lau 1979, 37–38). Through the process of *wen* education and enculturation, a man with the right amount of *zhi* substance will turn into a genteel *junzi*. *Wen* thus encompasses all the qualities that allow for nature to be refined into culture.

In practical terms, *wen* is the product of a proper education. It is said that Confucius taught four subjects: "cultural refinement [*wen*], moral behaviour [*xing*], loyalty [*zhong*], and faith [*xin*]" (Yang Bojun 1958, 78). Since the latter three of these are ethical concepts, we can assume that the skills we know he taught—literature, music, archery, charioteering, writing, and mathematics—belong to the category of *wen*. During the Communist era, these qualities became the subject of debates on education. Here, I should reiterate that, in general, the accomplishments Confucius considered to be the pre-conditions of *junzi*-hood apply only to men.

As a model of masculinity, the *junzi* is contrasted with the *xiaoren* (inferior man). The *Analects* contrasts the *junzi* and *xiaoren* in numerous places. Of most interest to us is the declaration by Confucius that "the *junzi* understands the importance of morality [*yi*] and the *xiaoren* understands the importance of profitability [*li*]" (Yang Bojun 1958, 42). In the context of the Spring and Autumn and Warring States periods this is an important pronouncement. The biggest challenge to Confucians at that time was the doctrine put forth by Mozi, who unashamedly advocated profit and utility as desirable goals. The Confucian hatred for the utilitarian profit-motive continued right into the twentieth century, with merchants and business people theoretically placed at almost the bottom of traditional Chinese society in terms of social status. One of the most striking illustrations of this Confucian outlook appears in the Qing novel *The Scholars* (Wu Jingzi 1972), where the ostentatiously unambitious and talented Wang Mian is touted as the ideal man and all the scholars and officials lusting after power, privilege, and money are portrayed as despicable fakes. In many ways, Wang Mian is the reincarnation of Yan Hui, Confucius' favourite student, a perfect *junzi* who died without achieving office, wealth, or fame and who has since been canonised as a sage.

This does not mean, of course, that Chinese concepts of masculinity tended towards asocial or apolitical behaviors, traits normally ascribed to the Daoists. Wang Mian did not actively seek office, but he gave advice freely to the ruler. Confucius, too, is said to have wandered from state to state seeking a kingly patron to whom he could offer counsel. (In contemporary terms, he was a political lobbyist.) By definition *wen* implied verbal skill, and *wenren* thus influenced society through rhetorical rather than more physical means of social action. In short, the *wenren* saw himself as an enlightened moral and spiritual guide to society. Confucius, certainly, sought only the company of the power elite and shunned the common folk, the *xiaoren*, and advised his followers to do likewise.

Confucius and the Sexes

Interestingly, in the same passage where Confucius admonishes his followers to shun the *xiaoren,* he directs them also to keep women at a respectable distance (Yang Bojun 1958, 198). Women, therefore, are another troublesome class of people to be eschewed. Since masculinity is often associated with sexuality and is also often analysed in terms of its relationship to femininity, it is important that the status of women in the *wen-wu* framework be clarified. I have shown elsewhere that the *wu* ideal has a multitude of defences against women, such that the *wu* god Guan Yu, as popularly imagined, would rather decapitate a beautiful woman than be tempted by her (Louie 1999). This attitude also underlies all the sadistic murders of women in the classic novel *Water Margin* (*Shuihu*; see Hsia 1968, 75–114). By contrast, in the typical 'scholar and beauty' (*caizi jiaren*) formulation of male-female affairs, the scholar always beds the girl. One would thus expect the *wen* god to be surrounded by women, but this is simply not the case—Confucius is never shown in the company of women. In traditional stories, *wen* men indeed consort with women in ways not possible for *wu* men, but this difference has little to do with ideal conceptions of masculinity. Indeed, although the *caizi jiaren* genre is by definition the "romance between talented men and beautiful women," the moral of most such stories is that it is foolish and even dangerous for scholars to become attached to women. The women in these stories are often prostitutes, demons, or fox-fairies who use their wiles to bewitch and ruin their men. Thus, although the impeccable Wang Mian has a significant man and a significant woman in his life, the man is his old peasant mentor and the woman is his old mother: he does not marry and has no romantic attachments as such.

This sexual exclusivity was traditionally taken for granted: women were barred totally from entering the realm of *wen-wu*. Those who did, such as Zhu Yingtai, who tried to gain recognition for *wen* accomplishments by entering a scholarly academy, had to do so in the guise of men and usually met with tragic ends. Similarly, women who were good at *wu*, such as the woman warrior Hua Mulan, had to conceal their sex in order to receive credit for their accomplishments. Once these women applied rouge and adopted feminine attire again, all their *wen-wu* attributes disappeared. *Wen-wu* is wholly a male quality and is never conferred onto women. If women were to worship at the feet of a Confucian idol, they did so to facilitate their sons' success at examinations. This is not a problem but for the fact that references to "the concept of man" are often confused with the concept of humankind, in which "man" is made a universal signifier for both men and women, so that gender and sexuality issues are ignored (see for example Munro 1969, 1977).

Indeed, as we observed above, Confucius himself unambiguously classed women with the detested *xiaoren* as a class of people to be avoided. He would rather have women kept far away than have them offering sacrifices at his feet. In the *Analects*, Confucius seems to live up to his principles in this regard. All of his disciples and associates are men, and all the exemplars in his teachings are male. He seems most at ease and happy in the company of men, and he is most openly and unashamedly grievous at the death of Yan Hui, his favourite student. The only challenge to this homosociality occurs when Confucius visits the beautiful Nanzi and is immediately criticized by his outspoken disciple Zilu, whose displeasure prompts the Master to protest innocence (Yang Bojun 1958, 68).

The homosociality and misogyny that characterize the *wu* god Guan Yu can thus also be found in the *wen* god, albeit in a different form and in a less dramatic way. While it may seem self-evident that Confucius' philosophy is male-centered, scholars have assumed that Confucianism does not discriminate on the basis of gender. In the *Analects* itself, the detested *xiaoren* is mentioned 24 times, mostly as a counter opposite to the *junzi*. But in keeping with the neglect of women in Confucius' time, the *Analects* makes no reference to women as a group, and the paucity of instruction regarding them leaves room for extravagant interpretations. As recently as a couple of years ago it was argued "that the teachings of Confucius are similar to those of some Feminists" (Sellmann and Rowe 1998, 1)! The authors justify this pious assertion by pointing out that Confucius' preferred notion of *"ren,"* in its written form, consists of "two parts, the figure of a person and the numeral two, and so we render it into English as 'person to person care' or just 'care' to be brief" (Sellmann and Rowe 1998, 4). In this instance, the authors are targeting a Western audience, which presumably favors Chinese culture but not its sexist tendencies, so Confucius is presented as a caring, loving man.

But for Chinese scholars whose most important audience for many years was the Chinese Communist Party, the question of Confucius' attitude towards women was not, and is still not, of primary concern. After all, the CCP explicitly subordinates women's liberation to class liberation. The major preoccupation of the CCP has been the assumption and continuance of political power, and women were welcome only in as far as they helped to achieve this goal. Similarly, in the *Analects*, whose explicit aim is the creation of states ruled by wise men and peopled by *junzi*, women are virtually nonexistent. This omission has by default led to a patriarchal system that was publicly denounced as such only with the advent of the May Fourth Movement in the early 1900s. Women were next recognized as significant members of society when the PRC was established. Under the new spirit of sexual equality in the early 1950s, some of the more strident critics, such as Cai Shangsi, whose May Fourth–style onslaught on Confucius as anti-women and anti-masses did continue to be promoted (Cai Shangsi 1950). The most damaging Communist criticism of Confucius in the 1950s and 1960s, however, came from younger scholars such as Zhao Jibin and Yang Rongguo, whose concerns were not with gender but with class. Their writings show that, contrary to the common belief that Confucius had discovered humanity in his notion of *"ren,"* he had only worked on behalf of the ruling elite; the "people" in *"ren,"* therefore, did not extend beyond the ruling class (Zhao Jibin 1962). Thus, say Zhao and Yang, that Confucius was politically reactionary even by the standards of his own time constitutes sufficient reason for not emulating the essence of his thinking (as distinct from the concrete manifestations of Confucianism in Chinese history) in the New China.

This very critical assessment of Confucius gained strength in the early 1960s and reigned supreme from the Cultural Revolution until the late 1970s. In such an anti-traditional environment, Confucius clearly could not be restored to his former glory. As an icon, he signified a superfluous fossil from a by-gone era, hardly a model for men. Yet, it was also obvious that *wen* as a predominant male virtue could not be so easily erased. Many scholars who had spent years learning the Confucian classics depended on the canonical acceptance of these classics for their authority and privileged positions. Whenever politically permissible, therefore, they defended Confucius. Mao's instruction to "sum up our history from Confucius to Sun Yat-sen and take over this valuable legacy" was reiterated ad nauseam to justify the continuing need for traditional Confucian values (see Louie 1980).

Nevertheless, while influential philosophers such as Feng Youlan valiantly attempted to find a place for Confucius in the New China, these attempts only served to further demystify him as a *wen* god. In arguing that Confucius made a valuable contribution to world culture through the discovery of "*ren*" and its implied love of the ordinary person, philosophers such as Feng Youlan tried to prove that Confucius had not advocated class oppression but rather a Chinese-style humanism. This argument proved so attractive that even in the 1980s some scholars still sought to demonstrate the superiority of Confucius' humanism to that of the Europeans (Chen Shigai 1986). But whatever their other effects, these efforts further demystified Confucius, who, if he were at best merely a humanist, could not possibly be restored to the godly status traditionally accorded him.

Indeed, in the first thirty or so years of the PRC, the State's propaganda apparatus was geared to producing new male prototypes for national adulation. These were the peasant-worker-soldier models, best illustrated by the Daqing worker Wang Jinxi and the Dazhai peasant Chen Yonggui; and the soldier hero Lei Feng. These ubiquitous worker-peasant-soldier images were projected as encapsulating the socialist ideal and dominated the media in the 1960s and 1970s. Ostensibly dedicated, selfless, and simple-minded, the worker-peasant-soldier icon confounded all former notions of masculinity in terms of *wen* and *wu* and shared none of the passions or ambitions characteristic of the traditional *wen* or *wu* gods. Their complete lack of interest in women was the only conspicuous commonality between them and the previous prototypes. In this climate of sustained attack on traditional *wen-wu* values, intellectuals had to comport themselves as reformed *wenren* in the new society.

In fact, in the early decades of the PRC very few *wen* models remained congruent with traditional norms. Intellectuals are notoriously difficult to fit into a class schema, and attempts to valorize intellectuals in the aftermath of the Cultural Revolution only produced such nerd-heroes as the mathematician Chen Jingrun. Although these awkward individuals reportedly were sought by some women as marriage partners, they were too insipid to inspire many followers. In a sense, even though the scholars of old achieved fame by passing examinations of rote learning and thereby gaining official status, they were, at least in the ideal, nonetheless thinking beings with a rich inner life. With Lei Feng and the other new male models, traditional respect for education and culture receded in the face of a new concept of the hero as one unthinkingly and willingly performing mindless chores as part of a bigger machine. The new ideal did not advocate excelling in either *wen* or *wu*, and to excel in either requires a certain degree of self-control and control over others. In effect, the new class analysis between 1949 and 1976, in positively discouraging any form of individuality that did not manifestly advance the good of the worker-peasant-soldiers, produced heroes who were decidedly anti-intellectual and therefore anti-*wen*.

Confucius as Teacher and Scholar

It therefore became a matter of utmost urgency for intellectuals of the *wenren* mold to justify their social usefulness on the new political scene. This they did in two stages, of which I will discuss the more orthodox first.

With the changed social situation in the early years of the PRC, it was obvious that Confucius could no longer be invoked as "the Sagely King, the Everlasting Teacher, the Protector of the People and the High Priest of the World" (Kang Youwei 1968, 5). However, except for a few years during the anti-Confucius campaign of 1973–74, almost all evaluations of Confucius since the PRC was established have contained at least a paragraph or two praising his contribution to education. Since the new *wenren* in socialist China could hardly claim to be a member of the "laboring masses," teaching and research provided an important vehicle for self-justification. Being a teacher is a legitimate and worthy profession, and the "paragon of teachers" (*wanshi shibiao*) is, of course, Confucius.

Apart from one's parents, teachers were traditionally those whom one most revered and esteemed. Mao Zedong's own expressed desire to be remembered as a teacher was likely not mere modesty or self-effacement but rather a strategic invocation of an enduring public veneration of teachers. As stated earlier, the idea of Communist leaders serving as exemplars of modal conduct accords well with the "Confucian philosophy of education [which] is the notion of education by example" (Ames 1983, 4). Calls to "inherit" Confucius' ideas on education and praise for his accomplishments as a scholar and teacher were routine in any discussion of him before the Cultural Revolution. Thus, as early as 1954, several articles appeared in the *Guangming ribao* (Guangming daily) extolling Confucius as an educationalist (see Louie 1984a). The first of these, by Xu Mengying, claimed that Confucian education encouraged people to practise benevolent government by teaching "the way of the *junzi*" (Xu Mengying 1954). Interestingly, Xu tried to argue that Confucius had extended the scope of *junzi* to connote not just the aristocracy but rather a complete code of behaviour, and that as such *junzi* remained relevant in contemporary socialist China.

The idea that the *junzi* was just someone who, because he loved the people, should be emulated in socialist society was stressed even more vigorously during the Hundred Flowers movement, when a whole book was published on Confucius as an educator. Written by Chen Jingpan, who taught education at Beijing University, the book presents Confucius as an educator who used the models of the sage (*shengren*) and gentleman (*junzi*) to enlighten his students (Chen Jingpan 1957) and whose pedagogy was based on the idea of self-cultivation (*xiuyang*). The use of the term *xiuyang* is important, as it is the basic tenet used by Liu Shaoqi in his book *On the Self-cultivation of a Communist Party Member*, which first appeared in 1939 (Liu Shaoqi 1962). By showing that Communist leaders such as Liu Shaoqi had extensively borrowed from Confucius for their model of the new socialist man, academics and intellectuals hoped to defend their idol's relevance in the new society. It is true that the Confucian revival had the blessing of some very powerful leaders, including not only Liu Shaoqi but also Zhou Yang, who organized the well-publicized commemoration of the 2440th anniversary of Confucius' death in 1962. However, these people unfortunately also belonged to the faction that lost power during the Cultural Revolution, with the result that their Confucian leanings also came under attack.

Despite these adversities, Confucian doctrine maintained some significance throughout the Communist period and in the anti-Confucius campaign of 1973–74 actually enjoyed a huge resurgence of popular interest, as evidenced by both the hundreds of articles and books about Confucius as well as the thousands of meetings held to "criticize" him. Cartoons and descriptions from this period depict him as a weakling resembling the decrepit scholar Kong Yiji painted so poignantly by Lu Xun. Because Confucius was thus held up as a "negative example" (*fanmian jiaocai*), the "positive man," presumably, was everything contrary to these representations. The depiction of Confucius as weakling may also have been a reaction to the 1960s, when sports educators attempted to promote him as a robust and physical person. Citing extracts from the *Analects* in which he is described as a tall and strong person, these commentators claimed that he did not just stress the *wen* type of education but considered physical education (as *wu*) as also important (Xin Lan 1962).

Thus, those who wanted to promote Confucius claimed that he did not neglect the physical. This assertion was made to justify "inheriting" him in the new socialist China, where models were supposed to engage in manual labour. The aversion of *wen* men for physical labor in traditional China is well known. Confucius in the *Analects* explicitly discourages his students from participating in productive labor, which he regards as not worthy of the *junzi*. *Wen-wu* is about self-control and control of others. Thus, *wu* implies not just physical strength but also how that strength is used. Productive labor such as that of the peasants is considered unskilled work not worthy of *wu*. Just before the Cultural Revolution, some academics such as Li Yinnong had abandoned the pretence that the model male must be the worker-peasant-soldier. Li claimed that Confucius had in fact made a greater contribution to Chinese civilization than had the peasants he chastised (Li Yinnong 1962).

It is not surprising that during the Cultural Revolution Confucius was most vehemently attacked for his educational ideas. In the new China, where "feudal" ways were to be abandoned, it was difficult to salvage the philosopher most closely identified with those ways. As we have seen above, education was the one area where many intellectuals felt Confucius could still provide a model. Through education and its associated *wen* values, the Chinese literati of the past and the intelligentsia of the present could continue to acquire a sense of meaning and power in society. This became patent as soon as the Cultural Revolution ended. The first piece of literature to question "Gang of Four" policies—Liu Xinwu's "Class Teacher"—was about education. Immediately after its publication, writers associated their own sexuality and masculinity with the power of the pen. This could be seen from short stories such as "Glasses" (Liu Fudao 1979) and the controversial novel *Half of Man Is Woman* (Zhang Xianliang 1985), which link political power, sexual potency, and desirability very closely with education, knowledge, and other *wen* achievements.

Wen masculinity was thus experiencing a phenomenal comeback in the early 1980s, and Confucius was once more elevated to a supreme position. His status as the paragon of teachers was used as a signal that this was a man well worth imitating. Throughout the 1980s and 1990s, it was generally agreed that a crisis of faith, especially among the young, was haunting China. It was felt that there was a moral vacuum after the disillusioning experiences of the Cultural Revolution. Thus, even as early as 1980, Confucian moral education was proposed as a means of filling this gap. This proposal was reiterated many times. Again, Confucius was held up as a man upon whom young people could model themselves. Thus, by highlighting the perception that the moral and educational situation had reached a crisis point, Confucius as *wen* god was again used to justify the privileged positions of scholars and intellectuals as indispensable elements of the social fabric.

By the early 1990s, Confucius and Mao Zedong were paired as the two greatest educators in Chinese history, one ancient, one modern. In a significant article on this topic, Xu Quanxing, a member of the CCP Central Committee Party School, argues that Mao Zedong had on numerous occasions wanted to be remembered as a teacher. Furthermore, he quotes Mao Zedong praising Confucius in many of his speeches and writings. One of the most interesting of the quotations is an assessment of Confucius given during a talk in 1938. After eulogizing Confucius, Mao asks rhetorically: "Why didn't Confucius become a Communist? That's because the masses those days did not want him to be a Communist: they wanted him to be a teacher. But today, the masses want us to be Communists" (Xu Quanxing 1993, 4). That is to say, if Confucius had been alive in the 1930s, he would have been a Communist leader. Such claims are almost clichés; what is remarkable about this one, however, is the manner in which it is used to help argue the paramount importance of the ancient sage for Chinese culture.

Critics like Xu Quanxing are not merely debating the merits of Confucian education. As a professor of the Communist Party School, Xu leaves little doubt as to the political motive behind his article. He concludes with a short comment to the effect that although Confucius' influence on Mao was generally positive, it also had a negative aspect. The biggest shortcoming in Confucius' educational thought, according to Xu, is his "emphasis on ethics and disregard for materiality" (*zhong renlun, qing wuli*; Xu Quanxing 1993, 6). Because of this, Chinese thinkers throughout the ages, including Mao, have paid insufficient attention to material and economic progress. Thus Mao Zedong was partial to political education and neglected modernization and economic production. By contrast, says Xu, "Deng Xiaoping rectified this bias in Mao Zedong. He [Deng] spoke about the importance of education for achieving modernization and catching up with the highest international standards. He pointed out that science and technology were the key to the four modernizations, and education provided the foundations" (Xu Quanxing 1993, 6). Presumably, if Confucius lived in the 1990s, he would be more than just a Communist leader: he would be a Communist entrepreneur!

Confucius as Entrepreneur: 1980s and 1990s

Given the fact that Confucius had for centuries been associated with the scholar class and was seen to be hostile to commerce and monetary concerns, it seems inconceivable that he could be portrayed as a business guru. Yet, as I will show, this is precisely what happened. As stated above, attempts to resuscitate the traditional image of the *wenren* as the conscience and guardian of Chinese values were often made by continuing to enshrine Confucius as the paragon of teachers. These attempts to privilege the social positions of the scholars, so successful in previous centuries, could have continued into the twenty-first century. The "contemporary neo-Confucianists" (*dangdai xin rujia;* Liang Xin 1986) such as Tang Junyi and Tu Wei-ming would certainly not have been averse to such a turn of events. For example, the *Journal of Confucius and Mencius Research* (*Kong Meng xuebao*), published since 1961 by the Confucius and Mencius Society in Taiwan, continues to propagate traditional Confucian values. In North America, academic associations such as the Canadian Culture and Regeneration Research Society, which publishes the quarterly *Cultural China* (*Wenhua Zhongguo*), have also been formed to revive traditional Chinese culture in the new world order. Significantly, since the mid-1980s, some "contemporary neo-Confucianists" outside China have attempted to modernise and internationalise Confucianism by linking Confucian education with the increasing economic prosperity in East Asia (Tu Wei-ming 1996). Studies of cultures in the social sciences have also projected Confucian values as a "dynamic dimension" in promoting economic growth (Hofstede 1997).

In mainland China, a similar shift in emphasis has also taken place. Since 1978, a major national or international conference on Confucius or Confucianism has taken place every year, indicating an unprecedented enthusiasm for the philosopher and his philosophy (Song Zhongfu et al 1991, 353). In the beginning, these conferences were held to repudiate the "Gang of Four" criticisms of Confucius. Very quickly, however, they became occasions for his adulation. The fact that the conferences were held on his birthday and almost always in Qufu, Confucius' birthplace, made the intentions of the organizers even more transparent. Thus, at the 1984 gathering, a ceremony was held to unveil Confucius' statue as well as to establish the Chinese Confucius Foundation, whose director was Kuang Yaming, the former President of Nanjing University. Kuang was a staunch Communist, and at the same time, a good Confucian. He was then about to release his new book calling for the "inheritance" of Confucius and his ideas (Kuang Yaming 1985).

In the same year, the International Confucian Association was established in Beijing, with former Singaporean Prime Minister Lee Kuan Yew elected Honorary Director. Lee's role was a clear signal that Confucianism was seen as not only compatible with but important to the building of a modern society. Since then, many more international conferences have been held to commemorate Confucius, with most foreign participants coming from East and Southeast Asia. The economic growth of the Asia-Pacific region throughout most of the 1980s and 1990s generated increasing interest in the search for "Asian values," of which Confucianism was an integral feature. In quick succession, a series of articles appeared showing how Confucianism had been essential for modernization in industrial countries in East Asia such as Japan and Korea (see for example Wang Ruisheng 1996 and Li Xianghai 1997).

Scholars who for many years had called for the "inheritance" of Confucius' educational thought were understandably very quick to cash in on the economic boom in East Asia in the 1980s and early 1990s. As early as 1979, the link between Confucian values and the quest for wealth and industrialization was expressed implicitly in the immensely popular prize-winning short story "Manager Qiao Resumes Office" by Jiang Zilong (Louie 1984). In the fields of philosophy and political commentary, this link was made explicit by the mid-1980s. By the 1990s the message was very forcefully promoted. From a sagely adviser to kings and statesmen, Confucius has been turned into a management consultant whose words set the benchmark for good business practice and whose morals are held up as exemplary because they are supposed to promote production and profit.

However, as pointed out earlier, the *Analects* unambiguously states that "the *junzi* understands the importance of morality (*yi*) and the *xiaoren* understands the importance of profitability (*li*)" (Yang Bojun 1958, 42).Thus, throughout Chinese history, good Confucians such as the neo-Confucian Zhu Xi eschewed talk of profit and business. This aversion to money and commerce would have to be resolved if the *junzi* model were to succeed in an era which measured success in economic terms. Confucians throughout the ages were supposed to have placed morality above profits and utility, whereas the Mohists took the reverse position. This is a major reason that Mozi has generally been ignored throughout history, including during the Communist period (Louie 1986). Interestingly, in the economically driven social climate of the 1980s and 1990s, it was felt that this premise needed to be reassessed. Articles discussing the relationship between ethics and utility usually concluded by arguing the need for some degree of morality in an age where "money is all" (Zang Hong 1986, 21). By 1989, when three international conferences were held in China to commemorate the 2540th anniversary of Confucius' birth, scholars, keen to connect Confucius' views on the profit motive to the modernization of China, embraced both *yi* and *li* as important in this age of rapid economic growth (Miao Runtian 1989). Kuang Yaming, in an influential paper "On Confucius' *yi-li* and Economic Affairs," contended that on close examination, Confucius did not really stress *yi* above *li*. In fact, his highest ideal was "the Great Commonwealth" (*datong shijie*), in which *yi* and *li* were in harmony and in unity (cited in Song Zhongfu et al 1991, 358–359). Confucius highlighted the conflict between *yi* and *li* because he realized "the Great Commonwealth" was difficult to accomplish in his time. He thus emphasized *yi* so that society could at least develop ethically.

By the end of the 1980s, therefore, there was a concerted effort to show that Confucius' ideas were beneficial to economic growth. As well as the appearance of many articles devoted to the relationship between Confucian ethics and business management, a number of conferences were held to examine traditional Chinese morality and the market economy (Hu Dongyuan 1996). Using the generally accepted view that the central core of Confucius' teaching is *ren*, and that *"ren"* meant the discovery of humanity in human relationships, scholars tried to show that this emphasis on the centrality of men was the essential element that had been missing in modern management (see, for example, Ye Ruixin 1998). Furthermore, it is often argued that there is a close connection between Confucian and socialist economic morality, so that in a developing socialist market economy, Confucian ethics should be used to combat the corrupting influence of money lust (Liu Minghua 1996, 29). This view was even more appealing because of the belief that first the Cultural Revolution and then modernity had had a dehumanizing and alienating effect on the people, especially the young (Song Xiren 1993).

Confucius is therefore being held up once more as a model for the young. More importantly, he is celebrated as the person who outlined a method whereby management can be carried out efficiently by humane cadres and managers. In a very detailed article, Beijing University economist Zhao Jing argues that Confucius' management techniques could be adopted by capitalist and modern enterprises. The thrust of his argument is aimed at "leaders" in both industry and politics. In particular, he claims that those who emphasized politics a few years ago were people who "did not understand our national character" and who wanted to rush straight ahead with communism without checking whether this was a realistic move or not (Zhao Jing 1989, 34). Zhao acknowledges that Confucius' lack of attention to the economic structure of nations had a negative impact on China. However, he believes that if Japan and Korea could modernize by adopting Confucius' management techniques, China could too. "Moral management" became a motto under which many writers advocated the return of Confucius in the new industrial China (Xu Qixian 1998).

Throughout the 1990s, therefore, the powerful forces of industrialization and consumerism pushed cultural artifacts, including masculinity, into the marketplace as commodities (Louie and Cheung 1998). Scholars and writers therefore had to satisfy consumers instead of each other, and their metamorphosis entailed a similar re-invention of their alter ego, Confucius. The *wen* god was thus reinterpreted as someone who did not suppress the profit motive but merely advocated righteousness (*yi*) as a means by which the *junzi* could have a moral standard to which to aspire (i.e., once he became economically successful; see Luo Guojie 1994). In the present climate, therefore, where luxury items are flaunted and unashamedly taken as signs of success, the Confucian icon has been stood on its head, with scholars such as Zhao Jing discussing the moral management techniques of Confucius with the ultimate aim of nurturing a generation of leaders who follow the reformed Confucius.

This does not mean, of course, that *wen* has been erased from the masculinity matrix. The new consumer society has unquestionably brought huge dilemmas for intellectuals and artists who cling to traditional ways. The changed make-up of Confucius, however, has provided a tremendous moral boost for the *wenren* who now "wade into the ocean of business dealings" (*xiahai*). By claiming that the venerated sage had over 2000 years ago discovered the secret to a humane leadership style suitable for the 20th century, these men are able to indulge in finance while at the same time feeling morally superior. They are the new *junzi*.

Thus, the commodification of intellect and morality is given a traditional and rationalized foundation. Most importantly, Chinese men's, particularly businessmen's, nationalist and masculine pride can be restored after so many years of uncertainty and anguish; Confucius can still be retained in the pantheon of Chinese gods as one of the most enduring icons. The Chinese search for wealth and power has produced some curious consequences in relation to this icon. It is now quite proper, for example, for graduates of commerce to hold their graduation ceremonies and have their photos taken at Confucian Temples. Also, the efficacy of relics connected with the *wen* god is now measured not by the virtues they inspire but by how much cash they generate: profitable tourism ventures linking Qufu and Confucius, for instance, are highly topical and greatly trumpeted (see Kong Xiangjin and Wang Xinhong 1999; Yu Xuecai 1990).

As the world becomes more accessible and interdependent through travel and finance, and as China, in response, becomes more international in outlook, the Confucian icon will likewise change. Given the divergent number of Confuciuses we have contended with in the past fifty years, we must indeed consider the man to be the consummate chameleon. In order for us to "inherit" (*jicheng*) his teachings, Confucius has been variously interpreted as sage, scholar, teacher, restorationist, and business guru. The latter of these is the last word on him. For example, in late 1998 and into 1999, when parts of East Asia were experiencing economic difficulties, journalists were quick to blame Confucius for the "five basic human relationships" which had apparently led to hierarchy, lack of rule of law, and transparency, resulting in an "Asian eclipse" (Backman 1999). Like it or not, the name "Confucius" will continue to be shorthand for Chinese culture no matter how this culture is interpreted.

Although discussions of Chinese society generally do not make gender issues explicit, the implicit perspective of such discussions is usually a male (*wen-wu*) one. More specifically, Confucius, being the *wen* god, will continue to exemplify this particular aspect of male culture. The *wu* component of masculinity is also changing and becoming more international, as can be seen in martial arts films such as those of Bruce Lee, Jackie Chan, and Sammo Hung. Thanks to the invention of cyberspace, images and models are available to many different cultures instantaneously. As a consequence, constructions of Chinese masculinity will need to be continually altered and modernized if they are to have meaning and relevance. By the same token, the basic *wen-wu* structure will also need to be transformed if it is to be maintained as a "national characteristic." As long as the man in question is Chinese—regardless, in other words, of whether he is to be a multinational entrepreneur or civil servant—his personality will be said to possess qualities consonant with the *wen* god Confucius. In this way, although *wen* has never before been rendered to mean business acumen and managerial skills, that unlikely signification seems to have been achieved in recent times.

References

Ames, Roger T. 1983. *The Art of Rulership: A Study in Ancient Chinese Political Thought*. Honolulu: University of Hawaii Press.
Backman, Michael. 1999. *Asian Eclipse: Exposing the Dark Side of Business in Asia*. Singapore: John Wiley & Sons.
Cai Shangsi. 1950. *Zhongguo chuantong sixiang zong pipan* (A comprehensive criticism of traditional Chinese thought). Shanghai: Dangdi chubanshe.
Chen Jingpan. 1957. *Kongzi de jiaoyu sixiang* (Confucius' educational thought). Wuhan: Hubei renmin chubanshe.
Chen Shigai. 1986. "Kongzi de lunli sixiang yu zichan jieji rendao zhuyi zhi bijiao yanjiu" (A comparative study of Confucius' ethical thinking and the humanism of the bourgeoisie). *Hubei daxue xuebao* (Hubei University journal) 2: 31–36.

Hall, David L., and Roger T. Ames. 1987. *Thinking through Confucius*. Albany: State University of New York Press.
Hodge, Bob, and Kam Louie. 1998. *The Politics of Chinese Language and Culture*. London: Routledge.
Hofstede, Geert. 1997. *Cultures and Organizations: Software of the Mind*. New York: McGraw-Hill.
Hsia, C.T. 1968. *The Classic Chinese Novel*. New York: Columbia University Press.
Hu Dongyuan. 1996. "Zhongguo chuantong wenhua, shichang jingji, daode jianshe" (Traditional Chinese culture, the market economy, moral development). *Xuehai* (Sea of learning) 1: 52–54.
Kang Youwei. 1968 edition. *Kongzi gaizhi kao* (A study of Confucius as reformer). Taipei: Taiwan shangwu yinshuguan.Originally written in 1899.
Kong Xiangjin, and Wang Xinhong. 1999. "Qufu choujian Kongzi wenhua guangchang" (Qufu raises money to build Confucius culture square). *Renmin ribao* (People's daily). 9 April.
Kuang Yaming. 1985. *Kongzi pingzhuan* (A critical biography of Confucius). Jinan: Qilu shushe.
Lau, D.C. 1979. "Introduction." *Confucius: The Analects*, trans. D.C.Lau. Harmondsworth: Penguin Books.
Lee, Leo Ou-fan. 1973. *The Romantic Generation of Modern Chinese Writers*. Cambridge, Mass.: Harvard University Press.
Li Xianghai. 1997. "Rujia lunli yu Dongya xiandaihua" (Confucian ethics and East Asian modernisation). *Zhongzhou xuekan* (Zhongzhou journal) 1: 64–69.
Li Yinnong. 1962. "Lun Kongzi dui laodong de taidu" (On Confucius' attitudes towards labour). *Yangcheng wanbao* (Guangzhou evening news). 22 March.
Liang Xin. 1986. "Shenme jiao 'dangdai xin rujia'" (What is a 'contemporary neo-Confucianist'?). *Wenhui bao* (Wenhui daily). 10 June.
Liu Fudao. 1979. "Yanjing" (Glasses). *Aiqing xiaoshuo ji* (Collected love stories). Shanghai: Shanghai wenyi chubanshe:1–21.
Liu Minghua. 1996. "Rujia yili guan yu fazhan shehuizhuyi shichang jingji" (On the Confucians'attitudes towards *yi-li* and the developing socialist market economy). *Guizhou daxue xuebao* (Guizhou University journal). 1: 24–29.
Liu Shaoqi. 1962 edition. *Lun Gongchandang yuan de xiuyang* (On the self-cultivation of a Communist Party member). Beijing: Renmin chubanshe. Originally written in 1939.
Louie, Kam. 1980. *Critiques of Confucius in Contemporary China*. Hong Kong: Chinese University Press.
———. 1984. "In Search of Socialist Capitalism and Chinese Modernisation." *Australian Journal of Chinese Affairs* 12: 87–96.
———. 1984a. "Salvaging Confucian Education (1949–1983)." *Comparative Education* 20 (1): 27–38.
———. 1986. *Inheriting Tradition: Interpretations of the Classical Philosophers in Communist China 1949–1966*. Hong Kong: Oxford University Press.
———. 1999. "Sexuality, Masculinity and Politics in the Yingxiong: The Case of the Sanguo Hero Guan Yu." *Modern Asian Studies* 33 (4): 835–860.
Louie, Kam, and Cheung Chiu-yee. 1998. "Three Kingdoms: The Chinese Cultural Scene Today." Ed. Joseph Y.S. Cheng. In *China Review 1998*. Hong Kong: Chinese University Press: 543–575.

Louie, Kam, and Louise Edwards. 1994. "Chinese Masculinity: Theorizing Wen and Wu." *East Asian History* 8: 135–148.

Luo Guojie. 1994. "Guanyu Kongzi yili guan de yidian sikao" (Some considerations on Confucius' attitudes towards *yi-li*). *Xueshu yanjiu* (Academic research) 3: 51–53.

Miao Runtian. 1989. "Qianlun Kongzi de yili guan ji qi xiandai yiyi" (On Confucius' attitude towards *yi-li* and its modern significance). *Qilu xuekan* (Qilu journal) 1: 55–59.

Munro, Donald J. 1969. *The Concept of Man in Early China*. Stanford: Stanford University Press.

———. 1977. *The Concept of Man in Contemporary China*. Ann Arbor: University of Michigan Press.

Nathan, Andrew J. 1997. *China's Transition*. New York: Columbia University Press.

Sellmann, James D., and Sharon Rowe. 1998. "The Feminine in Confucius." *Asian Culture* 26 (3): 1–8.

Song Xiren. 1993. "Rujia chuantong yili guan yu qingshaonian daode jiaoyu" (On the Confucians' attitudes towards *yi-li* and the moral education of the young). *Jiangsu shehui kexue* (Jiangsu social sciences) 6: 119–123.

Song Zhongfu et al. 1991. *Ruxue zai xiandai Zhongguo* (Confucianism in modern China). Zhengzhou: Zhongzhou guji chubanshe.

Tu Wei-ming (ed). 1996. *Confucian Traditions in East Asian Modernity: Moral Education and Economic Culture in Japan and the Four Mini-Dragons*. Cambridge, Mass.: Harvard University Press.

Wang Ruisheng. 1996. "Rujia sixiang yu dongya de xiandaihua" (Confucian thought and East Asian modernisation). *Zhongguo zhexueshi* (History of Chinese philosophy) 4: 7–11, 31.

Wu Jingzi. 1972 edition. *Rulin waishi* (The scholars). Hong Kong: Zhonghua shuju. Originally published in 1610.

Xin Lan. 1962. "Kongzi zai tiyu fangmian de shijian he zhuzhang" (Confucius' practice and principles in the field of sport). *Xin tiyu* (New sports) 8: 13–16.

Xu Mengying. 1954. "Kongzi de jiaoyu sixiang" (Confucius' educational thought). *Guangming ribao* (Guangming daily). 14 June.

Xu Qixian. 1998. "Lun rujia lunli yu daode guanli" (On Confucian ethics and moral management). *Zhongguo renmin daxue xuebao* (Chinese People's University journal) 1: 48–54.

Xu Quanxing. 1993. "Kongzi yu Mao Zedong: Gujin weida 'jiaoyuan'" (Confucius and Mao Zedong: great 'teachers' of the past and present). *Kongzi yanjiu* (Confucius research) 4: 3–9.

Yang Bojun. 1958. *Lunyu yizhu* (The Analects translated and annotated). Beijing: Zhonghua shuju.

Ye Ruixin. 1998. "Kongzi de yili guan" (Confucius' attitudes towards *yi-li*). *Shanxi daxue xuebao* (Shanxi University journal) 4: 33–37.

Yu Xuecai. 1990. "Rujia sixiang yu Zhongguo lüyou wenhua chuantong" (Confucian thinking and traditional Chinese tourist culture). *Kongzi yanjiu* (Confucius research) 2: 29–33.

Zang Hong. 1986. "Lüelun rujia de yili guan" (On the Confucians' attitude towards *yi-li*). *Xuexi yuekan* (Study monthly) 4: 16–21.

Zhang Xianliang. 1985. "Nanren de yiban shi nüren" (Half of man is woman). *Shouhuo* (Harvest) 5: 4–108.

Zhao Jibin. 1962. *Lunyu xintan* (A new exploration of the *Analects*). Beijing: Renmin chubanshe.

Zhao Jing. 1989. "Kongzi de guanli sixiang he xiandai jingying guanli" (Confucius' management ideas and modern administration and management). *Kongzi yanjiu* (Confucius research) 1: 26–37.

2

The Changing Concept of *Zhong* (Loyalty): Emerging New Chinese Political Culture

Godwin C. Chu

On October 1, 1949, Mao Zedong mounted Tiananmen in Beijing and declared: "The Chinese people have stood up!" Mao meant this to be a death knell for western imperialism in China. It was also his signal for ushering in a new political culture under the tutelage of the Chinese Communist Party.

Is there a new political culture in China today, fifty years later? The answer is yes, but not in a shape Mao had envisioned. My thesis is that there is a new political culture in China, centered in a fundamental change in the traditional concept of *zhong*, or loyalty. This change has emerged largely through an evolutionary process in which three major developments have played a critical part: (1) the revolutionary political campaigns that Mao engineered during his nearly three decades' dominance in Chinese politics, campaigns that changed the traditional concept of *zhong*; (2) the major social structural changes brought about by these political campaigns, which altered the concept of authority in traditional Chinese culture and changed the relations between the Chinese people and government officials; and (3) the subsequent economic development under Deng Xiaoping's open door policy and the easing of government regulation of resources and economic activities, which together have created a social and economic environment conducive to the emergence of a new political culture.

My analysis and discussion, hermeneutic in methodology, follow a broad historical and social structural approach. To establish a historical perspective, I first discuss political culture in traditional China. In doing this, I take political culture as a special domain of the broader culture defined by Chu in terms of the self's relations to his/her personal, material, and nonmaterial surroundings. I analyze the mass political campaigns Mao initiated in both rural and urban China from the early 1950s until his death in 1976, which effectively brought an end to the Cultural Revolution, and how these campaigns changed traditional Chinese social structure and cultural values. Finally, I identify the fundamental characteristics of the new political culture, including the supportive influence of ongoing economic development, and discuss the role of *zhong* in the present context of rapid socio-cultural change.

Political Culture in Traditional China

Political culture in China before Mao was highly traditional. Chu broadly defines culture conceptually as consisting of the self's relationship with (1) significant others in his/her life; (2) the material world within which those significant others play an indispensable role; and (3) the values, beliefs and attitudes that govern both (Chu 1979; Chu and Ju 1993). A particular society, such as traditional China, assigns specific dimensions that shape the three types of relationship in ways such that together they constitute its distinctive culture. Political culture embodies these same principal features more specifically determined. Thus, one's significant others in a political culture have mostly to do with the government, and one's relations with the material world manifest themselves primarily through (1) taxes and levies which the government collects and the various services which the government provides, and (2) material demands and other expectations of the people addressed to the government.. Both of these functions are facilitated, though not predetermined, by the relevant prevailing values, beliefs, and attitudes.[1]

In traditional Chinese culture, the core value was submission to authority (Hsu 1949, 1953), whether in the extended family or in the local community.[2] In political culture, this loosely defined authority permeated a rigid structure, consisting of layers upon layers of bureaucrats, in which subordinates bowed unquestioningly to their superiors.

The emperor, whose official title was The Son of Heaven and who was believed to embody Heaven's mandate, symbolized ultimate authority, although in reality many emperors were little more than puppet figureheads. In all cases, however, officialdom functioned on the assumption that supreme power rested with him. Indeed, his authority was such that if he wished an official dead, the official would dutifully submit to death as a behavioral enactment of *zhong*.

Largely as passive onlookers, the vast majority of the Chinese people remained on the periphery of the traditional political culture, which governed primarily members of the officialdom and the imperial household. Officials interacted little with the people, except to collect taxes and levies, deal with breaches of law and order, and facilitate conscription for public services, including military service. There were few government services to speak of, and the people had no meaningful role in the political system. Their duty was, simply, to submit to the authority of the local officials.

Rights and obligations exist in all social relations. In a traditional Chinese family the children bore lasting obligations to their parents, but the children also had some marginal rights in that their parents looked after their caring and feeding. In traditional Chinese political culture the situation was similar. In fact, Chinese people looked upon themselves literally as "children" (*zimin* 子民) and regarded the officials as "parents" (*fumuguan* 父母官). While children in the family had some rights, however, in traditional Chinese political culture the people had virtually none. Even at times of famines and natural disasters, the government rarely acted to ensure the people's welfare. Regulations on disaster relief were promulgated during the Qing Dynasty, but they were rarely implemented because of corruption. Indeed, corruption, generally considered a subsidy to the meager official salaries, was rampant. Bribery was accepted as a fee for service by anyone wanting action. Hardship was a way of life, and injustice was tolerated as a necessary evil. A popular motto, "Stay away from officials if at all possible," indicates the preferred means of dealing with the government. For the masses, the emperor was as far away as the heaven above.

The concept of culture as consisting of a series of relationships suggests that material relations and other aspects of political culture are related. Indeed, in traditional China relations with the material world supported an authoritarian political culture. People did not have high material aspirations. They considered acceptance of poverty to be a means of

achieving peace in life, known in Chinese as *anpin ledao* (安貧樂道).
One traditional saying describes a blissful life as "three acres of land, a
cow, and a wife in a warm clay bed" (*sanmu tiandi yitou niu, yige laopo
rekangtou* 三畝田地一頭牛, 一個老婆熱炕頭). The Chinese people
made few demands on the government. Easily satisfied and possessed
of a strong fatalistic sense coupled with an unusual capacity for endur-
ance, they readily accepted the unresponsive political system and meekly
submitted to the authority. Even in famines and natural disasters, they
blamed their hardships more on fate than on a corrupt officialdom. Only
when life became utterly unbearable under widespread suffering and
wanton oppression would the people rise up in revolt. Although this
happened numerous times, the uprisings typically were short lived, and
the system reasserted itself afterwards.[3]

Social Structure and Political Culture

An interactive bond holds social structure and culture together in a mutually supportive manner.[4] The core Chinese cultural value of submission to authority laid the cognitive and emotive foundation for the Chinese
social structure of the past. Chinese people accepted the rigid structure
of authority not only because they believed this was the proper thing to
do but, perhaps even more importantly, because they derived a sense of
meaning and self worth from doing it. In the extended family, the cultural value of submission to authority was embodied in the concept of
xiao, or filial piety. *Xiao* means more than taking care of the physical
well-being of the parents, or engaging in a pattern of behavior to please
the parents. There are many such stories in Chinese folklore. More significantly, *xiao* in the traditional context became a binding principle when,
in cases of serious conflict of purpose between parents and offspring, grown
children, regardless of their social status and wealth, were expected to
bow to the wishes of their parents, not so much as a sacrifice, but as a self-
motivated expression of *xiao*. Traditional Chinese literature is filled with
tragic stories of dutiful sons divorcing their beloved spouses in order to
please their parents, usually because the mother does not like the daugh-
ter-in-law. At the same time, the social structure, embodied in this case
in the extended family and the local community, reinforced the enactment of *xiao* by rewarding and honoring people who exemplified this
cultural value and despising and ostracizing those who violated it.

The same relationships between cultural values and social structure were found in China's political system. The dominant value here was *zhong*, or loyalty, instead of *xiao*. Just as *xiao* was unreservedly directed towards the parents, *zhong* ultimately implied obeisance to the emperor as the embodiment of supreme authority and to the entire imperial dynasty. *Xiao*, being a key value in traditional China, was surpassed in preeminence only by *zhong*. If a conflict arose between *zhong* and *xiao* such that it was not possible to fulfill both, *xiao* would be sacrificed in deference to *zhong*. The important point to bear in mind is that even though Chinese officials carried out their functions in broadly defined fields, their performance was necessarily guided by the concept of *zhong*. This is why many Chinese willingly sacrificed their lives to defend the Ming Dynasty when it fell, even though the Ming was among the most despotic of Chinese dynasties and was especially so during the cruel and misguided reign of the Ming's last emperor. Thus *zhong* is sometimes referred to as *yuzhong*, or blind loyalty. Because *zhong* and *xiao* both required total submission and absolute obedience, Chinese emperors were guided by the cardinal principle that if a man proved to be a filial son, he could be completely trusted as a subject.

Under such a political culture, rule of law became impossible since it directly challenged the supreme authority of the emperor. Alternatively, the political system rewarded acts of *zhong*. Only officials who had convincingly demonstrated *zhong* behavior were chosen for promotion and power. If their loyalty was so much as doubted, the consequences were disastrous, especially for ranking officials personally known to the emperor. Usually, the result was death, sometimes for the entire extended family. Indeed, the Ming Dynasty fell partly because of its last emperor's merciless execution of capable field commanders whose loyalty came under suspicion. Getting ahead in the political arena thus depended on two essential qualities: the ability to demonstrate *zhong* under all circumstances, and the ability to cast doubt on the *zhong* of competitors.

Although the traditional political system virtually ignored ability and efficiency, it managed to survive for millennia. It was able to do so largely because members of the ruling class fully internalized the critical cultural value of *zhong*. General Yuan Chonghuan, for example, was a brilliant military strategist who successfully defended China's northern borders against the Manchu in the final days of the Ming Dynasty. Nevertheless, he put up no defense when he was accused—falsely—of treason, and when the emperor ordered him dismembered, he submitted unquestioningly. But the traditional political system survived also because of an economic system in which relatively low levels of commerce and productive technology operated in a loose socio-economic organization, and in which expertise played a minor role. *Zhong*, not expertise, constituted the critical requisite for the political elite. Stylish prose grounded in Confucianism was taken as a measure both of intelligence and of *zhong*. Administrative and managerial ability was not required and could even become counterproductive. The best way to survive in the political arena was never to risk trouble by tackling important issues. Such considerations partly explain the failures of three major political and economic reforms in the post-Han period. And it certainly was no accident that China during the Manchu Dynasty proved totally incapable of coping with the external forces of western imperialism.

I have discussed the value of *zhong* in the political culture of traditional China in order to establish a historical context for my assessment of Mao's campaigns of revolutionary change and their role in the evolution of a new political culture in contemporary China. Indeed, there exist uncanny parallels between China's traditional political culture and the revolutionary political culture under Mao's tutelage.[5] Both the traditional system and Mao placed an enormous emphasis on *zhong*: in the past, *zhong* meant loyalty to the emperor; in Mao's China, it meant loyalty to the Chairman, to the Party, and to the lofty ideals of communism. The supportive role of minimal material life was also similar: the low material aspirations of the people and the control of material resources by the elite, whether dynastic or communist, made it easy for the unresponsive political system to remain in power. Both traditional and Maoist China minimized the importance of expertise in government administration. As we recall, Mao placed greatest importance not on expertise but on a demonstrated quality he called "being Red," by which he meant total loyalty to himself and unquestioning ideological dedication to his vision of communism. In fact, having expertise but no proven "Redness" was an unforgivable political sin. And finally, both in the traditional past and under Mao, the Chinese people were virtually bereft of rights, political or otherwise. Like the emperors, Mao allowed no rule of law.

Mao's Campaigns of Revolutionary Change

From the early 1950s till his death and the resulting end of the Cultural Revolution in 1976, Mao launched a succession of revolutionary campaigns. Did he really want to change China's political culture, as he implied when he said: "The Chinese people have stood up"? The answer is seemingly yes, but in reality no. Obviously, Mao understood from the beginning something that few in his time were able to grasp: that culture and social structure are inseparably conjoined. You cannot change one without changing the other. In political culture, it is extremely difficult to change the attitudes, values, and beliefs, especially of illiterate peasants, without first changing the social and political structures in the villages. This is what Mao set about doing when he took power.[6]

Although the founding of the Republic of China in 1912 ended dynastic rule, little occurred during the next four decades to change traditional Chinese political culture. In the early 1950s, however, Mao launched a series of violent mass movements in villages nationwide. Known as the Rural Land Reform, these programs eliminated the landed gentry as a class of local authority.[7] As a result, Chinese peasants not only acquired land but also learned to speak out against their former landlords, who used to hold undisputed authority in their villages. It was also from the ranks of peasants that the Party recruited cadres to replace the landed gentry and run village affairs. What Mao did in the villages was followed a few years later by a similar but much less violent campaign in the cities, where factories were nationalized, to be run by cadres chosen from among the workers.

After land reform, Chinese peasants worked and lived in a new era of local autonomy and prosperity. But this situation was short lived, for within a few years Mao initiated another series of mass movements, this time to take the land back from the peasants. The Mutual Aid Movement asked peasants to pool the use of their labor, cattle, and farm implements, while the subsequent Agricultural Cooperative Movement required peasants to submit their land holdings as shares in cooperatives. This led eventually to the People's Commune movement of 1958, the ultimate form of rural collectivization in which even family kitchens were replaced by commune mess halls. When the People's Commune as Mao had originally conceived it turned out to be a disaster, the Party, forced to backtrack, allowed the peasants small private plots and some limited individual work incentives. Family kitchens were restored. Mao found it necessary to step down as head of the state.[8] However, as commune members without land ownership, Chinese peasants found themselves economically little better off than they had been as landless tenants, except that they now worked for the state and earned work points instead of working for the landlords and surrendering part of their crops as rent.

Impact on Political Culture in Rural China

Mao's revolutionary campaigns in the villages both did and did not change political culture in rural China. In terms of major decision-making, the passive and peripheral role of Chinese peasants remained the same during the few short years of rapid transformation from family land ownership through land reform to the loss of land as a result of the People's Commune Movement. Ostensibly, each mass movement was initiated by the peasants themselves, who wanted to demonstrate their revolutionary fervor and their devotion to the proletarian cause of communism. During the People's Commune movement, the official media were flooded with enthusiastic affirmations by the peasants that the proletarian cause would be best served if they were allowed to return the land to the state. According to the official media, villages across the nation responded warmly to this idea and appealed for support to the Party leadership, which, in acceding, was merely bowing to the wishes of the people. In fact the idea for the communes came primarily from Mao himself, and it was left to the grassroots Party organizations to organize what appeared to be spontaneous popular events (Chu 1977). During the People's Commune movement, for example, many villages organized festive parades, complete with cymbals and gongs, to celebrate the return of their land to the state, but these affairs went forth without the peasants being consulted at all. They were simply organized to do, as if it was of their own volition, what the Party authorities had decided upon. To demonstrate their *zhong* to the Party, and particularly to Chairman Mao, they dutifully performed what was required of them, whether that be to organize initial petitions, express popular support for the Party, or give up the same land they had only recently acquired during the land reform.

On the behavioral level, the fundamental roles of Chinese peasants under the Communist Party differed little from those of their ancestors in imperial China; that is, they were expected to do what they were told to do, in much the same way as their ancestors. They were expected to submit to the authority of the Party hierarchy instead of to the landed gentry, and proclaim their *zhong* to Chairman Mao instead of the emperor. Once their land was taken away from them, their relations with the material world also were much the same as before. However, there were two highly significant differences from the past, one cognitive and the other social structural, that had unintended long-term implications for political culture in contemporary China.

We have discussed how Chinese peasants under Mao were organized to create the perception that they did what they did not merely to obey orders from the Party but rather to fulfill their own wishes. As it so happened, the environment of mass enthusiasm and participation generated in such campaigns often blurred the line between reality and perception. When Chinese peasants were placed repeatedly in such an environment, they generally developed two perceptions. Because they heard only a chorus of support in the village group meetings, and no dissenting voice, their first perception was that the required action—for example, to return the land to the state—had the unanimous backing of the villagers. Also, because each person was required to express his or her view in support of the action, their second perception was that they had a voice in deciding what action to take. Some Chinese peasants might have had initial doubts, but as this scenario was played out again and again, many came to believe they had indeed played an active role in initiating and implementing the movement. In time these perceptions led to an expectation among Chinese peasants to participate actively in the management of village affairs. After all, wasn't this what the Party leadership under Chairman Mao expected of them? This expectation would later have a profound but unintended impact on the evolution of a new political culture in rural China.

In addition to the cognitive implications of Mao's reforms, the replacement of the landed gentry by a core of cadres recruited from among the peasants radically altered the social structure of Chinese villages. To be sure, the newly installed cadres took their instructions from their superiors in the Party and had no say in the decision-making that affected life in their villages. Even the broadest policy outlines were clearly spelled out in Party directives. But the rural cadres' relations with other peasants were different from the erstwhile relations between the villagers and the gentry. The local authorities of the past, including landlords and officials, were remote and of a class above the villagers. The rural cadres, on the other hand, were peers of the villagers: both belonged to the same class of "poor and lower-middle peasants"; and they were personally known to each other, often intimately. Unlike the landed gentry, the rural cadres had no personal assets and no financial sources of influence. They earned work points in lieu of wages just like everyone else in the villages. The cadres and villagers addressed each other as "Old Zhang," "Old Wang," and the like. Significantly, the near equality between rural cadres and villagers in both social status and economic resources fundamentally weakened the social structural basis of submission to authority as a core traditional cultural value.

In the past, the officialdom was as far removed from village life as one could imagine. There was a popular saying: "The heaven is high above, and the emperor is far away" (*tian gao huangdi yuan* 天高皇帝遠). In Maoist China this was no longer true. The arms of the Party reached every village through the network of rural cadres, which functioned as a Party-controlled channel of communication to reach the villagers. But the cadre network could also serve as a channel for the villagers to air their complaints and grievances, although it did so but rarely, if ever, and at considerable risk. For example, during the initial stage of the People's Commune movement, agricultural production declined drastically while ripe crops were left unattended in the fields. Villagers and rural cadres alike knew that the commune system did not work, yet only rosy reports of success and fabricated statistics reached the Party hierarchy. The Party leadership had no sense of the actual conditions until the situation in the rural countryside became a colossal disaster and Party leaders who went to the fields for inspection tours could no longer cover it up. Only then were corrective measures taken (Chu 1977). Nevertheless, this channel of upward communication in the villages did inject into China's political culture a new dynamic that grew in importance after Mao's death.

The latent impact of Mao's revolutionary campaigns on the new emerging political culture in rural China began to manifest itself in two different and significant ways under Deng Xiaoping's Open Door and economic reform policies. The first impact is traceable to the redefined material relations in the villages. Under Mao, material aspirations had been totally suppressed. The Party had maintained complete control over rural production and distribution and had limited material rewards to a bare minimum. In this sense, Mao's policy was consistent with the essence of economic culture in traditional China. Under Deng Xiaoping's economic reforms, however, Party control was very much eased in rural China. The commune system was abolished, and land was returned to the peasants. This led not only to a speedy recovery of agricultural production but also to a revival of rural entrepreneurship. An in-depth study of village life in Eastern China in the early 1990s (Chu, Wu, and Yu 1993) found village residents to be actively engaged in various kinds of highly profitable commercial ventures the likes of which had been totally banned under Mao. One immediate impact of the new dispensation was the decline of status generally accorded to elders within the family. The family head was no longer the eldest male member but rather he or she who was most capable of managing the family business, usually someone of middle age, and quite often a woman. In terms of political culture, village residents became actively interested in government policy changes that might affect their business opportunities.

The other latent impact is reflected in the emergence of new communication channels in rural areas. As the control of the Party became gradually loosened under Deng's leadership, the upward channels of communication in the villages nominally initiated during the Mao era began to play a more active role in rural life. Village residents, sometimes with the tacit support of their local leaders, did not hesitate to complain to the Party through these upward communication channels, sometimes with real effect. The Party's recent decision to allow popular elections of village chiefs, for instance, can be seen as a result of the growing demands of the villagers. Such demands reflect a major change in values and political attitudes, from submission to authority to assertive expression, and from passive compliance to active participation. To a group of visiting American journalists and media executives in the fall of 1999, such elections, closely monitored as they were by Party officials, seemed more symbolic than substantive (Isaacson 1999). However, they may equally be seen as a fresh new page in the annals of political culture in rural China. The roots of this fledgling show of democracy in the villages can be traced back to the mass campaigns in which Chinese peasants were mobilized to participate during the 1950s and 1960s, and to the social structural change brought about by these mass campaigns.

Political Campaigns in Urban Areas

The experiences of urban Chinese were quite different from those of their rural counterparts. Social structural changes in cities and towns appeared to be less drastic than the radical and sometimes bloody changes in the villages. The mass campaigns in the cities started with the Three-Anti and Five-Anti movements in the early 1950s, which attacked corruption and weeded out remnants of the former regime, and continued through the Public-Private Joint Management campaign of 1956, which mandated the state take-over of all private enterprises. These campaigns were meant to reinforce Party control over the cities by replacing the power holders of the previous regime with Party cadres.[9] They modified (but did not completely redefine) the urban social structure by seizing the assets of industrial and business owners, who were given moderate compensation. For their own part, city dwellers initially seemed to welcome the change of regimes and the economic recovery that followed.

The first sign of mass purges did not come until 1957. Chinese intellectuals had enthusiastically greeted the People's Republic and its promise of a new democracy. The few minority democratic parties that had sided with the Communists during the civil war did not hesitate to support Mao's policies of rural and urban reforms. Their intellectual leaders saw hope for democracy in the new Communist government. However, the bloody manner in which the rural land reform was carried out, and the abrupt seizure of private enterprises in the cities in 1956, unsettled many intellectuals. The Hungarian Revolution in the winter of 1956 brought the widespread discontent among the Chinese intellectuals to the surface. Being an astute political leader, Mao felt the growing unrest and sensed the threat it posed for the Communist Party. So, in the spring of 1957 he launched the Hundred Flowers movement as a way of relieving some of the public frustration.[10] Borrowing two phrases from classical Chinese literature, he declared: "Let a hundred flowers blossom, and let a hundred birds sing" (*baihua qifang, bainiao qiming* 百花齊放百鳥齊鳴). He invited frank public criticisms of government failures, promising that anyone who spoke up would be held completely blameless.

Chinese intellectuals in the cities took him at his word. This was the moment they had been waiting for in order to foster a true democracy for new China. Teachers, university students, government employees, and even factory workers spoke up in group meetings sponsored by Party branches. They hung big character posters on public buildings. The bitterness of the criticisms and the severity of the exposés of Party policy failures took Mao by surprise. He kept his silence for the time being, but when summer came, he set his Anti-Rightist campaign in motion. Apparently, full records had been kept on all who had spoken up. The Party-controlled media launched a coordinated and relentless attack on the leaders of the democracy movement. Anti-democracy big character posters appeared everywhere. At the grassroots level, group criticism sessions were held in every school, every government office, and every factory. Targeted individuals were forced to make self-criticisms in mass rallies and confess their sins. They were condemned as "rightists" and sent to remote areas for labor reform. Being branded a "rightist" left one stigmatized for life, and the curse carried on to the next generation. Hundreds of thousands of Chinese intellectuals spent years, sometimes decades, in exile, until their "rightist" stigma was lifted after the death of Mao, that is, if they had survived so long. Untold numbers perished.

The Hundred Flowers movement and the Anti-Rightist campaign that followed left a mixed but lasting impact on Chinese urban intellectuals. Compared to the peasants, they went through a much more agonizing experience. The peasants had themselves participated in the mass campaigns and had unanimously supported the Party policies calling for the removal of the former village elite. The peasants themselves had not been targeted in the purges. The urban intellectuals, on the other hand, while starting as active participants in the Hundred Flowers movement, subsequently became targets of harsh condemnation during the Anti-Rightist campaign and ended up in labor camp exile. Their relations vis-à-vis the Party—the "self and significant others" relations in our conceptual framework—by and large changed from being enthusiastic and supportive to being doubt-ridden and distrustful. It is noteworthy that the 1957 experience does not seem to have dampened the faith some intellectuals had in the Party. Many ranking officials today had been branded as "rightists" for what they did or said during the Hundred Flowers movement; now they are back in the government and seem to be trying hard to build a new China within the existing Party framework. For others, such as the noted dissident Liu Binyan, the experience of 1957 gave them a new perspective to see things in contemporary China. Liu (1990), for example, speaks of a higher kind of *zhong*, not the blind loyalty that bound imperial officials of the past to their emperors, nor the unquestioning loyalty that Party members dedicated to Chairman Mao in the early days of the communist movement. The Hundred Flowers movement and the Anti-Rightist campaign proved the futility of this kind of unquestioning loyalty. To Liu, *zhong* has come to signify loyalty to the ideal of democracy, and to the belief that democracy alone holds the key to the future of China.

The impact of the political campaigns in urban areas manifested itself partly in social structural change, but mostly in change in political attitudes and beliefs. The yearning for democracy first sparked in 1957 lay dormant for the next decade. The ten years of Cultural Revolution beginning in 1966 suppressed it further, but did not completely smother it.[11] After the death of Mao and the downfall of the Gang of Four, the spirit of democracy resurfaced during the Spring of Beijing movement in 1978–79. It attracted attention both at home and broad; but like its predecessor of 1957, it proved short-lived. The seeds for democracy sown in the Hundred Flowers movement, however, remained, and for a brief few weeks Chinese intellectuals found their voice of freedom and democracy once again during the campus liberalization movement in the fall of 1986. Their voice was silenced only under enormous pressure from the Party.[12] Hu Yaobang, then General Secretary of the Party, had to step down because he sympathized with the students. Then in the early summer of 1989, the voice of democracy cried out yet again, this time through massive demonstrations at Tiananmen Square, initially in mourning of the death of Hu Yaobang and subsequently turning into demands for democratic political reform. At the height of the movement, more than one million people in Beijing participated—students, workers, journalists, housewives, and even grandmothers and grandfathers. Almost the entire city took the side of the students as popular sentiments ran high. As the outside world, stunned and hopeful, watched nervously, the democracy movement ended in the tragic Tiananmen massacre on the early morning of June 4, 1989.[13]

* * *

Relevant Survey Findings

Relevant survey findings that help us understand the emerging new political culture in China are sketchy. In late 1987, Chu and Ju (1993) conducted a survey of cultural values in China based on a sample of 2,000 respondents randomly drawn from urban Shanghai, small towns outside Shanghai, and villages in the surrounding area. According to the results, submission to authority remained a key cultural value. But only 50.3 percent of the respondents (no apparent differences between rural and urban respondents) said they felt proud that this was so. More than one out of six (17.1 percent) said the value of submission should be discarded, and another 32.6 percent were not sure. The erosion of this value in China was more or less the same among all age and educational subgroups. In comparison, a parallel survey conducted in Taiwan in mid 1990, and using the same wording, found that the traditional value of submission to authority was endorsed by nearly eight out of ten Chinese respondents (Wang, Chung, and Chu 1991).

Discretion for self-preservation, a traditional value contrary to assertiveness, was overwhelmingly rejected by 63.6 percent of the respondents in the Shanghai-based survey. Only 7.8 percent were proud of it, and another 28.6 percent were not sure. People having higher exposure to media news and those of higher education felt more strongly about abandoning this traditional value. Pleasing superiors, another traditional value with political undertones in China, was rejected by 55.8 percent of the PRC respondents. Only 6.9 percent said they felt proud of it, and the remaining 37.3 percent were not sure. The rejection was stronger among those of higher education and among urban dwellers.

As a measure of attitudes towards political participation, the respondents in the Shanghai survey were asked whether the way a government spends its money is the government's own business, or whether this is something the people have a right to know. A large majority (74.2 percent) said the people had the right to know; only 25.8 percent said it was the government's own business. Respondents with high exposure to media news had a stronger awareness of the right of the public to know than the low-exposure group.

We have suggested that belief in fate can be a relevant element in traditional Chinese political culture. Chinese in the past tended to see their sufferings as a manifestation of fate rather than a result of the government's failure to look after their welfare. Chu and Ju asked this question: "If someone does not do well all his life, do you think this is because he does not work hard enough, or he is treated unfairly by others, or it is his fate?" Even though the question does not mention government failures, the answers are revealing. Only 13.5 percent said it was due to fate. As many as 71.8 percent attributed one's failure to not working hard enough, and another 14.7 percent mentioned unfair treatment by others. Similarly, a survey of 7,600 readers of the *China Youth* magazine showed only 11.6 percent of respondents agreed that "it is best to leave our life to fate" and 88.4 percent disagreed (Bai and Wang 1987).

In a national survey of 2,896 respondents conducted in China in December 1990, Nathan and Shi (1993) presented this statement: "There are some people whose ideology is problematic, for example, they sympathize with the Gang of Four." The respondents were then asked whether such people should be allowed to express their views in public meetings, express their views as a teacher in a college, and express their views by publishing articles or books. Only 17.4 percent said that these people should be allowed to express their views in a public meeting; 10.3 percent would permit such expression in a teaching environment; and another 10.3 percent would permit the publication of these viewpoints. Nathan and Shi interpreted the results as indicating low tolerance of minority political views. The same results can be taken to reflect the unpopularity of the communist ideology as envisioned by Mao, nearly fifteen years after the purge of the Gang of Four.

The survey findings do not illustrate the evolutionary process of the emergence of a new political culture in China. They provide indicators of certain aspects of political culture in China in the post-Mao era that is consistent with our historical and social structural analysis.

* * *

Emerging New Political Culture

The emerging new political culture in China reflects a complex mixture of Mao's revolutionary campaigns, the social structural changes the campaigns caused, the varied responses of the rural and urban populations, and the undying yearnings for democracy among Chinese intellectuals dating back to the May 4th movement of 1919 (Chow 1960). If one word can characterize the essence of the new political culture, in a general sense, it is *assertiveness*, which stands in sharp contrast to *zhong* and submission to authority which for centuries bound traditional Chinese culture, whether political or otherwise. A popular saying circulated in Beijing in the mid 1990s vividly illustrates the concrete expression of this assertiveness:

> If you have something to say but do not say it, it will be in vain.
> But if you say it, it will still be in vain.
> Even in vain, you still want to say it,
> Until it is not in vain.

Youhua bushuo baibushuo	有話不說白不說
jiushi shuole yebaishuo	就是說了也白說
baishuo yeyao shuo	白說也要說
shuo dao bubaishuo	說到不白說

The tortuous path by which Chinese political culture freed itself from its submissive past and pushed into the assertive present is both surprising and revealing. Mao, perhaps inadvertently, played a critical role in setting the course of this historic change, even though the outcome seems to be quite different from what he had in mind.

What did Mao really do in his nearly three-decade rule? His rural campaigns, from the land reform in the early 1950s to the People's Commune movement of 1958, aroused the Chinese peasants from their millennia of submissive obedience. They began to hope for a new life of local autonomy and self-sufficiency. The enthusiasm with which they had responded to the land reform movement was dampened somewhat by the bloody purges of the landlords, not all of whom were corrupt and evil, but the peasants themselves neither initiated the movement nor had any input into the manner of its implementation. They certainly had no say in the subsequent movements that took the land away from them. Had they really stood up, as Mao, in 1949, declared they had? The answer is a qualified yes. In a way they had stood up, but only passively for the moment Mao told them to, and in a manner Mao prescribed. Mao wanted them to stand up primarily to carry out his campaigns to eliminate the landed gentry from the rural social structure.

He probably failed to see the other side of the coin, however. The very fact that the peasants had stood up, no matter how briefly and under what confined circumstances, seems to have left a lasting impact on the emerging new political culture in the vast countryside. The peasants saw how the traditional structure of village authority, embodied in the landed gentry, could be torn apart and thrown out. They believed that they had taken an active part in bringing down the landlord class. Authority was no longer permanent, as it was in the past. They were later surprised to learn that even the venerable Chairman Mao, the symbol of ultimate authority under communism in China, had to step down following the disastrous People's Commune movement. In subsequent political campaigns, beginning with the Four Clean-Ups movement in the early 1960s, which targeted rural cadres who deviated from Mao's policy of rigid collectivism, and continuing through the years of the Cultural Revolution, the peasants witnessed the successive purges of the Party's cadres who had been accused of being "capitalistic roaders."

The peasants did not understand what that term meant, but they knew that many of the "capitalistic roaders" had done well in protecting the material well-being of their villages. On what grounds were they removed? In terms of relations between the self and significant others, the peasants' respect for authority and confidence in the Party leadership, as embodied in the rural cadres, had eroded further. In terms of values and beliefs, the peasants' experiences in these later political campaigns cast doubt on the concept of *zhong*, in the sense of loyalty to the Party. If those rural cadres who seemed to be dutiful followers of the Party could be thrown out for no apparent reasons other than being "capitalistic roaders," how could one demonstrate loyalty to the Party? What did loyalty to the Party mean?

As long as the Party's control over the rural regions remained tight and rigid, these questions seemed irrelevant. Performance was motivated not so much by *zhong*, as in the 1950s, but rather by the necessity to endure. Both the peasants and the rural cadres tried their best to survive by strictly following the Party's collective imperatives. For example, in villages outside Shanghai City in the 1970s, each family was allowed to raise no more than three chickens. To enforce this policy, trivial as it may sound today, rural cadres got up at night and, with flashlight in hand, went around in search of excess chickens (Chu, Wu, and Yu 1993). But after the death of Mao and the downfall of the Gang of Four, rural policies went through fundamental changes. Beginning in the early 1980s, the communes were abolished and the land leased back to the peasants. The rigid political control over rural production and distribution was lifted. The change of economic relations altered the social structure set up by Mao's mass campaigns and generated pressure for the shift to a new political culture.

Events following the abolition of the People's Communes suggest that interest in a new political culture had existed already for some time in rural China but had remained latent as long as the Party's tight control was rigidly imposed. Once the revolutionary political straitjacket was loosened, however, the Chinese peasants seem really to have stood up. The abolition of the People's Communes deprived the Party of its powerful, pervasive means of controlling the economic life of the rural population, including the invisible collection of hidden taxes. This, together with the discontinuation of political campaigns, seriously weakened the Party's authority over the vast rural countryside. Most rural cadres, finding themselves divested of effective influence over the daily life in the villages, had to supplement their meager wages by working their own leased land just like other peasants.[14] Their roles were reduced to routine administration and the unwelcome duty of tax collection, something that did not exist under the commune system.

It did not take long before the process of tax collection became rife with corruption in the rural countryside. The situation was made worse by the uncodified and complicated ways in which the taxes were collected. In one program, the government purchased crops at below market prices. Rural cadres in many areas found they could make money by giving the peasants "white slips" (*bai tiao* 白條), I.O.U.s of sorts, for the crops purchased, instead of paying cash as the central government had directed. Such practices were not new in the Chinese bureaucracy, but what was new were the responses of the peasants. Traditionally, of course, the peasants simply accepted the local officials' abuse of power, no matter how great the unhappiness and resentment involved in doing so. The proverb "When treated unfairly, submit meekly" (*ni lai shun shou* 逆 來 順 受) reflects this attitude accurately. Now, however, the peasants neither submitted meekly nor blindly obeyed. Their material relations were fundamentally changed and were exerting pressure on the Party. The peasants had become property owners, though still in a marginal way, and they wanted to protect their economic gains. Although they may have lacked a clearly articulated concept of rights, they were conscious of what should be theirs to own and keep. They openly voiced their protests by taking their cases to the county governments and, failing to get a satisfactory hearing, by staging local demonstrations, sometimes involving hundreds and even thousands of peasants. In the mid 1990s, such demonstrations were reported in various places through grapevine channels, although such news was not reported in the official media. These grassroots protests did not, however, go unnoticed by the central government, which later prohibited the issuing of "white slips" to peasants. The Party's decision to allow village elections, first in a few experimental locations, and now reaching a broad section of the country, is undoubtedly another attempt to address the problems of local corruption and village discontent.

Behind the peasant demonstrations lie highly significant changes in the political culture. The past notion of blind loyalty is gone. Chinese peasants are beginning to become conscious of what is their right, and in consequence they have become assertive rather than submissive. An in-depth study conducted in rural areas around Shanghai in the early 1990s found the villagers to be keenly alert to possible policy changes that might affect their economic fortunes. They listened to radio news everyday for clues (Chu, Wu, and Yu 1993). They do not hesitate to stand up and voice their protests, and even more importantly, they are capable of organizing massive demonstrations, something they learned from their near thirty-years' participation in the mass campaigns under Mao. Even though village elections are currently conducted under close monitoring by Party officials (Isaacson 1999), the Party's tight control over the rural countryside during the reign of Mao is gone for good. Experiments with direct elections at the township level were already being planned early in the year 2000 (Lawrence 2000).

The situation in urban centers is somewhat different. Unlike the villagers, most urban dwellers are wage earners whose material relations have changed little. A small minority of successful entrepreneurs own businesses, and these rely on personal connections to protect their enterprises. Urban dwellers are interested in changes in economic policies, especially if such changes affect their own jobs. In the last couple of years, the possibility of downsizing in state-operated enterprises, for example, has worried many families in large cities. In terms of political culture, the forces of change originate from a different source from in the countryside; that is, in the cities change is stimulated by ideas coming from abroad under the open door policy. Urban dwellers, especially the young and better educated, are more actively concerned with freedom and democracy than their rural counterparts. During the month-long Tiananmen Square demonstrations for democracy, a number of large cities, including Shanghai, Wuhan, and Chengdu, witnessed mass demonstrations held in support of the students in Beijing. In Wuhan, students and workers staged days-long sit-ins to block the Yangtze River Bridge. In Shanghai, the demonstrators tried to occupy the railway station while in Chengdu students set fire to public buildings.

The quest for freedom and democracy by the urbanites has its recent roots in the Hundred Flowers movement and the subsequent crackdown during the Anti-Rightist movement of 1957. Urban dwellers also bore witness to the excessive violence and bloodshed during the early years of the Cultural Revolution. Even though many today were too young at the time to understand fully the import of those events, they remembered what happened to their parents. Stories were passed around and became an important source of knowledge about what happened during the Cultural Revolution.[15] During my own frequent visits to China I have heard a number of such stories, most of them ending with words like "I can never forget what I saw." Such bitter memories lay low and latent during the busy day-to-day activities for making a living, but they came forth vivid and strong whenever groups of students and intellectuals stepped forward to demand democracy and political reform, as happened during the Spring of Beijing movement in 1978–79, the political liberalization movement in 1986, and most of all, the Tiananmen Demonstration in 1989. A major influence was the influx of ideas of freedom and democracy from the West. The most dramatic example was the Goddess of Democracy set up at Tiananmen Square by Beijing students in 1989. In their East China survey, Chu and Ju (1993) found that even exposure to Western media entertainment subtly affected political attitudes in ways contrary to Party ideology. Not a single respondent in the heavy-exposure group (one of those rare zero percentages found in survey research), versus 4.9 percent in the low-exposure group, wanted to be a Communist Party cadre. Also, as many as 58.8 percent of respondents in the heavy-exposure group, compared with only 20.2 percent in the low-exposure group, rejected "study politics seriously" as an important criterion for promotion.

Ironically, Mao himself may have unintentionally paved the ground for the democracy movements in China. First promising Chinese intellectuals a bright future in his version of new democracy, he then dashed their hopes by persecuting those who had responded to his call and spoken up. The final blow came during the Cultural Revolution, when Chinese intellectuals who had dedicated themselves to *zhong* and thus to Chairman Mao suddenly found themselves "enemies of the people" (*renmin gongdi* 人民共敵).

Many did not know how to cope. At one of the large universities in Shanghai, for example, a female professor who had been tortured by the Red Guards, including some of her own students, for three days and nights, jumped from her third floor office. As she lay in a pool of blood on the cement below, she cried aloud over and over: "Chairman Mao, I have not betrayed you. Chairman Mao, I have not betrayed you." The whole campus listened in deathly silence. No one, not even her husband, also a professor, dared come to her aid. Her voice became weaker and weaker until she died a few hours later. In telling this story, my friend said this was something he could never forget. In a rhetorical sense, one could say that when this female professor died crying "Chairman Mao, I have not betrayed you," loyalty to Chairman Mao passed away with her. It is memories like this that prepare the way for Chinese intellectuals to turn away from communism and embrace the ideas of Western democracy as an alternative.[16]

In the emerging new political culture, China's rural countryside and urban centers present an intriguing picture of commonalities and contrasts. In both villages and cities we see a clear departure from the traditional value of submission to authority. In both villages and cities we sense the emergence of assertiveness as the cornerstone of a new political culture. In both villages and cities blind loyalty to the Party authorities is a passing phenomenon. Both villagers and urbanites now know how to organize mass demonstrations to express their protests. By way of contrast, although the villagers capably utilize their local channels of communication to organize demonstrations when necessary, they have no active concern for democracy. Their demonstrations are about local issues, mostly corruption and abuses of power by rural cadres. In urban centers, on the other hand, the cognitive roots for democracy are clearly part of their new political culture. Urbanites are very much concerned with freedom and political democracy. But control is much tighter in the cities. And they do not have readily available channels of communication by which they can turn the cognitions for democracy into concrete, organized movements. Since the Tiananmen demonstration, the Party leadership has blocked all communication channels that can potentially lead to an organized movement of a regional or national scale. Even the Internet is placed under close monitoring by the Party because it can potentially serve as a communication channel for political purposes.[17]

Summing Up

The emerging new political culture in China is a concoction of contradictions (*mao dun* 矛盾), a term Mao himself used to signify the driving force of revolution, the impetus for change. For one, the new culture represents a contradiction between Mao's rhetoric of new democracy and his unhesitant silencing of the voices of democracy whenever they threatened his totalitarian control. Secondly, the new culture represents a contradiction between the seemingly endless mass political campaigns orchestrated by the Party under Mao and the skills of organization and demonstration the Chinese people learned from participating in them. Also present is a contradiction between the traditional Chinese cultural value of submission to authority, which the Party demands from the Chinese people despite its rhetoric to the contrary, and the new assertiveness that now finds its vocal expressions in many events. This is the contradiction between blind loyalty, which the Party expects from the people, and the people's discerning ability to assess their situation and to protect their own interests. Finally, the new political culture represents a contradiction between the unyielding determination of the current Party leadership to remain in power at whatever price and the budding popular demands for freedom and democracy in the post-Mao era. The Tiananmen Square massacre of 1989 was a sad and painful consequence of such contradictions. Less severe but equally telling was the 1999 crackdown on the seemingly innocuous Falun Gong spiritual and physical exercise movement, which the Party apparently sees as a silent threat to its power (Pomfret and Laris 1999). What apparently worries the Party leadership in this latter case are not the forms of spiritual exercises practiced but the undetected channels of communication tying together millions of Falun Gong members nationwide.

In the emerging new political culture we see a new trend in the self's political relations with significant others, that is, with Party officials and the government itself. We also see a new trend in the self's relations with values and beliefs, as the Chinese people reject the traditional values of *zhong* and *yuzhong* and adopt in their place the new values of assertiveness and active protection of self interest. And we see a new trend in the self's aggressive relations with the changing material world, more apparent in rural areas than in urban centers, as the Party loosens its control over the distribution and utilization of material resources in ways that may have profound effects in the realms both of political relations and of values and beliefs.

The Chinese Communist Party found itself in a dilemma as it celebrated the 50th anniversary of the founding of the People's Republic of China. Few could dispute that Mao's nearly three decades of ultra-leftist economic policies had resulted in poverty and deprivation on a nationwide scale. The ten years of Cultural Revolution he launched in 1966 perpetrated unspeakable excesses of violence and brutality unprecedented in Chinese history, no matter how benign Mao's original intentions might have been. The combined impact of these events registered itself in an unforeseen loss of confidence in communism among the Chinese populace. Communism no longer seems to excite people either as a viable ideology or as a working goal for the nation. In fact, livelihood in China has greatly improved and prosperity has spread in cities in the coastal regions with its abandonment as a guiding principle of economic policies. China has made significant strides in many fields in the twenty years since Deng Xiaoping adopted his open door policy of economic reform. Visitors who return to China after merely a few years are generally impressed with the signs of prosperity they see in the cities. Some scholars in America, for example Schell (1994), are pinning hope for China's future on a new rising generation of entrepreneurs, dissidents, and technocrats. Whether this new generation will be able to transform China into a modern nation depends very much on political reform, which has been slow in coming. The Party leadership, in hesitating even to consider a partial loosening of political control, seems both unable to understand and unprepared to cope with the forces of the emerging new political culture inadvertently fostered by Mao's revolutionary campaigns and now gaining momentum in China's vibrant economy. The future of China in the 21st century rests on whether, when, and how the Party leadership will find its way to adapting to the emerging new political culture.

Notes

1. Political culture in contemporary China is discussed by Shiping Hua in the introductory chapter of the present volume. Also, see the chapters herein by Alan Liu, Edward Friedmen, Peter Moody, and Kalpana Misra. For a theoretical discussion of the concept of political culture in general, see Gabriel Almond, "The Intellectual History of the Civic Concept," in Almond and Verba (1980). Although the sociological contributions by Max Weber and Talcott Parsons are recognized by Almond, they do not appear to play a significant role in the formulation and empirical studies of civic culture and political culture.

2. The scholarly writings of Francis L.K. Hsu have approached the understanding of Chinese cultural values from a holistic, rather than a psychological viewpoint. For other discussions of traditional Chinese culture, see Fei Hsiao-tung (1939), Theodore de Bary, Wing-tsit Chan, and Burton Watson (1960), Liang Shu-ming (1963), Benjamin Schwartz (1985a), Benjamin Schwartz (1985b), Tu Wei-mng (1991), Wang Gungwu (1991), and Fei Xiaotong (1992) . The importance of social structure is manifest in the writings of Fei Xiaotong (Fei Hsiao-tung) on contemporary China. In my own conceptualization, as well as in the formulations of these scholars, culture is not embued with explanatory power in the behavioral science notion of causation. I have used culture as a conceptual framework in which we seek to understand the broad behavioral patterns of a people.

3. The concept of political culture in this hermeneutic discussion shares common ground with the concept of civic culture as first proposed by Almond and Verba (1963), but with a different orientation. Their theoretical emphasis is on the psychological dimension of politics. Some of these components of political culture are implicit in my discussion of political culture in traditional China. For example, in traditional China, people did not see themselves as participants in the political system other than in their roles as taxpayers and service providers. In fact, the notion of participation in the political processes was alien to them. They bore heavy obligations and possessed few of the rights implied in the concept of political participation. Hua (1999) has succinctly discussed the definition and methodology of studying political culture in China, including both hermeneutic and empirical, non-quantitative methods. Quantitative surveys of political attitudes are not readily available in

China. The relevant statistical data I have used in this paper come primarily from Chu and Ju (1993) and Nathan and Shi (1993). The study of the evolution of a new political culture in China necessitates a broad historical approach. In my overall conceptual framework, I have relied on a social structural perspective, without overlooking the psychological implications such a perspective entails.

4. There is academic debate over whether social structure or culture is a more powerful explanatory factor for understanding political behavior. See Dickson (1992). But it is pointless, as Pye (1988) has stated, to argue which one is a more powerful factor.

5. Pye (1988) has noted similarities between the Mandarin officials of the past and the cadres of the People's Republic of China. There are of courses differences.

6. In my conceptualization, social structure and cultural values are closely related and mutually supportive entities. Mao's thinking, however, leaned toward social structure as a primary force for bringing about changes in values and beliefs. Once the social structure is changed, Mao believed, changes in cultural values follow as a matter of course. Events in China have shown that Mao was right, although not in a way he had envisioned.

7. For a detailed analysis of the mass campaigns during the land reform movement, see Chu (1977), chapter 2, pp. 35–60. Also see Cell (1977, 1984), and Huang (1995).

8. For a discussion of the events during the People's Commune movement that led to Mao's stepping down as head of the state, see Chu (1977), chapter 4, pp. 187–214.

9. The political campaigns that converted more than seventy thousand private enterprises into state ownership, in what was known as the Public-Private Joint Management movement of 1956, are analyzed in Chu (1977, 43–46).

10. The Hundred Flowers movement and the subsequent Anti-Rightist campaign are analyzed in Chu (1977), chapter 7. pp. 215–252.

11. For detailed discussions of the Cultural Revolution, see Barnouin and Yu (1993). For a chronicle of the Cultural Revolution, see Gao Yuan (1987). Wen Chihua (1995) has analyzed the impact of the Cultural Revolution on the next generation.

12. Popular protest movements in modern China are analyzed in Wasserstrom and Perry (1994).

13. For a detailed account of the events that led to the Tiananmen massacre, see Morrison (1989). Also, see Yi Mu and Thompson (1990), Duke (1990), Saich (1990), Yang and Wagner (1990), and Hong Shi (1990). Reports from the provinces on prodemocracy protests outside the large cities are presented in Unger (1991).

14. Chan, Madsen, and Unger (1992) have conducted a comparative analysis of one village before and after the death of Mao Zedong.

15. Personal recollections and oral history have become important sources of knowledge about what happened during the Cultural Revolution. For example, see Cheng Nien (1987) and Feng Jicai (1991).

16. The potential impact of Western ideologies on contemporary China is analyzed in a collection of papers edited by Li Bulou (see Li Bulou 1991).

17. The extent the government's control over the Internet will be loosened after China's accession into the World Trade Organization (WTO) remains to be seen. Most likely the impact on China's political culture, if any, will initially be limited to Internet subscribers in the cities, but will eventually spread to urban residents in

general. The impact, however, will not be immediately observable. Together with e-mail, which is used among Chinese both at home and abroad, the Internet can be used as a channel of communication from foreign sources. For the audience at large in China, media news and messages from Western Internet sources will have to be translated into Chinese. Whether the translation is conducted at the source of origin or in China will be a relevant factor determining the impact of Western-originated news through the Internet.

References

Almond, Gabriel A., and Sidney Verba. 1963. *The Civic Culture*. Princeton, NJ: Princeton University Press.
———, eds. 1980. *The Civic Culture Revisited*. Boston, MA: Little, Brown and Co.
Bai Nanfang, and Wang Xiaoqiang. 1988. *The Social Psychology of Reform: Changes and Choices*. Chengdu: Sichuan People's Publishing House.
Barnouin, Barbara, and Changgen Yu. 1993. *Ten Years of Turbulence: The Chinese Cultural Revolution*. London: Kegan Paul International.
Brown, Archie, and Jack Gray. 1977. *Political Culture and Political Change in Communist States*. New York: Holmes and Meier.
Cell, Charles P. 1977. *Revolution at Work: Mobilization Campaigns in China*. New York: Academic Press.
———. 1984. "Communication in China's Mass Mobilization Campaigns." In *China's New Social Fabric*. Godwin C. Chu and Francis L.K. Hsu, eds. London: Kegan Paul International, 25–46.
Chan, Anita, Richard Madsen, and Jonathan Unger. 1992. *Chen Village Under Mao and Deng*. Berkeley, CA: University of California Press.
Cheng Nien. 1987. *Life and Death in Shanghai*. New York: Grove Press.
Chow Tse-tsung. 1960. *The May Fourth Movement: Intellectual Revolution in Modern China*. Cambridge, MA: Harvard University Press.
Chu, Godwin C. 1977. *Radical Change through Communication in Mao's China*. Honolulu, HI: University Press of Hawaii.
———. 1979. "Communication and Cultural Change in China: A Conceptual Framework." In *Moving a Mountain: Cultural Change in China*, Godwin C. Chu and Francis L.K. Hsu, eds. Honolulu, HI: University Press of Hawaii.
Chu, Godwin C., and Yanan Ju. 1993. *The Great Wall in Ruins: Communication and Cultural Change in China*. Albany, NY: State University of New York Press.
Chu, Godwin C., Shenling Wu, and Zhenwei Yu. 1993. *Rural Chinese Family in Transition: A Case Study in Qingpu County*. Shanghai: Academy Press.
de Bary, William Theodore, Wing-tsit Chan, and Burton Watson, eds. 1960. *"The Mean* (Chung yung)," *Sources of Chinese Tradition*. New York: Columbia University Press.
Devine, Donald. 1972. *The Political Culture of the United States*. Boston, MA: Little, Brown and Co.
Dickson, Bruce J. 1992. "What Explains Chinese Political Behavior? The Debate over Structure and Culture." *Comparative Politics* 25, no. 1: 103–118.
Duke, Michael S. 1990. *The Iron House: A Memoir of the Chinese Democracy Movement and the Tiananmen Massacre*. Laton, Utah: Peregrine Smith Books.

Fagen, Richard. 1969. *The Transformation of Political Culture in Cuba*. Stanford, CA: Stanford University Press.
Fei Hsiao-tung. 1939. *Peasant Life in China*. London: Kegan Paul.
Fei Xiaotong. 1992. *From the Soil: The Foundations of Chinese Society. A Translation of Fei Xiaotong's Xiangtu Zhongguo*, translated by Gary G. Hamilton and Wang Zheng. Berkeley: University of California Press.
Feng Jicai. 1991. *Voices from the Whirlwind: An Oral History of the Chinese Cultural Revolution*. New York: Pantheon Books.
Gao Yuan. 1987. *Born Red: A Chronicle of the Cultural Revolution*. Stanford, CA: Stanford University Press.
Goldman, Merle. 1979. "The Media Campaign as a Weapon in Political Struggle." In Chu, Godwin C. 1979, 179–206.
Hong Shi. 1990. "China's Political Development After Tiananmen: Tranquility by Default." *Asian Survey* 30, no. 12: 1206–1217.
Hsu, Francis L.K. 1949. *Under the Ancestors' Shadow*. London: Routledge and Kegan Paul.
———. 1953. *Americans and Chinese: Two Ways of Life*. New York: H. Schuman.
Hua Shiping. 1999. "Definition and Methodology of Political Culture Theory: A Case Study of Sinology." *Asian Thought and Society* 24, no. 70 (January–April, 1999): 23–41.
Huang, Philip C.C. 1995. "Rural Class Struggle in the Chinese Revolution: Representational and Objective Realities from the Land Reform to the Cultural Revolution." *Modern China* 21, no.1:105–143.
Isaacson, Walter. 1999. "Our Newstour to China—A Visit Reveals the Promise and Problems of Sweeping Change." *Time*, 11 October 1999, 6.
Lawrence, Susan V. 2000. "China: Village Democracy." *Far Eastern Economic Review*. 20 January 2000, 16–17.
Li Bulou, ed. 1991. *Chongji yu sikao: Xifang sichao zai Zhongguo* [Impact and reflections: Western ideologies in China]. Wuhan, Hubei: Hubei People's Publishing House.
Liang Shu-ming. 1963. *Zhongguo wenhua yaoyi* [The essence of Chinese culture]. Hong Kong: Jichen Publishing Co.
Liu Binyan. 1990. *A Higher Kind of Loyalty: A Memoir by China's Foremost Journalist*. New York: Pantheon Books.
Moody, Peter. 1994. "Trends in the Study of Chinese Political Culture." *China Quarterly*, no. 139 (September 1994): 731–740.
Morrison, Donald. 1989. *Massacre in Beijing: China's Struggle for Democracy*. New York: Warner Books.
Nathan, Andrew J. 1993. "Is Chinese Culture Distinctive?—A Review Article." *The Journal of Asian Studies* 52, no. 4: 923–936.
Nathan, Andrew J., and Tianjian Shi. 1993. "Cultural Requisites for Democracy in China: Findings from a Survey." *Daedalus* 122, no. 2: 95–123.
Pomfret, John, and Michael Laris. 1999. "China Confronts a Silent Threat—Despite Arrests, Falun Gong Continues Peaceful Protests." *Washington Post* Foreign Service, 30 October 1999, A01.
Pye, Lucian. 1968. *The Spirit of Chinese Politics: A Psychological Study of the Authority Crisis in Political Development*. Boston, MA: MIT Press.

————. 1988. *The Mandarin and the Cadre: China's Political Cultures.* Ann Arbor, MI: Center for Chinese Studies, University of Michigan.

————. 1992. *The Spirit of Chinese Politics.* Cambridge, MA: Harvard University Press.

Pye, Lucian, with Mary W. Pye. 1985. *Asian Power and Politics: The Cultural Dimension of Authority.* Cambridge, MA: Harvard University Press.

Pye, Lucian, and Sidney Verba. 1966. *Political Culture and Political Development.* Princeton, NJ: Princeton University Press.

Saich, Tony, ed. 1990. *The Chinese People's Movement: Perspectives on Spring 1989.* Armonk, NY: M.E. Sharpe.

Schell, Orville. 1994. *Mandate of Heaven: A New Generation of Entrepreneurs, Dissidents, Bohemians, and Technocrats Lays Claim to China's Future.* New York: Simon and Schuster.

Schwartz, Benjamin I. 1985a. *China's Cultural Values.* Occasional Paper No. 18. Tempe, AZ: Center for Asian Studies, Arizona State University.

————. 1985b. *The World of Thought in Ancient China.* Cambridge, MA: Harvard University Press.

Solomon, Richard. 1971. *Mao's Revolution and the Chinese Political Culture.* Berkeley: University of California Press.

Tu Weiming, ed. 1991. *The Living Tree: The Changing Meaning of Being Chinese Today. Daedalus* 120, no. 2 (Special Issue, Spring 1991).

Tucker, Robert C. 1973. "Culture, Political Culture, and Communist Society." *Political Science Quarterly* 88, no. 2 (June 1973): 173–90.

Unger, Jonathan, ed. 1991. *The Pro-Democracy Protests in China: Reports from the Provinces.* Armonk, NY: M.E.Sharpe.

Wang, Georgette, Wei-wen Chung, and Godwin C. Chu. 1991. "Cultural Value Survey in Taiwan." *Journal of Communication Arts, Special Issue on Cultural Change in Asia and the United States* (Chulalongkorn University, Bangkok, Thailand) 12, no. 2: 71–80.

Wang Gungwu. 1991. *The Chineseness of China: Selected Essays.* Hong Kong: Oxford University Press.

Wasserstrom, Jeffrey N., and Elizabeth J. Perry, eds. 1994. *Popular Protest and Political Culture in Modern China.* 2nd edition. Boulder, CO: Westview Press.

Wen Chihua. 1995. *The Red Mirror: Children of China's Cultural Revolution.* Boulder, CO: Westview Press.

Whyte, Martin K. 1992. "Urban China: A Civil Society in the Making?" In *State and Society in China: The Consequences of Reform,* Arthur Lewis Rosenbaum, ed. Boulder, CO: Westview Press, 77–101.

Yang, Winston L. Y., and Marsha L. Wagner, eds. 1990. *Tiananmen: China's Struggle for Democracy, Its Prelude, Development, Aftermath, and Impact.* Baltimore, MD: University of Maryland School of Law.

Yi Mu, and Mark V. Thompson. 1990. *Crisis at Tiananmen: Reform and Reality in Modern China.* San Francisco, CA: China Books & Periodicals.

3

New Confucianism: A Native Response to Western Philosophy

Roger T. Ames

The Problem

In response to the question "What has been the impact of Western cultural imperialism—what Edward Said has called 'cognitive imperialism'—on the Sinic world?, we can certainly observe that over the past century and a half "Confucianism," on the stock market of world culture, has experienced some rather wild swings in value. At one end of this pendulum Hu Shi's battle cry for the May Fourth reform was "Down with the House of Confucius"; at the other end is the banner of Tu Weiming's evangalizing anti-disestablishmentarianism: "Third-Wave Confucianism." We watched the "*pikong* (批孔)" anti-Confucius campaign during the Cultural Revolution; we are now tracking the rhetorical rehabilitation of Confucianism by Deng Xiaoping's reformist policies, which bills it as China's resource for human rights "with Chinese characteristics." Confucianism has been reviled by many as yellow silt clotting the arteries of China, retarding the vital circulation of those new ideas necessary to enable it to emerge into the modern world. At the same time others are celebrating it as that indigenous cultural resource

---

An earlier version of this article appeared in *China Studies* (*Zhongguo yanjiu*) No. 5 (1999): 23–52, and is reprinted here with permission.

which has made Asian economic development in recent decades the miracle we all know it to be. Turning from *Confucianism* to *Confucianist*, Guy Alitto has called Liang Shuming "the Last Confucian," thereby tolling the passing of this great tradition. Today, the Chinese academy is touting the same Liang Shuming as the first in the breed of "New Confucians" (*xinruxuejia* 新儒學家). For some, such as Joseph Levenson, Myron Cohen and Marjory Wolf,[1] Confucianism is an effete, patriarchal ideology whose welcome demise is making room for a long-needed cultural transformation; for others, the same Confucianism is a *sine qua non* for "Chineseness" and is alive and well in the modern world. Arif Dirlik rues what he takes to be an unholy tryst between Confucianism as an indictable "post-colonialist discourse," and the devil himself, capitalism. For him, the revival of Confucianism in modern Asia is oriental "Orientalism." It is at best a conspiracy between the State and freeloading intellectuals, or, as he says, "a foremost instance . . . of intellectual discourse creating its object."[2]

In order to assay the impact of Western philosophy on China's indigenous traditions and to assess the price China has had to pay for this engagement in terms of its own cultural integrity and autonomy, it is necessary first to determine what in Chinese culture has been put at risk in the relationship.[3] Given the confusion that frequently arises over the term "Confucianism," it would seem we must ask the question: What, after all, is "Confucianism?" What is it, precisely, that all the divided, conflicting, and mutually contradictory judgments of our best interpreters of modern China are directed at?

However, the philosopher's job is "meta": to worry about our basic presuppositions in engaging such a question. And the *comparative* philosopher's job is to worry about the uncommon assumptions that separate cultures: assumptions that are at once the greatest obstacle and the greatest opportunity in cross-cultural translation. As a starting point in this essay, I contend that framing our question in Western analytical terms as "What is Confucianism?"—or, in other words, essentializing Confucianism by treating it as a specific ideology that can be denoted with varying degrees of detail and accuracy—is an assumption that Dirlik begins from and is one likely to add confusion rather than provide resolution. *What* is an interrogative perhaps appropriate for attempts at systematic philosophy, from Plato to Freud, but it is not appropriate in reading a fundamentally aesthetic tradition which takes as its basic premise the uniqueness of each and every situation. Setting aside the "what" question, therefore, we need rather to ask: *How* does "Confucianism" function? Taking our cue from Chinese medicine, we have to think physiologically rather than anatomically: in understanding Confucianism, we might need to feel a pulse rather than locate an artery.[4]

Dao: The "Way" or the "Truth"?

We need to begin from an awareness of the contingency and cultural specificity of those exclusionary and imperialistic Cartesian assumptions that have driven the modern Western approach to self-understanding. As Tiles and Tiles contend:

> the very radical separation which Descartes achieved, a separation which distinctively marks off Cartesian epistemology from ancient epistemology, has continued to shape not only our philosophic tradition, but also the conception of science on which many of our institutions have been based. The dominant conception has been that science is a quest for truth, for objective knowledge, and as such is not and should not be concerned with practical, political and moral issues that might arise as a result of making its knowledge available for application.[5]

This attitude that cultural understanding can, as a kind of experimental science, be pursued as an encounter between a self-contained subject and an independently given object, stands in stark contrast to certain assumptions grounding the Confucian world view.

Chinese philosophy, like most things Chinese, must be understood in terms of process and continuities rather than abstract and essential truths. As Confucius, standing on the riverbank, remarked: "So it passes, never ceasing day or night" (*Analects* 9.17). Thus, any discussion of the cultural interests of contemporary China must begin with the "where" and the "when" of things. In contrast to a dominant theme of Western philosophy, beginning its career with the decontextualizing metaphysical sensibilities of the classical Greeks and later reiterating these assumptions with Cartesian objectivism, the Chinese tradition has tended to be historicist and genealogical. As such, it is resistant to articulation in theoretical and conceptual terms that presuppose unfamiliar notions such as objectivity and strict identity—notions that have underwritten dualistic thinking as a Western cultural dominant.[6] Conceptualization requires principles, univocal meanings, correspondence between propositions and states-of-affairs, and a sense of reference—all assumptions which, while of central importance in Western epistemology, have had minimal relevance in the axiologically driven Chinese traditions of ethics, aesthetics, and religion.

Yü Ying-shih in his role as a cultural historian, underscores the problem entailed by the wholesale application of Western structures to an understanding of the Chinese experience:

> I am far from proposing any kind of intellectual isolationism in the study of Chinese history. . . . However, it is imperative that Chinese historians begin to design and develop their own concepts and methods uniquely suited to coping with the particular shapes of Chinese historical experience independent of, but not in isolation from, theories and practices of history in other parts of the world including the West.[7]

Does this mean that, in registering entirely defensible suspicions about the sometimes scientistic pretences of historical positivists, we must abandon attempts at historical objectivity? Yü Ying-shih, citing the dangers of sliding into nihilism and relativism if we abandon objectivity, resists this assumption. But perhaps approaching the story of Confucianism as a continuing cultural narrative rather than as isolatable doctrines and ideologies opens a third position between positivism and relativism. While presenting us with a rolling, continuous, and always contingent narrative out of which emerges that tradition's own value and logic, this tradition alerts us both to the reflexivity entailed in telling the story as well as to the hermeneutical sensibilities necessary for any responsible attempt at cultural interpretation. But why, then, call it "Confucianism"? Because a narrative must have a proper name.

I.A. Richards, the Cambridge scholar, registers an important insight when he asserts in passing that the classical Chinese philosophers are closer to poets than to analysts, and that reading their key philosophical terms as concrete images rather than as concepts will take us much closer to the original intent.[8] Richards worries over the reductionism that has characterized most of our attempts at cultural translation:

> The problem seems to grow still more formidable as we realize that it concerns not only incommensurable concepts but also comparisons between concepts and items which may not be concepts at all. . . . In place of a baffling and obscure *concept*, translation has in such extreme cases to deal with a relatively describable blend of intention, feeling, and tone.[9]

Richards surmises, I think correctly, that if conceptual "analysis" is introduced as a methodology for understanding traditional Chinese culture, it smuggles in with it a world view and a way of thinking that is alien to the tradition itself. I cite him at some length:

> Our Western tradition provides us with an elaborate apparatus of universals, particulars, substances, attributes, abstracts, concretes, generality, specificities, properties, qualities, relations, complexes, accidents, essences, organic wholes, sums, classes, individuals, concrete universals, objects, events, forms, contents, etc. Mencius, as we have seen, gets along without any of this and with nothing at all definite to take its place. Apart entirely from the metaphysics that we are only too likely to bring in with this machinery, the practical difficulty arises that by applying it we deform his thinking. . . . The danger to be guarded against is our tendency to force a structure, which our special kind of Western training (idealist, realist, positivist, Marxist, etc.) makes easiest for us to work with, upon modes of thinking which may very well not have any such structure at all—and which may not be capable of being analysed by means of this kind of logical machinery.[10]

Following Richards, then, we might want to be suspect of analysis as a method for getting a handle on Confucianism and, again like Richards, rely upon some alternative approach.

In fact, we might do better, as Yü Ying-shih suggests, to take the Chinese tradition on its own terms. That is, we might do better to pursue a *narrative* understanding, an understanding we might arrive at by drawing relevant correlations among specific historical figures and events.

Perhaps an example taken from the dawning of Confucianism but still of contemporary relevance will help bring the difference between narrative and analytic modes of understanding into sharper focus and thereby suggest a way of "reading" the tradition. How, we might ask, should we read the *Lunyu* (Analects)? We can proceed with a conceptual reconstruction by isolating and attempting to stipulate the content of the key philosophical vocabularies: *ren* (仁), *yi* (義), *li* (禮), and so on. Alternatively, we can construct our understanding in a much less formal way, that is, analogically by associating one passage with another, and one historical example with another, so that *ren* is ultimately defined by the *way* or, using the vocabulary of the text itself, the *dao* (道) according to which central players such as Confucius himself, Yan Hui, and Guanzhong lived their lives. In this reading strategy, the reader's life experience is always brought to the interpretation, making each reading specific and unique. If *ren* means "achieved person," perhaps it refers to the unique ways of living and thinking of exemplary persons rather than to some formula.

A second example. If there is one exception to the otherwise sound assertion that the Indo-European and Sinic cultures developed almost totally independently of each other, it is Buddhism. One way of focusing on the difference between the analytic search for "truth" and the mapping of an appropriate and productive "way" (*dao*), then, is to examine the different interpretations which a story in the Pali canon has provoked within the traditions of Indo-European and Chinese cultures respectively. The story is of one Kisagotami, whose suffering as a Buddhist Job seems without limit:

> Going along, about to bring forth, I saw my husband dead; having given birth on the path, (I had) not yet arrived at my own house. Two sons dead and a husband dead upon the path for miserable (me); mother and father and brother were burning upon one pyre. . . . Then I saw the flesh of my sons eaten in the midst of the cemetery; with my family destroyed, despised by all, with husband dead, I attained the undying.[11]

As the story is recounted, Kisagotami "attained the undying" with the help of the Buddha. As a strategy for relieving her plight, Buddha instructed her to go around to the various houses in her village and return to him with a mustard seed from that residence which had not been visited by death.

A familiar Indo-European rendition of this story has it that Kisagotami, in going house to house in search of the mustard seed, came to realize that death always attends life. Death is a universal and inescapable truth, and the knowledge of this truth has set her free. Peter Hershock, in *Liberating Intimacy*, characterizes Kisagotami's epiphany in the following terms:

> According to our usual set of presuppositions, the point of this story is that suffering is universal. Kisagotami learns that grief is an experience common to all of us, one that is perhaps inevitable given the nature of sentient being. Among these presuppositions . . . is a more or less well-articulated belief in the objectivity of identity and hence in the reality of essences or universals. . . .[12]

Within the Chinese tradition, on the other hand, there is a narrative rather than a conceptual reading of Kisagotami's plight and her return to health. The basic unit of humanity and the pervasive cultural metaphor in China is the family. Kisagotami's predicament is that the traumatic serial deaths of her family members has led to her gradual disintegration from the village community. In the course of this growing isolation, there has arisen a challenge to her own life, for the loss of the roles and relationships out of which a person is constituted is indeed life-threatening. The Buddha, in his wisdom, sends Kisagotami back into her community, constituted as it is by those specific family members, neighbors, and friends from which her life narrative has been constructed. By rekindling and renewing these relationships, she is able to restore her sense of person. Far from attaining universal insight, Kisagotami, who has wandered from her own path and lost her direction, simply finds her way back and relocates herself. In reconstituting herself, she regains a sense of continuity, a trust in the community, a feeling of belonging. This smaller sense of truth—Kisagotami's trust in the shared narrative of her in the community—is the realization that restores her to her proper life's path.

Hershock characterizes this Chinese understanding of the story in the following terms:

> We have to recall that Kisagotami is not just "a woman," a faceless player in a generic tale, but someone known with greater or lesser intimacy by everyone in her village. When she knocks on a door and asks if a death has occurred in the home, rather than being answered with a brusque yes or no, her own pain will call forth that of the person she meets. . . . Hearing these stories and being drawn ineluctably back into the fabric of her neighbors' lives, their hopes and fears, their sorrows and joys, Kisagotami must have begun already to feel herself being healed. But it is only upon returning to the Buddha and reporting her failure to secure the mustard seeds that Kisagotami is said to have truly awakened. Relating the stories of her neighbors, Kisagotami actively understands that suffering is never merely objective or subjective, but profoundly and irreducibly interpersonal, shared. . . . *What* happens is decidedly less important than *how* it ramifies among all those whose stories are in even some very small way included in and inclusive of our own.[13]

In settling on a methodology for exploring Confucianism, we must be aware that the analysis of the Confucian world, or of the key philosophical terms that report on it, will prejudice our project by overwriting Chinese philosophy with Western assumptions. For example, in looking for a Chinese functional equivalent for *truth,* we should not limit ourselves to our philosophically dominant, and thus familiar, corresponding notions of truth but consider the alternative and more marginalized, pragmatic, and aesthetic meanings as well.

It is explicitly to avoid such cultural reductionism that Richards proposes his "multiple definitions" approach to cultural translation. His "technique for comparative studies" is both semantic and syntactical. In moving between the cultures, he recommends that we "vague up" the meanings of key philosophical terms by bringing the full range of possible meanings of any particular term into consideration. At the same time, we need to be critically self-conscious of what our implicit syntactic apparatus entails. In Richards' own words:

> What is needed, in brief, is greater imaginative resource in a double venture—in imagining other purposes than our own and other structures for the thought that serves them. . . . [Multiple Definition] is a proposal for a systematic survey of the language we are forced to use in translation, of the ranges of possible meanings which may be carried both by our chief pivotal terms—such as Knowledge, Truth, Order, Nature, Principle, Thought, Feeling, Mind, Datum, Law, Reason, Cause, Good, Beauty, Love, Sincerity . . . — and of our chief syntactic instruments, 'is,' 'has,' 'can,' 'of,' and the like.[14]

Richards believes that it is the acceptance of one definition as being opposed to another that locates us in different camps within our own philosophical dialectic and separates us from philosophical traditions that lie beyond our experience. Hence, in surrendering the specificity of our meaning we also surrender our imposed philosophical presuppositions.

In fact, as we reflect on the Chinese tradition broadly, we find that "reason" does not function analytically as some abstract, impersonal standard available for adjudication, but rather as a reservoir of historical instances of reasonableness available for analogical comparison. Similarly, "culture" is *this* specific historical pattern of human flourishing as it is lived out in the lives of the people; "logic" is the internal coherence of this particular community's narrative; "knowledge" is a kind of "know-how" evidenced in making *one's own* way smoothly and without obstruction in *this* particular locale; and "truth," or probably better the cognate idea of "trust," is a quality of relatedness demonstrated in *one's own* capacity to foster productive relationships that begin with the maintenance of one's integrity and extend to the enhancement of one's natural, social, and cultural contexts.

This specific narrative character of Chinese philosophy arises because a culture dominant in the tradition, now and then, has been the priority of process and change over form and stasis, a privileging, in other words, of cosmology over metaphysics. That the *Book of Changes* (*Yijing*) is the first of the Chinese classics in every sense, bears witness to the priority of prescriptive cosmological questions—"*How* should the world hang together?"—over putatively descriptive, metaphysical, and ontological questions—"*What* is the reality behind appearance?/ *What* is the Being behind the beings?/*What* is the One behind the many?"

On the Western side, truth is commonly conceived of as a correspondence between what is real—the Being behind the beings—and what is representational—a mental mirroring of reality. On the Chinese side, with its *how*-priority attitude, the ambition is of a different order. With no separation between phenomena and ontological foundations, "reality" is precisely that complex pattern of relationships which in sum constitute the myriad things of the world. Knowledge, then, is not abstract but concrete, not representational but performative and participatory; it involves not closure but disclosure and is not discursive but is, rather, concerned with the requisite know-how to effect robust and productive relationships.

"Knowing" in classical China, then, does not consist so much in knowing *what*—a kind of knowledge which provides some understanding of the environing conditions of the natural world—as in knowing *how* to be adept in relationships, and *how*, in optimizing the possibilities that these relations provide, to develop trust in their viability. The cluster of terms that define knowing are thus programmatic and exhortative, encouraging as they do the quality of the roles and associations that define us. Propositions may be true, but it is more important that husbands and friends be so.

Rather than a vocabulary characterized by oppositions like *truth* and *falsity*, *right* and *wrong*, *good* and *evil*, which speak to the "whatness" of things, we find *harmony* and *disorder*, *genuineness* and *hypocrisy*, *trust* and *dissimulation*, *adeptness* and *ineptness*, dichotomies which, being concerned as they are with "how well" things hang together, reflect the priority of the continuity that obtains among things. The epistemic commitment thus lies in "realizing" a viable community rather than "knowing" the truth about the world.

And it is particular exemplars that provide the bearings for continuing community. In lieu of gods as a separate order of being, the

Chinese tradition has seen fit to celebrate and elevate ancestral figures, cultural heroes, and supreme personalities. This need to emulate models, then, requires the philosopher to be a paradigmatic
individual—a scout to reconnoiter and recommend a "way" for the
generations to come.

Philosophers and *Philosophes*

Hence, as a narrative, Confucianism is biographical in that it highlights
the life stories of formative models. And in reflecting on the lives of
Chinese *philosophes*—often passionate, sometimes courageous intellectuals advancing their own programs of human values and social
order—we become immediately aware that any account of the existential, practical, and resolutely historical nature of this tradition stretches
it beyond the boundaries of what we might think of in a contemporary
Western context as "philosophers" doing "philosophy."

In both traditional and modern China, philosophy is much more (and
certainly in some ways, much less) than a professional discipline. Many
Chinese philosophers of our generation continue the tradition wherein
scholar-officials are institutionalized intellectuals who have the practical responsibility to forge a "way" for the daily workings of government and society. This is Yü Ying-shih's point when he draws a line
between the traditional literatus of imperial days and the contemporary intellectual:

> As much as I would like to distinguish the *shih* [*shi* 士] from the *chih-
> shih fen-tzu* [*zhishi fenzi* 知識分子] , I must point out that spiritually the
> latter has continued much of what had been cultivated by the former. For
> example, the idea that the intellectual must always be identified with
> public-mindedness is not a cultural borrowing from the modern West,
> but from Confucian heritage traceable ultimately to the sage himself.[15]

In the contemporary Chinese context philosophy continues to encompass the relationship between prevailing cultural values and the social
and political lives of the people. Philosophers have been and still are the
intellectual leaders of society. Hence, a reflection on Chinese philosophy from an internal Chinese perspective must be primarily a practical
survey of the intellectual discourse as it has driven and shaped social,
political, and cultural developments.

Confucianism as the Shifting Center of a Porous, Moving Line

Any particular doctrinal commitment or set of values that we might associate with Confucianism needs to be qualified by its resolutely porous nature, absorbing into itself, especially in periods of disunity, whatever it needs to thrive within its particular historical moment.

The porous nature of Confucianism makes it a persistently comparative tradition. In fact, a compelling argument can be made that China has been doing comparative philosophy since the introduction of Buddhism into China in the second century. Another wave of Indo-European ideas entered China with the Jesuits in the late fifteenth century, armed as the Jesuits were with religious convictions fortified by the best of classical Western philosophy. More recently, in the late Qing dynasty, Yan Fu (1853–1921) stands out at the beginning of an ambitious project to translate recent Western philosophical classics into Chinese. Soon thereafter, the Marxist heresy was appropriated by iconoclastic modernizers as a foundation for Chinese socialism.

The resilience of the indigenous values has caused history to repeat itself. When Buddhism was introduced into China through a largely Daoist vocabulary (*geyi* 格義), the foreign ideas were, in due course, overwhelmed by the vitality of the indigenous impulse, and Buddhism was effectively sinocized. Generally, but perhaps most clearly in its Sanlun, Huayan, and Chan incarnations, Chinese Buddhism has a closer correlation to the early Daoist classics than it does to its South Asian origins. Christianity melded with popular religions to spawn the Taiping rebellion, one of the largest uprisings in human history. And with Yan Fu's penchant for the arcane, evocative language of China's own philosophic tradition, the foreign ideas of modern Western thought were largely overwritten with traditional Chinese values and sensibilities.

In this pattern of assimilation and ingestion, China's Marxist experience has certainly been no exception. Chinese Marxism—most recently, Maoism—is a peculiarly Chinese run on Marx that has taken a doctrine which, in most interpretations, owned universalistic aspirations, and redefined it as a kind of neo–neo-Confucianism by historicizing, particularizing, and de-psychologizing it. And any reference to Chinese "democratic" ideals introduces terrible equivocations: the promotion of seemingly individualistic values in the absence of Western notions of the individual, of autonomy, of independence, of human rights, and so on. As soon as we get beneath surface impressions, we realize that contemporary Chinese philosophic developments are deeply embedded within traditional Chinese methods of philosophizing. By and large, Chinese philosophers continue to be concerned with the creative appropriation of their own cultural tradition. Marxian rhetoric and liberal democratic values are largely heuristic structures through which more fundamental traditional Chinese values are revisited, reconfigured, and sometimes, revitalized.

Syncretic Confucian Nativism

With the above contextualization of the Chinese philosophical tradition in place, we can now consider the contemporary status of Chinese philosophy within the Chinese world. In most traditions, patriotism is expressed as a kind of grudging conservatism, but in China, especially in this century, it has often driven radicalism, iconoclasm, and even revolution. Similarly, "nativism" in China has a paradoxical shape. In his research on the Chinese nativism in this century, Yü Ying-shih reports that "national essence (*guocui* 國粹)," a neologism coined in Japan, took on a rather curious meaning when imported to China. In describing the 1920s scholars who identified themselves under this banner, Yü Ying-shih observes:

> It might at first sight seem strange that a group of scholars professedly devoted to the preservation of China's national essence should rely so heavily on Western conceptual schemes and methods for the study of their own history. . . . Criticizing the Japanese scholar Inoue Kaoru (1835–1915) who identified "national essence" as something entirely indigenous, Huang Chieh [Jie] remarked that "national essence" consists not only in what is indigenous and suitable, but also in what is borrowed and adaptable to the needs of our nation.[16]

Similarly, Chang Hao, by telling the story of four of its most prominent intellectuals, demonstrates rather persuasively that neither discontinuity, as claimed by Levenson, nor the continuity referred to by Metzger[17] provides an adequate account of twentieth century China.[18]

Perhaps, in our attempt to evaluate the role of Confucianism in recent Chinese history, we are paying too much attention to the "*ru* (儒) " and not enough to the "*jia* (家) ." We might want to reflect on the import of *jia*, meaning "family" or "lineage." The centrality of this idea of family as the grounding metaphor in Chinese culture arises from two Confucian insights. If the family is that institution in which people give most wholly and unreservedly of themselves, how do we, beginning with family, extend this complex of roles and relationships to the community and the nation more broadly? How do we get the most out of our human resources?

Secondly, the continuity between humanity and the world leads to the singular importance of the family metaphor in the definition of relational order within Chinese culture. Benjamin Schwartz follows Donald Munro in challenging the suitability of Joseph Needham's use of the organic metaphor, preferring the family metaphor—ancestor, mother, womb, and so on—that we find reflected in the vocabulary of the early cosmologies and in fact defines the specifically genealogical cosmogonies.[19]

When we move from family to Confucianism as a cultural lineage, the question remains the same: How do we get the most out of the available cultural resources? The characteristic Confucian appropriation of what is fitting—*yi*(義)—is justified either as the adaptation of that which will fortify a continuing past, or as the revivification of resources already present in China's early past. Such appropriation constitutes a syncretism that seeks to get the most out of its ingredients under always specific circumstances. The degree of appropriation is a function of crisis and of opportunity. The irony is that so-called nativist intellectuals, in borrowing whatever they need from non-Confucian sources to achieve "productive continuity,"[20] provide a clear example of the characteristic "how" of Confucianism.

This lineage called Confucianism—vague and slippery—can be imaged in different ways. It is this moving line—in calligraphy, the brush stroke, in philosophical literature, the "way" (*dao* 道), in ornamentation, the fabulous "dragon" (*long* 龍) and phoenix (*fenghuang* 鳳凰) —that defines the ever changing, ever provisional, cultural horizon. The most obvious image is the one, cumulative *dao*, the progressive line of culture being continuously extended by the "road builders" of each generation. And the pursuit of wisdom has, from classical times, centered on finding a way to stabilize, to discipline, and to shape productively and elegantly the unstoppable stream of change in which the human experience is played out.

Although this way of living, this *dao*, has historical antecedents, it is not simply to be discovered and walked. As the *Zhuangzi* says, "The path is made in the walking." *Dao* means both to lead along a path and to be led along it. In the *Analects* 15.29 we read: "It is the human being that can broaden the way (*dao*), not the way that broadens the human being." The human being must be a road builder because human culture is always under construction.

Another way of imaging the Confucian lineage is as the key icon of the tradition, the *long* (龍)—unfortunately usually translated as "dragon." Undulating, sprawling, wriggling, coiling, spiraling, thrusting, and ultimately soaring through the clouds, this embodied moving line captures the notion of unrestricted transformation and articulation (*wenhua* 文化) across the axes of time, space, and light. This image dominates Chinese cosmology. Appreciating the energy inherent in and expressed by the line, Li Zehou develops an interesting analogy between the art of the line in design and calligraphy, and the rhythm and harmonies expressed in everything from musical composition to architecture. He draws a contrast between the nature of what he calls "formal beauty" on the one hand, which is standardized, static, and stylized, and the "significant form" inscribed by the line—vigorous, animated, and beautiful in its allusions to life.[21]

Where does the moving line as changing cultural horizons begin in the Chinese tradition? Fuxi and Nuwa, the ancestors to whom the fundaments of Chinese culture such as farming, fishing, and abstract symbols (the eight diagrams) are ascribed, are described and represented in the earliest texts as human figures with the bodies of snakes. In fact, this representation is typical of many of the gods, supernaturals, and cultural heroes remembered in ancient Chinese legends. Over time, this snake-like figure, now swallowing creatures whole, now shedding its skin, accumulated the features of "every animal" to become the generative and transformative symbol of Chinese culture—the totemic Chinese "dragon" (*long*).[22] Unquestionably the most substantial presentation of the dragon image is the Great Wall, composite of many walls, as it peaks and lunges, dances and glides, meandering across thousands of miles and countless generations to give expression to the cadence of time as much as to space.

Tu Wei-ming sees this *long* as a symbol of the process of accumulation and integration:

> As a composite totem, the dragon possesses at least the head of a tiger, the horns of a ram, the body of a snake, the claws of an eagle and the scales of a fish. Its ability to cross totemic boundaries and its lack of

verisimilitude to any living creature strongly suggest that from the very beginning the dragon was a deliberate cultural construction. The danger of anachronism not withstanding, the modern Chinese ethnic self-definition as the "dragon race" indicates a deep-rooted sense that Chineseness may derive from many sources.[23]

Turning from images to historical players, and from relatively abstract reflection to concrete examples, I want to explore two specific cases in recent scholarship in which contemporary Chinese philosophers—Li Zehou and Mou Zongsan [Mou Tsung-san]—have resisted Western cultural imperialism by appropriating Western resources, and the philosophy of Immanuel Kant specifically, to fortify their own tradition. I want to suggest that in so doing they continue to be Confucian in several ways. First and most obvious is that they continue the Confucian lineage by translating and in fact transforming their strongest rival, who is by intention exclusionary and imperialistic, into a vocabulary consistent with their own premises.[24] Secondly, given that the philosopher has a fundamentally different role in Chinese society than in the West, the question again concerns not so much *what* is appropriated as *how* the thing appropriated is applied in practical, perlocutionary ways to further the interests of the community. Thirdly, Li Zehou and Mou Zongsan use the terms "sedimentation" and "transcendence as immanence" respectively as a vocabulary for assimilating Kant to the Confucian tradition. These two terms do double duty. Not only are they specific examples of creative appropriation, but the manner in which their versions differ from the original source is itself an object lesson which reiterates the genealogical and historicist premises of the Chinese tradition.

How is Kant imperialistic? Julia Ching, in an essay entitled "Chinese Ethics and Kant," contends that

> Kant represents a kind of prototype Western philosopher who judges Eastern philosophies according to his own formalist preconceptions and prejudices, while failing to appreciate their basic intentions as well as their own inner dynamics.[25]

Is Ching overly severe? She translates Kant's own words:

> Philosophy is not to be found in the whole Orient. . . . Their teacher Confucius teaches in his writings nothing outside the moral doctrines

designed for the princes . . . and offers examples of former Chinese princes. But a concept of virtue and morality never entered the heads of the Chinese. . . .[26]

Li Zehou, "Sedimentation," and the Sinocization of Kant

The Kantian scholar Li Zehou is one of China's most prominent social critics. Work being done by several contemporary interpretive scholars, particularly Woei Lien Chong and Gu Xin at Leiden, and Liu Kang at Penn. State, testifies to Li Zehou's maturity of thought and his growing stature as a philosopher. Woei Lien Chong demonstrates specifically how Li's commentary on Kant is an integral and foundational element in his rejection of Maoist voluntarism—the idea that the power of the human will can accomplish all things.[27] Mao's voluntarism is not new but emerges out of and is consistent with the traditional Confucian position that human realization lies with the transformative powers of the unmediated moral will. Unbridled confidence in the moral will—a belief that translates into ideologically driven mass mobilization campaigns—has been responsible for China's contemporary crises from Western colonialization to the Great Leap Forward and the Cultural Revolution.[28]

The argument, simply put, is that Chinese philosophers from classical times have recognized a continuity, *tianren heyi* (天人合一) between human beings and their natural environments. The nature of this continuity, however, has often been misunderstood, to the detriment of the natural sciences. Instead of being a continuity between subject and object, respecting both the ability of the collective human community to transform its environment productively and the resistance of the natural world to this human transformation, it has been dominated by the belief that the moral subject holds absolute transformative powers over an infinitely malleable natural world. It has become a kind of raw subjectivism which discounts the need for collective human efforts in science and technology to "humanize" nature and establish a productive relationship between subject and object, a relationship that Li Zehou takes to be a precondition for human freedom.

Where does Kant come in? Li Zehou sees Kant as confronting a problem similar to contemporary Chinese intellectuals: how can "deterministic" scientific progress and its political expression, totalitarian socialism, be reconciled with human freedom? For Kant it was the reconciliation of mechanistic Newtonian science, Church dogma, and Leibnizian rationalism on the one hand, and Rousseauean humanism on the other. Kant's epistemic move is to claim that the forms and categories of science do not exist independently of the human being but constitute an active structure of the human mind. This a priori structure of the mind acts to synthesize our experiences and to construct our world of scientific understanding. Hence, scientific understanding, far from contradicting the possibility of human freedom, is an expression of it.

Li Zehou appropriates Kant's notion of categories of human understanding but attempts to sinocize it by historicizing and particularizing it.[29] How so? First, China, contrary to the passive Marxian "mirror" conception of mind, has traditionally embraced a resolutely active notion of heart-mind (xin 心) as expressed in the performative force of knowledge. Li extends this assumption by offering a theory of "sedimentation"—the form of the human cultural psychology (wenhua xinli jiegou 文化心理結構)—that is synchronic, diachronic, and evolutionary. The structure of human understanding—Li Zehou actually prefers the more processional formation as a rendering of jiegou—is not an a priori given but a dynamic function of shared human experience that is historically and culturally specific. As human beings transform their shared environment, the transformed environment shapes their categories of understanding.

Underscoring the power of the collective community, sedimentation is the accumulation of a contingent social memory through which each individual human being is socialized and enculturated. As Woei Lien Chong observes, it begins at the level of the human species through the designing and making of tools:

> The process of the "humanization of nature" (ziran de renhua 自然的 人化) works in two ways: mankind humanizes external nature in the sense of making it a place fit for human beings to live in, and at the same time, by this very activity, it humanizes its own physical and mental constitution by becoming increasingly de-animalized and adapted to life in organized society. [30]

Li Zehou moves the argument from the human being as a species to specific cultural sites and experiences when he insists that Chinese scholars look to their own traditional resources in shaping a vision for China's future. Chong summarizes her conversations with Li Zehou in the following terms:

When it comes to cultural regeneration, in Li's view, the Chinese should go back to their own heritage rather than start from premises derived from Western worldviews, such as Christianity, liberalism, and Freudianism. . . . These Western premises, Li holds, cannot take root in the collective Chinese consciousness, which is based on entirely different foundations.[31]

Jane Cauvel summarizes not two but three dimensions of sedimentation in her examination of Li Zehou's philosophy of art:

we all have what we might call a "species sedimentation," (those mental forms common to all human beings), and we also have a "cultural sedimentation," (those ways of thinking and feeling common to our culture), as well as a "subjective sedimentation," (those ways of looking at the world built up from our own individual life experiences).[32]

With his theory of sedimentation, Li Zehou, like Kant, is able to reconcile causal science and human freedom, but in a way that, from the Chinese perspective, resists Kantian imperialism. What begins early in Li's career as Kantian commentary becomes a turn in Chinese philosophy consistent with underlying premises of the Confucian tradition, releasing the dragon and imbuing it with new energy to continue on undeterred. The Kantian categories, far from providing a basis for discovering universal claims, become a dynamic process for formulating and respecting cultural differences. An indication of Li Zehou's continuing commitment to the aestheticism of the Confucian tradition is his belief that the highest form of cultural sedimentation is expressed as art.

Mou Zongsan and "Immanental Transcendence"

In *Thinking Through Confucius*, David Hall and I characterize strict transcendence in the following way:

a principle, A, is transcendent with respect to that B, which it serves as principle if the meaning or import of B cannot be fully analyzed and explained without recourse to A, but the reverse is not true.[33]

This epistemological characterization may, of course, be translated into ontological terms by the substitution of *being* for *principle* in the above sentence. But a coherent notion of strict transcendence requires a doctrine of external relations, and such a doctrine is more difficult to express than one might think.[34] The moment one begins to articulate the consequences of epistemological or ontological independence, incoherences and inconsistencies begin to multiply. How might one characterize a being externally related to oneself? Surely independence in this sense suggests complete ignorance of the object or entity. Whether Kant's noumenal realm, externally related to the phenomenal at the epistemological level, is populated by things-in-themselves or is one giant *Thing-in-Itself*; or whether "thing" language even applies in that realm is, of course, unknowable.

It is possible, of course, to use the term *transcendence* simply to mean "surpassing," "going beyond." Something may be said to be transcendent, then, when it serves as an pre-eminent model or ideal for possible emulation. In another context, "transcendent" language refers to the abstract and abstruse, something incomprehensible. In a more formal sense, the Scholastics used the term to refer to anything which could not be classified under the Aristotelian categories. This comes close to the later Kantian sense of the term as meaning that which is "beyond experience."

As applied to Deity, transcendence usually indicates "independence from the created order." In its earliest uses such transcendence entailed a denial of divine intervention with respect to the world. This suggested a bilateral transcendence in which, at least after the creative act, the world and God remained independent of one another. Later references, however, almost always refer to an asymmetrical relationship in which God transcends the world, but not vice versa. Li Zehou, in responding to his interpreters, makes the point that the Kantian notion of "transcendental" as an a priori given is not consistent with the Chinese historicist way of thinking because,

> filled with a sense of history, the Chinese mind always searches for some historical interpretation. Then the "transcendental" and the *a priori* must also have its roots in this world, in the proceeding of history.[35]

A discussion in the secondary literature has emerged following our own criticism of the contemporary "New Confucian" scholar Mou Zongsan for appealing to the transcendental language of Kant to explain what is unique and distinctive about Chinese philosophy.[36] According to Mou Zongsan:

The way of *tian* (天) being high above connotes transcendence. When the way of *tian* pervades the human person, being immanent in this person, it becomes one's nature. At this time, the way of *tian* is also immanent. This being the case, we can use an expression that Kant was fond of using and say that the way of *tian* on the one hand is transcendent, and on the other hand is immanent (transcendent and immanent are opposites). When the way of *tian* is both transcendent and immanent, it can be said to have both religious and moral import: religion stresses the transcendent meaning and morality stresses the immanent.[37]

Concerned to identify and preserve the difference between those assumptions about transcendence dominant in classical Western philosophy and those being attributed to the Chinese tradition, Mou continues:

In Western discourse on "human nature," the first letter of "nature" is written with a small "n," indicating that it belongs to the "natural" as opposed to the "supernatural." When this "supernatural" begins to have a transcendent import, it belongs to the nature of God rather than the natural world. Western philosophy then entifies it to arrive at a personal God, while the Chinese tradition treats it functionally to arrive at *tiandao* (天道). These are the different routes that the East and West have taken in understanding the existence of the transcendent.[38]

Mou Zongsan makes it clear that whatever might be construed as transcendent in classical Chinese thought is neither independent of the natural world nor is it theistic. Far from entailing the dualism entailed by Western models of transcendence, classical China's world order, according to Mou, is altogether "this worldly." By insisting on "function"—the *how* question—as the mediating concept, Mou seems to reject "agency"—the *what* question—as being an appropriate characterization of *tian*.[39]

For Mou Zongsan, the transcendence of the human heart-and-mind (*xin* 心) is expressed in terms of the ongoing active creation of new values. It is not, therefore, a simple reiteration and instantiation of what is theistically "given" to the human world. The nature and character of the human being is an ongoing creative process which both stimulates and is affected by change. John Berthrong makes much of this human plasticity in his analysis of the contributions of Mou Zongsan to contemporary Confucian-Christian dialogue:

Human nature can *change* and in fact is human nature because it is not structurally constrained as other animals seem to be bound by their naturees. The soul of the Confucian is what the person seeking sagehood decides to become—you are what you will to be, and you become more fully human as you create your own world as moral community.[40]

In fact, when Mou Zongsan turns to *tiandao* 天道 and *tianming* 天命 and their relationship with the notion of human creativity, he defines them ultimately as "the true impulse of ceaseless creativity" (*chuangsheng buyi zhi zhenji* 創生不已之真幾) or unbounded "creativity itself" (*chuangzaoxing benshen* 創造性本身).[41] This creativity is expressed as the ongoing transformation of the world at the synergistic interface between uniquely human achievements and the boundlessly fertile natural and cultural context in which humanity resides.

In contrasting the Confucian world view with the theologically anchored Western model, Mou places human effort at the center and dismisses explicitly any association one might make with notions of Divine volition. As Berthrong observes in his analysis of Mou Zongsan's commentary on the Confucian tradition, "humanity can participate in the creativity of the universe as a cosmotheandric agent of the highest order."[42]

For Mou Zongsan, then, it is the process of becoming fully human that constitutes the substance of Confucian religion, and it is the absence of real constraints to that process that prompts Mou to describe it as "transcendent." Since, however, Confucian spiritual sensibilities are human-centered in the manner Mou characterizes, there must be an explicit rejection of any notion of radical otherness or ontological disparity between what he calls the immanent and transcendent or the moral and religious aspects of that process. Mou affirms both the continuity between and the interdependence of humanity and *tian* as it is expressed in the phrase, *tianren heyi*—the continuity between *tian* and the human being. In one's attainment of Confucian sagehood, there is a mutual relationship between the profoundly religious human being and *tiandao*.

Berthrong defends Mou's qualified use of transcendence by arguing that, although what Mou actually means by this term is anathema to many of the irrevocable commitments of orthodox Western theology and philosophy, it does have a close ally in the movement of process theology originating with Whitehead and elaborated in the work of scholars such as Charles Hartshorne. But by attempting to align Mou's under-standing of transcendence with a radical, dare we say heretical posi-tion within Western philosophical theology, Berthrong only highlights the difficulty of discovering that notion in any strict form within Chi-nese speculations. For process philosophy departs from more ortho-dox understandings of transcendence but certainly does not wish to escape the notion altogether. The dualism of God and the material world is replaced, in part, by the dualism of God's two natures—in Whitehead's terminology, the "primordial" and the "consequent." It is this model of the deity, we will recall, which allows for the under-standing of relationships between God and the world as entailing both transcendence and immanence. But, though this model does better sat-isfy the intuitions of those who would claim that there must be a truly intimate relationship between God and the world, the model does not escape the sorts of incoherences that plague all understandings that require, as the process model does, a final resort to strict transcen-dence. Thus, in importing a version of the process model into Mou's thinking, Berthrong illegitimately introduces the language of strict tran-scendence into his thinking.

There are others in the transcendence debate who would wish to de-fend a stronger sense of the term than Mou Zongsan seems to do. A case in point would be Li Minghui. Li is clear on what is at stake here:

> The question of whether or not there is transcendence in Chinese thought is not simply a matter of defining transcendence, but extends to Confu-cian thinking and the very way of thinking presupposed in the entire Chi-nese culture and the *Weltanschauung* that it has fostered.[43]

He is also aware of what transcendence cannot entail in describing Chinese culture:

> Perhaps we can roughly say: The basic model of thinking for the Chinese tradition takes continuity as its foundation; the basic model of thinking in Western culture takes disjunction as its foundation. And the world view that these two cultures have fostered are distinguished on the basis of these unique characteristics.[44]

Taken in a strict sense, such a statement as this aptly characterizes in a general fashion our reason for denying the relevance of strict transcendence to traditional Chinese intellectual culture. For a variety of reasons, the disjunction entailed by strict transcendence has dominated Western philosophical speculations. That God should not be contingent upon the world requires that he be disjoined in some way from it. That human reason might have some unsullied realm untouched by the welter of concrete circumstances, and that causes might not be implicated in the clutter of passing facts so as to be clearly distinguishable from their consequences, disjunction was essential.

There seems no reason, nor any real disposition, for the Chinese to accept the same consequences of disjunction that have played themselves out in the Western tradition. The evidence for continuity as a preferred value is altogether persuasive in Chinese culture. In the Confucian model, the commitment to the processional and transformative nature of experience renders the "ten thousand things" (*wanwu,* 萬物 or *wanyou,* 萬有) which make up the world, including human beings, at once continuous with one another and unique. And the primary philosophical problem that emerges from these assumptions is *ars contextualis*—the art of contextualization.[45] How do we correlate these unique particulars to achieve the most productive continuity? The adoption of ancestor worship as the defining religious sensibility, family as the primary human unit, consummate humanity (*ren* 仁) and filiality (*xiao* 孝) as primary human virtues, ritualized roles, relationships, and practices (*li* 禮) as constituting communal discourse, are all strategies for achieving and sustaining the continuity of communal harmony (*he* 和).

In Li Minghui's survey of what the term *transcendence* actually signifies within the purview of Western philosophy, he recognizes that it is freighted with a whole range of different meanings. This being the case, Li argues that Mou Zongsan, a seasoned scholar who was entirely in control of the many uses of transcendence in European philosophy, is justified in retooling this allowably equivocal European notion as an instrument for making Chinese philosophy clear:

> It is difficult for us to imagine that Mou Zongsan who has studied Kant so thoroughly is not clear on what transcendence and immanence mean for Kant. Perhaps the most reasonable explanation is that Mou is certainly not relying completely on Kant's meaning in using these concepts.[46]

As I have argued above, Mou Zongsan is usually careful in his use of *transcendence,* maintaining a distance from *strict transcendence* as it has appeared in the Western tradition. But sometimes Mou becomes rather unclear, and in so doing, confuses the distance between Chinese and Western ways of thinking. For example, Li Minghui cites approvingly Mou's description of the transcendent aspect of *tianming* as:

> having imperceptibly within it an immutable and unchanging standard which causes us to feel as though under its sanction we must not err or transgress at all in our conduct.[47]

In classical China the inexorably dynamic process of existence is defined in correlative dyadic pairs such as *you* (有) and *wu* (無), *bian* (變) and *tong* (通), *shi* (實) and *xu* (虛), that capture the inseparability of change and continuity, function and formation, process and discernable regularity. This being the case, to characterize *tianming* as an "immutable and unchanging standard," without further explanation, evokes dualistic notions of transcendence, especially when Mou offers a comparison between *tianming* and the classical Greek notion of Justice (*dike*). Li Minghui explicitly defends Mou's comparison between Justice and *tian* in the following terms:

> As noted above, the new Confucians are certainly not using the concept of transcendence with the dualistic framework of a contrast between transcendence and immanence. For example, when Mou Zongsan says that *tianming* and *tiandao* are similar to the notion of Justice in Greek philosophy, he is obviously only saying that they are both "unperishing and unchanging standards," and is certainly not suggesting that he wants to understand the Confucian *tianming* and *tiandao* according to the dualistic framework of Greek philosophy. If it were otherwise, Mou would not say: "The meaning of the latter (*tianming* and *tiandao*) are a long way from the richness and remoteness of the former (Justice)."[48]

We could be sophistical and claim that it must indeed be "otherwise," since Li Minghui himself reverses Mou's order here: Mou's actual claim is that it is *tianming* and *tiandao* that are much richer and remote than the Greek notion of Justice, not the other way around.[49] But the problem is more serious. For Li, Mou's use of this language finally encourages him to ask: "But who can deny that the *tian* and *dao* of the Confucians is independent and eternal, and thus, on the basis of Hall and Ames's definition, can be regarded as transcendent principles?"[50] Li's ultimate position is that Chinese philosophy can be accommodated within the understanding of strict transcendence as stipulated in *Thinking Through Confucius* and recalled above.[51] What is at risk in using the language of transcendence to characterize the Chinese tradition, and why would Mou Zongsan take it? First, the incautious use of a vocabulary of transcendence may unwittingly contribute to familiar Western misreadings of the Chinese tradition. Secondly, understandings of Chinese philosophy aside, use of a language of strict transcendence might encourage subsequent generations of Chinese scholars—Li Minghui is an example—to claim the existence of altogether too much common ground between the classical Western and Chinese cultural traditions, and in so doing, to underappreciate Chinese philosophy as a real alternative to dominant Western sensibilities. Finally, a besetting irony of the present state of the conversations between China and the West should not be missed. Within contemporary Western academia—in theology, in philosophy, in science, and in social theory—there has been a serious decline in appeals to conceptual structures built upon notions of transcendence. Thus, any common ground sought by either Chinese or Western interlocutors by appeal to transcendent categories may be largely slipping away due to the diminishing importance of the concept of transcendence in the West.

I want to suggest that Mou Zongsan's reason for appealing to transcendence is, like Li Zehou's use of Kant rehearsed above, an attempt to co-opt Kant to reinstate a traditionally Confucian conception of religiousness. In fact, this is the substance of the analysis of Mou's work undertaken by Lin Tongqi and Zhou Qin in which they explore this transcendence debate.[52] Mou is concerned that Confucianism not be reduced to an exclusive secular humanism devoid of religious import. In fact, Mou's revisionist interpretation of the neo-Confucian thinkers and his rejection of Zhu Xi as the orthodox line are two parts of an effort to underscore the central importance of the religious dimension in Confucianism. Here again, Mou Zongsan is attempting to promote a "new Confucianism" fortified by the prestige and rigor of Kant, while at the same time resisting the cultural imperialism entailed by taking Kant on his own terms.

Notes

1. See Wolf (1994, 253): "The Confucian principles defining the propriety of hierarchical authority structures and the orderliness of the patriarchal family system

seem anachronistic in this age of multinational corporations in Fujian, and young people from Shanghai acquiring Stanford MBAs."

2. Dirlik (1995, 238). He goes on to identify the activity of reviving Confucianism as "a particularly egregious instance of collaboration between state and intellectual discourse" (242).

3. Dirlik (1995, 232) argues that "intellectual efforts to salvage Confucianism by connecting it to modern values of Euro-American origin seemed to serve only to further undermine it by compromising its integrity as a coherent philosophical system."

4. After all, the expression *zhenmai* (診脈) means "to take a pulse" rather than "to examine a blood vessel or artery."

5. Tiles and Tiles (1993, 79).

6. See Hall and Ames (1995) for a comparison of dualistic and correlative thinking. The history of *concept* as it is understood in Plato gives us hypostatized ideas (*eide*), and although Aristotle abandons the reification of concepts, he still insists that conceptual *eidos* is the universal of predication and the subject of definition. See the entry for *eidos* in Peters (1967, 46–51).

7. Yü Ying-shih (1991, 26).

8. Yü Ying-shih references Qian Mu who makes a similar observation in his *Outline History of the Nation*, described by Dennerline (1988, 66):

> The pattern . . . is China's, and it differs from the West's as a poem differs from a drama. . . . The one expands to fill a space when it is ordered and disintegrates when it is not. The other progresses from conflict to conflict toward some inevitable tragic conclusion. . . . The historians who tried to understand the course of Chinese history by applying Western science were right to look for facts. In this regard they surpassed the New Text revisionists. But they failed to comprehend that their theories presumed the universality of the dramatic form.

9. Richards (1932, 87–88).

10. Richards (1932, 89, 91–92).

11. Norman (1971, 24).

12. Hershock (1996, 15).

13. Hershock (1996, 15–16).

14. Richards (1932, 92–93).

15. Yü Ying-shih (1993, 145).

16. Yü Ying-shih (1994, 161).

17. Levenson (1959) and Metzger (1977).

18. Chang Hao (1987).

19. See Munro (1985, passim) and Schwartz (1985, 200, 416–418).

20. In traditional language, this is the achievement of *he* (和) : productive harmony.

21. See Li Zehou (1994).

22. A caution is needed here. To translate this icon as "dragon," as is conventionally done, reflects the difficulties encountered in cultural translation, *long* needing as it does to be clearly distinguished from its Anglo-Saxon cousin that met a proper end under the Christian foot of St. George. See Hay (1994).

23. Tu Wei-ming, "Chinese Philosophy: A Synopsis."

24. The most obvious example of this strategy in the classical period is perhaps

Xunzi. See Hall and Ames (1995, 204–210) for his coopting of the later Mohists and the School of Names in laying the ground for Confucianism as state ideology. A similar argument can be mounted for his appropriation of the Militarists with the "Debating the Military" (*yibing* 議兵) chapter. The extent to which this pattern is true of Xunzi has yet to be fully appreciated.

25. Ching (1978, 162).

26. Translation by Julia Ching cited from von Glasenapp (1954, 104). This Kantian perception of China as externally animated and internally inert is representative rather than unique. Hegel, for example, in his discussion of China, insists:

> Moral distinctions and requirements are expressed as Laws, but so that the subjective will is governed by these Laws as by an external force. Nothing subjective in the shape of disposition, Conscience, formal Freedom, is recognized. Justice is administered only on the basis of external morality, and Government exists only as the prerogative of compulsion. . . . Morality is in the East likewise a subject of positive legislation, and although moral prescriptions (the *substance* of their Ethics) may be perfect, what should be internal subjective sentiment is made a matter of external arrangement. . . . While *we* obey, because what we are required to do is confirmed by an *internal* sanction, there the Law is regarded as inherently and absolutely valid without a sense of the want of this subjective confirmation.

See Hegel (1956, 111–112).

27. I am indebted here to Woei Lien Chong (1996), and also to the responses to Chong's work by Li Zehou and Jane Cauvel that appeared in a special issue of *Philosophy East & West* 1999, guest-edited by Tim Cheek. For a bibliography of recent scholarship on Li Zehou, see Chong (1996, 142–143n12).

28. Chang Hao (1994) makes a similar point in his response to deBary's *Trouble with Confucianism*.

29. Li Zehou's reading immediately calls to mind Clarence Irving Lewis's and his "pragmatic" reading of Kant (Lewis 1955). See his attempt to repudiate idealism with the notion of the "pragmatic" a priori.

30. Chong (1996, 150).

31. Chong (1996, 141).

32. Cauvel (1999, 150).

33. Hall and Ames (1987, 13).

34. See the attempt of Hartshorne (1964) to develop a coherent doctrine of external relations.

35. Li Zehou (1999, 180).

36. See for example Li Minghui (1994), and Lin Tongqi and Zhou Qin (1995).

37. Mou Zongsan (1963, 20).

38. Mou Zongsan (1963, 20).

39. We have benefited in our appreciation of Mou Zongsan's contribution to this debate by John Berthrong's detailed account of it (Berthrong 1994). In describing our own position on transcendence as it is presented in *Thinking Through Confucius*, our only qualification would be to disassociate ourselves from Berthrong's claim that we allow that transcendence to become part of the picture beyond the classical Chinese tradition in later philosophical speculation—neo-Daoism, Buddhism, neo-Confucianism. We simply suspend judgment on this issue until we have had further time to study the original sources.

40. Berthrong (1994, 117). See Ames (1991, *passim*) in which I make a similar case for Tang Junyi's interpretation of *renxing*.

41. Mou Zongsan (1963, 21).

42. Berthrong (1994, 114). Berthrong is appealing to Hartshorne's version of process theism, which does not make the same metaphysical claims with regard to the primordiality of "creativity." There is no reason, therefore, for him to interpret Mou's rather elaborate and expansive speculations on "unbounded creativity itself" in metaphysical terms. On a Whiteheadian model, however, one might easily proceed to elaborate Mou's claims concerning "creativity" along ontological lines.

43. Li Minghui (1994, 148).

44. Li Minghui (1994, 148).

45. For an elaboration of this "art of contextualization," see Hall and Ames (1987, 1995).

46. Li Minghui (1994, 143).

47. Li Minghui (1994, 144), citing Mou Zongsan (1963, 21).

48. Li Minghui (1994, 145–146).

49. Mou Zongsan (1963, 21).

50. Li Minghui (1994, 142).

51. Hall and Ames (1987, 13 and *passim*).

52. See Lin Tongqi and Zhou Qin (1995).

References

Alitto, Guy S. 1979. *The Last Confucian: Liang Shu-ming and the Chinese Dilemma of Modernity*. Berkeley: University of California Press.

Ames, Roger T. 1991. "The Mencian Conception of Ren xing: Does it Mean 'Human Nature'?" In *Chinese Texts and Philosophical Contexts: Essays Dedicated to Angus C. Graham*. Edited by H. Rosemont, Jr. La Salle, IL: Open Court.

Berthrong, John. 1994. *All Under Heaven*. Albany: State University of New York Press.

Cauvel, Jane. 1999. "The Transformation Power of Art: Li Zehou's Aesthetic Theory." *Philosophy East and West* 49, no. 2:150–173.

Chang Hao. 1987. *Chinese Intellectuals in Crisis*. Berkeley: University of California Press.

———. 1994. "Response to Ted de Bary's Trouble with Confucianism." *China Review International* 1, no. 1: 14–18.

Ching, Julia. 1978. "Chinese Ethics and Kant." *Philosophy East and West* 28, no. 2: 161–172.

Chong, Woei Lien. 1996. "Mankind and Nature in Chinese Thought: Li Zehou on the Traditional Roots of Maoist Voluntarism." *China Information* 11, no. 2: 138–175.

Dennerline, Jerry. 1988. *Qian Mu and the World of Seven Mansions*. New Haven: Yale University Press.

Dirlik, Arif. 1995. "Confucius in the Borderlands: Global Capitalism and the Reinvention of Confucianism." *Boundary 2* (Fall): 229–273.

Hall, David L., and Roger T. Ames. 1987. *Thinking Through Confucius*. Albany: State University of New York Press.

————. 1995. *Anticipating China: Thinking Through the Narratives of Chinese and Western Culture*. Albany: State University of New York Press.

Hartshorne, Charles. 1964. *The Divine Relativity: A Social Conception of God*. New Haven: Yale University Press.

Hay, John. 1994. "The Persistent Dragon." In *The Power of Culture*. Edited by W. Peterson, A. Plaks, and Y.S. Yu. Hong Kong: Chinese University Press.

Hegel, G.W.F. 1956. *Philosophy of History*. Trans. J. Sibree. New York: Dover.

Hershock, Peter. 1996. *Liberating Intimacy: Enlightenment and Social Virtuosity in Ch'an Buddhism*. Albany: State University of New York Press.

Levenson, Joseph. 1959. "The Suggestiveness of Vestiges: Confucianism and Monarchy at the Last." In *Confucianism in Action*. Stanford: Stanford University Press.

————. 1968. *Confucian China and Its Modern Fate: A Trilogy*. Berkeley: University of California Press.

————. 1977. *Confucian China and Its Modern Fate*. Berkeley: University of California Press.

Lewis, C.I. 1955. *The Ground and the Nature of the Right*. New York: Columbia University Press.

Li Minghui. 1994. *Dangdai ruxue zhi ziwo zhuanhua*. Taipei: Zhongyang yanjiuyuan.

Li Zehou. 1994. *The Path of Beauty: A Study of Chinese Aesthetics*. Hong Kong: Oxford University Press.

————. 1999. "Subjectivity and Subjectality." *Philosophy East and West* 49, no. 2: 174–183.

Lin Tongqi, and Zhou Qin. 1995. "Dynamism and Tension in the Anthropocosmic Vision of Mou Zongsan." *Journal of Chinese Philosophy* 22, no. 4: 401–440.

Metzger, Thomas. 1977. *Escape from Predicament: Neo-Confucianism and China's Evolving Political Culture*. New York: Columbia University Press.

Mou Zongsan. 1963. *Zhongguo zhexue de tezhi*. Taipei: Xuesheng shuju.

Munro, Donald J. 1985. "The Family Network, the Stream of Water, and the Plant." In *Individualism and Holism: Studies in Confucian and Taoist Values*. Ann Arbor: University of Michigan Press.

Norman, K.R. 1971 (trans.). *The Elders' Verses II: Therigatha*. Pali Text Society Series No. 40. London: Luzac and Company.

Peters, F.E. 1967. *Greek Philosophical Terms: A Historical Lexicon*. New York: New York University Press.

Richards, I.A. 1932. *Mencius on the Mind*. New York: Harcourt, Brace and Co.

Schwartz, Benjamin I. 1985. *The World of Thought in Ancient China*. Cambridge: Harvard University Press.

Tiles, Mary, and James Tiles. 1993. *An Introduction to Historical Epistemology: The Authority of Knowledge*. Oxford: Blackwell.

Tu Wei-ming. 1997. "Chinese Philosophy: A Synopsis." In *A Companion to World Philosophies*. Edited by E. Deutsch and R. Bontekoe. Oxford: Blackwell.

von Glasenapp, Helmuth. 1954. *Kant und die Religionen des Osten*. Beihefte zum Jahrbuch der Albertus-Universitat, Konigsberg/Pr. Kitzingen-Main: Holzner Verlag.

Wolf, Marjory. 1994. "Beyond the Patrilineal Self: Constructing Gender in China." In *Self as Person in Asian Theory and Practice*. Edited by R. T. Ames, T. P. Kasulis, and W. Dissanayake. Albany: State University of New York Press.

Yu Ying-shih. 1991. "Clio's New Cultural Turn and the Rediscovery of Tradition in

Asia." Keynote Address to the 12th Conference, International Association of Historians of Asia. Hong Kong: University of Hong Kong.

——. 1993. "The Radicalization of China in the Twentieth Century." *Daedalus* 122, no. 2 (Spring):125–150.

——. 1994. "Changing Conceptions of National History in Twentieth-Century China." In *Proceedings of Nobel Symposium 78*. Berlin: Walter de Gruyter.

Part II

Socialization: Official Ideologies, Literature, and the Media

4

Still Building the Nation: The Causes and Consequences of China's Patriotic Fervor

Edward Friedman

Chinese nationalism could spark a major war.[1] This conclusion runs contrary to the dominant theme in the professional literature that Chinese nationalism is not worrisome,[2] that economic imperatives invariably rein in out-of-control patriotic passions,[3] and that Chinese nationalism is for domestic consumption only.[4] Actually, a dangerously chauvinistic and war-prone Chinese nationalism was manifested after 1992–1993, strongly rooted in the unifying patriotism born in the wartime struggle against Japan and persisting in the eras of both Mao Zedong and Deng Xiaoping. After 1974 the continuous encroachments against weaker southeast Asian neighbors in the South China Seas, after the 1995–1996 military threats against democratic Taiwan, and after the frenzied rage of 1999 rioters after NATO bombed the Chinese embassy in Belgrade, the serious question is the origin and dynamics of China's dangerous patriotic passions, not whether they even exist.

Just as ruling groups in China in the revolutionary, anti-imperialist 1950s, 1960s, and 1970s treated Moscow's policy of peaceful coexistence as an anti-China plot, so post-Mao ruling groups, in an era of economic reform, increasingly see American's policy of promoting win-win international exchanges as an anti-China plot. In both eras, Chinese patriots embraced self-wounding absurdities as profound nationalistic truths. Benign things are treated as deadly threats. It is as if they wanted to be fooled. To comprehend such a deep, pervasive, and powerful continuity requires grasping events which have become institutionalized in ways that blind and enchant an entire people. Such is the deeply structured history of Chinese patriotism.

Since 1979, but especially since 1992, an ever more virulent patriotism has been rising and spreading in China. By 1994, even in northern hinterland villages, people who paid attention to politics learned to hold America ultimately responsible for even local horrors. Inflation, unemployment, and corruption were all somehow America's fault. Supposedly, the United States wasn't allowing China's goods to be purchased in America and in international markets. Indeed, America was said to be bullying people all over the world, proving that America was, of course, trying to keep China down. The ultimate proof—the smoking gun— was America's alleged conspiracy in 1993 to prevent Beijing from hosting the year 2000 Olympics. America was hateful. Most analysts missed the anti-American mobilizing force of that vote against China by the International Olympics Committee.

This pervasive and potent nationalism has unleashed a dangerous political dynamic where ruling groups in China are increasingly legitimated by tough anti-foreign military talk, a logic of competing to prove one's patriotic credentials. Every voice demands action. Everyone is a super patriot. To be sure, not every Chinese actually hates Americans or Japanese or Taiwanese. Far from it. But the power of recent chauvinism has virtually silenced, at least temporarily, the non-haters and the open-minded.[5] As in the lead up to the Cultural Revolution, political discourse is ever more infused by a language of angry zealotry. The Mao era notion of left-is-better-than-right persists, with the content of the left altered to mean nativistic, as Hu Ping, an exiled democracy activist, has pointed out to me. As in the Mao era, believers and opportunists alike understand the political logic involved and act accordingly. A nasty nationalism strengthens. But that fervor has long and deep roots.

Even participants in the 1989 democracy movement actually insisted on describing their movement first and foremost as a patriotic movement. As cultural critic Linda Jaivin has pointed out, they helped turn Hou Dejian's mournful and nostalgic dirge, "Heirs of the Dragon," into a proud, strong, and loud assertion of Chinese identity, virtually of a racial sort, celebrating a people supposedly defined by black eyes, black hair, and yellow skin. Older liberals were appalled. But a decade later most liberals had joined the chauvinistic chorus. Nativism continues to strengthen. Even human rights activism can be suffused with racism, as when Chinese protested against the authoritarian Suharto regime in Indonesia, which permitted rapes of girls of Chinese ancestry in 1998–99. Patriots described the cruel criminality as a threat to the race, a challenge to which a truly Chinese government would respond forcefully.

As Jeffrey Wasserstrom perceptively noted at the time, the 1989 democrats indeed were already militant nationalists.[6] They particularly condemned privileged and unaccountable authoritarian elites for selling out the national patrimony for their own selfish gains, such as the means to purchase the most expensive foreign cars, usually German Mercedes Benzes. But the movement's patriotism turned Benzes into Toyotas. Patriotic anger had been directed at Japan for a long time.[7]

Anti-Japanese hatreds were stirred up even after the People's Liberation Army's conquest of China in 1949. Author Hong Ying notes that "In 1953, all Japanese married to Chinese were forced to leave the country." Subsequently, in campaign after political campaign, the offspring of such marriages were humiliated, publicly disgraced as treasonous "Jap brats."[8] Takeuchi Yoshimi, a Japanese China specialist who had spent much time in China, experienced that hate. He concluded at the outset of 1966 that "the Chinese deeply hate the Japanese . . . common people. . . . [E]ven if the Chinese today, for political reasons, say that they do not feel bitter, or that the [war] guilt does not lie in the Japanese people. . . . [T]hat hatred still lies deep. . . . [T]his bitterness will not vanish in one or two decades. . . ."[9] Chinese patriots had learned from family, friends, and neighbors that the Japanese in China were savage, and that while Communist martyrs gave their lives to end Japanese inhumanities to Chinese, Chiang Kai-shek's Nationalists did little to challenge that savegery.[10] Someone growing up in Tianjin after the war who took ill would be told by parents that, when the Japanese ran Tianjin, the Japanese regularly rounded up youth suspected of carrying contagious diseases, threw them into huge pits, covered them with lime, and buried them. The Japanese would not live where sick Chinese could spread disease. Liberation was liberation from Japanese inhumanity.[11]

When the Soviet Red Army marched into northeast China in August 1945, raping as it advanced, much as its soldiers had done in East and Central Europe, one popular Chinese Communist propaganda excuse was that the Russians could not distinguish Chinese from Japanese, implying that the gang rape of young Japanese girls was pardonable. By the time of the Cultural Revolution, in part an attack on Soviet Russian practices, the Russian Red Army was vilified for its earlier rapes in China, with people saying that the acts proved that Russians were as monstrous as Japanese, the standard for evil inhumanity.

Although the Cultural Revolution focused on Soviet Russian evils, attacks on Japanese never let up. A movie about the 1894–1895 war between China and Japan fought in and around Korea, which highlighted the innocent Chinese victims of Japanese inhumanity, continued to be popular presented as an opera. The opera *The Naval Battle of 1894*, racially denouncing the Japanese as "dwarf bandits" and featuring the sinking of the Chinese navy and the drowning of Chinese sailors, ended with the Chinese audience on its feet demanding vengeance and over and over "shouting 'Down with Japanese Imperialism'!"[12]

Highest-level Chinese researchers tell me that during the Cultural Revolution one of the few items of discontent to spread as far as Great Leader Mao Zedong was the discovery that, starting around 1963, Chairman Mao, in addressing Japanese visitors who spoke of Japan's need to indemnify China for the damage done by the Imperial Army, said that since his forces could not have won without the free supply of Japanese arms, maybe China actually should indemnify Japan.

In other words, the popular 1990s view that Beijing was not doing enough to stand up for Chinese dignity actually began even before reformers came to power in the post-Mao era and came under attack by conservatives and a new left for supposedly selling out the nation to international capital. If in 1989 there was naiveté in China about America, its locus may have been less among democratic students and more among anti-Japanese officials who believed that the U.S. Government was worried that "a divided and weak China would not have the power to check Japan."[13] It is noteworthy how many Chinese patriots believed America would want to join with China to check an allegedly militaristic Japan.

In 1989 passionately anti-Japanese young Chinese in Beijing knew that local taxi drivers condemned government policy which protected China's inefficient auto industry and made purchases of Japanese cars prohibitive. The drivers would have earned far more income if they could have purchased imported, easily serviced, fuel-efficient Japanese vehicles without extremely high Chinese protective tariffs and with low-interest bank loans. The northern intellectuals, however, felt themselves superior to these working people, felt themselves to be China's true patriots because they, in contrast to taxi drivers and others, would not concede to "mere" personal material interests and sell out the nation. In other words, many northern intellectuals chauvinistically treated trade that in fact benefited working Chinese as a kind of national betrayal. China's new patriotism is internally generated and diversely experienced.

Business people who work in southern cities like Shanghai still seldom encounter the North's vitriolic patriotism. I have often heard southerners boast that China's only post-Mao ideology is making money. They condemn foreign nations for causing problems with China by being ideological, when China supposedly lacks anti-foreign passions. The southerners conflate one region, their own, with all of China.

Passionately patriotic Chinese are often blind to their own national complexities, one of which is the growing gap between reality and perception. Since China is ever stronger, its neighbors worry about Beijing's expansive ambitions. Even Beijing's friend, Singapore's Lee Kuan Yew, noted in 1995 that "China . . . is a fierce animal that . . . could be easily agitated and become fierce again."[14] China has a large land mass, more people than any other nation, nuclear weapons, a UN Security Council veto, ambitions for predominance in Asia, and the fastest rising economy in the world since 1978. It is a power, the proverbial two-ton guerilla. But in popular perception, China is weak, poor, and unrespected. If it doesn't stand up toughly, others will continue to bully China. This Chinese perception of being endlessly insulted, this nationalism of victimization, is obviously generated by historical and internal experiences, not by contemporary international reality.

In short, if one is going to obtain an understanding of the complexities of how Chinese nationalism is contested, one wants to clarify China's actual history as well as its regional, occupational, and experiential diversity. It is misleading to assume that all Chinese are, and ever will be, naturally one brand of patriot. Takeuchi Yoshimi erred in implying that all Chinese equally hated the Japanese.

Women seem far less vengeful, far less militarily nationalistic than men. Were China a democracy, a gender gap might appear which would have significant peace-oriented policy implications. A democratic China could have a very different foreign policy.[15]

In today's patriarchal authoritarian China, however, there is no women's vote. Male chauvinists dominate.[16] Many were embarrassed by the great performance in the 1999 World Cup of the magnificent Chinese women's soccer team, feeling that it highlighted how poorly the men did. On the Sunday morning of the World Cup final, many

Beijing men almost surreptitiously rose early to root for China. When America won, the northerners "knew" this strengthened America's arrogant sense of superiority. They had no idea that in fact the victory was celebrated in the United States as proof that a 20-year-old law requiring equal funding for women's athletics was a success. That U.S. celebration of the rise of women would not have been much different if the opponent had been Norway instead of China. But in China in 1999–2000, a top issue was getting a new coach for the men's soccer team to get China among the world powers of soccer where it belonged.

Since not all Chinese patriots imagine the world the same way, it very much matters who and what wins in Chinese politics. The structure and rules of the political game—that is, who is marginalized and who is privileged—impacts heavily on the quality of policy outcomes. The point is not that all women or all southerners are less chauvinistic or less militaristic. During China's 1999 anti-American riots, prostitutes, even in the south-central city of Wuhan, asserted their patriotism by refusing business dealings with Americans. Also in the south, Nanjing people seem passionately anti-Japanese.

In fact, Nanjing, the victim of a 1937–1938 monstrous massacre by the Showa era Imperial Army, embodies China's anti-Japanese nationalism.[17] A story about Nanjing spread soon after Japanese Premier Tanaka Kakuei visited Beijing in 1972 to normalize Tokyo-Beijing relations. In the popular rumor, which may even be true, a young Chinese girl from Nanjing presented the Japanese premier with flowers when he alit at Beijing airport. Thrilled to represent China, the girl returned to Nanjing and boasted to her mother about the honor. The mother swiftly slapped the daughter sharply across the face and cursed her for dishonoring China.

One should not, however, describe any place's virulent nationalism as historically natural, not even Nanjing's. There is nothing historically natural about persistent hate. Politics always matters. If the hate was from the war, then one would expect it to have been greatest soon after the Japanese committed their atrocities and then, gradually, to have declined. Instead, it has dramatically risen almost two generations after the cruelties occurred. This unnatural trend requires a political explanation. Why, at a time when China is more secure, powerful, and wealthy than ever before in the modern era is anti-foreign hate intensifying?

While the nasty political trend is national, regional and political variations do not readily disappear. Nagasaki and Hiroshima, for example, are politically very different places in Japan, with almost opposite ideas about whom to blame for the American WWII atomic bombing they both suffered: people in Nagasaki are far more likely to name and blame the despotic Showa-era imperial system.[18] The politics of the two nationalisms are distinct.

It is therefore important, while not denying the spreading national potency in the 1990s and after of the northern passion, to get regional particulars right and not to invoke a homogeneous China as the agent of the complex currents of Chinese nationalism, as if there were nothing ambiguous or contested in Chinese identity. American media fixation in 1999 on what sells in the United States—that is, pictures of rocks through windows—focused on Beijing rioters outraged at the destruction of the Chinese embassy in Belgrade. Despite the natural shock and outrage among Chinese because of sovereign territory struck by American bombs, little attention was given in America to Shanghai, where little occurred.

Regional differences are of enormous political significance virtually everywhere. Deng's heir, President Jiang Zemin, was recognized and rewarded in 1989 for managing the patriotic democracy movement in Shanghai without having to resort to force, when, perhaps, it was less Jiang's unique political acumen and more a particular societal feature of the South that facilitated the peaceful situation in Shanghai. Most people in Shanghai, despite the city's hosting of the ultra-left in the Cultural Revolution, have little desire for a return to another era of political mobilization and economic decline. After all, Shanghai people were exploited in the Mao era. Jiang may be the beneficiary of historically particularized regional experiences.

When one focuses on regional particulars in China, one finds great diversity. Chengdu in western Sichuan was among the most violent sites in China's monstrous and deadly Cultural Revolution, an event where patriotic young vigilante torturers and murderers sought out so-called class traitors, supposed counter-revolutionaries who would then be treated, or mistreated, as it were, as running dogs of imperialism, spies, saboteurs, and national traitors. And so China's poisoned patriotism, after all, is not new. It is, of course, not only in Chinese nationalism that traitors deserve to die. But the popular quest for manufacturing traitors is not universal. Politics matter.

In the 1989 patriotic democracy movement Chengdu again was a most violent spot. And in the 1999 anti-American riots, yet once more, Chengdu was the most violent place, a city where the residence of the American consul was torched. While Chengdu people often laugh off the violence, saying that people who eat hot foods have hot tempers, my hypothesis is that this stronger, more virulent nationalism in Chengdu reflects the concentration of military power there. Chengdu was the heart of third front defenses in the 1964–82 era, a city full of military families and defense money and envisioning itself as the ultimate bastion whose sacrifice would save the nation. But some acquaintances of mine from Chengdu instead argue that the city sees itself as the largest metropolis in the farthest reaches from Beijing, a place and a community permanently angry at an uncaring national center for ignoring, marginalizing, and depreciating Chengdu's contribution.

Whatever the explanation for Chengdu, rather than treating Chinese nationalism as natural or homogeneous, a political analysis of contestation is required. Recent chauvinism is not simply a uniform historical legacy, although northern virulence ever more pervades the nation. Even after the UN in 1999 sanctioned the occupation of Kosovo, the Chinese media kept portraying Milosevic as an anti-fascist resistor and the Serbs as the victims of Nazi-like NATO aggression. Serbian crimes were almost unreported. New books were published, such as *The Nine Times China Said No*, hailing China as the heroic source of resistance against evil, American-led global forces. Decades of this hate-mongering have had their effect: proud nationalists want to believe worst-case stories about Americans, who are imagined as siding with and re-arming a militaristic Japan. Chinese patriots demand military action against peoples they have learned to hate.

Chinese commentators who are not sucked into patriotic passions tend to insist on the centrality of politics to those passions. Some interests benefit from promoting them. Sounding very much like the uniquely well-informed journalist Willy Lam in Hong Kong, a person who talks to a lot of these sharp people from China, these Chinese analysts see certain persons, institutions, and groups in Beijing using chauvinistic opportunities and a hard-line nationalistic discourse to advance their political fortunes. These nativists have been doing ever better since 1979. Despite the imperative of economic reform, nativistic and militaristic hard-liners have grown ever stronger since the humiliating defeat in 1979 of the Chinese invaders of Vietnam. Democratic critics were quickly silenced. A new nationalism was promoted. The return of Taiwan became a top priority. Actual recent political turning points in policy orientation are invisible to patriots who imagine a long history of Chinese victimization and a weak and belated governmental response.

While certain institutions and groups benefited more than others from joining the subsequent nationalist frenzy (*minzuzhuyi kuangre*), young patriots bravely imagine themselves as pure agents, ignoring the issue of which political interests they actually serve. They remind me of Mao's Red Guards with the major difference that the haters of traitors in the Mao era sought to attack and annihilate Chinese.

Still, Chinese politics is far more than chauvinism. In spring 1996, when the PLA tried to terrorize Taiwan toward submission, credible leaks revealed that power holders in China's southern provinces pressured Beijing to end a militarily provocative policy that threatened needed foreign investments. And most analysts agree that in 1999 such economic concerns were yet more widespread when Beijing-backed anti-American riots led to a loss of tourist money, to hotel room cancellations, to the calling off of visits by trade delegations and by potential investors, and to a drop in stock market prices. In 2000, people in Shanghai called themselves the peace party, referred to Beijing as the war party, and dubbed people further south in Xiamen as the surrender party. Given China's enormous economic problems, political elites, of course, have to heed major economic impacts. China is thus infused with contradictory internal political dynamics. While the domestic political struggle ensues, people all over China are preoccupied by a need to grapple with deep economic problems.

The hard-liners manipulate real patriotic passions to advance their political agenda. Nations and people wanting to do business with China often woo Beijing by reciting as much of Beijing's hard line on America, Japan, and Taiwan as possible, hoping to curry favor. Foreign news organizations in China are pressured to highlight the official propaganda or face costly restrictions, possibly even expulsion. Then the propaganda iterated by foreigners is presented back in China as proof that China's war-prone chauvinism is but a well-recognized defensive response to real foreign threats. The anti-openness forces are strengthened, and criticism of chauvinistic public sentiment becomes almost non-existent.

Optimistic analysts, however, tend to see economic factors as invariably trumping the chauvinism. Such observers usually conclude that, despite periodic emotional explosions, the imperatives of reform, openness, and growth will always compel Chinese leaders to rein in out-of-control patriotic forces, because China's continued economic rise requires good relations with the United States, Japan, and Taiwan. Hence, even soon after the NATO bombing of the Chinese embassy in Belgrade, Beijing agreed to the concessions required of it for entrance into the WTO.

Momentary outbursts are, in this economistic perspective, just that, momentary. Beijing has indeed regularly pulled back from the unintended consequences of treating the United States or Japan or Taiwan as an ultimate enemy. This creates the impression of a *yin/yang* power struggle, when in fact such drawbacks are only temporary adjustments in response to unwanted outcomes of a strengthening policy surge. Because the chauvinism is ever more hegemonic, Chinese returns to economic rationality are experienced internally as retreats.

As any visitor can quickly learn, Chinese patriots in places like Beijing and Chengdu see leaders as reining in patriots, see rulers as insufficiently patriotic, as squashing genuine nationalists, and therefore not truly standing up for China. The popular struggle against Japan's legal claim to the Senkaku Islands, a movement attractive even in Hong Kong and Taiwan yet, wisely, restrained by national leaders in Beijing, exemplifies this explosive prospect and its temporary dampening effect. There is no discussion as to why the Senkakus are Japanese.[19]

Given the surging strength of Chinese chauvinism, nationalistic passions could yet defeat economic reason and smear the economic reformers as new Wang Jingweis and new Li Hongzhangs—as, in fact, old traitors reincarnate. One already hears such language. While China's future is politically contingent, it is pure wishful thinking to see China as if a virulent nationalism were not ever more hegemonic.

Liberals and the huge cohort of proponents of economic reform also increasingly speak from inside the new Chinese nationalism. Although modern China has never been so strong or secure, they embrace a world view where this is an age of American hegemony, where that hegemony threatens the vital interests of a too-weak China, and where China has no choice but to defend itself. The reformers, however, may still contend that the Soviet Union destroyed itself by unnecessarily treating America as an enemy and trying to compete with America militarily. Therefore, the reformers argue, China must instead focus on economic reform and only respond defensively to specific threats. Calling attention to domestic problems, they further insist that it was minority ambitions and religious fanaticism that destroyed the Soviet Union and Yugoslavia, and that such ambitions and fanaticism must be ruthlessly crushed in China, however that looks to the international human rights community.

The reformers either accept the chauvinists' view that much of the world, led by a hegemonic America egging on Chinese sectarianism, is against China; or they see particular domestic forces using chauvinism only for internal political purposes, to legitimate, in other words, the repression of democratic urges. Foreigners who talk to these Chinese counterparts, usually good friends with like values, come away reporting wrongly that Chinese nationalism is only for domestic purposes, arguing as if military hardliners have not become ever stronger. In either case, it is obvious why China will not cooperate on multilateral security issues. The international security system, and indeed the United Nations itself, is perceived or at least self-interestedly described in China as an American tool institutionalizing American hegemony—an interpretation that may come as a surprise both to the AFL-CIO and to U.S. Senator Jesse Helms.

But patriotic Chinese see themselves as having been forced to agree to the UN-sanctioned war against Saddam Hussein in 1991 and as having not been able to block the NATO-sanctioned occupation of Kosovo in 1999, although both actions were experienced as being against China's vital interests. While some critically-minded Chinese wildly imagined the Chinese military in the spring of 1999 loading the Chinese embassy in Yugoslavia with anti-aircraft intelligence to challenge NATO bombing and to help Milosevic, even happily voicing fraudulent boasts about Chinese responsibility for the shooting down of a U.S. stealth bomber, most reformers accept the Chinese chauvinistic world view of China as still weak and disrespected. Strong reformers tend to argue for military restraint lest China destroy itself in an un-winnable arms race, as did the Soviet Union. Yet, ever more voices condemn the authorities in Beijing for already having made too many concessions to the allegedly American-run international system. A peaceful outcome is not guaranteed.

A dangerous new dynamic has been spawned. Whatever power-holders do, most Chinese living inside of heightened patriotic passions tend to judge rulers as being insufficiently patriotic, if not unpatriotic. This is precisely how leaders of the 1989 democracy movement already saw the top residents of Zhongnanhai. While Chinese like to insist that their strong nationalism of 1999 was very different from a craven giving-in to America in 1989, they in fact self-interestedly misremember 1989. A close analysis of the patriotic discourse from 1989 to 1999 reveals great continuity with a continual deepening of a quite similar chauvinistic passion, one promoted by state leaders since at least 1979, after China's defeat in Vietnam.

None of this is to suggest that anti-China acts do not occur, but rather that the Chinese patriotic response to such deeds has a vengeful Manichean content. Sometimes foreign pragmatists inadvertently strengthen Beijing's ability to portray the world as a contest between an innocent Chinese victim wishing only to do good, and an evil world unfairly vilifying and bullying China. In the early 1980s, when I worked for the U.S. House of Representatives Committee on Foreign Affairs, the U.S. Drug Enforcement Agency was frustrated in its efforts to get the PRC to close a methaqualone plant in the Canton region, whose exports, trans-shipped via Hamburg, ended up in Columbia, where drug cartels turned the chemicals into qualudes, which then were illegally smuggled into the United States. I was asked to chat with acquaintances in the Chinese embassy in Washington. They eventually suggested that, if the United States would drop its accusations, then China would, at the next meeting of the international drug enforcement agencies, announce that Beijing had discovered the methaqualone plant and shut it down. The world would congratulate China.

Pragmatists dealing with China were pleased to get the outcome they wanted. They did not worry about mere Chinese verbiage. In like manner the Chinese ship *Yin He*, meant to carry chemical weapons to Iran, could be found innocent. The pragmatists would be silent if they got what they wanted. Chemical weapons stopped going to Iran. But the popular and elite Chinese experience propagandized to the Chinese people—that of an innocent and pure China unfairly attacked by American-led evil—is misshaping Chinese political culture into an explosively resentful nationalism.

This nasty division of the world into a pure China and an evil external anti-China was manifest in the popular Chinese response to racist comments made during the 1996 Atlanta Olympics by an NBC television commentator.[20] When the Chinese team marched in during the opening ceremony, the NBC sportscaster declared that Chinese athletics was marred by drug scandals. Chinese everywhere were outraged. There indeed was a drug problem with some members of an Asian Games women's swimming team. But rather than name the individuals, as announcers did with Canadian sprinter Ben Johnson, China was smeared as a national entity. Ben Johnson was Ben Johnson, but the women swimmers were non-persons, just Chinese. None of the guilty Chinese women swimmers had been allowed on the Olympics team. The announcer indeed mischaracterized Chinese policy and spoke in a racist manner. His introductory comment was disgraceful. But no Chinese response was tempered by any recognition that the Chinese women's swim team had problems.

Even after the Olympics, the coaches of China's women's swim team promoted the illegal use of drugs by their athletes and were again caught, this time in Australia. Particular disqualifications followed. There was a continuing problem that would never be mentioned by outraged Chinese defending a pre-suppositionally pure and innocent China. These angry patriots had little interest in complex truths.

Chinese sports actually had been reformed in the American direction. In fact, Chinese coaches no longer were part of some big, red, centralized, bureaucratic machine, as was still the case in Cuba. Indeed, contrary to prevailing assumptions, even the offending Chinese swimmers were not coached by exiles from the former East Germany, where drug usage in fact reached deadly scandalous proportions. NBC had its data very, very wrong. But the outraged Chinese patriots were not interested in the facts, and there grew a Chinese movement to get the NBC announcer fired. The enemy had to be destroyed. Compromise was surrender. Chinese insisted that NBC had politicized a friendly sporting competition, that NBC was part of a vast American conspiracy to besmirch China's good name, a conspiracy involving human rights crusaders such Harry Wu and the Dalai Lama as well as supposedly false charges about Beijing's involvement in illegal weapons proliferation. Chinese external relations were imagined in terms of truth and justice resisting demonic slander. The issue was not that some athletes had been wronged but that an innocent nation had been victimized. The Chinese discourse was similar to that of Mao-era vigilante class struggle where adversaries were 100 percent evil and had to be literally smashed to smithereens by pure reds. The language was similar to 1966, when young Chinese proved their loyalty and patriotism by turning Mao's call for a Cultural Revolution into an orgy of torture and murder aimed at purported traitors. Great, murderous, patriotic continuity had a new target. While China was still an endangered victim, now it needed to strike out at foreign forces to survive and protect its honor.

Actually, the Beijing government greatly politicizes sports. It does not engage in friendly competition for competition's sake. Who does? During the Atlanta Olympics, Beijing ordered that the achievements of people born in China now on other teams be down-played and that American victories be marginalized in Chinese reporting. Chinese sports reportage regularly blamed Chinese losses on cheating by foreigners, especially by allegedly biased judges supposedly chosen by the host Americans, which, of course, is not how the International Olympics Committee actually runs the games. The media message for China as always was that, were it not for an international anti-China conspiracy, a misunderstood, glorious, and struggling China would have prevailed. The message was not about the Olympics but about a good China's rightful place in an evil, anti-China world. What is so noteworthy is how welcome that propaganda line was even among supposedly open-minded Chinese with access to the international media. This deep patriotism was passionate and pre-suppositional. Given that the great Chinese teams in Atlanta actually performed magnificently, there is a mystery as to why world-class strength in a rising China is accompanied by the claim of extreme victimization crying out for vengeance against alleged enemies supposedly keeping China down.

This dangerous chauvinism has a long and deep history. Japanese students of Chinese nationalism stress the strength of historically structured forces in China in generating both the political contestation of the national identity struggle in China and a panicky and out-of-control quality to that nationalism caused by a feeling that everything is at risk. As Sharif Shuja says, "Japanese have doubts about China's prospective political stability."[21] Japanese scholars such as Tokyo's University's Masahiro Wakabayashi contrast China's anti-Japanese nationalism with the postcolonial nationalism of long-term imperialist colonies.[22] China's postcolonialism is special because China was never fully controlled and administered by Japan for a sufficiently extended time for sustained peaceful progress to be possible. Only the Northeast enjoyed such benefits. Much of China was never conquered by Japan at all; while some parts, as in the north, suffered fantastic cruelty under Japan's murderous "three all" campaign, with little modernizing gains. Given such historical variation, Chinese do not have a uniform experience of the Japanese invaders.

Professor Nishimura Shigeo of the Osaka University of Foreign Studies stresses the incomplete natures of Chinese nationalism and nation-building, which combine to perpetuate the ancient imperial project which subordinates Japan to Chinese hegemony,[23] and to produce a felt need in post-Mao Beijing for leaders to target a hated foreign enemy in order to create sufficient political glue and loyalty for Chinese society not to surrender to fissiparous forces.[24] The key under-appreciated facilitating factor of this nativistic mobilization is, for Nishimura, Mao Zedong's failure in nationalistic construction. The Mao era was a waste that permitted a popular subsequent chauvinism. It fixates on an unchanging militaristic Japan. However much Japan has actually been transformed two full generations after the Nanjing massacre, social surveys in China, according to political scientist Stanley Rosen, find Chinese still identifying Japan with the war criminal Tojo and still thinking of the democratic, inward-looking Japanese as "cruel." This is not a natural legacy. China's political imagination has been filled with fantasies that legitimate anti-Japan military actions by China in Asia.[25] The Chinese press selects and distorts. It will not inform its people that in June 1999 Japan Airline pilots urged JAL to ban soldiers wearing battle fatigues from JAL flights since the uniform made passengers "feel uncomfortable," hardly an action that fits with Beijing's propagandistic portrayal of a militaristic Japan.[26]

As Nishimura describes the historical process producing China's legitimating fantasies, China's imperial rulers, long proud of their unique imperial greatness, were slow to respond to the challenge of modern state capacity, including new military technologies impinging on China from Europe, Japan, North America, and Russia. Only at the start of the 1930s did a broad-based consciousness grow of a need to build modern national loyalties to buttress the integration and institutions required for independence and development. Just then, Japan launched an all-out invasion. Anti-Japanese sentiments naturally flowed into the still existing nationalistic vacuum. The particular late or slow developing history of Chinese nation-building permitted China's anti-Japanese nationalism to become peculiarly strong. It defined and infused Chinese patriotism.

This sudden and complete legitimation of anti-Japan fury is hidden from Chinese by the official story they have imbibed in which Chinese nationalism from 1895 is singularly anti-Japanese. The anti-Japan litany from 1895 includes the treaty Japan imposed at Shimoneseki after the war with China in Korea, Japan's twenty-one demands on China's sovereignty in 1915, Japan's Nishihara loans, and China's patriotic May Fourth movement. Actually May Fourth was far less a nationwide anti-imperialist struggle than was the 1925 anti-British mobilization following the gunning down of Chinese strikers. Anti-British actions spread everywhere in China, even in Xinjiang in China's far west. Chiang Kaishek's Nationalist Party was based in China's south, where British imperialism was the natural focus. During the 1920s, Japan proposed "forging a united front with China to counter Western influence."[27] Beijing's subsequent anti-Japan discourse diminishes China's earlier, powerful anti-British nationalism. Japan was not always Enemy Number One for Chinese patriots.

According to Gerald Horne, in China as indeed almost everywhere people feared European domination, "Russia's defeat at the hands of Japan" in 1905 was interpreted as the start of a general crisis of European, or white, superiority. Chinese nationalist leader Sun Yat-sen experienced the impact of "Tokyo's victory over Moscow" as proof that "'blood is thicker than water,' which is why the British were saddened by Russia's defeat."[28] Sun went to Taiwan to deal with Japanese colonialism, imagined as a friend of China's national liberation from the Manchu rulers of China and their Czarist Russian supporters. Indeed, as Jung Chang notes, "Twenty years after the [1911] republican revolution, there was still no unified nation to replace the rule of the emperor, nor, in Manchuria, did the people have much concept of being citizens of something called 'China.'"[29] For the first third of the twentieth century even Chinese patriots who joined the Chinese Communist Party went to Japan to learn how to become modern, free, and strong. The Japanese scholars are right that the unifying glue of anti-Japanese nationalism that helped Mao to power was a blinding and lasting 1930s patriotic explosion.

However, once in power, Mao Zedong did not use this shared patriotism to build a modern nation. Instead, as an internationalist and a communist, Mao launched campaigns of so-called class struggle, actually vigilantism which labeled many Chinese as enemies and traitors. A national vulgate language did not spread. Economic integration was not advanced. The institutional practices of a modern nation-state, other than the military, were left frail and fragile. Consequently, the military and its notion of patriotism gained unusual weight. And instead of developing the integrating institutions of a modern welfare state, as even the Soviet Union did, Beijing after 1949 ordered each unit to fund its own local schools, health facilities, housing, and so on. Whereas Moscow built on the inherited Russian state after a quick 1917 coup, Beijing, after a long period of devastation, invasion, and civil war, left many crucial governmental functions to local units (danwei) rather than building national, vertical administrative bureaucracies. With power thus dispersed, the modern nation-state remained unrealized.

Economic reform in the post-Mao era has begun to foster language and economic integration. But reform inevitably also decentralizes power, intensifies local identities, and weakens the tax power of the center relative to the strong provinces. Ruling groups face enormous problems in reforming the economically irrational Leninist command economy. The Mao era legacy of a weak nation-state greatly worsens the difficulties confronting reformers. Chinese everywhere quite rationally fear the nation falling apart, falling into civil war, chaos, and violence. Nationalism therefore seems to be needed for integration, and post-Mao nationalism consequently feels healthy to most Chinese. It is experienced as that which keeps the nation together, as the single most important source of unity and stability. To question its dangerous chauvinism is to sound like you wish to see China divided, in disarray, declining, suffering, weak.

What is usually invisible is the political content of this nationalism, that is, its political bias. Unintentionally, but ever more strongly, it benefits those promoting military action to deny Japan, as an American surrogate, hegemony in Asia. Chinese patriots imagine a twenty-first century Asia where China predominates. Such nationalism is presuppositional. Anti-Japanese hardliners who are not friends of openness and reform are consequently major beneficiaries of a popular Chinese patriotism one-sidedly imagined by many good people either as a mere domestic ploy of hardliners or as a healthy source of unity, stability, and pride. After all, Chinese patriots all wish to see China great again. That means preventing a presumably innately evil Japan from gaining too much influence in Asia. If Chinese wish to prove they are truly patriotic, then never again should Japan rise in Asia. Chinese patriots want to show that ruling groups wrongly ignored their true nationalism in the Mao era. Even Chinese in Hong Kong and elsewhere can feel this passion. They become 110-percenters. Their nationalism feels natural, which is to say historically infused with an anti-Japan content.

Central leaders, while at times restraining such patriotic passions, have generally chosen to make use of this virulent chauvinism. Hence it has grown stronger and stronger. It seems to do so many things for their leadership. It helps keep the country together and allows reform to move ahead. But it also serves certain particular interests. It has a potentially perverse anti-reform logic and energy. It engenders a backlash which challenges international openness and militarily threatens neighbors in the region with Chinese vengeance, with a return to Chinese hegemony. How else deny the region to a supposedly militaristic Japan?

Of course, particulars of nationalist history are not the sole sources of China's ultra-patriotism. After all, any formerly occupied colony tends to spawn a strong nationalism in its struggle for independence. This holds from India to the United States. But, in addition, anti-imperialist Leninist tyrannies create a peculiarly strong patriotism in each citizen. Sufferers in such countries all know how useless their government and its domestic policies are. Yet merely to take care of their family members, people must cooperate daily with Leninism's pervasive hierarchical authoritarianism. Citizens from Cuba to North Korea tend to rationalize their humiliating complicity by turning themselves into super-patriots, believing that the foreign policy line, at least, is true. Their good conscience for quotidian complicities requires being fooled and used in international affairs. In the worst days of Stalin's terror, even innocent victims of that paranoid despotism struggling merely to survive in a slave labor gulag volunteered to fight and die in the front lines to prove that they were genuine loyal patriots.[30]

So it has been in China. Even during the death plague of Mao Zedong's great leap–era famine, Chinese chose not merely to believe the official lies of how weather and Moscow were the true causes of the huge death toll but actually to invent credible details to lend the government's cover-up some verisimilitude. As Ting-xing Ye learned,

> The Soviet Union, our 'elder brother,' . . . had turned against us and was forcing us to pay back our debts all at once [in exporting Chinese] rice and milk [needed by starving Chinese]. . . It was rumored that [exported Chinese] apples . . . were checked one by one by the Russians for desired color and shape. The unwanted fruit was not sent back to China, where people were hungry, but dumped and left to rot in heaps. Eggs that failed the size test were smashed and discarded; in Shanghai's black market one egg cost more than a worker's daily salary.[31]

In like manner, Chinese patriots at the turn of the millennium innovated details to lend credibility to anti-China tales of perfidy by Washington, Tokyo, and Taipei. Former President Lee of Taiwan was said not to worry about the trouble he caused because he could flee, just as the worst Chinese exploiters did in 1949. President Lee's private plane was said to be ready to fly him into exile in Japan. The more politically sophisticated patriots reassured themselves that President Lee's seeming insanity in supposedly provoking China irrationally is explained by this or that narrow political motive. The one thing that Chinese patriots and their foreign apologists would not entertain was the possibility that the apparently crazy president of Taiwan, with the overwhelming and enthusiastic support of the people of Taiwan, just might be worried about

preserving a precious and precarious autonomy which seemed to be eroding because of a successful Beijing diplomatic offensive, yet that is how
it in fact looked on Taiwan.

Except for 1989–1992, a period when Beijing tried to woo and con-
ciliate neighbors by advancing the cause of peace and mutual benefit—
a most successful policy meant to end economic sanctions imposed
internationally in response to the June 4, 1989, Beijing massacre—this
virulent Chinese chauvinism, with its anti-Japanese thrust, has grown
ever stronger. Since Taiwan's democratic identity in the Lee Teng-hui
era, a time when Taiwan's president announced that only at age 23 did
he realize he was not Japanese, embraces the larger part of the Japanese
colonial experience—as some Indians can do with Britain, as some
mainland Chinese in the Northeast once did with Japan—Taiwan is seen
among anti-Japanese Chinese patriots as the evil heir to the murderous
Japanese who perpetrated barbarism in China. Democracy in Taiwan is
consequently intolerable. That is, Taiwan is considered a continuation
of Japanese conquest, a humiliation to be ended by any means necessary, and as soon as possible. China's anti-Taiwan patriotism legitimates
armed conflict. Taiwan is the most likely flash point for a larger war.

This anti-Japan nationalism is no longer a northern particular. It has
even begun to spread to the south, where it often takes on a more economic form, one which legitimates acceptance of northern Chinese hatreds. In the south, it will be said that Asia will grow better without too
much Japanese aid, trade, and investment. The Japanese forms of these
activities are described, even condemned, as one-sidedly benefiting only
Japan, as causing trade deficits, never transferring advanced technology, and never promoting and training skilled management. Consequently, increasingly, strong action against a narrowly selfish Japan seems
legitimate. The north's anti-Japanese hatred increasingly infects the south.
One patriotic Hong Kong legislator told me that he had come to hate
things named *Zhongshan*, the well-known short-hand of Sun Yat-sen,
the father of the 1911 republican revolution. *Zhongshan* was Sun's alias
in Japan. It made him Mr. Nakayama, a Japanese name. This southern
Chinese patriot experienced a hated Japanese hegemony each time he
encountered the once revered name *Zhongshan*, the now detested Japanese Nakayama. Patriots demand anti-Japanese actions.

The Chinese people's just demands seem unmet by a Beijing government imagined as groveling to Japan. Why, people ask, did President
Jiang invite the Japanese emperor to China when Japan's imperial in-

stitution is purportedly the heartbeat of a revanchist Japan? Changes in northeastern China are also indicative of this intensifying and virulent anti-Japan trend that can turn actual economic pragmatism into a charge of treason. When Mao died and China opened to the world, northeastern Chinese were most warm to Japan, as were Taiwanese. Many had benefited during Japan's occupation. Millions had fled from North China chaos to Japanese safety in the Northeast. A significant number spoke Japanese and resumed ties to Japanese acquaintances in the post-Mao era. Children of such families predominated among privately funded Chinese students in Japan. Beijing conservative leaders cursed pro-Japanese sentiments in China's Northeast. But entering the twenty-first century, this is all changing. Post-Mao government-promoted reminders of Japanese savagery, as, for example, memorials to Showa-era biological warfare and medical experiment centers, seem to be turning Chinese in the Northeast away from reconciliation with Japan and toward vengeance.

However deeply felt the anger at Chinese traitors, the real difference between patriots and traitors is often accidental, more a matter of geography and history, rather than character, determining who is good and who is bad. In North China, the so-called traitors are the folk who lived, usually along railroads, in Japanese-occupied areas and had to get along with those wielding power in order to care for their families, while the so-called patriots are those who lived away from railroads, where they could be mobilized by anti-Japanese resisters. They are all Chinese. Surely if each had lived in the other's spot, each would have done as the other did. Accident has been politically legitimated to create beloved heroes and hated villians.

This vengeful nationalism in China is deep and visceral. It is promoted in popular song and folk humor. Indeed it beats strongly and proudly even in Chinese hearts in open democracies abroad. That is, its political logic is usually invisible. It is not affected by access to new information. It already seems the truth. Chinese nationalists experience themselves not as victims manipulated by political interests at the state center but as pure patriots who know the truth and will not be fooled. These patriots are outraged and demand action, sooner rather than later. They are standing up for China. They actually totally invent history. In the new nationalism, Mao stood strong and firm; in contrast, Deng was weaker, and Jiang weaker still. Actually, Mao's military was so weak that in 1979 second-rank Vietnamese troops demolished it. The policies of Mao's successors, Deng and Jiang, have actually built China's military into a potent force to be reckoned with.[32] But the Chinese patriotic mind-set, demanding assertive military—even nuclear—action, criticizes Jiang for stopping nuclear testing and imagines Mao as he never was, as China's hawk. The real Mao, after all, did not even commemorate the Nanjing massacre. Such a silence is unthinkable for late–twentieth century Chinese haters of Japan. Their Mao, their Japan, their America, their history—it is all a fantasy. But it is not a harmless daydream. In short, domestic forces in China re-imagine history to legitimate surging Chinese strength. That is, expansive military action is interpreted as merely an end to post-Mao supine-ness, which is surely not what China's worried neighbors experience.

There has grown in China a racially informed chauvinist mind-set similar, as one liberal intellectual in China put it to me, to what rose in Japan in the 1930s.[33] This mind-set is ever more impervious to fact, logic, or economic interest. Patriots "know" that America, Japan, and others do not wish to see China's return to glory, and therefore they conspire to humiliate China. Foreigners, Chinese patriots agree, invariably strive to keep China down. The seminars on Chinese campuses after the May 1999 bombing of their embassy in Belgrade took it as their goal to reveal the true essence of America's anti-China global policy of hegemonism. In this peculiar Beijing perspective, Kosovo was not about Europe or NATO but instead a preparation for continuing American hostility in Asia against China.

These Chinese haters of America and Japan ignore the fact that for Washington and Tokyo the Cold War is over. Japan is actually the major source of China's bilateral economic aid. Chinese patriots also forget that China is the number-one recipient of inexpensive World Bank loans, an impossible status were Japan and the United States actually opposed to China's rise. The Chinese patriots ignore that sales to the American market are the major source of the foreign exchange that China uses to purchase advanced technology to speed China's rise. Living within internally generated Chinese chauvinistic passions, these patriots make invisible the real international world that benefits them and then fabricate another world, which they treat as truth.

Central to this dangerous presuppositional paranoia is the Chinese outrage in 1993 when the International Olympic Committee did not reward Beijing with the year 2000 Olympics. Living within their skewed patriotic mind-set, the Chinese "knew" that America, in order to humiliate and suppress China, had denied them the right to host the Olympics as Olympic-host Japan had done in 1964 and as Olympic-host South Korea had in 1988.[34] With America accused of conspiring to keep China down, "to make China the enemy,"[35] hatred for America intensified after 1993 to the point that anti-Americanism became pervasive. Be that as it may, the Chinese political claim in 1999 that the murderous NATO bombing of the Chinese embassy in Belgrade for the first time ended a naive Chinese love affair with America is obviously a lie. The same language of innocence and disillusion had already been invoked in 1993, and the patriotic hates actually even preceded 1993, as the resurgent post-Mao anti-Japanese venom proves.

The logic of injured Chinese nationalism is patterned: A pure and vulnerable China is the innocent victim of anti-China foreigners; China must therefore act such that the insulting and bullying ends, must reassert itself in Asia, build a military capable of imposing its will in Asia, and regain what rightfully belongs to it. Such is justice.

This reactive and defensive discourse is actually a popular legitimation for Chinese military hegemony in East and Southeast Asia. The Chinese accusation that America seeks hegemony in Asia has little to do with American behavior. From India to Singapore to Japan, many Asian governments actually fear American withdrawal from Asia and are anxious over a growing American isolationism or unilateralism. The uniquely Chinese view of a militarily expansionist America rationalizes Chinese ambitions as defensive. China assumes "grievances with the current world order, illustrating U.S. dominance, highlighting China's relative weakness."[36]

This is clear in Chinese critiques of American foreign policy stances toward Milosevic and Saddam Hussein. What is at issue is not the rightness or wrongness of U.S. actions in Kuwait or Kosovo. Given the amorality of international relations, it is inconceivable that American actions be beyond reproach. But Chinese patriots fantasize those actions as no one else in the world. They brush aside matters of oil in the former case and NATO's future in the latter, and imagine events in Kuwait and Kosovo as basically preparation for more serious American military intervention in Xinjiang, Tibet, Taiwan, and North Korea. What is happening is the Chinese nationalistic rationalization of Chinese regional hegemony in Asia. In the words of Xiaorong Li, "Government leaders in China . . . dress up xenophobic nationalism as concern for protecting national sovereignty."[37]

This is obvious when one examines the Chinese response to the 1993 rewarding of the year 2000 Olympics concession to Sydney, Australia. As everyone now surely knows, Sydney bought the needed votes just as had Atlanta, Nagano, and Salt Lake City. America was irrelevant to the 1993 choice. But in 1993 the Chinese were fully persuaded, not to mention self-persuaded, even "self-illusioned." As with the Cultural Revolution–era propaganda about a Soviet revisionist threat, this time it was an American plot that challenged China, costing it the year 2000 Olympics.

But facts are not the issue. The accusations against America are rooted in nation-state domestic insecurity, injured innocence inherited as a discourse from the anti-Japan war, and a will toward historically legitimated regional predominance. A lack of evidence did not stop the Chinese rioting in 1999 against U.S. installations in China from "knowing" that U.S. President Bill Clinton, pictured as America's Hitler, intentionally bombed the Chinese embassy in Belgrade in order to humiliate China. (Personally I do not want to speculate about the bombing. I will continue only to state facts and offer factual explanations.) But that President Clinton chose to bomb China's embassy is a claim that contradicts Clinton's politics and interests. Apparently senior leaders in Beijing soon realized that it was absurd to believe that Clinton could benefit from such a bombing. High-level friends in Beijing tell me the Chinese leadership realized that, had they concluded that Clinton had intentionally bombed the embassy, they would have had to respond as if America had declared war on China. But the government never told the people their conclusions or their dilemmas. They seldom do.

No one has been told that the 1993 campaign against America for supposedly costing China the Olympics was a big lie. Consequently, the poisoned propaganda launched by Beijing time and again comes back at the leadership in a super-patriotism that threatens economic reformers in Beijing by demanding tough action against nations needed as partners in the reform venture and against reformers who cooperate with such nations. Vacuous yet virulent charges against these foreign partners and domestic reformers are relentless.

Thus, despite the Clinton administration's lack of human rights activism, China accused it of continually harassing China on the issues of Tibet and human rights. In fact, the Chinese are yet again persuading themselves of their insulted innocence. They are being self-persuaded that Washington is the leader of a foreign human rights crusade aimed at subverting Beijing's sovereignty when, actually, America is a laggard on international human rights, having both rejected a land mine treaty at the end of the 1990s and long opposed participation in an international criminal court. China has actually signed some human rights covenants that the sovereignty-drunk unilateralists in the U.S. Congress have put on hold. Indeed, as international relations analyst Samuel Kim has pointed out, China's discourse of sovereignty over human rights is largely borrowed from a prior American discourse, at times phrase by phrase. Yet the Chinese insist that America is leading a human rights crusade against China when in fact it isn't.

Since the foreign provocations that patriotic Chinese attack do not exist, one must look within China for the sources of Chinese superpatriotism. These origins are in the late history of Chinese nationalism and the Mao-era failure to build a modern nation-state. The Revolution failed, but its debris is life-threatening.[38] Various observers will, of course, balance the nationalist, political, and economic factors somewhat differently, but the general trend is indisputable. There are few, if any, liberal or internationalist Chinese voices left to openly challenge the chauvinism. The Chinese have, for the most part, long since chosen nationalism over democracy. The political atmosphere in China makes it almost impossible, even politically suicidal, for voices of common sense to be persuasive against expansive nationalism. In 1999, on viewing the play *Between Life and Death*, Susan Lawrence noted that "Beijing's cultural elite break into fervent applause when Japanese are killed on stage."[39]

Yesterday's liberals today usually also insist on standing up for a vengeful and militarily tough China. They see their special role in the new nationalism as building the nation, the task Mao ignored. They will insist on succor for people injured by the creative destruction attendant to global market integration. They are still building the just state, as Mao did not. They are still building a national identity, too, one infused with hate and contempt for Japan, America, and Taiwan. This nationalism, however, benefits China's military, China's hardliners, and China's conservatives. Fervent Chinese patriots often do not fully appreciate the consequences of their actions and beliefs, which they feel is mainly a matter of standing up for China and keeping China united. But this nationalism is infused with hate and legitimates military action. This nationalism is vengeful and outward thrusting, while it rationalizes itself merely as necessary defensive measures to hold the country together and not allow China to be bullied.

It is useful to analogize China entering the twenty-first century to

Japan entering the twentieth century, when that country too still had a great potential for political reform. It too continued to join international bodies and to benefit from that participation. Yet, at the same time, a militaristic nationalism, imagining Japan as the innocent victim of an unjust international regime, grew stronger and stronger, gradually eroding more hopeful possibilities. An analogy, of course, is not an identity. The constitutional thrust in China seems far weaker than in Japan; the chauvinistic dynamic seems stronger in China. But in both cases, the future was and is contingent on imponderables, open to multiple possibilities.

This essay's description of Chinese political tendencies and their deep sources is not meant as a prediction. The future is contingent on too many unknowns to risk a sure prognostication. Mao's death and the rise of Deng changed much between 1976 and 1978. China can again change its course for the better. The economic imperative, after all, is as pressing as ever. But it is Chinese who will decide. Personally, I favor policies toward China of total engagement with quiet vigilance. Such cooperative actions by Washington and Tokyo, however, have not slowed the surge of Chinese chauvinism. That dynamic is domestic. It has unleashed a vicious cycle, a downward spiral, creating frightening future portents. And so the new patriotic fervor augers ill. It insists on changing the international rules. Typical of this Chinese consciousness is the popular explanation of why the great 1999 Chinese women's soccer team barely lost the World Cup final to a most fortunate U.S. team. The gossip was that only because an American referee (who did not in fact exist) wrongly disallowed a Chinese goal did China lose. China is always the innocent victim of anti-China foreigners and unfair international rules. China, in this Chinese perspective, would be on top but for American-institutionalized anti-China international unfairness.

The deeply structured continuity of nation-building/nationalism sketched herein did not suddenly rupture at the death of Mao Zedong. However great the change initiated by the reform policies of Deng Xiaoping, everything did not totally change. Even in the post-Mao era, there is a community of leaders who identify with the salvation of China from foreign threats, people who identify with a unique role for a heroic China surviving an anti-China environment. That survival, that greatness, is experienced as the virtually sacred task of the continuing leadership, of the heirs of the martyrs who sacrificed that this great China should live. This is not a political community readily prone to self-destruction tomorrow through an opening to political uncertainty for itself via democratic contestation.

In fact, very soon after Deng initiated reforms premised on joining the World Bank set of institutions to benefit from the win-win game offered by such things as IDA soft developmental loans; foreign investment; international trade; and scientific, technical, and cultural exchanges, Deng and his reforms came under criticism at the highest levels for being too soft on America, Japan, and a hostile global capitalism. China has ever since been riven by a debate in which the institutions and ideas inherited from the era of the anti-Japan war have increasingly challenged the hope of a win-win game premised on international exchange inherent in the original Deng reform thrust which grabbed the momentary opportunity made possible by the demise of Mao and the opening to change offered by the accession of a new state leadership.

While future openings for further reforms made possible by a politics taking advantage of crisis cannot be ruled out, the post-1992 trend has clearly been toward a reassertion of the world view and values of a uniquely great and internationally challenged China imagining a zero-sum world order in which China must use its power to stave off foreign threats. This tendency of the nationalistic past to return and challenge to take the lead in policy, momentarily repressed by the hope of Deng-era reform, continues to strengthen. Increasingly China is seen by Chinese leaders as uniquely capable (given its economic growth) and courageous (given its nationalist history of heroic struggle and ultimate sacrifice) to resist and reverse a world tide where a super-powerful but cowardly America would command global hegemony and dominate and pollute the world. Indeed, as with Kuwait and Kosovo, so with economics: the rules of the dominant global institutions are seen in China as unfairly skewed to serve immoral America's hegemonic purposes.

Presupposing therefore that a risen China is central to an anti-hegemonic project which serves the interests of truly sovereign states everywhere, as the Beijing leadership does indeed assume, old Sinocentic myths and ambitions become increasingly important to the national dynamics born in China earlier in the twentieth century. Beijing imagines itself as gloriously pioneering an anti-hegemonic path that others such as Russia and India should also join. (Beijing's special relationship to Pakistan built over forty years has been somewhat sacrificed to this Chinese-led counter-hegemonic politics which challenges both alleged American hegemony and the real premises of the Deng reform thrust.)

Because of the contradictions, tensions, and ambiguities in Beijing's continued building of a great nation, China would both join the core of great powers in order to act as one of the few leaders of its institutions and, at the same time, challenge the core, seeing it as a threat to China and all other sovereign states, except the hegemonic United States. This latter policy line, embedded and empowered by the nationalist forces explored in this essay, rejects the Deng reform vision of joining a world of international institutions, finding in them not a win-win game but an anti-China logic. Consequently, concessions to join the WTO or to open up on information technology are long resisted in order to preserve the domestic institutions and political interests of the authoritarian community whose leadership supposedly can save China and the world. Much of the economy of the authoritarian state therefore remains unreformed, remains the power base of China's authoritarian nationalism.

The continuing strength of this logic of nation-building means that success for the economic reform project is far from guaranteed. Because politics and policy resist basic change, post-Mao China may be caught in the same quandaries as post-Nagy Hungary. In Kadar's economically reformist Hungary, after 1956, economic growth was extraordinary for about a quarter of a century. But then the limits placed on reform by the entrenched power of the old Leninist center hindered further rapid growth and intensified societal contradictions. Those tensions are strengthening in China, too.

Yet the two trajectories are unlike. Hungary's political breakthrough after 1989 was not purely a matter of economic evolution defeating political stagnation. Instead it took a foreign *deus ex machina*, Gorbachev, to change the balance of forces in Hungary. Given the independence of China and the power of Chinese nationalism, no similar savior seems in the cards for China. For the moment, it is the long-entrenched nation-building forces of China which are winning out over the Deng-era reform vision of joining an international world and benefiting from its win-win possibilities. The consensus of Chinese leaders across the legitimate political spectrum is that only naive dupes of American hegemonic ideology could embrace that win-win worldview. Consequently, the popular vision among analysts that the reform initiatives of 1978 constitute a second revolution, a rupture from the Mao era, may, despite all the manifest and magnificent Hungary-like progress, be as misleading as Mao-era notions that the Great Leap or the Cultural Revolution constituted a unique rupture on to a special path. Instead, China seems still headed on the dangerous nation-building path first legitimated and institutionalized in the anti-Japan nationalism of the 1930s, a path which threatens to deny the Chinese people the further benefits of more open international exchange. In short, once again, the Chinese revolution's peculiar nationalistic content may work against the better interests of the Chinese people in advancing a world of mutual prosperity and peace.

China is increasingly driven to act strongly in Asia to change the rules and the regional reality. That agenda, however, conflicts with the presence of other militaries in the region. War could occur. To be sure, Beijing does not seek a war with America. But given the felt Chinese need to stand up by using its might as Mao did not, the new military-oriented nation-state seems natural, historical, and reasonable common sense to ever increasing numbers of Chinese, when, in fact, it is political, passionate, popular, and just beginning. It is the result of political forces taking advantage of Mao's failure to build the nation, experienced as a legitimation of strident nationalism on behalf of unity and stability. The political dynamics of this patriotism, however, serve chauvinistic political forces in China, interests which urge that the military be allowed to prove that China has at long last once again stood up and forced the world to respect it. However much President Jiang Zemin's aura rests on international sophistication and on delivering the economic benefits flowing from good relations with America, it is not easy for a Chinese leader to transcend a shared elite Chinese world view which treats bilateral dealings with other powers as zero-sum struggles over power between us, China, and the enemy, them.[40]

In short, the origins of China's patriotic fervor are readily identifiable. They are not responses to foreign threats. Not only are they ever more poisonous and ever more pervasive, they are deeply rooted and branching out. Their rise threatens all the good done in China by post-Mao reformers and also threatens peace and prosperity in the region. The long-term consequences of China's historic twentieth century failure to build a competent and stable nation-state looks like it could constitute a challenge to regional peace well into the twenty-first century.

Notes

1. Patrick Tyler, *A Great Wall* (New York: Public Affairs, 1999).
2. See Suisheng Zhao, "'We Are Patriots First and Democrats Second,'" and Jianwei Wang, "Democratization and China's Nation Building," in *What if China*

Doesn't Democratize? Implications for War and Peace, eds. Edward Friedman and Barrett McCormick (Armonk, NY: M.E. Sharpe, 2000), 21–73. Other articles in the volume detail reasons for anxiety over the direction of Chinese nationalism.

3. Erica Stecker Downs and Phillip Saunders, "Legitimacy and the Limits of Nationalism," *International Security* 23, no. 3 (Winter 1998/99). For a broad historical analysis countering this vision of peaceful economics in command, see Norrin Ripsman and Jean-Marc Blanchard, "Commercial Liberalism Under Fire," *Security Studies* 6, no. 2 (Winter 1996/97).

4. Yongnian Zheng, *Discovering Chinese Nationalism in China* (Cambridge: Cambridge University Press, 1999). My rejoinders are in *The China Journal*, no. 43 (January 2000): 160–162 and *American Foreign Policy Interests* 21, no. 6 (December 1999): 57–58.

5. Chen Pi-chao notes of the authors of a book courageously advocating political legal reform (Dong Yuyu and Shi Binhai, eds., *Zhengzhi Zhongguo* [Political China] [Beijing: Jinri Zhongguo chubanshe, 1998) that in today's "xenophobic China" no one even dares to promote liberal democracy lest they be denounced as subversive and pro-Western (*China Perspectives*, no. 24 [July–August 1999]: 90–95).

6. Jeffrey Wasserstrom, "Student Protests in Fin-de-siècle China," *New Left Review* (2000): 52–76.

7. Edward Friedman, "Preventing War Between China and Japan," in *What if China Doesn't Democratize? Implications for War and Peace,* eds. Edward Friedman and Barrett McCormick (Armonk, NY: M.E. Sharpe, 2000), 99–128.

8. Hong Ying, *Daughter of the River* (New York: Grove Press, 1999), 200.

9. Takeuchi Yoshimi, "Asia as Method," *Asian Cultural Studies* (Tokyo) 5 (October 1966): 7.

10. Meihong Xu, *Daughter of China* (New York: John Wiley and Sons, Inc., 1999), 6–11, 121.

11. Ting-xing Ye, *A Leaf in the Bitter Wind* (St. Paul: Hungry Mind Press, 1999).

12. Ha Jin, *Waiting* (New York: Pantheon, 1999), 51.

13. Nicholas Kristof and Sheryl WuDunn, *China Wakes* (New York: Times Books, 1994), 403.

14. Unryu Suganuma, *Sovereign Rights and Territorial Space in Sino-Japanese Relations* (Honolulu: University of Hawaii Press, 2000), 144–145.

15. Friedman and McCormick, eds., *What if China Doesn't Democratize? Implications for War and Peace* (Armonk, NY: M.E. Sharpe, 2000).

16. For studies of the relation of gender to nationalism, see "The Body in Contemporary China," *China Information* 13, no. 2/3 (autumn/winter 1998–1999).

17. Honda Katsuichi, *The Nanjing Massacre* (Armonk, NY: M.E. Sharpe, 1999).

18. Norma Field, *In the Realm of a Dying Emperor* (New York: Vintage, 1993).

19. See Unryu Suganuma, *Sovereign Rights and Territorial Space in Sino-Japanese Relations* (Honolulu: University of Hawaii Press, 2000), and Greg Austin, "Japan's Superior Rights in the Sentaku Islands," chap. 6 in *China's Ocean Frontier* (St. Leonards, Australia: Allen and Unwin, 1998).

20. See Suping Lu, "Nationalist Feelings and Sports," *Journal of Contemporary China* 8, no. 22 (1999): 517–533.

21. Sharif M. Shuja, "Warming Up," *Harvard Asia/Pacific Review* 3, no. 2 (Summer 1999): 40.

22. Masahiro Wakabayashi, "Two Nationalisms Concerning Taiwan," in *Divided*

Nations, ed. Jaushieh Joseph Wu (Taipei: National Chengchi University Institute of International Relations, 1995), 170–192.

23. Nishimura Shigeo, "A Perspective for Understanding Twentieth-Century China," in *Structural Change in Contemporary China* (Osaka: Osaka University of Foreign Studies, 1998),

24. This is also the thesis of Yongnian Zheng, *Discovering Chinese Nationalism in China* (Cambridge: Cambridge University Press, 1999).

25. Catherine Rose's *Interpreting History in Sino-Japanese Relations* (London: Routledge, 1998) is an excellent study of how Beijing manipulates myths about a revanchist Japan to serve a legitimating nationalism in China.

26. "JAL Pilots against GSDF Riders in Fatigues," *Japan Times,* June 25, 1999.

27. Fred Yen Liang Chiu, "Suborientalism and the Subimperalist Predicament," *Positions* 8, no. 1 (2000): 115.

28. Gerald Horne, "Race from Power," *Diplomatic History* 23, no. 5 (Summer 1999): 443, 444.

29. Jung Chang, *Wild Swans* (New York: Doubleday, 1991), 37

30. Eugenia Ginzburg, *Journey Into the Whirlwind* (1967; reprint, New York: Harcourt Brace and Company, 1995).

31. Ting-xing Ye, *A Leaf in the Bitter Wind* (St. Paul: Hungry Mind Press, 1997), 26.

32. You Ji, *The Armed Forces of China* (London: I.B. Tauris, 1999).

33. Barry Sautman, *Relations in Blood: China's 'Racial Nationalism'* (Seattle: University of Washington Press, forthcoming).

34. It is a fact that the U.S. Congress, only three years after the Beijing massacre, did not wish to see Beijing and its mayor, Chen Xitong, a leader of China's pro-massacre forces, rewarded while the innocent victims and their hundreds of thousands of grieving friends and family members were ignored. Surely it is not illegitimate to express such concern in a non-binding resolution, which Congress did.

35. Cited in Yongnian Zheng, *Discovering Chinese Nationalism in China* (Cambridge: Cambridge University Press, 1999), 3.

36. Bates Gill, "Limited Engagement," *Foreign Affairs* 78, no. 4 (July/August 1999): 70.

37. Xiaorong Li, "The East Asian Challenge for Human Rights (book review)," *Dissent* 46, no. 3 (Summer 1999): 118–120.

38. This point was detailed in a 1990 paper republished as "Was Mao Zedong a Revolutionary?," ch. 11 in Friedman, *National Identity and Democratic Prospects in Socialist China* (Armonk, NY: M.E. Sharpe, 1995).

39. Susan Lawrence, "Life and Death," *Far Eastern Economic Review,* August 5, 1999, 22.

40. The conclusion of Qian Yuwei, a Chinese diplomat in *The Inside Story of the Diplomacy Between Communist China and America* (in Chinese) (Taipei: Chongcheng Publishers, 1999), 345.

5

Curing the Sickness and Saving the Party: Neo-Maoism and Neo-Conservatism in the 1990s

Kalpana Misra

The Democracy Movement of 1989 and its suppression marked a watershed for developments in post-Mao China. Deng Xiaoping's relative dominance within the system from the late 1970s to the late 1980s gave way to declining participation in the post-Tiananmen phase and to the steady consolidation of power by Deng's appointed successor, Jiang Zemin. The centrality of the ideological and political conflict between moderates and radical reformers in the previous period was replaced by a more complex and uncertain phase of transition in the decade following the events of June 4, 1989.

There were fundamental similarities and continuities between the pre- and post-Tiananmen periods. China's rapid economic growth, the erosion of the planned and state sector, the marketization of economic life, and the pluralization of society continued as before. Perhaps even more significant and cogent than in the earlier decade were the attendant problems and concerns over the adverse consequences of reform. In contrast to the intellectual dynamism and vitality which characterized theoretical discourse in the pre-Tiananmen era, ideological debate in the 1990s was muted both by the official crackdown on dissent within China and the exile of the most influential intellectual voices for radical reform. Nevertheless, rising levels of inequality and socio-economic tension, declining social mores, and pervasive official corruption provided the context for heightened apprehensions regarding an ideological vacuum; and the search for a "new ideology"—some sort of coherent framework of beliefs and values—to unify and guide the society and state through a crucial phase of transition acquired an acute sense of urgency in the post-Tiananmen decade.

The perception of the need for a coherent set of core beliefs and values was linked directly to the failure of the gigantic ideological reorientation effort that was undertaken to justify reformist policies since the December 1978 Third Plenum of the 11th Central Committee, and was reflected both in pervasive mass apathy and cynicism toward the ruling ideology, as well as in the steady erosion of support for officially sanctioned doctrinal norms among the intelligentsia. The ideological stalemate that characterized official circles and the intellectual elite in early 1989 was broken by the May–June developments in China and the successive collapse of communist governments in Eastern Europe later that year. In the immediate aftermath of these events the democratizing liberal orientation of the most radical reformist theorists such as Su Shaozhi and Li Honglin stood discredited as either "romantic utopianism" or an insidious counter-revolutionary theoretical current aimed at undermining the authority of the Party-state. The unprecedented challenge posed to the regime and the socio-economic order by rapid change and decentralization became the new focus of intellectual attention and prompted the resurgence of two trends of thought which had played a much more inconsequential role in the preceding decades—neo-Maoism and neo-Conservatism.

A Return to Mao

One of the ideological trends that has undergone a partial revival is that of neo-Maoism. For the leftists in the political leadership and the intellectual establishment, the catastrophic developments leading up to the Tiananmen Incident and the successive collapse of communist governments in Eastern Europe and the Soviet Union were an unhappy vindication of their fears that unchecked intellectual liberalization would entail too fundamental a revision of official doctrine, and consequently undermine the Party's normative authority. The support rendered to students and liberal democracy activists by industrial and commercial interests further underscored their belief that social polarization generated by economic reform had facilitated the emergence of new bourgeois groups that were now seeking to establish their own political authority and accomplish a restoration of capitalism.

In the months following the Tiananmen crackdown, terms such as *class struggle* and *dictatorship of the proletariat,* which had almost vanished from the Chinese Communist media, were encountered repeatedly in speeches and articles denouncing bourgeois liberalization and warning against "peaceful evolution" (Wang 1989; Duan 1991; Zhong 1991). The dangers of a gradual and subversive expansion of bourgeois influences imported from the West and growing out of the capitalist policies implemented by the Party leadership had been emphasized by moderate reformers in the 1980s. However, in the aftermath of the "political turmoil" of 1989 in China and the dismantling of the Soviet Union, the calls for preempting capitalist restoration were informed by a more imminent sense of urgency and foreboding. In the wake of the failed August 1991 coup in the Soviet Union a *Renmin ribao* commentator's article reminded readers that

> Chairman Mao was the first to raise this question…[t]he actual development over the past few decades has fully proved that the hostile forces at home and abroad have never stopped attempting to subvert the Communist party's leadership and undermine the socialist system—they are largely relying, to an increasing extent, on the 'war without the smoke of gunpowder' for fulfilling their goal. We will grieve if, instead of gaining a keen insight into the real threat of peaceful evolution, we lower our guard against it (*BBC Summary of World Broadcasts FE/1154*, 19 August 1991, B2/4).

In his public speeches during the days leading up to the 70th anniversary celebrations of the establishment of the CCP, Hu Qiaomu asserted that "those who recognized proletarian dictatorship but not class struggle were not Marxist-Leninists" (Meng 1991) In justification of the military action at Tiananmen, Hu noted, with some satisfaction, that "in the ever stormy situation around the world" after 1989, socialist China appeared more stable, but since the international and domestic class struggles were protracted the guard against peaceful evolution could not be relaxed (Hu 1991).

> In the changing international community today we should understand and recognize class struggle, the struggle between various strata, class

struggle objectively existing at home, two line struggle and ideological struggle within the Party, the struggle between real and sham Marxism, and the struggle between Marxists and democratic socialists. He who does not recognize this is not a good Communist leader. At least he is not a real Marxist (Meng 1991, 2).

Radical reformist exhortations to adopt "completely new forms of thinking and not be restrained by the difficult question of whether something is socialist or capitalist in nature" (*Jiefang ribao*, 22 March 1991) not surprisingly provoked neo-Maoist responses which directly equated economic restructuring with capitalist reform. While political figures like Deng Liqun minced few words in asserting that "reform and opening up is itself a banner for peaceful evolution in China" (Deng 1991, *FBIS*, 7 January 1992, 24), writers in *Guangming ribao* and *Dangdai Sichao* distinguished between socialist and capitalist reform and two kinds of communists, "those who persist in reform and opening up, safeguard state sovereignty and socialist dignity, and regard reform and opening up as a way to realize the Communist ideal . . . and those who deviate from the socialist orientation, forfeit the moral integrity of the state, party and people to willingly serve as dependencies of the Western bourgeoisie" (Wei 1991).

The influence of neo-Maoist ideological positions in the early 1990s was reflected in Jiang Zemin's address on the 70th anniversary of the founding of the CCP as well. Jiang (1991) praised the brilliance of Mao Zedong Thought and emphasized the need to maintain the people's democratic dictatorship and to persist in centralized economic planning and socialist ownership. His speech echoed the Party Elders' views on the intense struggle between infiltration and counter-infiltration, subversion and counter-subversion, and peaceful evolution and opposition to peaceful evolution. However, on the question of class struggle, Jiang struck a less strident note and reiterated the Party line that had been laid down by Deng Xiaoping in 1979; that is, class struggle was no longer the principal contradiction in China even though it still existed in certain spheres and could intensify under certain conditions. Mindful of Deng's policy preferences, Jiang downplayed the international aspect of class struggle and emphasized the need for a peaceful global environment to build socialism with Chinese characteristics. In the domestic context class struggle was reduced to the conflict between bourgeois liberalization and the Four Cardinal Principles "with the central question of political power being the central issue."[1]

Deng Xiaoping's celebrated southern tour of early 1992 and the subsequent Fourteenth Party Congress's shift of emphasis to accelerated and more extensive reform reversed the leftist ascendancy within the ranks of the political leadership and undermined their ideological influence in the official media and the central propaganda apparatus. But the nostalgia for the Mao era and increasing dissatisfaction with socioeconomic disparities and the alarming decline of public morality now found a broader audience. The best-selling *Looking at China Through A Third Eye* and its sequel deplored the new social polarization and class conflict, and advocated a return to revolutionary ideals and Mao Zedong Thought (Luo 1994; Wang Shan 1996). Apprehensions about the undesirable and destabilizing consequences of unbridled reform and marketization continued to find an echo in academic analyses as well. In an article entitled "The First Anniversary of the Market Economy," the economist Yang Fan (1993, 26) pointed out:

> Utilitarian standards replace rational standards as the basis for judging things, the ideological standard of surnamed socialism or surnamed capitalism is replaced by the standard of productive forces, and the standard of morality and conscience is replaced by the standard of money. . . . Stimulated by a small minority getting rich quickly, people's desire to pursue wealth has become unprecedentedly strong, and the principles of the commodity economy have corroded everything. . . . The activity of the whole society revolves around the word "money". . . . It can be said that the secularization of China's society is complete and that it is developing in an unhealthy direction.

Others went even further to defend Mao not only for his intellectual vision but also for such policies as the Great Leap Forward and Cultural Revolution, which had been the focus of much criticism and derision in the previous period. Cui Zhiyuan (1994; 1996) refuted Western models of economic liberalism and neo-classicism and argued that Mao's socialism being native to China was a more appropriate model of development. The commune system and the Great Leap Forward had laid the foundations of local autonomy and village and township enterprises, according to Cui, while the Cultural Revolution was a necessary experiment against bureaucrats. For the neo-Maoists, even the cult of personality had served a useful purpose on the argument that the supreme leader's persona had symbolized values and ideals that brought people together and promoted social cohesion and public morality (Luo 1994).

In the early 1990s the focus of leftist theorizing was the corrosive influence of bourgeois ideas and declining commitment to socialist norms among Communist cadres and in Chinese society in general. He Xin (1989, 3) set the tone for ideological orthodoxy by maintaining that Marxism was both the spiritual source of the cohesive and dynamic forces in society as well as the "intellectual guarantor of stability and peace." In a vast and complex country such as China "the demotion of Marxism from state doctrine to just one of a hundred schools of thought could only serve as a prelude to a great upheaval." By the mid-1990s, however, the concern with ideological contamination and decline had broadened and escalated to a deeper apprehension about the more fundamental changes that were being wrought on the social structure and the economic base. Between 1995 and 1997 a series of 10,000 character statements (variously attributed to Deng Liqun, his son Deng Yingtao, and larger study groups associated with leftist journals like *Zhenli de Zhuiqiu*, *Gaoxiao de Zhanxian*, and *Dangdai Sichao*) presented detailed and systematic analyses of the specific economic and sociological changes that had been effected by the expansion of market forces and China's integration into the global capitalist economy.[2]

The most striking and significant issue raised by these articles was their assertion that a re-stratification of Chinese society had occurred and that the reforms thus far had already contributed to the emergence of a non-governmental bourgeois class as well as the embryo of new bureaucrat and comprador bourgeoisie classes. According to the first article, entitled "Several Factors Affecting China's State Security" (1996), the objective basis for the crystallization of new social formations was the shrinking role of the public sector and the rapidly expanding shares of the collective and private sectors in the national economy. In the fourteen years from 1980 to 1994, it was pointed out, the proportion of the state sector dropped from 76 percent to 48.3 percent while that of the collective sector increased from 23.5 percent to 38.2 percent and that of the private sector, including foreign funded enterprises, went up from 0.5 percent to 13.5 percent. With the introduction of the shareholding system, corporate property rights, and the leasing, sale, and mergers of existing state-owned enterprises, it was estimated that by the year 2000 the proportion of the public sector would constitute only a quarter of the gross industrial output value while the collective and private and individual sectors would account for 50 percent and 25 percent, respectively. The changes effected in the ownership system had resulted, according to the article, in a massive drain of over 500 billion yuan of state assets from 1982 to 1994, and it was this turnover of state assets from public to private hands that had been the main source of the primitive accumulation of the new bourgeoisie.

For the leftists, whose definition of socialism centered on the predominance of public ownership and the implementation of "distribution according to work" as a remunerative principle, these trends represented the possibility of an imminent change in the class character of the Chinese state. The article continued to argue that the increasing political activities of the new entrepreneurs; their significant presence in the Chinese People's Political Consultative Conference (CPPCC), the Youth League, the Women's Federation, and other administrative posts such as mayors and people's deputies; their use of money in local elections; and their subsidizing of newspapers and magazines had already brought about an alliance with liberal intellectuals which would facilitate the transformation of the new bourgeois class-in-itself to a class-for-itself.

And, finally, the author pointed out that preparations for the wresting of power away from the dictatorship of the proletariat and into the hands of the new exploiting classes had begun with a two-pronged strategy of fomenting corruption and inner-party struggle within the ruling group. The new bourgeoisie provided support to those cadres in the Party who were inclined towards the capitalist road and attacked and isolated those who adhered to the socialist line. The Communist Party, which ordinarily could be expected to serve as a bulwark against the drift towards capitalism, was rendered ineffectual both as a consequence of the astounding corruption within its ranks and its growing estrangement from its traditional constituency, the laboring people. For the working class and the broad masses of the peasantry the large scale layoffs, increasing insecurities about jobs and livelihood, and the reemergence of exploitative relationships between workers and domestic and foreign business people had promoted the perception that the Communist Party "loved rich rather than poor people" and represented the interests of those who had "knowledge, capability, and wealth." At a critical juncture, similar to the August 1991 incident in the Soviet Union, the Party would not be able to hold on to power if a sizeable chunk of its membership made opportunistic choices to desert its ranks, and the workers and peasants declined to back the Party leadership.

The author of the second 10,000 character statement also warned that Moscow was a "mirror" for Beijing and that the reality of "polarization and the rise of a new bourgeoisie" in present day Russia was now "coming true at an accelerated pace" in China.[3] Countering the three criteria for evaluating reform which were attributed to Deng Xiaoping—whether or not reform could (1) reinforce national strength, (2) raise living standards, and (3) develop social productive forces—this piece suggested that on the economic front reform should be judged a failure if it undermined public ownership and gave rise to polarization and a new bourgeoisie. In the political sphere, reform would be considered unsuccessful if it either led to the moral degeneration of the Communist Party and drove it out of office or deprived people of their political power and turned the Party into the agent of the bourgeoisie.

Continuing the theme of threats to national security that were arising as a consequence of reformist policies, the second 10,000 character statement also emphasized that the penetration of China by international capitalism had reached a critical stage. With the entry of Western businesses into sensitive areas like finance, insurance, and telecommunications, China's formal economic independence was at stake at the same time as many individual sectors and markets were also coming under the monopolized control of foreign companies. The rise of a comprador bourgeoisie with extensive links to international capitalism was promoting an alliance that would facilitate the Western strategy to bring about a peaceful transformation to capitalism in China.

The third and fourth 10,000 character statements began circulating in 1997 and were signed by the Editorial Department of *Dangdai Sichao* and *Xin Mao,* respectively. Together, the two articles presented a strong defense of public ownership, collectivist ethos, normative incentives, and egalitarian practices. Their major arguments refuted radical reformist claims that leftist policies had contributed to sluggish economic growth and dampened worker enthusiasm in the decades prior to reform. The superiority of public ownership over individual or private ownership had been demonstrated adequately both by the rapid industrialization of the Soviet Union prior to World War II and by the remarkable industrial growth and economic development which took place in China after the Communists took control. While the previous system had worked out a balance between equity and efficiency and given workers a sense of being "masters of enterprises," reform was pursuing growth at the expense of equity as workers faced massive layoffs and increasing insecurity, while managers behaved like capitalist bosses and siphoned off state assets for private enrichment (for a more detailed analysis, see Feng 1991).

Reformist policies which attacked the concept of the "iron rice bowl" and linked high productivity to material incentives were based on the assumption that social progress could only follow from the pursuit of individual benefit and advancement. Such ideological positions were influenced by capitalist rather than socialist theories of human nature, and it was inevitable that reformist policies following such a premise would shake the foundations of the socialist system and lead to a capitalist restoration similar to the one that had already occurred in the Soviet Union and Eastern Europe.

Clearly, the return of the vocabulary of class and class struggle, of the two-line struggle between capitalist roaders and socialist roaders, and of dictatorship of the proletariat and capitalist restoration warrants the label neo-Maoist for this recent theorizing. However, it is important to note that these leftist analyses of contemporary Chinese society and state structure are a logical extension of the moderate reformist positions that had been staked out in 1979 and through the early 1980s. The moderate reformist leadership of Chen Yun, Peng Zhen, Hu Qiaomu, and Deng Liqun had early on emphasized the economic determinants of class and premised the identification of China as a socialist society on the extent of the nationalization of the economy and the pattern of "distribution according to work." Although the moderates conceded the need for "re-adjustments" to accelerate rates of growth, eliminate sectoral imbalances, and expand the role of the technical and professional intelligentsia, their emphasis had always been on efficient and rational macro-control mechanisms, the precedence of the state sector, nationalized industry, and the plan over the market. The attempts of radical reformers variously to switch to political and behavioral criteria to describe "progressive" rural capitalists and urban entrepreneurs as members of the working class, to considerably stretch the definition of "distribution according to work," to distinguish between ownership and management, and to innovatively reinterpret social and individual ownership were resisted by the moderate reformers throughout the 1980s.

The political timing of the circulation of the 10,000 character statements and the publication of articles critical of the capitalist orientation of reform could, no doubt, be linked to perceptions of shifting power configurations as Deng Xiaoping faded from the scene and personnel arrangements were being finalized for the Fifteenth Party Congress. However, the resurgence of Maoist analyses was more closely related to events in Eastern Europe, which clearly vindicated the deceased

Chairman's views, and to the crucial phase that the reformist process had entered in China. By the mid 1990s the cumulative effects of the economic policies that had been followed in the last decade and a half were becoming much clearer: unemployment, both rural and urban, was estimated at 20 percent by the World Bank; rural inequality had registered a sharp rise between 1988 and 1995; and the respective gaps between urban and rural areas, coastal and inland areas, and the various urban industrial sectors had increased considerably (*China News Digest* 1997). According to Khan and Riskin (1998), whose estimates for urban inequality were 18 percent higher than those of the State Statistical Bureau (SSB), the increase in urban inequality was proportionately greater than the increase in rural inequality over the same period, and, overall, China in 1995 was among the more unequal Asian developing countries.

Moreover, the rapid growth of inequality could be directly attributed to regressive policies such as the dis-equalizing systems of net subsidies that aggravated income disparities, or the rural fiscal policies which placed the burden of net taxes and other transfers of income from households to the state and collective sectors principally on the poorest households. Even more significantly, the Khan and Riskin studies point to a big gap between the growth of personal income and GNP as well as a sharp decline in the share of government revenue in GNP (from 15.7 percent to 10.9 percent between 1988 and 1995), which suggests that macroeconomic policies were indeed redistributing incremental income into business accumulation.[4]

At this juncture, the reformists' calls for "bold experimentation" and new forms of economic ownership, organization, and management, including the selling of shares in state enterprises, appeared to set the stage for a sweeping change which could bring about a qualitative transformation of the Chinese economy (Jiang 1997). Jiang Zemin's ambitious plan for the reform and reorganization of State Owned Enterprises (SOEs) envisaged both the merger of approximately 1,000 of the largest or "pillar" industries into corporate conglomerates with dominant state ownership and autonomous corporate management, as well as the conversion of the remaining large and medium sized ones into "mixed" firms with less than predominant equity held by the state (*Far Eastern Economic Review*, 9 October 1997). The clarification of property rights and the establishment of "standard corporations" had been endorsed by the Third Plenum of 1994, and since 1996 the policy of "grasping the large, letting go of the small" (*zhuada fangxiao*) had been promoted to permit the disposition of the 85,000 or so small industrial enterprises as "joint stock cooperatives," with equity shares offered to management, staff, and workers (*Asian Wall Street Journal*, 23 September 1997).

Jiang's (1997) report to the Fifteenth Party Congress drew attention to the vigorous growth of "self-employed and private businesses" and asserted that "even if the state owned sector accounts for a smaller proportion of the economy, this will not affect the socialist nature of our country." Such claims clearly did not find acceptance among the leftists. Not only was the vast expansion in "mixed" collective-private sectors of the economy seen as incompatible with socialism, but the introduction of the shareholding system for the SOEs and the proposed property rights reform were tantamount to undermining public ownership as the "foundation" of the national economy (Chou 1996). The process of enterprise conversion, it was feared, would most likely result in "asset stripping" and "spontaneous privatization" by corrupt factory managers while masses of workers would simply face factory closures and destitution (*Asian Wall Street Journal*, 23 September 1997).

The publication of the 10,000 character statements indicated a significant ideological divide within the Party in the period intervening between the Fourteenth and Fifteenth Party Congresses (1992–1997). Although the leftists were in a minority, the greater coherence and systematization of their arguments against the latest policy proposals made their stance more threatening than in previous years. Radical reformist intellectuals seemed little prepared on an intellectual level for responding to the leftist offensive. Cao Siyuan's "What are Those Negating Reform and Opening Up Up To?" (1996) in *Jingji Gongzuo Yuekan* sounded an alarmist note by accusing the left of trying to begin a new Cultural Revolution but provided no substantive arguments to refute the concerns that had been raised by the statements.

The decision of the Party leadership to ban Cao's article was obviously related to its mediocre content and to the fact that his extensive use of quotations from the 10,000 character statements would, in fact, result in a further publicization of leftist arguments against the new economic policies. A similar directive was issued to suppress the article, "Unshakable Reform and Opening Up—Commenting on Deng Liqun's 'Ten Thousand Character Memorial,'" by Fan Liqin (*Ching Pao*, 1 September 1996). The unwillingness of the leadership to engage in ideological debate—attributed to the need to promote unity and focus on economic development—more likely stemmed from ideological defensiveness and an awareness that the leftist critique could find a very sympathetic audience in a disgruntled constituency of unemployed workers and impoverished and uprooted peasants.[5] Herein lies the significance of the resurgence of neo-Maoism. The passing of the Old Guard of Chen Yun, Hu Qiaomu, and Wang Zhen together with the political eclipse of individuals like Deng Liqun have resulted in a much smaller base of leftism within the Party; but the appeal of Maoist ideas has strengthened and broadened beyond the Party membership due to the adverse social and economic consequences of reformist policies. As an intellectual trend, neo-Maoism has experienced a revival because it provides a much more compelling theoretical construct for understanding present reality than the official hodge-podge of "socialism with Chinese characteristics."

As I have argued elsewhere in greater detail, the massive ideological reorientation begun in late 1979 failed in its attempt to satisfactorily and conclusively set aside the Maoist legacy (Misra 1998). Expanding privatization of the economy, increasing inequality, and particularly the emergence of the cadre capitalists in the 1980s and 1990s all confirmed Mao's fears of capitalist restoration and vindicated his preoccupation with the phenomenon of the Communist Party itself becoming the major obstacle to the achievement of socialism. The consequences of the socio-economic policies so enthusiastically embarked upon by the reformist leadership had been predicted with extraordinary foresight by the leftist radicals (Yao 1975), and throughout the Deng era the Maoist prognosis returned to haunt both the moderate leaders who agonized over China's "peaceful evolution towards capitalism" as well as the radical reformers and liberal intellectuals who echoed the ultra-leftist denunciations of a new exploitative class of communist bureaucrats in socialist systems. The nostalgia for the Maoist era and the Mao fever of the 1990s, for all its eccentric and commercial manifestations, underscored and reflected at a deeper and more serious level the shortcomings of the intellectual effort to provide a sufficient theoretical basis or guideline for the reform program. The theoretical tenets that the Party upholds to justify its continuity in office no longer appear to restrict significantly its policy choices, but they do provide credible ammunition for critics who are less complacent about the ever widening chasm between ideology and practice.

Neo-Maoist theorizing is, for the most part, not a return to Cultural Revolutionary ultra-leftism, as alleged by its detractors. Its proponents draw attention to the undesirable and destabilizing effects of reformist policies, but in a telling illustration of how fundamentally China has changed, the leftists do not suggest an abandonment of reform. Rather, their concern is to reassert the normative goals espoused by the Party and the state and to ensure that there is a balance between equity and growth, distribution and development, and collective interests and private benefit. References to a bureaucratic class do appear in neo-Maoist writings, but they are relatively muted and far less frequent than the allusions to the newly emerged capitalist class and the comprador bourgeoisie. A far more serious concern for the neo-Maoists is the question of political power, because the Party's loss of control, in the ultimate analysis, will spell the end of the socialist system.

The erosion of socialist norms threatens the very existence of the Party because it encourages and promotes corruption within the rank and file at the same time as it weakens the organic links with the industrial working class and the peasantry. As Zhong Shuqiao put it:

> The loss of political power often starts with corruption. . . . [I]f we do not pay genuine attention to and effectively carry out the struggle against corruption, it will spread like pestilence, the Party will destroy itself and, because of the loss of the Communist party leadership, the state will be thrown into chaos and will regress.[6]

Needless to say, the neo-Maoists overlook the fact that while opportunities for corruption have multiplied significantly as a consequence of liberalization, misuse of official authority and control over resources, privilege seeking, and arbitrary exercise of power were also structural characteristics of the pre-reform period.

In emphasizing the new sources of tension and potential instability within the system and asserting the need for a stricter dictatorship of the proletariat, the neo-Maoists have identified an issue that is increasingly of concern to broad sections of Chinese society. However, the neo-Maoist apprehension that increasing economic pluralism will be accompanied by a widening and more insistent appeal for political liberalization has been misplaced, and the trend in intellectual theorizing in the past decade has, in fact, been more supportive of political authoritarianism. One such trend that appears to have gained extensive currency among Chinese students and intellectuals in recent years is that of neo-conservatism.

The Rise of Neo-Conservatism

For a core group of Chinese intellectuals quite favorably disposed toward the marketization of the Chinese economy and the open door policy, the fate of the East European communist regimes and subsequently the Soviet Union itself promoted the realization that the survival of the Chinese state and its continued progress on the path to economic development and modernization could be guaranteed only by a strengthened monopoly of power in the hands of the Party elite. The forerunner of this ideological trend was the theory of neo-authoritarianism that had gained currency among a section of Zhao Ziyang's supporters in late 1988 and early 1989. Against Hu Jiwei, Su Shaozhi, Yan Jiaqi, and others who argued for immediate democratization and the elimination of monopoly of state ownership as a solution for the decentralization/centralization–reform/crisis/reform cycle, Zhao advisors Wu Jiaxiang, Chen Yizi, and Wang Xiaoqiang along with intellectuals like Zhang Bingjiu, Yang Baikui, and Xiao Gongqin advocated "enlightened despotism" to guide the transition to a full-fledged market economy.[7] These neo-authoritarians claimed a commitment to political liberalism but argued that pluralist democracy could only be the "result of reform in China, not its precondition." Immediate introduction of political democracy before the consolidation of a capitalist economic order would be inefficient and prolong the transition to market relations (Yang 1991; Cao 1991).

The open advocacy of free enterprise, the creation of a solid middle class of property owners, and rule by a modernization-oriented social group consisting of industrial and commercial circles and intellectuals who possessed the "consciousness of modernity" brought criticism and persecution for the theorists of neo-authoritarianism in the period of leftist ascendancy during and immediately after the Tiananmen crackdown. But in the neo-authoritarian emphasis of political control and stability as well as of an instrumental approach to socialism and capitalism there was much to attract incumbent leaderships like those of Jiang Zemin and Deng Xiaoping, and it was not very surprising that the basic ideas of neo-authoritarianism survived and emerged repackaged in the form of neo-conservatism in the 1990s.

The major differences between pre-Tiananmen neo-authoritarian thinking and post-Tiananmen neo-conservative arguments stem principally from changed political, social, and intellectual circumstances. In 1988 and 1989, writers like Xiao Gongqin were enunciating their ideas within a context of massive introspection about Chinese culture and civilization, Marxist ideology, socialism as a system or model of development, and insistent demands for greater intellectual pluralism and political liberalization. In an intellectual climate where the terms of discussion were largely set by radical reformers, neo-authoritarians went to great lengths to highlight their similarities with liberal democrats and their commitment to the goal of a market economy. Their preference for market relations was premised on the perceived weakness of the planned economy and its consequences for both economics and politics. Neo-authoritarians agreed with their radical reformist colleagues that "vague and unclear property-rights relationships" embodied in state ownership prevented the effective utilization of productive property and obscured social responsibilities and the pursuit of individual interests (Rong 1990–91, 62). In theory, the state represented society in possessing and managing the means of production, but in actual practice public property was carved into "vertical strips and horizontal blocks" and fell under the ownership of departments, units, and localities. More often than not, state ownership tended to degenerate into either "individual bureaucratic ownership" or the "feudal warlords" economy that turned competition into "civil wars" among government departments (Wu 1990–91, 40–41).

Echoing the "totalist" argument, neo-authoritarians also pointed out that the complex macroeconomic regulation required by a planned economy produced an intense concentration of power in the state and a politicization and bureaucratization of the entire society.[8] The interests and demands of various classes, strata, and groups could be reflected only through a single political channel, and political clout became the "most effective and convenient shortcut" for the pursuit of economic and other interests (Rong 1990–91, 56). A full-fledged market would "reduce to a minimum the scope of public power and the number of political decisions" (Wu 1990–91, 36). The gradual emergence of autonomous and organized economic interests premised on equality, mutual benefit, and contractual relations in a privatized economy would undermine the fusion of politics and economics and contribute to the "pluralization and contractualization" of the political sphere.

However, in the transitional phase, Yang Baikui and others argued, the combination of a weak market with an imprecise delineation of rights and responsibilities would raise "transactional political costs" enormously as more and more people sought political power for economic benefit. The emergence of a healthy market would also be obstructed by the "delinquent behavior of vested interests." As Wu Jiaxiang observed, "the consumer would want to avoid the higher prices of the open commodity and labor-services markets and seek the lower priced or free-of-charge products and labor services of the internal market. . . . [T]he laborer would want to avoid the labor market" and become an "imperial worker with a guaranteed income." Such resistance to the market on the part of political constituencies necessitated "coercive guidance or propulsion" by a "power elite" to guide and push the whole society from tradition into modernity and oversee the transition to a market economy and liberal democracy (Wu 1990–91, 40).

In the early and mid 1990s, neo-conservative theorists built on earlier arguments in support of market reform and a commodity economy but differed from the radical reformers in their greater appreciation of macroeconomic control and planning. Neo-conservative theorists also are far more assertive and forthright in their opposition to democratization and support for authoritarian rule, or what is euphemistically termed "orderly change from above." The subtle shift in emphasis from the economic sphere to the political one (as in the case of neo-Maoism) was made in response to challenges perceived internationally and within China. Ethnic unrest, political disintegration, and the unruly economic transition in the former Soviet bloc apparently vindicated the views of the Chinese leadership that had prioritized economic liberalization over political democratization. Chinese students and intellectuals who had raised the issue of immediate political reform were now seen simply as romantic utopianists who had demanded radical change without considering its feasibility or practicality (Chen 1994; Xiao 1995). Internally, China's own daunting and ever increasing problems of corruption, unemployment, socio-economic polarization, crisis of values, and particularly the erosion of central authority seemed to underscore the need for tighter controls and a reassertion of ideological norms and beliefs (Xiao 1994b and 1996; Yi 1994; Li and Wang 1994). The prescription of a strong and enlightened dictatorship acquired even greater significance for the neo-conservatives at this time, not simply for guiding the transition to a market economy but also as the most important mechanism for arresting political decline and preventing the total collapse and disintegration of the system itself.

For neo-conservatives in the 1990s and into the present century the goal of political stability to offset the crises sparked by rapid economic growth has become an overriding priority. Just as Jin Guantao and others had linked the inability of the Communist system to achieve modernization and intellectual enlightenment to the ultra conservatism of the Confucian order, neo-conservative theorists like Xiao Gongqin employ a historical perspective to demonstrate the repeated tendency in Chinese politics toward radicalism, political romanticism, and idealism, a tendency which constantly overstepped historical phases and attempted total transformation of values and institutions and ended up only retarding progress and causing massive dislocations in the economy and in society generally (Xiao 1995). Both the mass mobilization of the Cultural Revolution variety and the activities of latter day liberal democrats were doomed to failure because in the absence of the necessary conditions for democratic institutions and processes they merely provided sporadic outlets for mass grievances. It was irresponsible and unrealistic to promote Western-style democratization in a society such as China that lacked both the civic culture and the historical and social contexts that were necessary for the proper functioning of such institutions.

In the more chaotic climate of the post-Tiananmen period, the neo-conservative preference for orderly change from above envisages an enhanced role for political institutions and central authority in exercising macroeconomic control and in arbitrating conflicts of interest. For Hu Angang and Wang Shaoguang, a major source of concern is the decline in the Chinese state's political capacity and financial strength as a result of the devolution of authority and control over revenue and resources from the center to the provinces (Hu and Wang 1994). "A Heart to Heart Talk with the General Secretary" (Wang 1996), published under the auspices of the Chinese Academy of Social Sciences (under the sponsorship of Liu Ji, an advisor of Jiang Zemin), reiterates the views of Wang and Hu that reformist policies of "grant power and yield interests" have been counter-productive because they serve only to expand centrifugal forces and foster lordly attitudes in rival special interest groups which feud with one another and are increasingly difficult to control. The enhanced regionalism and growing clout of provincial governments could well end up with the transfer of political allegiance from the center to local groups, as in the case of Yugoslavia. Thus, the prospect of "political decline and erosion of authority leading to social disintegration and [the splitting] up of the country" was one which must be borne in mind (Hu and Wang 1994). In arguments reminiscent of Gunnar Myrdal's "soft state, hard state" thesis, neo-conservatives point to the market-oriented yet state-dominated modernization strategies of East Asian states, with their ideologies of nationalism and political conservatism, as models for China to emulate.[9] Inspired both by the examples of these countries that had accomplished "economic miracles" under the "visible guiding hand of autocratic governments" as well as by the gradual evolutionary approach of late 19th-century and early 20th-century indigenous reformers like Yan Fu, the neo-conservative strategy for China's transition from tradition to modernity stresses a blend of selective Western ideas and institutions (to promote economic rationality, market forces, autonomous interests, and eventually a middle class which could serve as the basis for a pluralist democratic social order) and the traditional Chinese values of collectivism and patriotism propagated and maintained by the Party elite (Xiao 1994a).

The resurgence of neo-conservative thought and its increasing attraction to wide sections of Chinese officialdom and intellectual elite can be related to some extent to the incarceration and exile of the more vociferous liberal democratic critics of the regime. However, its broader appeal is linked in no small measure to the fact that the vast body of writing that can be characterized as neo-conservative is based on theoretical assumptions that are common to a variety of Chinese political opinions ranging from liberal democrats to neo-Maoists. Neo-conservative arguments in favor of market forces and a capitalist economy flow naturally from the ideological evolution set in motion with the critiques of ultraleftist voluntarism and the valorization of the role of productive forces after the December 1978 Third Plenum. The triumph of economic determinism was evident in the adoption of the "Primary Stage of Socialism" thesis by the Party's Thirteenth Congress in 1987 that consigned the goal of socialist society to a very distant horizon and paved the way for theories marginalizing teleological concerns and rationalizing the immediate and complete transition to a market economy. Neo-conservatism's vague promises of liberal democracy after the consolidation of a solid middle class and the establishment of an advanced economy has parallels with the reformist leadership's own extended time frame establishing democracy and socialism after a several-decades and even centuries-long period of "primary socialism." The reassertion of planning and administrative controls have also brought the proponents of neo-conservatism closer to political leaders like Chen Yuan who shared the neo-conservative gradual and incremental approach to change and, particularly, the prescription for a more active governmental role for addressing politically divisive issues such as unemployment and social inequality.

Moreover, the distinction between the instrumental rationalism of the political pluralism advocated by liberal democrat intellectuals, on the one hand, and the civic or technocratic dictatorship favored by neo-authoritarians and neo-conservatives, on the other, is far narrower than would be warranted by such labeling of the two groups. Prior to the events of 1989 the extent of political reform demanded by most radical reformers would also lead to the establishment of an elite democracy. Li Honglin, Yu Haocheng, Su Shaozhi, and Hu Jiwei were a minority who extended the application of democratic rights to workers and peasants. Most of their colleagues emphasized the criteria of education, training, and professional skills for participation in policy making and politics (Ding 1994). Indeed, on the question of participatory democracy, there has been a remarkable congruence of views across the Chinese political spectrum. Fang Lizhi, widely known as "China's Sakharov," advocated wholesale Westernization but maintained that intellectuals were an "independent stratum occupying a leading place" while the broad masses of the peasantry were not quite ready for democracy.[10] Fang's characterization was not far removed from that of the leftist hard-liners who justified their rejection of political democratization by pointing out that, "China must take into account . . . its people's limited capacity to withstand political and psychological strains . . . and their lack of democratic practice, experience and habit. . . . When many people are still preoccupied with the daily toil of basic survival, it is impossible to expect from them a high degree of democratic participation" (Zheng 1989, 3).

On the eve of the Tiananmen crisis, neo-authoritarians, to justify their arguments for a "civic dictatorship" of technocrats, elite intellectuals, and political leaders in favor of free enterprise, echoed liberal democratic sentiments about the "priceless" role of the intellectuals' modern consciousness and values in a society that "lacked a middle class and modernizing forces" (Xiao and Zhu 1989). Contemptuous of the "backwardness of the economic and educational standards of the vast majority of the masses," neo-authoritarians also recommended a polity in which a "power (or intellectual) elite" would "occupy the positions of leadership, represent the masses," and oversee the transition to a market economy (Yang 1991). In the 1990s, neo-conservatives repeat all of the earlier arguments against participatory democracy and point out that the incorporation of mass democratic movements in national politics can only produce negative outcomes.

It would not be an exaggeration to say that the neo-conservative solution to China's problems is deceptively simple and woefully inadequate. The significance of neo-conservatism lies in its identification of the varied and serious challenges faced by the Chinese state in an era of rapid development and change. Its most important contribution lies in refocusing attention on the factors of competent and efficient governance and cohesive ideological norms for generating support and legitimacy for authority. Its glaring weakness is its inability to provide satisfactory answers to the questions it raises.

The need for augmenting performance-based legitimacy with ideological norms that would unite the population behind the leadership and mobilize it voluntarily for the pursuit of elite-defined modernizational goals has been emphasized by most neo-conservative theorists. The increasing difficulty of maintaining law and order, the rising incidence of crime and corruption, and the declining capacity of the state are seen to be linked in one way or another with the dissipation of moral and ethical values; yet neo-conservative writing provides few substantive details about the normative framework that needs to be put into place. In 1991 a document entitled "Realistic Responses and Strategic Choices for China after the Soviet Upheaval" (1991, 35) suggested nationalism as a renewed rallying and cohesive force within an ideological framework combining Western rationalism and the "lofty and noble traditional culture of the Chinese people." Based on the East Asian experience, a focus on cultural nationalism and a revival of Confucian values to fill the ideological vacuum created by cynicism toward socialist ideas would seem to be a logical choice, and it has indeed been reflected in the receptivity to the ideas of new Confucianism introduced by overseas scholars like Tu Wei-ming. The Confucian concepts of self-cultivation and inner-sageliness do not simply provide a key to improved ethical standards for both elite and masses; they also assist in national rejuvenation by reorienting the country's search for a value and belief system separate from the West and in line with indigenous traditions.[11] However, given the neo-conservative instrumental approach to ideology, it is not surprising that the reevaluation of Confucianism is cursory and inadequate. It is, moreover, compromised and contradicted by the calls for adhering to the Communist Party's leadership and the Four Cardinal Principles.

The more obvious inconsistency between the neo-conservative commitment to the market economy as a teleological goal and its support for the incumbent political leadership and "socialism with Chinese characteristics" is problematic both for neo-conservative theorizing as well as for the ruling elite whose legitimacy it is trying to enhance. For the Party elite, neo-conservative advocacy of its claim to leadership at best reinforces neo-Maoist accusations that it has allowed itself to become a vehicle for the evolution towards capitalism. At worst, it exposes the neo-conservative utilitarian perception of Marxism-Leninism-Deng Xiaoping Theory as simply an integrative myth and makes the Party a conscious ally in a cynical ploy to use ideology as a cloak for the pursuit of diametrically opposed interests.

Perhaps the most serious shortcoming of neo-conservatism is its inability to explain how a strengthening of dictatorship or a greater concentration of powers in a centralized bureaucracy will resolve the problem of pervasive official corruption that is the greatest contributor to economic crime and mass cynicism about authority. In the late 1980s, neo-authoritarian theorizing had identified the structural basis for corruption and the misuse of official position in the concentration of power in the state and the "supra-economic coercion mechanism" that provided for "bureaucratic manipulation and extraordinary interference in all spheres of society" (Wu 1990–91; Yang 1991). However, neither then nor at the present time do Xiao Gongqin and others explain how the institutional arrangements of the "enlightened despotism" or "civic dictatorship" would preclude and eliminate such an inherent defect (Xiao and Zhu 1989, 5).

For the neo-conservatives it would seem that it is solely a matter of faith in the sincerity and ethical standards of a "power elite" that can guarantee honesty and integrity in public office. In this resort to explanations of bureaucratism and corruption as being individual behavioral problems rather than as arising from a social structural base, the neo-conservatives are in agreement with both the official position as well as that of neo-Maoist thought. One can recall that even the ultra-leftists in the 1960s and 1970s, who had first raised the issue of bureaucratic capitalism and rejected the distinction between legal ownership and control of productive property, had suggested a strengthening of the dictatorship of the proletariat, rather than the placing of limits or checks on authority, as a solution. It would seem that the historical and cultural appeal of rule by a few virtuous individuals still retains a powerful hold over a broad spectrum of political thinkers today.

Ideology in the Jiang Zemin Era

The post-Tiananmen period has seen an emphasis on ideology as both neo-Maoists and neo-conservatives have focused on the serious consequences of ideological and political fragmentation. There has also been a resurgence of ideology, in an abstract way, in official proclamations and programmatic documents. The neglect of ideological work and an overemphasis on economic construction, first noted with regret in 1986 and then reaffirmed as a major mistake by the Sixth Plenum of the 14th Central Committee, has brought forth a renewed initiative for building socialist spiritual civilization (CCP Central Committee 1996). However, what constitutes a socialist spiritual civilization is far from clear, although Deng Xiaoping Theory as the ideal embodiment of "socialism with Chinese characteristics"; patriotism, collectivism, and socialism as normative ideals; and the reassertion of the thesis of the primary stage of socialism have all been put forward as the main components of official ideology or Marxist-Leninist theory in the current phase.

More significant than the meager content of the official discourse on ideology is the fact that the initiative for outlining or enunciating doctrinal norms and providing authoritative conceptual lenses for understanding present reality seems to have passed from the top leadership of the Party to other groups such as the neo-Maoists or neo-conservatives. This development, if it continues, has long-term implications for the Party's hegemony over ideological discourse; but in the immediate context the ruling group has benefited, for the most part, from the climate of opinion that has been created from objective developments, nationally and internationally, as well as from the trend of intellectual evolution in the 1990s. As Edward Friedman argues elsewhere in this volume, the "pervasive and potent nationalism" that has been proliferating in China since 1992 has unleashed a political dynamic where ruling groups find legitimacy through tough anti-foreign action and rhetoric. The backlash against the wholesale Westernization and cultural and national nihilism of the previous decade has allowed the Party to recoup a measure of legitimacy on the basis of past achievements in repulsing imperialism and, in the present context, to promote itself as the defender of Chinese sovereignty and national interests in a post–Cold War world marked by the resurgence of a United States now poised to contain China. As Western imperialism rather than enlightenment values have incited popular imagination in recent years, the Party has not been slow to turn the new tide of nationalist sentiment to its advantage.

It is interesting to note that here, too, the Party, rather than establishing its own hegemonic discourse, has benefited from the discursive invention of the nation by other groups. There are, of course, problems inherent in the fostering of nationalist sentiments as a rallying force or as spiritual motivation because a too-assertive manifestation can escalate internal ethnic tensions. In foreign policy the outpouring of nationalism can serve the needs of the leadership, as in the case of the NATO bombing of the Chinese embassy, but it can also undermine and restrict a policy orientation stressing close ties and a "strategic partnership" with the United States. The ambivalence of official policy was reflected in the enthusiastic reporting of the runaway success of *China Can Say No!* in the official media as well as in the subsequent decision to ban it. In general, Party and government formulations have tried to avoid controversy by using the term *patriotism* rather than *nationalism*.

The revival of neo-Maoism in the post-Tiananmen period has put the Party on the ideological defensive, and the refusal of the top leadership to engage with the neo-Maoist critiques further undermines its claims as the fount of ideological authority. The much broader appeal of neo-conservatism among influential sections of Chinese society strengthens the position of Party leaders who share the neo-conservatives' orientation toward market forces and preference for a more aggressive governmental role to reverse the trend of ideological and political disintegration that threatens to erode central authority and undermine the social fabric. It has even been argued that a new core of leading figures may not be averse to co-opting the ideas of neo-conservatism as "pragmatic statecraft" for promoting capitalist policies under authoritarian rule (Feng 1997). This may be so, but it is premature to conclude that the ideological ambivalence and legitimacy crisis that has characterized CCP policy in recent years will be resolved either by making a decisive move toward neo-conservatism or by backtracking toward neo-Maoism. Neither of the two alternatives as currently formulated provide any satisfactory long-term solutions to the dilemma of half-way economic reform or the problem of ensuring responsible and accountable political leadership, and eventually participatory political development. These are serious shortcomings because, as Godwin Chu's research demonstrates, contemporary Chinese political culture is marked by a "rejection of traditional values of submission to authority, and the inculcation

of new values of assertiveness and active protection of self interest."
Under these circumstances the paucity of theory continues to place ever
more strain on the system, as it raises enormously the costs of any fail-
ings in the performance of the regime. Thus, the central issue of normative legitimacy and the resolution of China's century-long "orientational
crisis" remains an elusive goal on the eve of a new millennium.[12]

Notes

I am grateful to the Institute of Chinese Studies, New Delhi, for granting me the
generous use of its facilities and resources in the summer of 1999. An earlier draft
of this article was presented at the Institute in August 1999, and I want to thank the
participants of the Wednesday Seminar, especially Manoranjan Mohanty, Giri
Deshingkar, Patricia Uberoi, and Alka Acharya for their incisive comments and
feedback. Special acknowledgement is also due to Hua Shiping and K.K. Misra for
their insightful suggestions, and to Thomas Buoye for clarifying certain terms for
me.

1. In the aftermath of Deng Xiaoping's southern tour Jiang Zemin made a decisive shift to the radical reformist camp. Prior to that he proved himself adept at
playing to both galleries—the left and the right. For instance, in a speech on "theory
building" he emphasized the role of ideology by recalling the Maoist view of the
reaction of spirit on matter, of social ideology on social being, of production relations on productive forces, of the superstructure on the economic base. In a clever
twist of words, however, he also promoted the radical reformist cause of taking
"economic construction as the center" by pointing out, "in my opinion, under the
condition that our economy has lagged behind that of the developed capitalist countries the danger of capitalist restoration and peaceful evolution always exists. Socialism will eventually defeat capitalism. In the final analysis, it should have higher
labor productivity than the capitalist countries." See "Jiang Zemin on Enhancing the
Party's Theory Building," *Qiushi*, no. 12, 16 June 1991.

2. I want to thank Hua Shiping for pointing out the significance of the use of the
number ten thousand for these statements. The Chinese like to play with numbers
and ten thousand denotes large size, key importance, auspicious nature, and so on.

3. The author was Wu Yifeng of People's University according to Hong Kong
sources. See Chou Ying-jiu, "Political Situation as Viewed from Two '10, 000 character statements,'" *Ching Pao*, 1 August 1996, pp. 23–26.

4. Khan and Riskin (1998, 235) point out that from the point of view of stratification, the significance of the slower growth in personal income as compared to
the GDP is that rapid economic growth will not alleviate the effects of widening
inequality and even a small adverse change in distribution will have a deleterious
effect on the poor.

5. Deng Xiaoping's unwillingness to dwell on ideological concerns was reiterated during his southern tour. See "Key Points of the Talks in Wuchang, Shenzhen,
Zhuhai, and Shanghai," *Deng Xiaoping Wenxuan*, Beijing: Renmin chubanshe, 1993,
pp. 372–73.

6. Zhong Shuqiao, "Unswervingly Carry Out Struggle Against Corruption and

Degeneration," *Hebei ribao*, 4 July 1991. Jiang Zemin was also quoted as saying that if the costs of continuing economic growth were more bribery, embezzlement, and corruption, the CCP would become divorced from the masses and "we will collapse." *RMRB*, 25 January 1995.

7. For a detailed presentation and analysis of neo-authoritarianism see Stanley Rosen and Gary Zou, eds., "The Chinese Debate on Neo-Authoritarianism," *Chinese Sociology and Anthropology* (CSA), Winter 1990–91, Spring 1991, and Summer 1991; Mark Petracca and Mong Xiong, "The Concept of Chinese Neo-Authoritarianism," *Asian Survey*, vol. 30, no. 11 (November 1990), pp. 1099–1117; Barry Sautman, "Sirens of the Strongman: Neo-Authoritarianism in Recent Chinese Political Theory," *The China Quarterly*, no. 129 (March 1992), pp. 77–102; Ting Gong and Feng Zhen, "Neo-Authoritarianism in Mainland China,' *Issues and Studies*, January 1991, pp. 84–98.

8. Radical reformers argued in the mid and late 1980s that the combination of Party-state economy had produced a bureaucratic stratum with "total control over society."

9. In his *Asian Drama: An Inquiry into the Poverty of Nations* published in 1968 Gunnar Myrdal distinguished between "soft states" and "hard states" in that the former adopted developmental policies that were piecemeal and gradualist, and avoided the "use of force for social ends." "Hard states," on the other hand, would not shrink from authoritarian methods and violence to push through radical reform and enforce social discipline.

10. In a 1987 interview Fang Lizhi maintained, "I feel those uneducated peasants, living under traditional influence, have a psychological consciousness that is very deficient. It is very difficult to instill a democratic consciousness in them, they still demand an honest and upright official; without an official they are uncomfortable." "Conversation of Fang Lizhi with Wen Hui and Ming Lei," *Zhengming*, no. 117, 1987, p. 20.

11. Li Xiguang for instance urges the Chinese to resist American cultural imperialism and "draw sustenance from our own national culture and traditional values." See, "The Inside Story of Demonization of China," translated in *Contemporary Chinese Thought*, Winter 1998–99, vol. 30, no. 2, p. 66.

Also Li Xiguang and Liu Kang, "A Look at the Coverage of China by the Mainstream US Media," in *FBIS*, 30 July 1996, pp. 4–8.

12. I borrow the term from Chang Hao. See, "Intellectual Crisis of Contemporary China in Historical Perspective," in Tu Wei-ming, ed., *The Triadic Chord: Confucian Ethics, Industrial East Asia and Max Weber*, Singapore: Institute of East Asian Philosophy, 1991.

Bibliography

Barme, Geremie. *Shades of Mao: The Posthumous Cult of the Great Leader*, Armonk, NY: M.E. Sharpe, 1996.
Cao Siyuan, "What Are Those Negating Reform and Opening Up Up To?" *Jingji Gongzuo Yuekan*, no. 7, 1996. Reprinted in *Ming Pao*, 16 August 1996.
Cao Yuanzheng. "The Model of a Market Economy Under a 'Soft Government,'" and "The Model of the Market Economy Under a 'Hard Government,'" *Chinese Sociology and Anthropology* (hereafter *CSA*), vol. 23, no. 3 (Spring 1991), pp. 24–31 and pp. 32–38.

CCP Central Committee. *Resolution on Some Important Issues in Strengthening the Construction of Socialist Spiritual Civilization*, Beijing: Renmin chubanshe, 1996.

Chang Hao. "Intellectual Crisis of Contemporary China in Historical Perspective," in Tu Wei-ming, ed., *The Triadic Chord: Confucian Ethics, Industrial East Asia and Max Weber*, Singapore: Institute of East Asian Philosophy, 1991.

Chen Lai. "Radicalism in 20th Century Culture Movements," *Dongfang*, no. 1, 1994.

Chou Ying-jiu. "Political Situation as Viewed from Two '10, 000 character statements,'" *Ching Pao*, 1 August 1996, pp. 23–26.

Commentator. "Why Is It Necessary to Unswervingly Oppose Bourgeois Liberalization?" *Renmin ribao*, 24 April 1991.

Commentator. "Build Up a Great Wall of Steel Against Peaceful Evolution," *RMRB* 16 August 1991.

Commentator. "Let Us Ask If Reform and Opening Up Are Socialist or Capitalist in Nature? *Guangmin ribao*, 7 August 1991.

Cui Zhiyuan. "System Innovation and the Second Thought Emancipation Campaign," *Ershiyi shiji*, no. 8, 1994.

———. "Mao Zedong's Idea of Cultural Revolution and the Reconstruction of Modernity," *Hong Kong Journal of Social Sciences*, no. 7, Spring 1996.

Deng Xiaoping. "Key Points of the Talks in Wuchang, Shenzhen, Zhuhai, and Shanghai," *Deng Xiaoping Wenxuan*, Beijing: Renmin chubanshe, 1993, pp. 372–73.

Ding Xueliang. *The Decline of Communism in China: Legitimacy Crisis 1977–1989*, Cambridge: Cambridge University Press, 1994.

Duan Ruofei. "Persist in People's Democratic Dictatorship, Oppose, Prevent Peaceful Evolution," *Renmin ribao*, 5 June 1991.

Feng Chen. "An Unfinished Battle in China: The Leftist Criticism of the Refom and the Third Thought Emancipation," *The China Quarterly*, no. 158 (June 1991), pp. 447–467.

———. "Order and Stability in Social Transition: Neo Conservative Political Thought in Post-1989 China," *The China Quarterly*, no. 151 (September 1997), pp. 593–613.

Fewsmith, Joseph. "Neo-Conservatism and the End of the Dengist Era," *Asian Survey*, vol. 35, no. 7 (July 1995), pp. 635–651.

Friedman, Edward. "Democracy and 'Mao Fever,'" *The Journal of Contemporary China*, no. 6 (Summer 1994), pp. 84–95.

He Xin, "Sober Thoughts on the June 4 Turmoil," *Zhongguo qingnian bao*, 6 December 1989.

Hu Angang and Wang Shaoguang. *A Report on China's State Capacity*, Hong Kong: Oxford University Press, 1994.

Hu Qiaomu. "How the Chinese Communist Party Has Developed Marxism—Written to Commemorate the 70th Anniversary of the CCP," *Renmin ribao* (overseas edition), 25 June 1991. Also in BBC, Summary of World Broadcasts-Far East, (hereafter *SWB-FE*), no. 1113, 2 July 1991, pp. B2/1–12.

Huangfu Ping. "Reform and Opening Up Requires New Train of Thinking," *Jiefang ribao*, 2 March 1991; "More Greatly Enhance the Sense of Opening Up," *Jiefang ribao*, 22 March 1991.

Jiang Zemin. "Speech on the 70th Anniversary of the Founding of the CCP," *SWB-FE*, no. 1114, 3 July 1991, pp. B2/1–12.

————. "Hold High the Great Banner of Deng Xiaoping Theory For An All-Round Advancement of the Cause of Building Socialism With Chinese Characteristics into the 21st Century," Report to the Fifteenth Party Congress, *Beijing Review*, October 6–12, 1997, pp.19–21.

Khan, Azizur Rahman and Karl Riskin. "Income and Inequality in China: Composition, Distribution, and Growth of Household Income, 1988–95," *The China Quarterly*, no. 154 (June 1998), pp. 221–253.

Li Xiguang. "The Inside Story of Demonization of China," translated in *Contemporary Chinese Thought*, vol. 30, no. 2, Winter 1998–99.

Li Xiguang and Liu Kang. "A Look at the Coverage of China by the Mainstream US Media," in *FBIS*, 30 July 1996, pp. 4–8.

Li Zehou and Wang Desheng. "The Dialogue on the Cultural Status Quo and Moral Rebuilding," *Dongfang*, no. 5, 1994.

Luo Yi ning ge er. *Looking at China Through a Third Eye*, translated by Wang Shan, Taiyuan: Shanxi People's Publishing House, 1994.

Meng Lin. "Hu Qiaomu Criticizes Pro-American Faction inside CCP," *Ching Pao*, 5 August 1991. Also in *SWB/FE*, 10 August 1991, no. 1147, pp. B2/2. "Several Factors Affecting China's State Security," text in *The China Quarterly*, no. 148, (December 1996), pp. 1426–41.

Misra, Kalpana. *From Post-Maoism to Post-Marxism: The Erosion of Official Ideology in Deng's China*, New York: Routledge, 1998.

Myrdal, Gunnar. *Asian Drama: An Inquiry into the Poverty of Nations*, New York: New York Twentieth Century Fund, 1968.

Petracca, Mark and Mong Xiong. "The Concept of Chinese Authoritarianism," *Asian Survey*, vol. 30, no. 11 (November 1990), pp. 1099–1117.

"Realistic Responses and Strategic Choices for China After the Soviet Upheaval," *Zhongguo zhi chun* (New York), no. 104, 15 December 1991, pp. 35–39.

Rong Jian. "Does China Need an Authoritarian Political System in the Course of Modernization?" *CSA*, vol. 23 (Winter 1990–91), pp. 46–68.

Rosen, Stanley and Gary Zou, eds. "The Chinese Debate on Neo-Authoritarianism," *CSA*, Winter 1990–91, Spring 1991, and Summer 1991.

Sautman, Barry. "Sirens of the Strongman: Neo-Authoritarianism in Recent Chinese Political Theory," *The China Quarterly*, no. 129 (March 1992), pp. 77–102.

Ting Gong and Feng Chen. "Neo-Authoritarianism in Mainland China,' *Issues and Studies*, January 1991, pp. 84–98.

Wang Guofa. "Democracy Should Not Go Beyond Social Development," *Liaowang*, 7 August 1989, p. 17. Also in *FBIS*, 21 August 1989, pp. 32–33.

Wang Jiemin. *A Heart to Heart Talk With the General Secretary*, Beijing: Zhongguo shehui kexueyuan chubanshe, 1996.

Wang Shan. *Looking at China Through a Fourth Eye*, Hong Kong: Mingbao chubanshe, 1996.

Wei Xing. "Several Methodological Issues Regarding Study of Party Building," *RMRB*, 8 July 1991. Also in *SWB/FE*, 22 July 1991, no. 1130, pp. B2/1–2.

Wu Jiaxiang. "The New Authoritarianism: An Express Train Towards Democracy by Building Markets," *CSA*, vol. 23 (Winter 1990–91), pp. 36–45.

Xiao Gongqin. "Yan Fu's Reflections on China's Modernization and its Lessons," *Zhongguo qingnian bao*, 6 February 1991.

———. "East Asian Authoritarian Politics and Modernization," *Zhanlue yu guanli*, no. 3, 1994a.

———. "Nationalism and Ideology in China During the Period of Transition," *Zhanlue yu guanli*, no. 4, 1994b.

———. "Ideological Innovation and Political Stability," *Shanghai lilun neikan*, vol. 20, no. 2, 1995.

———. "The History and Future of Nationalism in China," *Zhanlue yu guanli*, no. 2, 1996.

Xiao Gongqin and Zhu Wei. "A Painful Dilemma: A Dialogue on the Theory of Neo-Authoritarianism," *Wenhuibao*, 17 January 1989, p. 5.

Yang Baikui. "Democracy and Authority in the Course of Political Development," *CSA*, vol. 23, no. 3 (Spring 1991), pp. 67–80.

Yang Fan. "First Anniversary of the Market Economy," *Zhanlue yu guanli*, no. 1, 1993, p. 26.

Yao Wenyuan. "On the Social Basis of the Lin Biao Clique, *Hongqi*, no. 4, 1975, pp. 20–29.

Yi Baoyun. "Nationalism and Modern Economic Development," *Zhanlue yu guanli*, no. 3, 1994.

Zheng Wen. " China Can Never Copy Wholesale the Western Democratic System," *Jingji ribao*, 18 July 1989, p. 3.

Zhong Shuqiao. "Unswervingly Carry Out the Struggle against Corruption and Degeneration," *Hubei ribao*, 4 July 1991. Also in *SWB-FE*, 27 July 1991, no. 1135, pp. B2/1–4.

6

The Antipolitical Tendency in Contemporary Chinese Political Thinking

Peter Moody

Twentieth-century Chinese culture was highly politicized. Political questions were often couched in terms of culture, with political "discourse" shaped around the affirmation or rejection of the Confucian heritage or the various contenders' versions of it, and many issues of culture—the non-biological aspects of human life—were open to political contention or intrusion.[1]

The politicization of all aspects of life is sometimes said to be a characteristic of totalitarianism. Friedrich and Brzezinski identify as part of that syndrome the presence of an "elaborate ideology, consisting of an official body of doctrine covering all vital aspects of man's existence to which everyone living in society is supposed to adhere, at least passively" (Friederich and Brzezinski 1966). According to Hannah Arendt (1958, 382), totalitarian movements may develop when there is no clear criterion of truth apart from political definition, where people (i.e., "the masses") "think that everything [is] possible and nothing [is] true."[2]

Promiscuous politicization may indeed be a general trend in modern political life in mass democracy as well as in totalitarianism, promoted particularly by those who wish to change the existing order or condition of things (Ellul 1967; Schattschneider 1975). On a somewhat arcane level, the postmodernist analysis of our world as "constructed" may be hypostasis of the totalitarian vision, extrapolating the nightmares both of Hannah Arendt and of George Orwell (1949) onto the general human condition.[3] On a less bookish level, "cultural" or "lifestyle" politics has become familiar in liberal democracies, mainly, perhaps, in the United States, but elsewhere as well.

The politicization of Chinese culture may have come in part from causes endemic to modernity generally and in part for reasons peculiar to China: China was challenged and its system assaulted by modern Western culture, and the dominant response has been, in reaction and defense, to seek to expand the scope of political power (and, hence, it is thought, control) and to strengthen its intensity (Hoston 1994).[4] Since the "traditional culture" (however various trends of opinion may have "constructed" it) was seen as a major reason for China's vulnerability, there were also attempts totally to recast it in a coherent, systematic way through deliberate political choice (Fitzgerald 1994).

Politicization may be a weapon of the weak, whereby those lacking money, status, respect, or some other value may attempt individually or collectively to call in political power to redress the defect. But under some circumstances—particularly under a totalitarian regime as in Maoist China—politics itself (rather, say, than economic exploitation) may become a major source of human misery, "liberating" people from what they desire and value, forcing them into molds which hurt them to fit. "Antipolitics" is one reaction against this tendency.

The term *antipolitics* is a neologism with no intuitively clear meaning. In this essay it refers to a principled rejection of politics, at a minimum an attempt to keep those matters of legitimate political concern confined to the narrowest possible scope. To be antipolitical in this sense is not to be apolitical or nonpolitical, although all these conditions may share certain traits. Antipolitics, rather, is itself a form of politics—just as, insofar as I understand it, the physical concept of antimatter does not refer to something non-material but to matter of a particular (and, fortunately for us, rare) kind.

There is a long tradition of antipolitics in Chinese culture. Antipolitical themes became a part of Chinese political discourse and, possibly, daily life after 1976 in reaction to the radical Maoist past. This trend may have received tacit and ambivalent regime endorsement, especially after 1992. This essay examines contemporary Chinese antipolitics, with a special focus on some works of the writer Wang Meng, which it attempts to place in their wider context.

Antipolitics and Contemporary Chinese Politics

Antipolitics, both as a word and as a concept, figures in different ways in political analysis. John Bunzel's reflections on the "anti-political temper" focus on how certain American "extremist" groups, especially right-wing but some pacifists as well, treat political issues as if they were exclusively moral in nature, substituting moralistic denunciation for the more "normal" political practices of courting support, bargaining over interests, and accepting compromise (Bunzel 1967). This kind of antipolitics supposedly threatens the democratic process. Students of Latin American politics have used the term to describe the circumvention of the older political order by military-imposed technocratic developmental dictatorships (Loveman and Dairen 1989). A particular political goal, such as economic development of a certain kind, is defined as unproblematic, the only available rational option. Force is used to silence alternative visions, and the achievement of the proposed goal is treated as a technical rather than a political issue. Andreas Schedler (1997) identifies two versions of antipolitics. One rejects the "basic premises" of politics (perceiving uniformity instead of plurality, necessity instead of contingency). The other is "colonizing" antipolitics, an attempt to reshape politics according to a "rationality" different from the prevailing one (technique, morality, rational choice, aesthetics). In practice, perhaps, these types may blur into each other, as they seem to in the movements analyzed by Bunzel or the Latin Americanists. Contemporary Chinese antipolitics tends toward the "colonizing" type (whereas Maoism, it could be argued, is a manifestation of the other type), although the word *colonizing* may imply an aggressiveness that is not present.

Contemporary Chinese antipolitics is perhaps closest to that outlined by some Eastern European intellectuals toward the end of the communist era. George Konrád (1984, 92, 101), apparently a colonizer, considers antipolitics on one level a "radical alternative to the philosophy of a nuclear *ultima ratio* [final justification]" which is to say, to the threat of nuclear war that hovered over the entire Cold War period. But his main interest, in fact a fairly standard liberal one, is more domestic in extension and points toward keeping the "scope of government policy (especially that of its military apparatus) under the control of civil society."

Because politics has flooded every nook and cranny of our lives, I would like to see the flood recede. We ought to depoliticize our lives, free them from politics as from some contagious infection. We ought to free our simple everyday affairs from considerations of politics. I ask that the state do what it's supposed to do, and do it well. But, it should not do things that are society's business, not the state's. So I would describe the democratic opposition as not a political but an antipolitical opposition, since its essential activity is to work for destatification (Konrád 1984, 229).[5]

The guiding slogan in Mao's China, especially since the Great Leap Forward, was "Politics Takes Command." The Chinese people were "poor and blank." Because they were poor, they wanted revolution; and because they were blank—without preconceptions—they could take political action to make themselves anything they wished. By an act of political will ("consciousness"), people could change material reality. The failure of the Leap, in the Maoist interpretation, reflected not poorly thought-through policies but, rather, backward and erroneous perceptions which needed to be changed through a Cultural Revolution.[6]

In reaction, the post-Mao leadership reverted to a more standard scholastic Marxism, stressing determinism over human will. Existence determines consciousness: the way people think is shaped, ultimately, by their material circumstances, not the reverse. This culminated in Deng Xiaoping's (or, rather, Hu Yaobang's) thesis that practice is the criterion of truth.[7] This eventually came to mean that whatever contributed to economic development was orthodox socialism (although "practice" did remain hedged: it had to conform, somehow, to "socialism," Mao's Thought, Marxism-Leninism, and especially to the continued primacy of the communist party).

The tenor of the economic reforms was that economic development and efficiency required respect for the "objective laws of economics," not the distorting of these laws through political intervention. Early during the reform era some began to articulate the proposition that politicization was as harmful to other spheres of life as it was to the economy. In March 1983, Zhou Yang, during the 1950s China's most visible literary inquisitor and scourge of the liberal intellectuals,[8] raised the question of whether "alienation" (yihua) could exist under socialism, asserting that China's political order could not overcome any such alienation unless it would first own up to it.[9] Zhou coupled his musings on alienation with a call to return to traditional ideas of humanism (whether Western or Confucian is not clear, but perhaps either or both would do), repudiating the Maoist view that in "class society" there is no human nature but only class nature.[10] The practical import of the Maoist vision is that there can be no bonds of human sympathy crossing class boundaries, with classes, in Maoist society, defined by those in political power. This meant also that feeling sorry for a class enemy made a class enemy of oneself.

In some of his earlier writings Karl Marx had pondered the alienating effects of life under capitalism, of the essential inhumanity of the social relations produced by the economic changes of the early Industrial Revolution. Later, though, when Marx spoke of alienation at all, he restricted his meaning to the appropriation of surplus value from the worker by the employer—that is, to economic exploitation. "Western"— or "neo"— Marxists reintroduced the young Marx's musings on alienation, but the older orthodoxy of the ruling parties, the Marxist-Leninist-Stalinist tradition, generally disdained the concept (Xiong Fu 1983). The ideological problem, of course, was that if alienation were held to result from a socialist political structure, the legitimacy of communist party rule could be called into question. As the conservative reformer Hu Qiaomu (1984) pointed out, it is understandable that some who came to grief in the Cultural Revolution might trace their discontent to alienation, but the criticism is in fact identical with that the Maoists leveled against the persons in power inside the Party taking the capitalist road (that is, Red Guards or the Gang of Four might complain about alienation, but good comrades will not).

The Party's theoretical organ, *Red Flag* (see nos. 22 and 23, 1984), published a kind of syllabus of errors against those who found the existing order alienating: there is no abstract humanism which transcends social class; Marx never used the term alienation to describe socialist society (and, on the other hand, the role of reform is to eliminate alienation); citizens are not alienated from the socialist state and the socialist system of ownership is not something alien to the laboring people; so forth, and so on. But even those who defended the basic soundness of the current order acknowledged the critics did have a point:

> The enemies of socialism curse us as "inhumane," "anti-humanistic." This is counterrevolutionary nonsense issuing from their reactionary standpoint. But it must also be admitted that our rejection of humanism since the end of the 1950s contains not a few errors (Tao Dalin 1984).

In fact, the official line continued to reject the notion of alienation but came tacitly to accept that Marxism did entail at least a certain kind of humanism, rejecting (tacitly) the attempt to define what constituted humanity in terms of the political convenience of the existing order.

The import of the alienation theme was that the political order, designed to eliminate economic exploitation, itself entailed a violation imposed from the outside of the human person, the person swallowed up by the claims of politics. The "humanists," then, asserted a moral autonomy against the claims of politics. A complication was that some claims to autonomy had an ambivalent moral content. In one construction, Maoist politics could be considered a negation of morality, with morality reduced to class struggle and moral reasoning to a power struggle. But Maoist politics had also been made the public touchstone of morality, with everyone expected to be totally and selflessly dedicated to the right side in the class struggle.

The supposedly objective laws of economics which the reforms were supposed to allow assumed that people acted rationally to satisfy their own interests and that the pursuit of individual economic interest would generate economic growth and material comfort. In the opinion of many comrades, not only Maoists, this meant the reforms encouraged selfishness and greed. The theorist Wang Bosen pointed out that, according to Marx, "The standard for judging whether a morality is progressive or not must be the nature of the economic relationships it maintains." He concluded from this that "it is not economic reform which hinders moral progress but old [that is, Maoist] moral concepts which hinder economic reform" (Wang Baosen 1984). Given how politicized morality had been, some Party conservatives feared that to detach morality from politics would lead to the abandonment of morality—and more radical reformers agreed, identifying morality itself with the vicious and inhuman demands of Maoist politics. The regime began to grumble about "spiritual pollution" (Gold 1984).

Spiritual pollution meant anything from support for democracy to a taste for pornography to a belief in religion. The attacks on it did not remain very intense for very long, but many within the leadership continued to worry about a loss of ideals among the younger generation. To some extent this loss meant simply skepticism about the claims of political propaganda, skepticism which in the more relaxed conditions was easier to express than it had been before. But it could also imply an antisocial hedonism and the crasser aspects of consumerist materialism. The Cultural Revolution had bred an endemic distrust of all authority, and their exposure to "political thought work" from elementary school onward left many young people who grew up in that era with a general detestation of all politics (Liu, Zhang, and Jiang 1989, 92, 257). The heroes of the youth of the 1980s were (supposedly) Sartre, Nietzsche, Schopenhauer, and Freud (124; also Wang Shubai 1998, 31) all of whom, old fashioned gentlemen though they may have been, showed, I guess, our conventional beliefs to be so much sham and hypocrisy (as did Marx—but given the company he hobnobbed with, he was no longer to be taken seriously).

In "society," then, the reform era meant a retreat from politics. The Cultural Revolution generation had led the way to both economic and political reform but by the late 1980s had abandoned any role as "revolutionaries" in favor of withdrawal, perceiving political action as requiring ethical compromise (Chen Xiaoyu 1995). Their younger siblings were apparently both more vivacious and more shallow, focusing on the TOEFL, business, and dancing (Liu, Zhang, and Jiang 1989). A scandal of sorts blew throughout much of 1988, when a set of Party intellectuals, giving a pep talk to some workers in the Special Economic Zone of Shekou, urged their listeners not to degenerate into mere gold diggers. Someone in the audience questioned them: What's wrong with gold digging? Isn't that how the American West was won? In the ensuing extended series of newspaper discussions of this little exchange, one side was shocked by the flippant, ungrateful attitude of kids nowadays,while about as many others were disturbed that the speaker should, in this enlightened era of reform and opening, respond by demanding the name and "unit" of the smart-aleck would-be gold digger. A summary comment on the incident concluded that "the young people of Shekou have a relatively strong profit-oriented mentality. This, obviously, is related to the development of the commodity economy." But "the kind of equality found in a commodity economy leads to the strengthening of the democratic mentality of young people (Ma Licheng 1989; see also Luo Xu 1995).[11]

The events of 1989 show that many of the young people of that time were not simply the bubble-headed hedonists they might have seemed the year before and that their withdrawal from politics reflected to a great extent a sense of lack of political opportunities. But these same events did nothing to induce anyone to idealize politics, or at least the existing political process, or to cause hope for its rapid transformation. After the Tiananmen massacre and, especially, Deng Xiaoping's Southern Tour of 1992, something like the Shekou attitude may have become a general norm, not particularly resisted by the regime despite sporadic aspects by Jiang Zemin and the like to revive a sense of the importance of "politics" (Jiang Zemin 1996). A representative or at least widely publicized cultural figure of the early 1990s was the iconoclastic writer Wang Shuo, famous for works of "thug literature" (*pizi wenxue*), stories of rudderless young ne'er-do-wells as contemptuous of conventional virtues and duties as they were (on the surface, anyway) empty of ordinary human decency (Barmé 1992). These would seem to be the outcome of an alienating, overly ambitious political world. His thugs represent an urban youth subculture (*ya wenhua*), a "marginal culture of young people resisting the subjective centralization of ideology." There remains, as might be expected, a certain sentimentality. Wang Shuo "places his characters on the anti-social margins. They mark allegations of value but in the end are unable to extricate themselves from traditional romantic passions."[12] Another critic explains that Wang Shuo represents an extreme reaction to Cultural Revolution politicized morality. Just as for Nietzsche the death of God did not really mean a rejection of all values but, rather, the valuing of having no values, so the disillusionment following the Cultural Revolution can be taken, however perversely, as a kind of liberation.[13] For Wang Shuo (1998, 4–5) himself, his thuggishness is simply a rejection of hypocrisy and bookishness.

The Shekou people were antipolitical by implication and Wang Shuo more by attitude than by any explicitly thought-through conviction. A more systematic working through of the antipolitical conviction can be found in at least some of the work of an older writer, Wang Meng (b. 1934). Contemporary Chinese intellectuals are sometimes fond of classifying each other by "generation," and Wang Meng has been called the most "avant-garde" of the "clan of 57," a cohort of young socialist writers who took Chairman Mao's call around that time for blooming and contending seriously and were to suffer as a consequence (Fan Xing 1993).

Wang Meng engaged in underground communist activity while still in high school and later served as a Youth League secretary in Peking.[14] In 1956 he published his maiden story, "The Young Newcomer in the Organization Department," which details the disillusionment of a young Party worker who finds his colleagues, all experienced revolutionaries who suffered prior to Liberation to bring to birth a new China in a new world, to have grown accustomed to the comforts and privileges of power, to be concerned primarily about their personal lives, and to treat their jobs as bureaucratic routine. The story occasioned much discussion, but its theme fit with Mao's program then to shake the Party out of just such a lethargy by mobilizing complaints from educated public opinion. By 1958 the climate had changed, and Wang Meng was expelled from the Party, condemned as a "rightist," and "sent down" to physical labor. According to a biographical chronicle, the rightist label was removed in 1961, but a couple of years later Wang was sent to the border region of Xinjiang, to what seems to have been, although the chronicle does not say so, internal exile. Around 1971 Wang served a stint in a May 7 cadre school. From about 1978, however, after the death of Mao and the triumph of Deng Xiaoping and reform, he was able to publish his fiction again. On trips abroad he defended the Beijing regime (so that writers from Taiwan who turned up at the same conferences took good-naturedly to calling him the Old Man from the Organization Department). In 1986 he rose to be the PRC's Minister of Culture. He lost that position after the Tiananmen events but was not otherwise molested.

Wang Meng is by no means a "dissident" writer, but some of his works do seem subversive of at least some versions of the existing order. A recurring theme is disillusionment. In the "Young Newcomer" there is a sense of great promise unfulfilled; in the later works the promise itself turns out to be an illusion, even a pernicious one. A 1989 story, "Thin Hard Gruel" (or, in another translation, "Stubborn Porridge"; the Chinese is *Jian ying de xizhou*) is less a political satire than a burlesque. The story, such as it is, details efforts by a family to embrace modernity by adopting a Western rather than a Chinese style breakfast. The process is initiated and presided over by Grandfather (an obvious figure of Deng Xiaoping), who is enthusiastic for modernization and democracy as long as he always gets his own way. In the end, everyone gradually loses interest:

> Time passed. People were vaguely aware that all things in heaven and earth find their own balance. So after a while, our fever of excitement over the great eating debate finally fizzled out, and the heat of controversy over theory and terms of methodology and experimentation gradually cooled down. We did not rack our brains over whether it was a technical problem or a cultural issue, a question of institutional structure or something never dreamed of in our philosophy. We stopped racking our brains over the problem. It seemed that without solving these knotty problems, we still managed to feed our bellies (Wang Meng 1994, 35).

Politics is superfluous and intrusive, vain in its content and silly in its methods. Ordinary life takes care of itself.

The Politics of Antipolitics

A more probing study of the antipolitical tendency, both less good humored and less bitter, is "The Butterfly," one of the first of Wang Meng's stories to be published after his own post-Mao reappearance.[15] It describes the ups and downs of a Party cadre, Zhang Siyuan, from the time of Liberation through the various campaigns of the 1950s, the Cultural Revolution, and the early reforms. It is a kind of ground-level view of Chinese history during the communist era. Wang Meng is supposed to be something of an avant-garde writer, so the episodes are not in chronological order and there is considerable interior dialogue and the like—so a summary of the plot may give a misleading impression of the story, where the stream-of-consciousness style represents the protagonist's attempt to understand and sort out his life.

The plot, roughly, is this: The young communist cadre Zhang Siyuan, a peasant lad, meets the even younger urban schoolgirl, the enthusiastic and infatuated Haiyun. They marry and have a child. After the beginning of the Korean War Siyuan is busy from morning until late into the evening doing all kinds of propaganda work and uncovering counter-revolutionaries. He hardly ever gets to go home. One day, "during an important meeting," Haiyun phones: The baby has a fever. Siyuan scolds her for bothering him when he is busy but later, feeling a little ashamed, decides to go home after the meeting—which does not break up until 1:30 in the morning. When Siyuan does get home, the child is dead. "Blaming himself," the narrative picks up, "he broke down and fell on his knees in front of the dead child and the young mother." Not very good at this sort of thing, all he can think actually to say is: "You must not just think of yourself, Haiyun! . . . We aren't ordinary people. We're Party members, Bolsheviks. This very second, American planes are bombing Pyongyang, thousands of Korean children are being killed by napalm. . . . That was the start of their estrangement" (Wang Meng 1981, 12). Siyuan, no doubt in a defensive frame of mind, decides that Haiyun remains, after all, a "petty bourgeois intellectual" (13). He encourages her to continue her schooling, while he moves on to ever greater successes in his administrative and political career. "Considering himself a part of a vast machine imbued him with vision, energy, and a sense of responsibility. This gave his life meaning" (20). Haiyun becomes pregnant again and her oaf of a husband suggests an abortion. The reason, he says, is that babies get in the way of work, although we may perhaps be permitted to think that the real reason is that they sometimes die and so are a cause of heartache and also, perhaps, of division between husband and wife. Haiyun does in fact have the baby and, after a year's maternity leave, returns again to college, where she drifts into a love affair with another student. Siyuan, however, pleads with her "for the sake of the child," and she breaks with her lover.

On the surface, anyway, Siyuan is more disturbed by Haiyun's political defects than by her adultery. In the aftermath of the Hundred Flowers she had been "labeled a Rightist" for "praising anti-Party novels" (among them, it is hinted, *The Young Newcomer*—Wang Meng likes his little jokes). Siyuan hectors her: "'You must admit your fault and turn over a new leaf.' . . . He was appalled by the icy look in her eyes." A month later Haiyun asks for a divorce. He still wants to save their marriage, but it is clear that they would have to split up. The last time he sees her, after their divorce, he is furious to see her face so radiant: "She really has degenerated," he told himself (15)

Eventually Siyuan marries again, through the influence and pressure of his co-workers. His new wife is one Meilan, a shallow, vulgar woman. In his feckless way he tries to remain close to his son, Dongdong, partly, no doubt, to compensate for what he cannot but see as his failure with Haiyun. But from a very early time the relationship between father and son is forced and strained, probably because Dongdong sees Siyuan as somehow having injured his mother, Haiyun. Dongdong rejects gifts of food from his father during the famine following the Great Leap Forward, and he thinks of Haiyun's new husband, her former lover, as his real father. Siyuan feels somehow vindicated by Haiyun's remarriage however much he retains a vague, unarticulated sense of guilt. In the meantime, his political career continues to prosper.

The Cultural Revolution comes, and Siyuan feels "both elated and tense." "He believed this struggle was to combat revisionism, to revolutionize China . . . for the Party's sake he must not be soft-hearted."

> The papers kept issuing warnings to beware of capitalist roaders who victimized subordinates to save their own skins. So, to find a more highly placed scapegoat, he hardened his heart and denounced the head of the municipal propaganda department. And then a vice secretary in charge of

education. As more and more cadres were overthrown, he himself became more exposed and vulnerable. And finally his turn came (18).

Zhang Siyuan is "dragged out" by the Red Guards and accused of
being a counterrevolutionary. In the meantime, Haiyun has been viciously
beaten by the Red Guards and has committed suicide. Dongdong is part
of the Red Guard group denouncing his father, and he even slaps his
father's face during the struggle that ensues at the meeting. After three
years' solitary confinement as an accused counterrevolutionary, Siyuan
is "sent down" to a mountain village, deprived of his official position
but (as was the practice of the time) retaining his salary. Meilan, of
course, divorces him as soon as trouble starts, but "this . . . piece of news
affected him not at all" (23).

Cadres rusticated to remote areas were supposed to learn from the
peasants, and, perhaps surprisingly, Siyuan actually does. He thrives on
the fresh air, the hard work, and the (perhaps idealized) company of the
villagers, with their honest good humor and rustic simplicity. No longer
a high official, he has become merely "old Zhang." Dongdong, as it
happens, had earlier been sent to the same village, and the two achieve a
partial reconciliation. Zhang learns that Haiyun had defended him to
Dongdong after he had been denounced, and Dongdong said he had
beaten his father not because he blamed Siyuan for what happened to
his mother but from simple cowardice in the face of peer pressure. However, Siyuan, in spite of everything, continues to believe in the revolution, while Dongdong has become completely disillusioned and
embittered.

Siyuan also becomes friends with Qiuwen, a woman doctor who seems
to be the story's spokesperson for clear-eyed, down-to-earth good sense
(and is not, I think, a successfully realized character). But one day a car
rattles into town and Siyuan learns that he has been rehabilitated. He
returns to work, continuing the rise interrupted for nine years by the
Cultural Revolution. He continues to think about his time in the countryside and eventually returns to the village to ask Qiuwen to marry
him, the narrative of this trip framing the entire story.[16] He is rejected
and, with much bittersweet musing about how everything in the end is
connected with everything else, how all things ultimately come together
for good, and how ordinary life is always getting better and better, Siyuan
returns to work:

It seemed many people were watching him, supporting him, hoping great things from him.

Tomorrow the pressure of work would be even greater (55).

Siyuan's time in the countryside probably made him an even better cadre than he had been previously, but being a good cadre still means submerging oneself and one's own judgment in the ever shifting Party policy:

The second letter [to Qiuwen after his rehabilitation] was written in the spring of '76, when he had to go along with the campaign against Deng Xiaoping. In that political climate he wrote forcefully, using the language of editorials. "We must trust that Chairman Mao's revolutionary line will win the final victory." "The peasants welcome you back here any time to remold yourself through labour," she had replied. "Materialists are fearless. Communism is a militant philosophy."

Zhang Siyuan had understood . . . (50).

But, in fact, the sarcasm is entirely lost on him. It is probably this little performance that causes Qiuwen to refuse his later proposal, not because she dislikes him but because it shows their fundamental incompatibility. For at least the second time, Siyuan has altered the entire course of his life by mechanically opting for political correctness over instinctive human sentiment.

The last words of the story, "Tomorrow the pressure of work would be even greater," are ambiguous and very sad. On one level they can be considered upbeat, a concluding "Hurrah for communism!" Zhang Siyuan, like the Party itself, has had his ups and downs, has done much good and some bad, has had his share of disappointments. But on balance life is getting better and there is work to be done. And we are, I think, supposed to assume that that work is genuinely worthwhile.

On a personal level Siyuan's concluding thoughts can be taken as a rationalization for his private disappointments. More deeply, however, he is one who has always allowed his work to dominate his life: "He lived solely for his work" (19). He meets to the full all demands placed on him by the political order, the organization. He is not at all a bad man, despite some unpleasant compromises. He loves Dongdong, Haiyun, and, in a more distant way, Qiuwen, however much he puts duty above such sentiments. He upbraids Haiyun for her thought problems, and remaining married to a Rightist would certainly damage his precious career; but he is not the one who initiates the divorce. The turning point in the story comes very early, with the death of the first child and Zhang's inadequate reaction to it; but there is never hinted that, had he returned home earlier, the baby would have lived—not that that is the point.

Zhang is not a bad official, either. It would be easy enough to denounce communist totalitarianism by pointing to all sorts of deliberate cruelty and injustice, but Wang Meng does not do this. He describes the totalitarian functionary at his best. Zhang does do a few bad things. It turns out that only a few of the "scoundrels" he "exposed" for corruption in the early 1950s are guilty of anything (13), and at the beginning of the Cultural Revolution he is as eager as anyone to implicate others as capitalist roaders; but in both cases he is acting as the Party desires. There are indications that before the Cultural Revolution he may have been getting too comfortable; but if that is a sin it is a venial one, and the implication is mainly that *he* is worried that he might be getting too comfortable: in both his public and private dealings he is highly scrupulous, in both the healthy and unhealthy senses, and is given to many internal worries, regrets, and fussings. At his root he is neither cruel nor corrupt. From the perspective of the Party, to which he is totally and selflessly dedicated, he is a good cadre, and what faults he has are the excesses of his virtues. And precisely because he is such a good cadre, he is not much of a human being.

During his rustication Zhang takes to worrying about his identity: who is he, really? Is he the young peasant kid hiding from the Japanese, the guerrilla in the mountains, the handsome young political organizer, the counter revolutionary criminal, "old Zhang," or the high official in the central government?

> The ancient philosopher Zhuangzi dreamed that he turned into a butterfly flitting this way and that. He awoke to a problem of identity. Was he Zhuangzi, awake, or a butterfly having a dream? (24)

Zhuangzi's famous parable comes at the end of the second chapter of his book, the chapter given the title *Ji Wu Lun* and translated by Wing-tsit Chan (1963, 179–180) as "The Equality of Things." This work purports to show that in the Tao (the "way"), there are no ultimately valid distinctions—*nothing* has its own unambiguous "identity." Zhuangzi begins with what some nowadays might call a deconstruction of the concept of self. We experience feelings, emotions, and thoughts: there must be something that does the experiencing, but there is nothing to be identified apart from the experiences themselves. Zhuangzi moves on to disassemble language—we create meaning by assigning names, but the names are arbitrary—and then value and reason. The butterfly story climaxes a discussion of the inability to distinguish truth and illusion or, more accurately, the lack of any reliable distinction between them. So in the end, I think, it is not that Zhuangzi is unable to tell the difference between "real life" and dreams. Rather, real life has its reality and dreams have theirs, and there is nothing apart from the two to privilege either. This is called the "transformation of things" (*wu hua*).

In Wang Meng's story the butterfly is an ambiguous symbol. Most of the time it refers to Siyuan's life in the countryside, free from the pressures and distortions of the political world. In this respect the story fits into venerable Taoist themes, contrasting the realm of nature and authenticity with the artificialities, burdens, hypocrisies, and cruelties of social and political life. But there is also a hint that the political world is itself a butterfly dream, or nightmare: As Zhang flies home, following his final encounter with Qiuwen, "The plane banked to change course as they reached the right altitude, higher by far than a butterfly could fly. . . . No matter how high the plane flew, it came from the earth and must return to earth. Men and butterflies alike were the earth's children" (Wang Meng 1981, 53). From the perspective of natural or normal life, the political world is unreal. From the broader perspective, perhaps, each is equally real or unreal, a world where Zhang Siyuan can have no authentic identity, or where authenticity is a concept without meaning. What identity he has is determined by his situation, by where he is and what he is doing at the time, and most of his situation is defined by the political process. Zhang's identity, his personality, is "constructed" by politics.

A Marxist or postmodernist reaction might be: So what else is new? For isn't everything constructed by politics (in Marxism, politics as mediated by the economic relations of production)? This, however, does not seem to be the perspective of the story. This kind of politically-shaped personality is not, apparently, part of the general human condition. The other characters—Haiyun, Dongdong, the peasants, Qiuwen, even the vulgar Meilan—are all, with different consequences for their personal happiness and in their different ways, adequately rooted in their own places, persons, interests, and values. Zhang Siyuan did not have to be what he was. He is constricted by his own choice, by his commitment to (to use Ellul's term) the political illusion.

The theme, in gross terms, is universal: The person who stunts himself by exclusive commitment to his work, particularly when the ends of that work are set by forces outside of him, can probably be found in most cultures and historical eras. A "totalistic" commitment to democratic politics is probably as "alienating" as one to the autocratic variety, if perhaps generally less damaging to other people. A similar totalistic commitment to any sort of work, or even to the pursuit of pleasure—anything which allows a necessary but partial and subsidiary part of life to become its whole—will tend toward limiting the person's opportunities for fulfillment. This message, however, was especially relevant in China in the wake of the Cultural Revolution's excesses of politicization.

Dongdong, a proto–Wang Shuo, although of a somewhat morose variety, represents the hostile rejection of politics. During their time in the village, Siyuan happens to glance at Dongdong's diary: "It was cynical, decadent. Dongdong had written, 'I've had enough of these swindlers' lies, hypocrisy, and high-falutin' talk. . . . People are utterly selfish. . . . Life's hell on earth.'" And Siyuan thinks: "Was it for this that our generation battled, slaved, and shed blood day and night? For you, who have had it so easy, to moan in this despicable way?"(28). Wang Meng, if we treat him as a preacher and a moralist rather than simply a storyteller, is not as shocked by all this as Siyuan, but neither does he fully approve.

In "The Butterfly" and other works by Wang Meng there is a clear recognition that politics is necessary and valid within its own sphere—but only there. Life is richer than politics, even though Chinese politics, at least, attempts to flatten life out. Politics implies, among other things, control, and tries to shape our lives to its own advantage; but life fights back, and not always in the most morally or aesthetically attractive ways. Thus, Wang Meng comments that Wang Shuo, whatever his limitations, has brought a new freshness to the language as well as some insight (perhaps) into such insalubrious but nonetheless interesting things as juvenile delinquency, illicit sex, and the world of petty gangsters. Reading him, says Wang Meng, is like playing mahjong or smoking: "not very nutritious, not very healthy," but for all that fun and satisfying. It would be hard to take if everyone were like Wang Shuo; but it is good there is at least one of him, which there would not be in a world in which political values were unchallenged (Wang Meng 1996, 230, 67–68).

Wang Meng rejects political idealism, particularly the form holding that the problems of humanity would be solved by giving political power to the idealists and allowing them to remake the world according to their ideals. The highest ideals cannot be realized in human life anyway, he says (27). And utopian thinking is pernicious precisely because it combines the idea that there is nothing that cannot be done, on the one hand, with the sense of our personal inability to do anything, on the other *(yi bian shi wu suo buneng, yi bian shi wuneng wei li).*[17] "Ideals leading to Heaven in reality," says Wang, "pull us down into the mud. The consequence of accepting all that is false, exaggerated, and empty is to take us in the opposite direction, to doubting everything and to servile hypocrisy" (Wang Meng 1996, 23).

It might be wondered, though, whether Wang Meng is focusing too much on yesterday's evils. In contemporary China, perhaps because politics had engulfed any alternative set of ideals, the retreat of politics sometimes seems to have left no value behind other than pleasure and the means to acquire pleasure, mostly, or most conveniently, by buying it. This is the Shekou mentality the more old-fashioned authorities used to complain about. Western observers comment on the new totalitarian domination of the "market," which has come to "envelop all within its fold," which has "ripped the social fabric of Chinese society." Consumption has replaced politics in determining identity, and "the market consumes government as much as it does the consumer" (Dutton 1998, 270, 273, 279–280).

Wang Meng is not as upset by all this as perhaps he should be. In practical terms, his antipolitics implies an affirmation of market economics, both as a way to enhance personal well-being and as a way to accommodate the diversity of individual preferences. Market economics, to be sure, are not so soul-stirring as Maoist political economy:

> Obviously a market economy is not a romantic, heroic economy. Market activities are relatively open. The market has no way to conceal its many shortcomings or the defects and crimes people fall into under the name of free trade. But it is relatively compatible with the laws proper to economic life, which is to say that it fits with the actual motives of behavior and the limits placed on behavior (Wang Meng 1996, 59).

Market economics, like all economics, including, presumably, the Maoist version, work on the principle of human selfishness; but the market economy brings this selfishness out into the open (Wang Meng

1996, 59–60). Wang is impatient with worries that all this crass commercialism will damage the quality of higher culture:

> Forgive me for being blunt, but I don't see why other countries can have a market economy for centuries on end and still produce so many great authors, artists, thinkers, and other cultural figures. But our own intellectuals, and no one else, are so weak and whiny that they must pull in their heads as soon as they see a market economy (64–65).

While Wang leaves this point implicit, there is perhaps no reason to think that works produced to satisfy market demand need be of any lower quality than those produced to satisfy the tastes and ambitions of political authority.

Wang Meng speaks of laws proper to economics. There are also, perhaps, laws proper to politics or to culture, none of which embrace all of life but all of which are included in what makes life pleasant. Wang Meng's antipolitical vision may in the end actually be somewhat Taoist. Zhuangzi is not a butterfly and the butterfly is not Zhuangzi, but both are children of the earth, are part of the same reality, and to define either as the other requires an arbitrary imposition.

The Limits of Antipolitics

In some contexts Wang Meng's antipolitical vision is highly subversive. Seen simply as what it is, with no thought for the context that generated it, it may seem no big deal. What reasonable person would take politics as the end-all and be-all of life anyway? But, in fact, lots of people do just that. In modern life generally so many issues which once were thought to be part of the private realm (or the public realm, as distinct from the realm of the state[18]) have become politicized. Politicization, for that matter, is not always in itself illiberal, and one function of democracy is to bring matters previously handled by elites among themselves into general political contestation (Schattschneider 1975). Politicizing the private (or the "personal") sphere is one of the ways workers can prevail against the bosses, women against their fathers and husbands, and environmental activists against owners of land. It is only recently that students of democracy, especially democracy in non-western societies, have rediscovered the attractions of limited government (O'Donnell 1994; Zakaria 1997). The antipolitical temper can be hos-

tile to democracy as well as to totalitarianism. Or, to put it more positively, it can be both a cure for an ill and an antidote for too much of a
good thing.

There is precedent in the People's Republic of China for the
antipolitical position attributed here to Wang Meng, especially, in the
aftermath of the Great Leap, in the work of Deng Tuo and the Three
Family Village, much of whose work at the time affirmed the routines
and pleasures of ordinary life in the face of the "politics in command"
atmosphere which had produced the famine (Moody 1977; Goldman
1981; Hamrin and Cheek 1986). At the outset of the Cultural Revolution this was denounced as vile subversion, a vicious attack on Chairman Mao and the Three Red Flags, an attempt to restore capitalism.
When Deng Tuo and his collaborators were rehabilitated (after their
deaths) in 1978, the new line denied they had any subversive intent. No
doubt this is true, for Deng Tuo did not really want to restore capitalism.
But his writings from the early 1960s certainly constitute political criticism. To be antipolitical is not to be apolitical.

But neither is it, usually anyway, to be *actively* political. An
antipolitical strain runs deeply through the Chinese heritage. Its most
direct expression is in the Taoism of Zhuangzi, and it reappears, among
other places, in poetry, good and bad, extolling a life of retreat in the
mountains and beside streams, away from the cruelties, vanities, snob-
bery, and humiliations of life at court. But even mainstream Confucianism has a streak of antipolitics. In Confucian thought there may be some
concept of politics in the modern sense, the competition among different trends of opinion or interest to shape public policy. But this conflict,
to the extent it is legitimated at all, takes place within a settled, objectively grounded moral order. In Confucianism, government, at its heart,
is more properly moral than political; it is the exercise of justice, prefer-
ably in a loving manner. This limits the degree to which politics can be
construed in terms of choice, since there is no *valid* choice against what
is objectively good and right. And this is also why Confucianism could
be used, or abused, to place the status quo beyond criticism or question.

In modern conditions (and probably a lot of the time in traditional
conditions as well) politics construed as morality implies a politicized
morality, with the good and the just defined in terms of what is politically expedient for those who already have power and privilege, and
opposition in terms of moral depravity. Wang Meng may have some of
the Confucian as well as the Taoist temperament, but he also has some

acerbic comments on what he takes to be traditional morality. The rejection of political morality in the antipolitical strain has some ambiguities. Those of the Cultural Revolution generation (it is said) who have rejected politics have done so not from lack of ideals but from overly exalted ideals. They are too high minded to "perceive reality, especially to perceive [it would be more accurate, I think, to say *accept*] the evil and the ugly" (Chen Xiaoyu 1995, 153). What seems to be a rejection of morality, even, probably, in the likes of Wang Shuo, is at bottom a moral position rejecting politics as the standard of morality.[19]

In reaction to Maoism, antipolitics has permeated the general culture since the onset of reform. In both popular literature and in the overall culture, commerce has replaced politics as the commander (or the "soul," as Lin Biao used to say), resulting in works not necessarily of higher quality but possibly less obnoxious than the earlier norm.[20] Among the more self-consciously literary there was a disinclination to deal with political subjects at all, in favor of what the solemn considered trivial subjects.[21] There was more appreciation of figures such as Zhang Ailing (Eileen Chang), one of China's most outstanding contemporary writers, whose works, say one pair of critics, "are not in the epic style. . . . She pays no attention to the fate of the nation, society, or humanity. She lacks insight into the historical and cultural conditions of actual life" (Wang Weiping and Ma Lin 1997). Ironically, this alleged lack of insight is probably much of the reason for Zhang Ailing's appeal. The good guys and bad guys in historical fiction no longer depend simply on whose side they happened to be on; and history itself is seen by many writers as the concatenation of chance events rather than the operation of social laws.[22]

This is all evidence of a freer, more varied, more normal life (here in the intellectual realm, but there are analogous developments in other spheres as well), the re-emergence, as it were, of China from the People's Republic.[23] The antipolitical theme regards politics as being close to intrinsically evil, something which cannot but be brutal, corrupt, demeaning. The theme stands in the way of any reversion to totalitarian domination.

But however subversive antipolitics may be of Maoism, and however unattractive its vision of their vocation, it may also be that the ruling elite of the 1990s was more than willing to live with some forms of it, and may even share some of its premises. This is one impression left by the reception of the 1990 television "maxiseries" (50 episodes, each roughly an hour long) *Kewang* (Yearning), a celebration of conventional morality which was written in part by, of all people, Wang Shuo, and which seems to have fascinated everyone from the men and women in the lanes and alleys all the way up to Deng Xiaoping.[24] As a work of popular commercial art the series was very well done, while in linguistic terms it was a veritable banquet of the Peking vernacular.

The convoluted story is itself interesting as a vision of Chinese social history from the Cultural Revolution through the reform era. The characters are perhaps stereotyped and sometimes overdone. The heroine, the proletarian young lady Huifang, is so, so good that some viewers took to calling her the "Mother Mary of the East," although the less jaded pronounced her the true model of oriental (*dongfang*) womanhood. She is a paragon of wisdom, beauty, good sense, gracious kindness, patience, and selflessness. The other "proletarian" heroes are less admirable: Huifang's mother is good-hearted enough, but grumpy and tediously garrulous; and her mates at the factory are prone, when exposed to temptation, to corruption and sexual immorality. The intellectuals of the older generation are out of place in the People's Republic but have a certain dignity and integrity. Huifang's intellectual husband, Husheng ("Shanghai-born," a no-doubt significant name) is, until he finally shapes up, conceited, fickle, cowardly, unprincipled, weak.

The antipolitics of *Yearning* is stronger and less subtle than that of "The Butterfly." Again, politics, intruding first as the Red Guards (depicted here as burly thugs who like to beat people with big leather belts, not as fanatical, know-it-all, callous, self-admiring teenagers), appears as the alien force gratuitously ruining the lives of happy, harmless people, bringing out, in many, bad traits of character which otherwise would remain only potential. The message would seem to be that if only people were left alone, and they in turn would mind their own business and do the right thing, then everyone could live in peace and be happy in his work (*an ju le ye*). And what more could anyone want? After the Cultural Revolution proper and the democratic "turmoil" of 1989, this kind of admonition certainly could be just what the rulers want. In Mao's day the goal was to revolutionize the people, to mobilize them, and to remold them. Now it's sufficient if they keep quiet and don't make trouble.

Yet any hypothesis of ruler indifference should not be taken too far, particularly in view of the crackdown on the new religious movement, the Falun Gong, in the summer of 1999. There remain, it would seem, limits to any toleration of even ostensibly non-political activity which enjoys broad popular support, has efficient internal communications, and is not under Party-state control. The meditations and the exercise regimens endorsed by the cult owe some of their appeal, probably, to the moral vacuum left by the retreat of politics and by the dizzying social change resulting from the economic reforms. While on its face nonpolitical, the movement may have been covertly antipolitical, although it did not directly challenge the existing distribution of power and privilege. The irony is that this movement, like other religious movements from the Han Dynasty on, may become politicized precisely because the authorities see it as a move against it. Politicization, or political action generally, in China today may be largely a defensive move, with people being forced to climb Liang Mountain (*bi shang Liang shan*), to use politics to defend themselves against attempts of the Party-state to reassert itself against their otherwise innocent undertakings. This kind of action may be either a promise or a threat—the promise of more open and democratic participation, and the threat of fanaticism competing against fanaticism by violent means for supremacy—and the sort of antipolitics attributed here to Wang Meng may not be very helpful in leading such politicization in its most promising direction.

This, at any rate, can be extrapolated from the opinions of the exiled communist idealist Liu Binyan (1995), who notes the enthusiasm of the authorities for *Yearning* and similar works. He questions Wang Meng's repudiation of political ideals: given the endemic corruption, social collapse, and moral decline in China, perhaps the "excess of idealism" Wang Meng so frets about is not really China's dominating social problem. Wang Meng's repudiation of past fanaticism becomes "a negation of the future as well," an "eternal perpetuation of the current condition" (54). In repudiating all political action and all political vision, in the posttotalitarian phase it amounts, "objectively," as the Marxist-Leninists would say, to an endorsement of the status quo.

An attempted rebuttal of Liu's criticism makes some valid points but also reinforces its general theme. Wang Meng is perhaps not opposed to idealism as such but to fanaticism, and Liu should keep in mind China's vile internal environment—one which produces the circumstances described in the fiction of Wang Shuo and allows one to be a degenerate but not a loyal minister (*zhong chen*, one who speaks truth to power, even unappetizing truth):

> In America a complete rejection of idealism is, of course, a sign of decadence. . . . But in China a liberal intellectual of conscience has no oppor-

tunity to express his own ideals, so sometimes he will take a position in opposition to idealism and morality (Song Ling 1995).

Under totalitarianism, antipolitics is a form of resistance. Under garden variety authoritarianism (or other political forms) it is a refusal to participate in the corruption, cruelty, and hypocrisy that politics entails. But in itself it generates no pressure for political change, so it may tacitly endorse that cruelty, corruption, and hypocrisy. Since any political order is likely to be deficient in terms of human value, it is hard to reject completely the antipolitical stance. Since some political orders are likely to be better than others, and since any political order can operate more humanly or less, it may also be that antipolitics must be at best a limited form of political action.

Notes

1. For early manifestations, see Lin (1979). For a brief overview, see Wang Furen (1998). On the continued relevance of Confucianism, and for different interpretations of that relevance, see the contributions to this volume by Roger Ames and Kam Louie, respectively.

2. For an exploration of some of the ambiguities of this contention, see Lee (1997).

3. The protagonist of *1984* at one point asserts that freedom consists in the ability to say that two plus two equals four, that is, I think, to conceive of truth independently of anyone's will.

4. For a critique of the uses of nationalism and patriotism, see the chapter by Edward Friedman in this volume.

5. David Ott (1990, 75) describes the success of Solidarity in Poland in 1980 as the "crowing triumph of the antipolitical strategy of democratizing society rather than the state."

6. For a systematic, relatively sympathetic rendering of Maoist voluntarism, see Wakeman (1973).

7. Schoenhals (1991, 243–268). For a memoir by a participant, see Sun (1998). For the place of this controversy in the evolution of contemporary cultural politics, see Wang Shubai (1998, 29).

8. Goldman (1967). Zhou was among the earliest victims of the Cultural Revolution, probably more for his factional affiliations than for any public stand he took. Red Guard sources, however, assert that what Zhou Yang said in public was one thing and what he did behind the scenes was something else. He may have been considerably more broadminded when not on public display.

9. For an overview of this rather broad term, see Seeman (1959, 783–791). For Chinese discussions of the term and its various usages, see Yuan Yayu (1982) and Gu Zhengshen (1998).

10. Zhou Yang (1983). For a fictional rendition of how Chinese communist society produced alienation, see Dai (1981).

11. The most senior of the Party spokesman at Shekou, Qu Xiao, had himself been persecuted right out of college in 1957 for uttering liberal sentiments and had been attacked again during the Cultural Revolution. At an earlier forum he had expressed some understanding about why contemporary youth might be less than ardent supporters of the Party, although he urged them to keep the faith (Qu 1985).

12. See the comments by Chen Shaoming appended to Wang Shuo (1993, 363, 365).

13. Wang Shixian, in Wang Shuo (1993, 343). The Tiananmen events must certainly have reinforced any such tendency.

14. Wang Meng (1996, 306–311) contains a chronology of his life.

15. It was first published in *October*, no. 4, 1980; here I am using the translation in *Chinese Literature* (January 1981): 3–55.

16. Qiuwen's husband had been imprisoned during the Hundred Flowers, and she had divorced him to make things easier for him. But she also remained faithful, continuing to regard herself as genuinely his wife. Siyuan comes to propose to her after he learns of her husband's death.

17. Wang Meng (1996, 19). There is some affinity here with Hannah Arendt's (1958, 382, 436–437) analysis of totalitarianism as built on the notion that all things are possible.

18. The concept of civil society has now become banal, its revival after several decades of neglect perhaps having run its course. In one influential usage, the concept postulates a "public" sphere which is distinct both from the purely private and also from the institutional life of the state or other political authority. The public civil society functions to limit the power of the state and helps the ordinary person, particularly if he is organized, privileged, or relatively well-placed, to have some influence on the politics of the state. For the work which brought about the revival of the concept once it had been translated into English, see Habermas (1989). The original was written in the early 1960s, when the theme was also being explored by Establishment political scientists in the United States. For an application to imperial China, see Rowe (1989). The concept's possible relevance to contemporary Chinese society has been extensively discussed, as, for example, by White (1994) and He Baogang (1997). I would argue for reasons extraneous to the present essay that China did not and probably does not have a civil society in quite the Western sense; the "culture" does have, however, an analogous understanding of the public sphere, with the word *gong* having the same ambiguous connotations as the English public: in Legalist theory (and Maoist practice) *gong* is political and state-centered, but in Confucian usage it is more social and moral. For some discussion of this, see Watt (1972).

19. Wang Meng (1996, 293–295) waxes nostalgic about, of all things, Stalin-era Soviet fiction. He apparently finds its content, propagandistic as it may have been, more human and humane than its Maoist imitations. In Orwell's *1984*, personal (in the book, sexual) immorality becomes an assertion of freedom against the all-encompassing moralized demands imposed by political power.

20. Hao Sunsu (1995). As long ago as the early 1980s, it is said, 85 percent of published fiction was about knights errant, ghosts, crime, or romance. Yu Ping (1985) complains, in effect, that people are being given what they want, not what their betters think they should have.

21. Liang Heng (1998). The author quotes the "old writer" Feng Mu complaining of having to read a passage of 3000 words on the changing of a diaper.
22. Shu Ye (1997). This author asserts, however, that the reaction against the old official politicization has resulted in a "counter-politicization" which takes the form of historical nihilism.
23. On the possibilities of a new political culture, see Godwin Chu's chapter in this book.
24. For a commentary, see Shao Daosheng (1991).

Bibliography

Arendt, Hannah. 1958. *The Origins of Totalitarianism.* New York: Meridian Books.
Barmé, Geremie. 1992. "Wang Shuo and *Liumang* ('Hooligan') Culture." *Australian Journal of Chinese Affairs* 28 (July): 33–64.
Bunzel, John. 1967. *Anti-Politics in America: Reflections on the Anti-Political Temper and Its Distortions of the Democratic Process.* New York: Knopf.
Chan, Wing-tsit. 1963. *A Source Book in Chinese Philosophy.* Princeton: Princeton University Press.
Chen Xiaoyu. 1995. "Seeing Through the Fad for the Culture of the 'Three Old Terms.'" *The East* 2. Reprinted in *Xin Hua Wenzhai,* June 1995, 151–153.
Dai Houying. 1981. *Ren, ah Ren* (Humanity, oh, humanity). Guangzhou: Huacheng chubanshe.
Dutton, Michael. 1998. *Streetlife China.* Cambridge: Cambridge University Press.
Ellul, Jacques. 1967. *The Political Illusion.* New York: Knopf.
Fan Xing. 1995. "The Fate of the 'Clan of 57.' " *Literary Review* 2. Reprinted in *Xin Hua Wenzhai,* July 1995, 113–118.
Fitzgerald, John. 1994. *Awakening China: Politics, Culture, and Class in the Nationalist Revolution.* Stanford: Stanford University Press.
Friedrich, Carl J., and Zbigniew Brzezinski. 1965. *Totalitarian Dictatorship and Autocracy.* Second edition. Cambridge: Harvard University Press.
Gold, Thomas. 1984. "'Just in Time!' China Battles Spiritual Pollution on the Eve of 1984." *Asian Survey* 24, no. 9 (September): 947–974.
Goldman, Merle. 1967. *Literary Dissent in Communist China.* Cambridge: Harvard University Press.
———. 1981. *China's Intellectuals: Advise and Dissent.* Cambridge, MA: Harvard University Press.
Gu Zhengshen. 1998. "The Translation of Foreign Technical Terms and Chinese Scholarly Issues." *Peking University Journal* 4. Reprinted in *Xin Hua Wenzhai,* November 1998, 121–126.
Habermas, Jürgen. 1989. *The Structural Transformation of the Public Sphere: An Inquiry into a Category of Bourgeois Society.* Cambridge: MIT Press.
Hamrin, Carol, and Timothy Cheek, eds. 1986. *China's Establishment Intellectuals.* Armonk: M.E. Sharpe.
Hao Sunsu. 1995. "The Choices and Fate of Contemporary Intellectuals." *Literary Contention* 4. Reprinted in *Xin Hua Wenzhai,* September 1995, 1180–1120.
He Baogang. 1997. *The Democratic Implications of Civil Society in China.* New York: St. Martin's.

Hoston, Germaine. 1994. *The State, Identity, and the National Question in China and Japan*. Princeton: Princeton University Press.

Hu Qiaomu. 1984. "On the Question of Humanism and Alienation." Speech of March 1. Printed in *Xin Hua Wenzhai*, April 1984, 1–15.

Jiang Zemin. 1996. "On Paying Attention to Politics." *Qiushi*, July 1.

Konrád, George. 1984. *Antipolitics: An Essay*. New York: Harcourt, Brace, Jovanovich.

Lee, Theresa Man Ling. 1997. *Politics and Truth: Political Theory and the Post-Modernist Challenge*. Albany: State University of New York Press.

Liang Heng. 1998. "Advocacy of Writing About Great Deeds, Great Emotions, Great Principles." *Renmin ribao*, July 17.

Lin Yusheng. 1979. *The Crisis of Chinese Consciousness: Radical Antitraditionalism in the May Fourth Era*. Madison: University of Wisconsin Press.

Liu Binyan. 1995. "Denial of Revolution, Affirmation of the Status Quo." *Beijing zhi chun*, November.

Liu Guangming, Zhang Zhongqiu, and Jiang Haohua. 1989. *Zhongguo zhi lei* (China's tears). Shijiazhuang: Hunan renmin chubanshe.

Loveman, Brian and Thomas M. Davies Jr., eds. 1989. *The Politics of Antipolitics: The Military in Latin America*. Lincoln: University of Nebraska Press.

Luo Xu. 1995. "The 'Shekou Storm': Changes in the Mentality of Chinese Youth Prior to Tiananmen." *China Quarterly* 142 (June): 541–572.

Ma Licheng. 1989. "The Beginning and End of the Shekou Storm." *Wen Hui Monthly* 2. Reprinted in *Xin Hua Wenzhai*, June 1989, 129–143.

Moody, Peter. 1977. *Opposition and Dissent in Contemporary China*. Stanford, CA: Hoover Institution Press.

O'Donnell, Guillermo. 1994. "Delegative Democracy." *Journal of Democracy* 5 (January): 55–69.

Orwell, George. 1949. *1984*. New York: Harcourt Brace.

Ost, David. 1990. *Solidarity and the Politics of Anti-Politics: Opposition and Reform in Poland Since 1968*. Philadelphia:Temple University Press.

Qu Xiao. 1985. "Life, Ideals, Quest." *Shanxi Daily*, April 26 and 27.

Rowe, William. 1989. *Hankow: Conflict and Community in a Chinese City, 1796–1895*. Stanford: Stanford University Press.

Schattschneider, E. E. 1975. *The Semisovereign People: A Realist View of Democracy in America*. Hinsdale, IL: Dryden Press.

Schedler, Andreas, ed.1997. *The End of Politics? Explorations into Modern Antipolitics*. New York: St. Martin's

Schoenhals, Michael. 1991. "The 1978 Truth Criterion Controversy." *China Quarterly* 126 (June): 243–268.

Seeman, Melvin. 1959. "The Meaning of Alienation." *American Sociological Review* 24, no. 6 (December): 783–791.

Shao Daosheng. 1991. "The 'Yearning' Craze and Traditional Culture." *Renmin ribao*, March 8.

Shu Ye. 1997. "New Historical Fiction." *Literary Studies* 6. Reprinted in *Xin Hua Wenzhai*, March 1998, 118–121.

Song Ling. 1995. "How to Look at China from Abroad." *Beijing zhi chun*, December, 63–66.

Sun Changjiang, as told to Cheng Mingyang. 1998. "The Inside Story, Before and After Publication." *Southern Weekly*, May. Reprinted in *Xin Hua Wenzhai*, September 1998, 2–4.

Tao Dalin. 1984. "On Several Questions Concerning Two Kinds of Theoretical Principle." *Yangtse-Han Review* 5. Reprinted in *Xin Hua Wenzhai*, August 1984, 23–26.

Wakeman, Frederic. 1973. *History and Will: Philosophical Perspectives on Mao Tse-tung's Thought.* Berkeley: University of California Press.

Wang Bosen. 1984. "An Attempt to Discuss the Relationship Between Economic Reform and Moral Progress." *Wen hui bao*, July 23.

Wang Changgui. 1992. "Commenting on 'Thin Hard Gruel.' " *Wenyi bao*, January 25.

Wang Furen. 1998. "Several Great Controversies in Contemporary Chinese Academic Culture." *The Age of Openness* 5. Reprinted in *Xin Hua Wenzhai*, December 1998, 142–144.

Wang Meng. 1956. "The Young Newcomer at the Organization Department." *Renmin wenxue*, September 19, 29–43.

———. 1981. "The Butterfly." *Chinese Literature*, January, 3–55.

———. 1994. *The Stubborn Porridge and Other Stories.* New York: George Braziller.

———. 1996. *Xueshu wenhui sui bi* (Notes on scholarship and culture). Beijing: Zhongguo qingnian chubanshe.

Wang Shubai. 1998. "Remembrance of Four Cultural Discussions over the Past 20 Years." *Eastern Culture* 4. Reprinted in *Xin Hua Wenzhai*, December 1998, 29–33.

Wang Shuo. 1988. *Zi xuan ji.* (Self-selected collection of Wang Shu's works). Beijing: Huayi chubanshe.

———. 1993. *Qing chun wu hui* (No regrets for passing youth). Beijing: Zhongguo shehui kexue chubanshe.

Wang Weiping and Ma Lin. 1997. "Review of 50 Years of Studies of Zhang Ailing." *Scholarly Monthly* 11. Reprinted in *Xin Hua Wenzhai*, February 1998.

Watt, James. 1972. *The District Magistrate in Late Imperial China.* New York: Columbia University Press.

White, Gordon. 1994. "Democratization and Economic Reform in China." *Australian Journal of Chinese Affairs* 31 (January): 49–72.

Xiong Fu. 1983. "We Need a Clear Understanding of Marx's Use of the Concept of 'Alienation.' " *Hongqi* 21. Reprinted in *Xin Hua Wenzhai*, December 1983, 15–19.

Yu Ping. 1985. "We Must Pay Attention to Research into and Guidance of Spiritual Consumption." *Social Science Review* 5, in *Xin Hua Wenzai*, February 1986, pp. 6–7.

Yuan Yayu. 1982. "The Theoretical and Practical Significance of the Concept of Alienation." *Social Science Research* 4. Reprinted in *Xin Hua Wenzhai*, December 1982, 15–17.

Zakaria, Fareed. 1997. "The Rise of Illiberal Democracy." *Foreign Affairs* 76 (November/December): 22–43.

Zhou Yang. 1983. "On the Exploration of Several Theoretical Issues of Marxism." *Renmin ribao*, March 16.

7

Political Culture as Social Construction of Reality: A Case Study of Hong Kong's Images in Mainland China

Jonathan Jian-Hua Zhu and Huixin Ke

Drawing on the theory of social construction of reality, we conceive political culture as the process and outcomes of interactions among three types of political reality: the objective reality, the subjective reality, and the symbolic reality (Adoni and Mane 1984). The *objective reality* is the real world out there, manifested by the occurrence of events with political significance (e.g., election, legislation, protest, war, etc.). The *subjective reality* is what the public learns, interprets, and remembers from the objective political reality. As the modern society becomes increasingly complex and remote from people's direct experience and observations, the objective reality is most often "out of sight, out of reach, out of touch" (Lippman 1922). Therefore, people become increasingly dependent on the mass media to learn about the world outside (Ball-Rokeach and DeFluer 1976). Mass media and other communication channels form the *symbolic reality* that mediates between the objective reality in the outside world and the subjective reality in people's minds (Gamson, Croteau, Hoynes, and Sasson 1992). As scholars of social construction of reality have argued, most, if not all, our knowledge of the objective reality is socially constructed (Berger and Luckmann 1966; Boulding

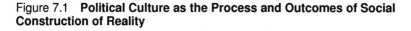

Figure 7.1 **Political Culture as the Process and Outcomes of Social Construction of Reality**

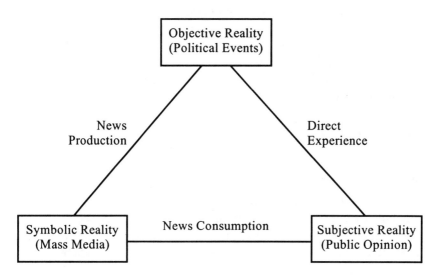

1969; Searle 1995). That is, rather than a mirror reflection of the objective reality, the subjective reality in people's minds is primarily formed and altered by the symbolic reality (see Figure 7.1).

To test these theses of theory of social construction, this current chapter focuses on a case study of how the public in mainland China forms its knowledge of, perception of, and attitudes toward Hong Kong. A city of currently six million people, Hong Kong was under British colonial rule for almost 150 years. In 1984, Britain agreed to return Hong Kong to Chinese sovereignty on July 1, 1997, under the "one country, two systems" arrangement under which Hong Kong, as a Special Administrative Region of China, would maintain the existing political and economic systems while handing over its defense and foreign affairs to the central government in Beijing. The return of Hong Kong to China was a major event in political discourse in China throughout the 1990s. On the one hand, it provided a rare opportunity for the Chinese government to boost its efforts in promoting patriotism and nationalism in the population, which has been a central theme of government propaganda efforts since the 1989 Tiananmen movement (Zhu 1997). From that point of view, the more positive the imagery of Hong Kong, the more significant the handover of sovereignty in 1997. On the other hand, a positive imagery of colonial Hong Kong may provide a sharp contrast to the problems in the mainland and thus raises serious questions in the public's mind about the socialist system and the Communist government in the mainland. This predicament provides an interesting context for us to examine the public opinion process underlying the construction of Hong Kong images among Chinese mainlanders.

Study Objectives

Knowledge of Hong Kong

The first objective of the current study is to investigate the cognitive base of Chinese public opinion about Hong Kong: How much do the ordinary mainland Chinese know about Hong Kong and its people? How much do they think they know about Hong Kong? Where do they get to know Hong Kong? What consequences does an accurate knowledge of Hong Kong have? And what consequences does an inaccurate but falsely trusted knowledge of Hong Kong have? A study of knowledge about Hong Kong is important not only in and by itself, but also because it provides a basis for us to assess the extent to which the Chinese public's perceptions and attitudes about Hong Kong, Hong Kong people, and the handover in 1997 are informed and rationalized (Zhu, Milavsky, and Biswas 1994).

Perceptions of Hong Kong and Its People

Our next aim is to zero in on the perceived images of Hong Kong and its people as perceived in the mainland Chinese's mind: What images do they have in mind about Hong Kong and its people? How are the perceived images of Hong Kong and Hong Kong people related? Where do these images come from? As documented in the rich literature on images, images of other people are most of the time biased and dominated by stereotypes (Buchanan and Cantril 1954; Carter 1962; Scott 1965). An earlier study of mutual perceptions and images among the residents in Beijing, Hong Kong, and Taipei has revealed persistent stereotypes across the three Chinese communities (Wang and Liang 1993). The images of Hong Kong and its people held by mainland Chinese seem to carry particular importance on the eve of Hong Kong's reunification with China.

A particularly important aspect of the images is crime and social order in Hong Kong. As predicted by the cultivation theory, ordinary citizens learn social reality not from direct observations but from largely distorted images transmitted by the media, especially television (Gerbner, Gross, Morgan, and Signorielli 1980; Gerbner and Gross 1976). Scholars have been debating the causal sequence between television viewing and perceptions of the outside world as a mean and scary world because it is often difficult to separate the two (Potter 1994). The current study provides an effective control over the causal link, if any, since most of the Chinese audiences have never been in Hong Kong. They acquire the images of Hong Kong only through the media.

Attitudes toward the Handover in 1997

In addition to the general questions about knowledge and images of Hong Kong, we also seek to explore the urban Chinese residents' attitudes toward the forthcoming return of Hong Kong to China: What do they think about the return of Hong Kong to China in 1997, e.g., what does it mean for China, for Hong Kong, and the chances of a successful and smooth transition? What factors affect these attitudes? These questions provide a new testing ground of the effectiveness of Chinese media, in light of competition from overseas media, especially Hong Kong–based television in this case.

Our earlier studies have shown that the effectiveness of Chinese media is conditioned by whether the audiences have access to information from overseas (He and Zhu 1994; Zhu 1995). However, the access to overseas media has never been so widespread as the Hong Kong–based television in Guangdong province in South China, from which half of the sample under study was drawn. A recent study of the impact of Hong Kong television on the residents in Guangzhou has uncovered a strong correlation between viewing Hong Kong television and a series of questions on ideological values such as money, premarital sex, and social relations (Chan 1996). The study has not taken into account the competitive influences from the Chinese media on the same issues, however. This will be a focus of the current study.

Perceived Issue Salience

What do the public in mainland China think about Hong Kong people's views about the return of Hong Kong to China in 1997? For example, what issues do mainland Chinese estimate as important for Hong Kong people to be concerned about? What factors have caused the estimated issue salience? This line of inquiry follows the research tradition on media agenda-setting that has demonstrated both short- and long-term impact of issue salience on individual and institutional behaviors (McCombs and Shaw 1972; McCombs and Zhu 1995). What is new here is that we are studying the "second-order" issue salience as projected by mainland Chinese to their counterparts in Hong Kong. As pointed out by McLeod and Chaffee (1973) in their coorientation theory, what people think about how other people think is often more consequential than what people themselves think. Thus, the current study will provide baseline data for comparing and contrasting the coorientation process between the mainland and Hong Kong Chinese before and after the handover.

Methodology

Sampling

The current chapter is based on a secondary-data analysis of a large-scale survey conducted by the Statistics and Survey Institute of the Beijing Broadcasting Institute in September 1995, which was less than two years prior to the handover of Hong Kong to China in July 1997. Four metropolitan cities were selected as the survey sites, including Beijing, Shanghai, Guangzhou, and Shenzhen. Beijing and Shanghai are not only the largest cities but also the national political, economic, cultural, and media centers in China. Guangzhou and Shenzhen, on the other hand, are chosen mainly for their proximity to Hong Kong, with Guangzhou being 100 miles away and Shenzhen right on the border between China and Hong Kong. Largely because of their closeness to Hong Kong, Guangzhou and Shenzhen have been among the most developed areas in China. In short, the residents in all of the four chosen cities are by no means the *average* citizens of China. Instead, they represent the most knowledgeable and influential segment of the population, and often lead the nation in major social trends. Although we cannot project from this upscale sample to the entire nation at the present time, the results from the survey are still informative for exploring the future trajectory of China.

The sample was drawn through a three-stage procedure. In the first stage, we randomly selected thirty residential blocks (*juweihui*) in each of the four cities to form an initial pool from which further sampling could be made. In the second stage, we selected twenty households from each of the thirty chosen residential blocks. At the end of this stage, we obtained 600 households per city, or 2,400 households in total. In the final stage, we sent interview staff to each of the chosen households to interview an individual at 16 years of age or older from the household. The individual was selected based on a pre-prepared random-number table to ensure that each qualified member of the household had an equal opportunity to be interviewed. The whole procedure resulted in a sample of 2,400 individuals.

Our survey team in each city included a supervisor and thirty locally recruited interviewers. Once the selection procedure was completed, the interviewers went to each of the chosen households to identify the qualified respondent and ask the person to fill out a self-administered questionnaire; the same person was revisited a few days later to collect the completed questionnaire. The survey achieved a high cooperation rate of 98 percent (i.e., the number of successful interviews divided by the total number of eligible respondents who were contacted).

We compared the sample with the adult population in each city in terms of the proportion of sexes and age groups. While most of the differences between the population and the sample were within the range of random errors, a few sex-age groups were significantly under- or over-sampled. In the Shanghai sample, for example, women between 25 and 34 were under-represented by 8 percent whereas men between 35 and 44 were over-represented by 14 percent. Therefore, the sample was weighted based on the population profile for each city to adjust the under- or over-representation by certain demographic groups.

Measurement

Knowledge of Hong Kong

The respondents were asked to answer eighteen factual questions, ranging from the economy and the political system to popular culture and media outlets in Hong Kong. The correct answers were then summarized into a knowledge score. Since these questions can be objectively verified, the summary knowledge score is labeled below as "Objective Knowledge." Thus, a score of 50 percent on objective knowledge means that the individual could answer nine out of the eighteen questions correctly.

In addition, a "Subjective Knowledge" score was created based on a battery of four questions asking self-reported knowledge of events related to Hong Kong's return to China in 1997. A score of 100 percent for subjective knowledge would indicate that the individual thought he or she was "Completely Knowledgeable" about the four questions whereas a score of 0 percent means the person gave "Not Knowledgeable At All" answers to the four questions.

Images of Hong Kong Society

The respondents were asked to express their agreement, on a five-point scale ranging from "Completely Agree" to "Completely Disagree," with ten statements describing certain characteristics of Hong Kong, such as its prosperity, freedom, streets, crime, and police. Some of the statements (mostly related to Hong Kong's economy) were worded in a positive tone whereas other items (mostly about crime and social order in Hong Kong) were worded in a negative tone. In the analysis, we used factor analysis to identify two separate themes underlying these statements, one representing a positive image for Hong Kong ("The Prosperous Hong Kong") and another a negative image ("The Dangerous Hong Kong"). Two image indices were subsequently created. The exact wording of the constituent items for both image indices and their internal consistency (i.e., Cronbach's α) are given in Appendix 1.

Images of Hong Kong People

The respondents were also asked to evaluate, on a similar five-point scale, twenty statements about Hong Kong people. Similar to the image items about Hong Kong society, some of the statements about Hong Kong people have a clearly positive connotation whereas other statements are unambiguously negative. However, the majority of these statements are more descriptive than judgmental and thus not included for further analysis.[1] Based on a similar factor analysis procedure, we created a positive image index ("The Generous Hong Kong People") and a negative image index ("The Apathetic Hong Kong People"). See Appendix 1 for the wording of the constituent items and their internal consistency (α) for the indices.

Attitudes toward 1997

In addition to the general image questions, the respondents were asked to evaluate, also on a five-point scale, fifty specific statements regarding the return of Hong Kong to China in 1997. Again, we used factor analysis to identify seven common themes underlying twenty-five of the statements. Consequently, we created seven attitudinal indices based on these twenty-five items. The remaining twenty-five items, most of which are either spreading over two or more factors (i.e., showing no unique meaning) or form a single-item factor by themselves, are excluded from further analysis. Three of the seven resulting attitudinal indices are in the positively worded direction, such as "UK: The Trouble Maker," "China's Benefits from the Handover," and "Hong Kong's Benefits from the Handover." The other four composite indices are worded in a negative direction, including "Displacement of Hong Kong," "Ineffective Government and Corruption after 1997," "The Death of Hong Kong after 1997," and "The Deserted Hong Kong after 1997." The exact wording of the constituent items and their internal consistency (α) for the indices are given in the Appendix (see pages 211–214).

Perceived Issue Salience

The respondents were asked to estimate from a checklist of six items what Hong Kong people would be most concerned about after 1997. The listed areas of concern include "Erosion of the Legal System," "Corruption," "Isolationism" (i.e., closed door to the outside world), "State Capitalism" (i.e., capitalism controlled by the state), "Lack of Freedom," and "Decline in Prosperity." Since the respondents were allowed to check as many concerns as possible from the list, we created six dichotomous variables (i.e., questions with "yes" and "no" answers), each representing a particular concern named. For example, if the respondent thinks that Hong Kong people would be concerned about corruption after 1997, a score of 1 will be assigned to "Corruption" for the person. Conversely, if the respondent does not mention corruption as an area of concern for Hong Kong people, then the person will receive a zero on "Corruption." The Appendix gives the wording of these issue-salience variables.

Media Exposure

The respondents were asked to indicate, on a four-point scale, ranging from "Never" and "Sometime" to "Often" and "Almost Everyday," how often they were exposed to domestic newspapers, domestic television channels, and Hong Kong television channels. The measure of exposure

Table 7.1

Which of the Following Is Your Primary Source of Information about Hong Kong? (select one only)

Source of Information about HK	South (%)	North (%)	Total (%)
Domestic media	31.2	72.7	51.8
HK/Macau/Taiwan media	43.1	2.5	23.0
Other overseas media	1.1	1.5	1.3
Political studies at workplace	1.3	2.0	1.6
Friends & relatives	5.8	5.6	5.7
Mainland Chinese who have visited HK	3.1	2.3	2.7
Visitors from HK	4.4	1.1	2.8
Purely self guess	3.8	6.5	5.1
Other sources	2.5	0.7	1.6
DK/No answer	3.7	5.0	4.4
Total	100.0	100.0	100.0
Number of cases	1,235	1,215	2,450

to Hong Kong television is a central variable for this study because half of the sample (i.e., those living in the two southern cities, Guangzhou and Shenzhen) had access to Hong Kong television programs from local government-run cable stations whereas the other half (i.e., those living in the two northern cities, Beijing and Shanghai) did not have such direct access. In the survey, we also asked the respondents to indicate among nine options their primary source of information about Hong Kong. As shown in Table 7.1, nearly three-fourths (73 percent) of the residents in Beijing and Shanghai relied on domestic media for information about Hong Kong whereas a similar proportion (74 percent) of the residents in Guangzhou and Shenzhen depended on a combination of the domestic and Hong Kong media.

Television ratings data, originally collected by the Central Viewer Survey and Consulting Center (CVSC), which is the audience research unit of Chinese Central Television (CCTV), show that the residents in Guangdong province, where Guangzhou and Shenzhen are located, spent about half of their total viewing time watching Hong Kong–based channels and the other half watching domestic channels. For example, based on our reanalysis of CVSC rating data, during September 1995, when this four-city survey was conducted, the residents in Guangzhou spent 96 minutes per day (or 57 percent of their total viewing time) watching the two Hong Kong–based Chinese-language channels (i.e., TVB-Jade and ATV-Home), and the residents in Shenzhen spent 70 minutes per day (or 44 percent of their total viewing time) watching the same two channels. The same ratings data do not register any viewing time on Hong Kong television by the residents in Beijing or Shanghai simply because physical access to Hong Kong television does not exist anywhere outside Guangdong province.

Analytical Strategy

The geographic division between the South (Guangzhou and Shenzhen) and the North (Beijing and Shanghai) represents two different sources of influence on the residents: cultural affinity and media access. Cultural affinity refers to the fact that the majority of the residents in Guangzhou and Shenzhen share a similar cultural tradition and language (i.e., Cantonese dialect) with the residents in Hong Kong. Media access refers to the direct access to Hong Kong–based television channels that the residents in the two cities have enjoyed since 1993. Thus, any difference between the South and the North sectors of our sample could be attributed to either the long-standing cultural affinity or the recently available media access (or a combination of both). While a complete separation of the two factors is impossible, we have adopted an analytical strategy that may partial out media effects from cultural affinity to some extent.

Under this analytic strategy, we have divided the four cities into two regional sub-samples, with Guangzhou and Shenzhen being the "South" sub-sample and Beijing and Shanghai being the "North" sub-sample. Regression analysis has been performed separately for each sub-sample. All independent variables in the regression analysis (representing various sources of influence on people's knowledge, attitudes, and perceptions) except one are identical for both sub-samples. The only difference is the presence of "Exposure to Hong Kong Television" in the regression analysis for the "South" sub-sample. This strategy will allow us to test the impact of Hong Kong television among the residents in the South and compare the impact of other sources of influences between the North and the South.

Findings

Knowledge of Hong Kong and Its People

On average, the residents in the four cities we surveyed have a 50 percent correct rate in answering the eighteen factual questions that can be

Figure 7.2 **Knowledge of Hong Kong**

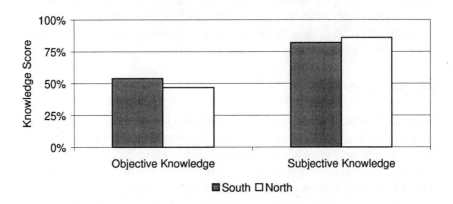

independently verified. As shown in Figure 7.2, between the two sub-samples, the knowledge level is higher in the South (54 percent) than in the North (47 percent). On the other hand, people in both regions felt they knew far more about Hong Kong than what they actually correctly answered. The average level of subjective knowledge, which is the self-claimed knowledge that cannot be verified by any objective criterion, is 84 percent for the entire sample, as compared to 50 percent for the objective knowledge. More interestingly, the subjective knowledge score is *higher* for the northern sub-sample (86 percent), who actually know less, than for the southern residents (82 percent). At the individual level, the two knowledge measures are weakly correlated, with $r = 0.10$ for the overall sample. The weak correlation suggests that how much a person claims to know is not related to how much the person actually knows. However, the correlation is stronger for the South sub-sample ($r = 0.17$) but weaker for the North sub-sample ($r = 0.08$). By and large, the subjective knowledge held by Chinese residents is largely a measure of self-confidence without much factual basis.

To explore possible sources of both objective and subjective knowledge about Hong Kong, we turn to the regression analysis results in Table 7.2. The numbers in the table are regression coefficients that describe the impact of independent variables (i.e., influential sources) on knowledge scores. The coefficients have been standardized so that their values range from 0 to ± 1, with 0 indicating no effects at all whereas ± 1 indicates fullest effects. To help read the results, we only present coefficients that reach statistical significance at $p < .05$. The non-

Table 7.2

Standardized Regression Coefficients Predicting Knowledge of Hong Kong (only significant coefficients shown)

	Objective knowledge		Subjective knowledge	
	South	North	South	North
Media exposure				
HK television	0.147***	N/A		N/A
Chinese television			0.096**	
Chinese newspapers			0.072*	0.134***
Control variable				
Age[L]	−0.079*	−0.129***	0.113***	0.090**
Sex (female=0)[D]	−0.098**			
Education	0.136***		0.197***	0.151***
Income[L]		0.078*		
CCP membership[D]		−0.066*		0.074*
Adjusted R²	0.059	0.035	0.087	0.066
Number of cases	1,095	1,086	1,095	1,086

[D] dichotomous variable.
[L] log-transformed.
$* p < .05;$ $** p < .01;$ $*** p < .001$

significant coefficients are omitted from Table 7.2 and all subsequent tables because they represent a relationship that is not likely to hold true in the population.

Because the regression coefficients are standardized, they can be directly compared with each other. The larger the coefficient (regardless of its positive or negative sign), the more the influence the independent variable has on one's knowledge. A positive coefficient illustrates the independent variable has a positive effect on the knowledge score. For example, the coefficient .147 in column one and row one of Table 7.2 means that the more Hong Kong television an individual in South China watches, the higher the level of objective knowledge the person holds about Hong Kong. Conversely, a negative coefficient suggests a negative impact of the independent variable on knowledge. Therefore, the coefficient .079 in column one, row four, indicates that older people hold lower levels of objective knowledge than younger cohorts do.

Taken together, the data in Table 7.2 show differential roles between domestic and Hong Kong media. Exposure to Hong Kong television, which is only available for the southern residents, has a significant and positive impact on the objective knowledge but no impact at all on the subjective knowledge. That is, watching Hong Kong television helps mainland Chinese, at least those living in the South, to improve their factually based knowledge about Hong Kong. On the contrary, exposure to both domestic television and domestic newspapers has no impact on the objective knowledge but a significant and positive impact on the subjective knowledge. This pattern holds in both sub-samples. These findings suggest that Chinese media contribute little to factual knowledge but help create a false perception among all Chinese, North and South, that they know a lot about Hong Kong. Between the two types of domestic media (i.e., broadcast or print), it appears that television is more effective in the South but newspapers more influential in the North in boosting the subjective knowledge.

Images of Hong Kong and Its People

On average, the respondents in our sample hold a neutral or slightly positive image of Hong Kong and its people. For example, on a five-point scale (with 3 being neutral, 4 agree, and 5 completely agree), the average image score of the entire sample is 3.4 for the image of "Hong Kong is rich," 3.5 for "Hong Kong is dangerous," 3.6 for "Hong Kong people are generous," and 3.0 for "Hong Kong people are apathetic." The two sub-samples differ slightly in the two positive image indices, with the southern sub-sample being somewhat more favorable of Hong Kong (mean = 3.4) and Hong Kong people (3.7) than the northern sub-sample (3.3 and 3.4, respectively). If one assumes that prosperity is a positive image for a place whereas danger is a negative image, then mainland Chinese seem to project both a prosperity image and a danger image onto Hong Kong. Likewise, they see Hong Kong people in both positive (e.g., Hong Kong people are ethical, helpful, and neat) and negative lights (Hong Kong people are naive, cowered, and isolated). These findings suggest that mainland Chinese held mixing feelings about Hong Kong and its people who would join the mainland family in less than two years.

Table 7.3 displays regression coefficients that test the impact of domestic and Hong Kong media on the perceived images of Hong Kong and its people, respectively. We can interpret these coefficients the same way as in the case of Table 7.2. The results suggest that exposure to Hong Kong television appears to have no impact on any image of Hong Kong and its people, in both sub-samples. On the other hand, exposure

Table 7.3

Standardized Regression Coefficients Predicting Images of Hong Kong and Its People (only significant coefficients shown)

	The prosperous Hong Kongers		The dangerous Hong Kongers		The generous Hong Kongers		The apathetic Hong Kongers	
	South (mean=3.4)	North (mean=3.3)	South (mean=3.7)	North (mean=3.4)	South (mean=3.0)	North (mean=3.0)	South (mean=3.5)	North (mean=3.5)
Media exposure								
HK television		N/A		N/A		N/A		N/A
Chinese television							0.071*	
Chinese newspapers		−0.078*	0.088*			0.075*		0.072*
Knowledge of HK								
Objective			0.097**					−0.081**
Subjective	0.098**	0.087**			0.069*	0.093**		0.069*
Control variable								
Age^L	0.090*	0.095**	0.069*		0.109**			
Sex (female=0)^D			−0.176***	−0.138***				
Education						−0.072*		
Income^L	−0.079*						−0.063*	−0.081*
CCP membership^D						0.091**		
Adjusted R^2	0.027	0.014	0.047	0.015	0.027	0.016	0.013	0.016
Number of cases	1,058	1,059	1,058	1,059	1,058	1,059	1,058	1,059

^{D} dichotomous variable.
^{L} log–transformed.
* $p < 0.05$; ** $p < 0.01$; *** $p < 0.001$

to Chinese media could do some damage to the images of Hong Kong and Hong Kong people. For example, reading Chinese newspapers by the residents in the North has a negative effect on the perceived prosperity of Hong Kong but a positive effect on the perceived apathy of Hong Kong people. Likewise, watching Chinese television by the residents in the South enhances the chances for them to see Hong Kong people as apathetic. The only positive effect of Chinese media is the fostering of a prosperous image of Hong Kong among the southern residents.

The two types of knowledge (i.e., objective or subjective) about Hong Kong seem to contribute differently to the perceived images. The objective knowledge primarily enhances the positive image of "Generous Hong Kong People" among the southern residents and suppresses the negative image of "Dangerous Hong Kong" among the northern residents. While the subjective knowledge helps foster a positive image of "Prosperous Hong Kong" among both northern and southern residents, it increases the likelihood that the northern sample will view Hong Kong people as cowed, isolated, and lonely.

Attitudes toward the Handover in 1997

Of the seven indices that represent attitudes toward the handover of Hong Kong to China in 1997, three were worded positively and the other four negatively. Overall, our sample moderately endorses the three positive views, with a mean score of 3.8 on a five-point scale for "UK is the trouble maker," 4.1 for "China will benefit from the handover," and 3.7 for "Hong Kong will benefit from the handover."[2] The mean score between the southern and northern sub-samples is identical on all three positive indices. Conversely, the sample as a whole leans toward the rejection of the four negative views, with a mean score of 2.8 for "Hong Kong will be displaced by Shanghai or Guangzhou after 1997," 2.8 for "The government in Hong Kong will be inefficient and corrupted after 1997," 2.1 for "Hong Kong will die after 1997," and 2.9 for "Capital and immigrants will flee out of Hong Kong after 1997." Of the four negatively worded attitudes, the two sub-samples differ somewhat about "the displacement of Hong Kong," with the South being neutral (3.0) and the North opposing the notion (2.7), and about "the death of Hong Kong," with the South disagreeing more (2.1) than the North (2.2).

Table 7.4

Standardized Regression Coefficients Predicting Positive Attitudes toward the Handover of Hong Kong to China (only significant coefficients shown)

	UK trouble maker		China gains from handover		HK gains from handover	
	South (mean=3.8)	North (mean=3.8)	South (mean=3.2)	North (mean=3.1)	South (mean=3.7)	North (mean=3.7)
Media exposure						
HK television	0.121***	N/A	0.122***	N/A	0.171***	N/A
Chinese television						
Chinese newspapers						0.075*
Knowledge of HK						
Objective	0.080**		0.148***			
Subjective	0.257***	0.325***	0.222***	0.175***	0.168***	0.207***
Control variable						
Age^L	0.142***				0.189***	
Sex (female=0)^D						
Education	0.084*	0.076*				
Income^L	-0.064*		-0.062*	-0.116***		-0.097**
CCP membership^D	0.077*					
Adjusted R^2	0.162	0.134	0.126	0.046	0.127	0.057
Number of cases	1,058	1,059	1,058	1,059	1,058	1,059

^{D} dichotomous variable.
^{L} log-transformed.
* $p < 0.05$; ** $p < 0.01$; *** $p < 0.001$

The regression coefficients reported in Table 7.4 describe the relative impact the same influences examined in Table 7.3 had on the seven attitudinal indices regarding the 1997 handover. It is quite clear from the table that the positive attitudes are primarily cultivated by the domestic media. In particular, domestic television channels have a strong impact on the residents in the South. The impact of domestic newspapers is largely confined to the northern population on one issue ("Hong Kong will gain more from the handover"). Surprisingly, exposure to Hong Kong television does not seem to have any impact, one way or the other, on the southern residents. Also evident from Table 7.4 is the strong impact of self-reported subjective knowledge on the acceptance of all three positively worded indices by both southern and northern subsamples. Factual objective knowledge also helps raise the support for these views in a more limited capacity (only among the southern residents on two of the three issues).

A somewhat different pattern emerges in the case of four negatively worded attitudes, however. As indicated in Table 7.5, exposure to Hong Kong television helps viewers reject both the notion that either Shanghai or Guangzhou will replace the strategic position Hong Kong has occupied and the view that Hong Kong will collapse right after the handover in 1997. Exposure to Chinese television seems to reinforce, instead of offset, the impact of Hong Kong television. However, reading domestic newspapers will make the southern residents *more* supportive of the possibility that Hong Kong will be displaced by Shanghai or Guangzhou after 1997. Knowledge of Hong Kong, either factual or self-imagined, seems to diminish the support for all these negatively worded attitudes.

Perceived Issue Salience

Table 7.6 shows both the percentage and rank order of six issues our survey respondents thought Hong Kong people might be concerned about after 1997. As shown in column 1 of the table, the respondents thought "Lack of Freedom" would be the number one concern (endorsed by 55 percent of the sample), followed by "Decline in Prosperity" (53 percent), "Corruption" (48 percent), and "Erosion of Legal System" (46 percent). The two issues that the Chinese respondents believed that Hong Kong people would not be concerned about are "State Capitalism" (24 percent) and "Isolationism" (14 percent). However, there are substantial

Table 7.5

Standardized Regression Coefficients Predicting Negative Attitudes toward the Handover of Hong Kong to China (only significant coefficients shown)

	Displacement of HK		Gov't. corruption in HK		Death of HK		HK deserted	
	South (mean=2.7)	North (mean=3.0)	South (mean=2.8)	North (mean=2.8)	South (mean=2.1)	North (mean=2.2)	South (mean=2.9)	North (mean=2.9)
Media exposure								
HK television	-0.060*	N/A		N/A	-0.094**	N/A		N/A
Chinese television			-0.128***	-0.097**			-0.085*	
Chinese newspapers	0.096**							
Knowledge of HK								
Objective	-0.116***		-0.065*		-0.111***			
Subjective	-0.070*	-0.103**	-0.128***	-0.098**	-0.233***	-0.230***	-0.093**	-0.036
Control variable								
Age^L	-0.131***	-0.081*		-0.116***			-0.081*	
Sex (female=0)^D							-0.085**	
Education				-0.083*				
Income^L	-0.187***				-0.068*			
CCP membership^D						0.072*		
Adjusted R^2	0.059	0.020	0.044	0.045	0.106	0.076	0.053	0.001
Number of cases	1,058	1,059	1,058	1,059	1,058	1,059	1,058	1,059

^{D} dichotomous variable.
^{L} log-transformed.
* $p < .05$; ** $p < .01$; *** $p < .001$

Table 7.6

Which of the Following Issues Do You Think That Hong Kong People Will Be Concerned with Most after 1997? (select as many as applicable)

Issue	Total %	Total Rank	South %	South Rank	North %	North Rank
Freedom	55.3	1	60.4	1	50.2	2
Prosperity	52.5	2	47.6	4	57.4	1
Corruption	48.1	3	54.9	3	41.1	3
Law	45.8	4	57.4	2	34.1	4
State capitalism	23.5	5	26.7	5	20.3	5
Isolationism	14.2	6	12.9	6	15.5	6

Spearman's rank-order correlation between South and North = .60, p > .20.

differences between the two regional sub-samples when assigning relative importance to this list of issues. For example, the southern sample rated "Prosperity" as the number four concern whereas the northern sample ranked it on the top of the list. In fact, the two sub-samples differ in three out of the six issues in terms of their salience. The Spearman's rank-order correlation coefficient, which measures the consistency between two lists of rank ordered items, between the two sub-samples is not significant, suggesting that there is a substantial disagreement between the two regions in their estimates of what Hong Kong people are concerned about after 1997.

Table 7.7 reports the impact of the same independent variables we have examined so far on the likelihood of identifying any of the six issues as an area of concern for Hong Kong people after 1997. Because these six issues are coded in a dichotomous fashion (i.e., "yes" or "no"), a special statistical technique called logistic regression was applied to the data. To help interpret the results, we have transformed the logistic regression coefficients to their anti-log values. A coefficient greater than 1.00 indicates a higher probability of naming a particular issue as the most concerned whereas a coefficient smaller than 1.00 signals a lower probability.

As shown in Table 7.7, exposure to Hong Kong television does not have any impact here. On the other hand, use of domestic television or newspapers has a significant impact in five out of the six issues. More interesting is the direction of the impact induced by the domestic media. For example, the more a person in the South watches Chinese televi-

Table 7.7

Anti-logged Logistic Regression Coefficients Predicting the Perceived Issue Salience Held by Hong Kong People

	Erosion of law		Corruption		Isolationism		State capitalism		Lack of freedom		Decline in prosperity	
	South	North	South	North	South	North	South	North	South	North	South	North
Media exposure												
HK television	N/A		N/A		N/A		N/A		N/A		N/A	
Chinese television					1.46***				0.86*			
Chinese newspapers				0.79*				0.67***			0.79**	
Knowledge of HK												
Objective	17.5***		5.50**	2.51*					12.3***	7.79***	3.45*	3.11*
Subjective			1.94*			0.40*			2.43**			
Control variable												
Age^L		1.58*	0.54**		0.36***	0.58*	0.36***					
Sex (female=0)^D										0.69**		0.49***
Education	1.20**	1.32***					0.86*			1.15*	1.20**	1.21**
Income^L		0.70**	1.60***	1.30*			1.41**					
CCP membership^D												
Adjusted R^2	0.055	0.025	0.038	0.011	0.031	0.016	0.031	0.025	0.032	0.028	0.019	0.028
Number of cases	1,002	988	1,002	988	1,002	988	1,002	988	1,002	988	1,002	988

^{D} dichotomous variable.

^{L} log-transformed.

* $p < 0.05$; ** $p < 0.01$; *** $p < 0.001$

sion, the *more* likely the person is to think "isolationism" would be an issue of concern for Hong Kong people, but the *less* likely the person is to name "lack of freedom" as a potential problem. Reading Chinese newspapers seems to have a "comforting" effect since the more frequently a person reads domestic newspapers, the less likely he/she is to identify "corruption" or "state capitalism" as a concern (if living in the North) or "decline in prosperity" (if residing in the South). Finally, knowledge of Hong Kong also has significant impacts on the perceived issue salience. For example, objective knowledge has the strongest effects on "erosion of legal system," "lack of freedom," and "corruption," especially among the southern respondents, suggesting that the perceived issue salience is indeed an informed opinion with a substantive knowledge basis.

Conclusions and Discussion

What have we found from this survey of 2,400 residents in four metropolitan cities in China? First, the study has revealed that the residents in the four cities have a half-true and half-false knowledge (i.e., an average 50 percent accuracy rate) about Hong Kong and its people, with those in the two southern cities (Guangzhou and Shenzhen) knowing more than those in the two northern cities (Beijing and Shanghai). However, many of the respondents in all four cities think they know a lot more about Hong Kong (i.e., an average 84 percent self-estimated knowledge level) than they really do. The objective knowledge and the subjective knowledge are only weakly correlated, suggesting that those with a higher score of self-estimated knowledge are not necessarily those who are most knowledgeable.

This study has identified four specific images of Hong Kong and its people from a list of thirty questions: Hong Kong is a prosperous place but also a dangerous place with crimes involving gangs and even police; Hong Kong people are generous and helpful, but also naive, inactive, and isolated. The sample as a whole moderately subscribes to the first three images (a rich but scary place, and a generous people) while holding a neutral position on the last image (an apathetic people). The residents in the South are more positive than those in the North about Hong Kong and its people.

When asked of their opinions on the scheduled home-coming of Hong Kong in 1997, the respondents in the survey appear to agree with the Chinese government's official line by attributing all the disputes and

Table 7.8

A Summary of Media Effects
(based on results shown in Tables 7.2–7.5 and 7.7)

	HK television		Chinese television		Chinese newspapers	
	South	North	South	North	South	North
Knowledge of HK						
Objective	+	N/A	0	0	0	0
Subjective	0	N/A	+	0	+	+
Image of HK society						
Rich	0	N/A	0	0	0	–
Dark	0	N/A	+	0	0	+
Image of HK people						
Generous	0	N/A	0	0	+	0
Apathetic	0	N/A	0	0	0	+
Attitudes toward 97						
UK troublemaker	0	N/A	+	0	0	0
China benefited	0	N/A	+	0	0	0
HK benefited	0	N/A	0	0	0	+
Displacing HK	–	N/A	0	0	+	0
Corruption after 97	0	N/A	–	–	0	0
Death of HK	–	N/A	0	0	0	0
Deserting HK	0	N/A	–	0	0	0
Issue Salience						
Erosion of law	0	N/A	0	0	0	0
Corruption	0	N/A	0	0	0	–
Isolationism	0	N/A	+	0	0	0
State capitalism	0	N/A	0	0	0	–
Lack of freedom	0	N/A	–	0	0	0
Prosperity	0	N/A	0	0	–	0

+: A significantly positive impact.
–: A significantly negative impact.
0: A non-significant relationship.
N/A: the variable is not available in the sub-sample.

problems in the handover to Britain; by viewing the handover as beneficial to both China and Hong Kong, with Hong Kong gaining more than
China; and by rejecting several negative or pessimistic predictions for
Hong Kong after 1997, such as the death of Hong Kong, the displacement of Hong Kong by Shanghai or Guangzhou, ineffective SAR government, corrupt politics in Hong Kong, and massive outflow of capital
and manpower. However, many of the same respondents, especially those
living in the South, are also aware of the concerns Hong Kong people
have over personal freedom, the legal system, and corruption in the postcolonial period.

In exploring possible sources of such knowledge, images, attitudes, and issue salience, we have looked into three types of mass media that the Chinese respondents depend on the most for information about Hong Kong: domestic newspapers, domestic television, and Hong Kong–based television (only accessible to the southern sub-sample). Table 7.8 summarizes the effects of these media as identified by the current study. It is clear from the summary table that the most significant impact of Hong Kong television on the southern audiences is the acquisition of factual knowledge of Hong Kong. In addition, exposure to Hong Kong television appears to help offset the dim predictions for Hong Kong's death or replacement.

Exposure to Chinese television appears to be more influential than that to Hong Kong television or to domestic newspapers. However, the effects are largely confined to the audiences in the South (with eight significant instances), rather than in the North (only one significant case). For the southerners, watching domestic television leads them to believe that they are well-informed about Hong Kong; to see Hong Kong as a dangerous place; to attribute all blame to the UK; to reject the notion that Hong Kong people are concerned about the lack of freedom after 1997; and to believe variously that China will benefit from the handover, that inefficiency and corruption won't be a problem, and that money and people will stay in Hong Kong after 1997.

On the other hand, Chinese newspapers seem to have more influences on the residents in the North, often in the same direction as Chinese television has influenced the southern audiences described above. In particular, reading Chinese newspapers leads the readers in both North and South to believe that they are well-informed about Hong Kong affairs. It also raises doubts about the prosperous images of Hong Kong among the northern readers and reduces the likelihood that northern readers will see corruption as an issue of concern by Hong Kong people.

These patterns point to the complexity of media effects in China. The most puzzling question is, naturally, why Chinese television's influence is found not in the North but in the South, where the residents have already had easy access to Hong Kong television. A few speculations here on the matter might stimulate further investigation into the question. One possibility is that the residents in the South are much more visually oriented than their counterparts in the North, partly due to the cultivation of an expressive cultural lifestyle by Hong Kong television in recent years. Another possible explanation involves the way the audiences in the South watch both domestic and Hong Kong–based television programs. Anecdotal evidence suggests that the audiences in the South watch primarily entertainment programs on Hong Kong television and turn to central or local channels for news. In an on-going study, we are linking the viewing data with program content to determine whether this is indeed the case.

Going back to the central thesis proposed by scholars of social construction of reality, the current study clearly demonstrates that how much people in mainland China know about and how they think of an outside society and its people have actually less to do with the objective characteristics of that society and that people than with the portrait of the society provided by the mass media. When there is more than one version of the symbolic reality (i.e., the information environment in Guangzhou and Shenzhen where the mainland and Hong Kong media coexist), the knowledge of, perception of, and attitudes toward Hong Kong tend to become more diverse and balanced. However, even in these localities, what people know about and how they view the world outside, with Hong Kong as the case in point, are still not an accurate picture of the actual world but rather constitute different, and sometimes contrasting, versions of a socially constructed reality.

Appendix

Question Wording for Image and Attitudinal Measures

The Prosperous Hong Kong ($a = 0.48$)
D1. Hong Kong is the easiest place in the world to make money.
D3. There is more freedom in Hong Kong than in Taiwan.
D4. Trading with Hong Kong plays a very important role in the mainland economy.
D5. Hong Kong's prosperity is far beyond the imagination of those mainland Chinese who have never been there.

The Dangerous Hong Kong ($a = 0.75$)
D6. The triads in Hong Kong are very active and powerful.
D7. There are many crimes of all kinds in Hong Kong.
D8. Many Hong Kong police officers are well connected with the triads.

The Generous Hong Kong People (a = 0.63)
 E2. The Hong Kong people have a very high standard for social morality and ethics.
 E5. The Hong Kong people love to help others.
 E6. The Hong Kong people love to keep the place clean.

The Apathetic Hong Kong People (a = 0.54)
 E4. The Hong Kong people are politically very naive.
 E9. The Hong Kong people try to stay away from any trouble.
 D10. The Hong Kong people do not interact with each other a lot.

UK The Trouble Maker (a = 0.71)
 G16. Hong Kong Governor Chris Patten has ruined the harmonious partnership between China and the UK by carrying out his political reform plan.
 G17. Hong Kong Governor Chris Patten has finally done something good by promoting democracy in Hong Kong through his political reform plan (reversed in the analysis).
 G18. It is the Chinese side that should bear the responsibility for the Sino-UK disputes over Hong Kong (reversed in the analysis).
 G50. It is the UK side that should bear the responsibility for the Sino-UK disputes over Hong Kong.

China's Benefits from the Handover (a = 0.84)
 G3. Hong Kong's return helps reunify China.
 G4. Hong Kong's return helps preserve national dignity.
 G5. Hong Kong's return helps enhance economic development in China.
 G6. Hong Kong's return helps enhance political development in China.
 G8. Hong Kong's return helps open up China to the outside world.

Hong Kong's Benefits from the Handover (a = 0.72)
 G2. Hong Kong can keep its prosperity after 1997.
 G10. Hong Kong will benefit tremendously from the "one country, two systems."
 G19. Hong Kong's return helps economic development in Hong Kong.
 G20. Hong Kong's return helps political development in Hong Kong.

Displacement of Hong Kong after 1997 (a = 0.89)

G21. Shanghai or Guangzhou will replace Hong Kong to become an international finance center.

G22. Shanghai or Guangzhou will replace Hong Kong to become an information center.

G23. Shanghai or Guangzhou will replace Hong Kong to become a trade center.

Ineffective Government and Corruption in Hong Kong after 1997 (a = 0.70)

G27. It will be difficult for the SAR government in Hong Kong to be in charge after 1997.

G28. It will be difficult for the SAR government in Hong Kong to sustain "high efficiency and low corruption."

G39. Hong Kong's return will help businesses in Hong Kong and government in the mainland to forge an alliance to transfer part of the economy in Hong Kong into a state-capitalist economy.

G40. Corruption will be exported from the mainland to Hong Kong, to undermine the legal system in Hong Kong after 1997.

The Death of Hong Kong after 1997 (a = 0.78)

G44. The financial market in Hong Kong may crash within a few minutes after Hong Kong's return.

G47. The arrival of 1997 will be the "death of Hong Kong."

G49. Hong Kong will no longer be the "Pearl of the Orient" after 1997.

The Deserted Hong Kong after 1997 (a = 0.71)

G45. There will be another flood of outgoing immigration in Hong Kong right before 1997.

G46. There will be a massive outflow of capital from Hong Kong right before 1997.

Perceived Issue Salience

H1. What concerns do you think the people in Hong Kong have about the return in 1997?

1. Erosion of the legal system
2. Corruption
3. Closed-door to outside world

4. State capitalism

5. Lack of freedom

6. Decline in prosperity

Notes

The preparation of the chapter has been supported in part by a Competitive Ear-marked Research Grant from the Hong Kong Universities Grants Council (CityU1018/97H).

1. For example, "Hong Kong people are very practical," "Hong Kong people have a strong business mind," "Hong Kong people pay a lot of attention to dressing," and "Many Hong Kong people have a religious belief."

2. The index is considered positively worded from the Chinese point of view because a low score (< 3) suggests that China is responsible for all the disputes over the handover.

Bibliography

Adoni, Hanna, and Sherill Mane. 1984. "Media and the Social Construction of Reality: Toward an Integration of Theory and Research." *Communication Research* 11: 323–340.

Ball-Rokeach, Sandra, and Marvin DeFluer. 1976. "A Dependency Model of Mass Media Effects." *Communication Research* 3:3–21.

Berger, Peter L., and Thomas Luckmann. 1966. *The Social Construction of Reality.* Baltimore, MD: Penguin Books.

Boulding, Kenneth E. 1969. *The Image: Knowledge in Life and Society.* Ann Arbor, MI: University of Michigan Press.

Buchanan, William, and Hardley Cantril. 1954. "National Stereotypes." In *The Process and Effects of Mass Communication*, edited by Wilbur Schramm and Donald F. Roberts. 191–216. Urbana, IL: University of Illinois Press.

Carter, Richard F. 1962. "Stereotyping as a Process." *Public Opinion Quarterly* 26:77–91.

Chan, Joseph M. 1996. "Penetrating China's Cultural Shield: The Impact of Hong Kong Television on Guangzhou Residents." Paper presented at the Conference on Patterns of Communication in Cultural China, Chinese University of Hong Kong.

Gamson, William A., David Croteau, William Hoynes, and Theodore Sasson. 1992. "Media Images and the Social Construction of Reality." *Annual Review of Sociology* 18:373–393.

Gerbner, George, and Larry Gross. 1976. "Living with Television: The Violence Profile." *Journal of Communication* 26:173–199.

Gerbner, George, Larry Gross, Michael Morgan, and Nancy Signorielli. 1980. "The 'Mainstreaming' of America: Violence Profile No. 11." *Journal of Communication* 30:10–29.

He, Zhou, and Jian-Hua Zhu. 1994. "The Voice of America and China: Zeroing in on Tiananmen Square." *Journalism Monographs,* vol. 43.

Lippman, Walter. 1922. *Public Opinion*. New York: Harcourt Brace.

McCombs, Maxwell E., and Donald L Shaw. 1972. "The Agenda-Setting Function of Mass Media." *Public Opinion Quarterly* 36:176–187.

McCombs, Maxwell E., and Jian-Hua Zhu. 1995. "Capacity, Diversity and Volatility of the Public Agenda: Trends from 1954 to 1994." *Public Opinion Quarterly* 59:495–525.

McLeod, Jack M., and Steven H. Chaffee. 1973. "Interpersonal Approaches to Communication Research." *American Behavioral Scientist* 16:469–499.

Potter, W. James. 1994. "Cultivation Theory and Research: A Methodological Critique." *Journalism Monographs*, vol. 147.

Scott, William A. 1965. "Psychological and Social Correlates of International Images." In *International Behavior: A Social-Psychological Analysis*, edited by Herbert C. Kelman. 70–103. New York: Holt, Rinehart & Winston.

Searle, John. 1995. *The Construction of Social Reality*. New York: Free Press.

Wang, Soon-Yin, and Qing-Rui Liang. 1993. *Liangan Shandi Renmin Yinxiang Zhi Yanjiu* (Mutual images among residents in Taiwan, Hong Kong, and China). Unpublished report. Taipei, Taiwan: Department of Mass Communication, Tam Kamg University.

Zhu, Jian-Hua. 1995. "Information Availability, Source Credibility, and Audience Sophistication: Factors Conditioning the Effects of Communist Propaganda in China." *Political Communication* 12:347–348.

———. 1997. "Political Movements, Cultural Values, and Mass Media in China: Continuity and Change." *Journal of Communication* 47:157–164.

Zhu, Jian-Hua, J. Ronald Milavsky, and Rahul Biswas. 1994. "Do Televised Debates Affect Image Perception More Than Issue Knowledge? A Study of the First 1992 Presidential Debate." *Human Communication Research* 20:302–333.

Part III

Comparative Political
Culture Studies: Social
Strata and Regions

8

Diversification of Chinese Entrepreneurs and Cultural Pluralism in the Reform Era

Cheng Li

Cultural changes in China during the reform era are largely attributed to the dynamism of the Chinese economy. Rapid economic growth, the structural transition to a market economy, China's wide-range integration with the outside world, and the rise of consumerism all have a strong impact on Chinese culture. Economic transformation has deeply affected people's lives and influenced their values. A market economy enables Chinese consumers to encounter a world of differences, choices, and various ways of thinking.

Close interaction between economic reform and cultural changes has aroused much scholarly attention. Tu Weiming, a Harvard historian on Chinese culture, argues that: "If economic development serves as the 'engine of change,' the transforming culture may determine the 'direction of change.'"[1] Probably no other term more adequately characterizes the overarching trend in Chinese cultural change at the turn of the century than "pluralism." Cultural pluralism can be seen in all aspects of Chinese life today: in fashion, diet, music, dance, the arts, movies, advertisements, social interaction, public opinion, societal tolerance, and political attitudes. As Elizabeth Perry, a political scientist at Harvard, recently observed, "Renewed interest in local dialects, histories, customs and cuisines is emblematic of a growing geographical differentiation with potentially momentous implications" (Perry 1999, 1). Cultural pluralism is reflected in the resurgence of provincial/municipal identities (as described in Alan Liu's chapter in this book) and ideological fragmentation (as described in both Kalpana Misra's and Peter Moody, Jr.'s chapters). Political decentralization, economic liberalization, and consumerism have led to a renewed sense of locality, individuality, and diversity.[2]

This development is in sharp contrast with events during Mao's era, especially those during the Cultural Revolution, when cultural diversity was strictly suppressed and a "monochromatic socialist culture" was the only accepted norm in the country. For example, Arthur Miller, a distinguished American playwright, and his photographer wife traveled to China prior to the reform in 1978. They noted the Chinese all wore exactly the same clothing—the Sun Yat-sen jacket (Westerners call it the Mao jacket) in grey or dark blue.[3] Conformity in behavior, in clothes, and in color is the way that totalitarian regimes destroy individuality and plurality within society. The result of conformity is uniformity. As Vaclav Havel, the former dissident and present president of the Czech Republic, observed, "standardized life creates standardized citizens with no wills of their own."[4]

China's rush to a market economy in the reform era is also a rush toward individual liberty. Now people not only have the chance to choose what to wear, but can decide where to work and how to live. Work units (*danwei*), which served as an institutional means for the government to determine both the political and economic life of individuals, are losing importance because people are now able freely to choose *danwei* or start their own private "*danwei*"(Lu and Perry 1997). The rapid industralization and privatization have also led to probably the largest rural-urban migration in Chinese history. This immense labor mobility may challenge not only the agrarian nature of the Chinese culture, but also contribute to the formation of a civil society (*gongmin shehui*).[5]

During the 1990s, especially in its coastal cities and towns, China has witnessed the rapid growth of teahouses, coffee shops, Internet cafes, karaoke bars, disco clubs, private bookstores, fitness centers, private salons, and private theaters. If one accepts Habermas's argument that the pubs and coffeehouses of seventeenth-century London were the real force behind the formation of British civil society, the surge in places for informal association in reform China also signifies the emergence of

Chinese civil society. These cultural and social changes will probably have a more profound political impact than the Tiananmen protests and other political rallies because the latter have been what a foreign observer calls "movements of masses rather than of citizens" (Chamberlain 1994, 116).

Central to all these developments is the role of the emerging entrepreneurial class. The upward social mobility of entrepreneurs represents a historical change in Chinese society. Traditional Chinese society, which was dominated by the gentry-scholar class, tended to devalue merchants (now called entrepreneurs). According to the late John King Fairbank, capitalism failed to grow in China during the late 19th and early 20th century because the Chinese merchant class did not break away from its dependence upon officialdom. In other words, it failed to create an independent entrepreneurial power outside the "control of the gentry and their representatives in the bureaucracy" (Fairbank 1983, 51).

The anti-merchant tendency reached its climax during the first few decades of the People's Republic of China (PRC). Throughout the Mao era, the role of entrepreneurs was strictly restrained and marginalized. The four million private firms and stores that had existed in China prior to the 1949 Communist Revolution had all disappeared by the mid-1950s.[6] During the Cultural Revolution, even petty bourgeoisie such as the owners of "Mom & Pop stores" were considered to be "the tails of the bourgeoisie"; and thus were often "cut off."

The rapid rise of the entrepreneurial class, China's "nouveaux riches," during the reform era created a new "entrepreneurial culture" in Chinese society. Like elsewhere in the world, factors such as social acceptance of economic competition, the glorification of material success, the entrepreneurial work ethic, the existence of laissez-faire capitalism, the interaction between power and wealth, and consumer demand have led to the prevalence of commercialism in society, and have made the ascendance of Chinese entrepreneurs possible. The upward social mobility of entrepreneurs has profoundly changed the economic structure and social norms of the country.

Although Chinese entrepreneurs have only recently re-emerged as a distinctive social class, they are not a monolithic group, and there is not a homogenous entrepreneurial culture. On the contrary, Chinese entrepreneurs have different origins and different means through which they are engaged in entrepreneurial activities. This study examines the characteristics of Chinese entrepreneurs, including their social backgrounds, occupational identities, political attitudes, value orientation, and especially their internal diversification within the entrepreneurial class. This diversification will likely further contribute to the growing cultural pluralism in the country.

Chinese Entrepreneurs: Definition and Characteristics

The term *entrepreneur* is widely used, but rarely defined. In the West, entrepreneurs are seen as business people who assume the "risks of bringing together the means of production, including capital, labor, and materials, and receive reward in profit from the market value of the product."[7] According to Joseph Schumpeter, one of the most influential scholars in the study of entrepreneurs in the West, entrepreneurs are primarily innovators whose dynamic "creative response" to the economic environment makes them central to the promotion of material growth (Schumpeter 1975, 132). Entrepreneurs are characteristically engaged in risk-taking in a market economy.

In the Chinese context, an entrepreneur is defined as a manager and/ or owner of private property—a person who has managed to possess property either through capitalization of personal income or through the private operation of a collective, public, or joint-venture enterprise (Zhang 1995, 33). The rapid development of rural industries, rural-urban migration, urban private enterprises and joint ventures, a stock market and land lease, technological revolution, and e-commerce has contributed to the birth of this new social class in the PRC.

Since their re-emergence in the 1980s, Chinese entrepreneurs have already experienced some important changes. The composition of this new entrepreneurial class has been diverse and dynamic. There are three distinctive groups of entrepreneurs: (1) "self-made entrepreneurs"— peasants-turned-industrialists in rural areas and owners of small business firms in cities; (2) "bureaucratic entrepreneurs"—corrupt officials and their relatives who have made fortunes by various forms of power abuse in the process of marketization and privatization; and (3) "technical entrepreneurs"—computer and Internet specialists who have become wealthy as a result of rapid technological development and the impact of economic globalization. Each of these three groups has a distinctive occupational background and each reflects a particular socio-economic environment from which it has ascended.

"Self-Made" Entrepreneurs: The Emergence of China's Private Sector

The first group consists largely of people who became rich as the result of the rapid growth of the Township and Village Enterprises (TVEs) in rural China or who opened private restaurants, shops, and other enterprises in urban areas in the early 1980s. Most of these entrepreneurs were from the less privileged, less educated, and less respected part of Chinese society. They are often "self-made men and women" who do not have much formal schooling or other privileges. In fact, many of them were either jobless youths who had just returned to urban areas after being sent to the countryside during the Cultural Revolution or landless peasants who sought opportunities in rural enterprises (Chen 1994).

For example, Li Xiaohua, a self-made billionaire, was born in a poor worker's family in Beijing. When he was in junior high school, the Cultural Revolution took place. He was sent to Beidahuang (the Great Northern Wilderness) in the northeastern part of China, where he worked as a farmer. As a Beijing youth who returned to his native city, Li started his business career with a single 4000–yuan beverage machine in 1981, selling cold drinks at a summer resort. Now he has become one of the ten richest men in China, someone whose wealth compelled the Chinese government to name a newly found star in the galaxy in his honor. He recently donated over 100 million yuan (or about US$12 million) to educational and sports programs in the country (Xiao 1999, 270).

In Jiangsu Province's Huaxi Village, a showcase of Chinese entrepreneurship, about 85 percent of families own cars (the same model—Volkswagen Jettas; the same color—red). The wealth of the village has been largely attributed to the rapid development of TVEs (Li 1997, 243–262). A majority of peasant-turned-entrepreneurs did not receive much formal schooling. Wu Renbao, the head of the village, for example, did not have even an elementary school education. According to the census of 1990, out of over 1,200 adults in Huaxi Village, only one attended a four-year college and only three graduated from two-year colleges. Over 52 percent of the villagers received only an elementary school education or were illiterate (Lu 1992, 357).

The peasant origin and the lack of educational credentials of entrepreneurs in Huaxi Village are by no means unique. According to a comprehensive survey of 1,440 private entrepreneurs conducted by China's

Table 8.1

Previous Occupation and Father's Occupation of China's Private Entrepreneurs (percentage) (N=1,440)

Occupation	Entrepreneurs (previous occupation)		Family background (father's occupation)	
	Rural area	Urban area	Rural area	Urban area
Peasant	53.5	17.2	68.9	35.2
Cadre (officials)	17.0	22.1	7.9	19.4
Industrial worker	11.6	25.2	7.9	17.4
Technical personnel	4.1	12.1	3.5	9.4
Peddlers/small business people	6.1	9.2	—	—
Commercial staff	2.7	7.6	6.0	10.1
Soldier	0.7	1.2	—	—
Others	4.1	5.5	5.8	8.5
Total	100	100	100	100

Source: Lu Xueyi et al., "Woguo siyou qiye de jingying zhuangkuang yu shiyou qiyezhu de qunti tezhen" (Operational conditions of private enterprises in China and the group characteristics of private entrepreneurs), *Zhongguo shehui kexue* (Social sciences in China), no. 4 (1994): 70.

Table 8.2

Previous Occupation of Entrepreneurs in 19 Provinces, 1993 (N=2,991)

Previous occupation	Number	Percentage
Peasant	1,367	45.7
Self-employed (*getihu*)	492	16.4
Resigned	324	10.8
On-leave	308	10.3
"Job-waiting" youths	181	6.1
Retired	158	5.3
Unemployed	68	2.3
Others	93	3.1
Total	2,991	100.0

Source: Zhu Guanglei, *Dangdai Zhongguo shehui gejieceng fenxi* (Analysis of social strata in China) (Tianjin: Renmin chubanshe, 1998), 372.

Table 8.3

Formation of Self-Employed Industrial/Commercial Entrepreneurs in Shanghai

	1985 Survey		1993 Survey	
Origin	Number	%	Number	%
Urban residents	53,864	48.12	79,022	43.16
Unemployed	26,283	23.48	23,161	12.65
"Job-waiting" youths	8,765	7.83	11,555	6.31
Retired workers	7,858	7.02	17,980	9.82
Resigned workers	5,93	5.30	19,037	10.40
Released prisoners	5,026	4.49	7,289	3.98
Rural-urban migrants	58,073	51.88	104,074	56.84
Total	111,937	100.0	183,096	100.0

Source: Chen Baorong, "Jiushi niandai Shanghai geti siying jingji fazhan yanjiu" (Study of the development of the private economy in Shanghai in the 1990s), working paper, Shanghai Academy of Social Sciences, 1994, 14.

Academy of Social Science in 1992, 53.5 percent of entrepreneurs in rural areas were former peasants (see Table 8.1). A majority of entrepreneurs in both rural and urban areas come from peasant-family backgrounds. Of all entrepreneurs in rural areas, 68.9 percent list their father's occupation as that of peasant. This is corroborated by a 1993 study of 2,991 entrepreneurs conducted by the State Commission for Restructuring the Economy (see Table 8.2). About 45.7 percent of entrepreneurs were originally former peasants, and 16.4 percent were self-employed industrial and commercial entrepreneurs (*getihu*). In another nationwide survey of 1,450 private entrepreneurs, 34 percent of them were former peasants.[8]

Table 8.3 presents two large surveys of *getihu* in Shanghai conducted in 1985 and 1993; more than half of the entrepreneurs were migrants from rural areas. A significant number of them were previously unemployed, and some were released prisoners. They became entrepreneurs not because of convenience or choice, but because this was the only way for them to make a living. The change in their social status shows the rapidity and scale of the upward social mobility in Chinese society during the reform era.

Table 8.4 shows the educational background of entrepreneurs. As compared with the national work force, the educational level of the group

Table 8.4

Educational Background of China's Private Entrepreneurs, 1992
(N=1,440)

Educational level	Percentage
Illiterate	1.0
Elementary school	9.9
Middle School	36.1
Senior high school/technical school	35.9
Two-year college	11.7
College	4.7
Post-graduate	0.6
Total	100.0

Source: Lu Xueyi et al., "Woguo," p. 70.

was relatively high.[9] Yet, almost one half of entrepreneurs (47 percent) did not receive education beyond the level of junior middle school. Approximately 10 percent of entrepreneurs went only to elementary school. Some other case studies also reaffirm the findings in the 1992 survey presented above. Two studies of private entrepreneurs in Shanghai conducted in 1988 and 1993 show that a majority of them received only a junior high school education or less (82.6 percent and 44.4 percent respectively; see Chen 1994 and Zhu 1998, 376). In Hunan Province, those who attended college account for only 0.3 percent of the total number of entrepreneurs, while 44 percent of them received merely an elementary school education or are simply illiterate (Zhongguo siying jingji yanjiuhui 1994, 16).

There are a number of factors that contribute to the lack of educational credentials of China's entrepreneurs. The 1992 survey shows that the average age of entrepreneurs was 42.9 years (Project Group for Research on Private Entrepreneurs in Contemporary China 1995, 61). Another case study of heads and deputies of six towns and fifteen TVEs in a county of Jiangsu Province shows that over 80 percent of them are around 40 years old (Wang 1994, 22). These studies suggest that a majority of Chinese entrepreneurs grew up during the Cultural Revolution. They are the "lost generation" who did not receive formal education. More importantly, few of China's college graduates have been allocated to collective enterprises or other non-State firms, especially to those in the rural areas.

Table 8.5

Growth of Private Enterprises (1989–1999)

Year	Number	Employed	Registered assets (billion yuan)
1989	91,000	1,850,000	na
1990	98,000	1,700,000	na
1991	108,000	1,830,000	na
1992	140,000	2,310,000	45.2
1993	238,000	3,720,000	68.03
1994	420,000	6,350,000	138.9
1998	1,201,000	17,091,000	757.9
1999	1,480,000	19,000,000	na

Sources: Economic Information Daily, May 31, 1994, 4; *Renmin ribao*, January 11, 1995, 2; and *China News Analysis*, February 15, 1995, 2; National Bureau of Statistics, PRC, *China Statistical Yearbook* 1999 (Beijing: China Statistics Press, 1999); http://www.duoweinews.com, January 22, 2000; and "China to Release Official Data of Private Sector," *Renmin ribao* (English online), January 11, 2000.

The rise of both the entrepreneurial stratum and private enterprises is a recent phenomenon. In fact, private enterprises began to reappear only in the mid-1980s; at that time each private firm was allowed to hire no more than eight workers. Then, the legal status of these small private businesses was ambiguous. In 1988, the Seventh National People's Congress passed a constitutional amendment that authorized the legitimate status of the private economy.[10] The State-owned sector still dominates the Chinese economy, but private enterprises have made enormous strides in recent years. Table 8.5 shows that the number of private enterprises in the country increased from 91,000 in 1989 to 1,480,000 in 1999, a sixteen-fold increase in a decade. In 1999 alone, about 280,000 private enterprises were established. In addition, thousands of private stores have spread throughout the country. About 80 percent of the 140,000 shops in Beijing, for example, are either owned or run by private entrepreneurs.[11] Meanwhile, the number of *getihu* expanded to more than 31 million in urban areas all over the country at the end of 1999.[12]

Private enterprises have not only increased quickly in number, but have also expanded in size and in type. Private schools, private hospitals, private churches (which do not receive financial and institutional support from the State), private banks, private airline companies, and private satellites have all developed in China in recent years. The State Administration for Industry and Commerce, which oversees the eco-

Table 8.6

Output of State-Owned, Collective, and Privately Run Enterprises As a Percentage of China's Total GNP (%)

	1988	1991	2000 (estimated)
State-owned enterprises	76.0	51.3	27.2
Collective enterprises	23.5	36.9	47.7
Private-run enterprises	0.5	11.8	25.1

Source and Note: Figures from the State Information Center, Beijing, reported in *Zhongguo shibao* (China times), Taibei, July 16, 1992, 10. Quoted from Chang Chenpang, "The Resurgence of the Bourgeoisie in Mainland China," *Issues and Studies* 30, no. 5 (May 1994): 42.

nomic activities of private enterprises, reported that the registered capital of private enterprises increased from 68.03 billion yuan in 1993 to 757.9 billion yuan in 1998 (see Table 8.5). In Shanghai, the average registered capital of private enterprises increased from 275,200 yuan in 1994 to 696,000 yuan in 1999. According to an estimate made by China's State Information Center, the private sector is soon expected to constitute 25 percent of the output value of the country's economy (see Table 8.6).

The rapid development of the private sector has brought enormous wealth to Chinese "nouveaux riches." Private savings of Shanghai residents, for example, increased from 3 billion yuan in 1980 to 237 billion in 1998, a seventy-nine-fold growth in eighteen years. Nationwide private savings increased from 21 billion yuan in 1978 to 4,628 billion yuan in 1998, a 220–fold growth in twenty years (basically within a generation).[13] In addition, Chinese citizens now have total foreign currency savings of US$40 billion, 800 billion yuan in cash, 400 billion yuan in bonds, and 350 billion yuan in stock.[14] The growth of the private sector, however, is only one of the many causes for the accumulation of private savings. Billionaires such as Li Xiaohua are only the tip of the iceberg of China's self-made entrepreneurs, because a majority of them are merely small business people. They have continued to constitute an important part of China's entrepreneurial class, but other groups of entrepreneurs with different social backgrounds and different means for upward mobility have become prominent since the 1990s. The loss of state property, especially through official corruption, is another reason for the rapid accumulation of private savings in the country.

Bureaucratic Entrepreneurs: Official Corruption and "Capitalization of Power"

The second group of entrepreneurs is comprised mainly of corrupt officials and their children, who may be identified as "bureaucratic entrepreneurs" since many of them have gotten rich through political power and bureaucratic status. A majority in this group emerged after the late 1980s, especially after Deng's southern journey in 1992. The nature of the reform, as many Chinese public intellectuals observe, is the transfer and redistribution of property.[15] It is not surprising that those Communist leaders who controlled resources under the planned economy took advantage of their political power and converted the wealth of the state into their own wealth during the reform. This is what some Chinese scholars call the "marketization of power" (*quanli de shichanghua*) or the "capitalization of power" (*quanli ziben*).

The transfer or redistribution of state property, as Yang Fan, a Chinese economist, describes it, has been achieved in four distinctive ways during different phases of the reform. First, during the late 1970s and early 1980s, when China adopted the rural household contract responsibility system, about two billion yuan in collective property went to rural cadres. Second, during the early 1980s, when more autonomy was given to firms engaged in domestic and foreign trade, about 5,000 billion yuan in commercial capital was transferred from the state to private enterprises. Third, the two-track pricing system allowed corrupt officials, by issuing certificates, business permits, and quotas, to profit from the 70–billion-yuan difference between the two tracks. The Chinese have coined the term *guandao* (official turnaround) to refer to the process in which officials buy raw materials or commodities at a fixed price and then "turn around" and sell them on the private market, thus reaping huge profits. It is estimated that 35 billion yuan went into officials' pockets through *guandao*. And fourth, during the late 1980s and early 1990s, when China established a stock market, mutual funds, private real estate, and leasing of land to foreigners, about 10,000 billion yuan in state assets was lost.[16]

The figures provided by Yang Fan are only calculated estimates. Nevertheless, the loss of state assets during the reform has been enormous. According to official data, in the year 1999 alone, about 15,000 government officials and managers of state-owned enterprises were sentenced for corruption charges. Among them, over 2,100 were officials at the county level or above. About 790 cases involved embezzlement or bribery of over one million yuan.[17] The major corruption cases reported, such as the embezzlement by Chen Xitong (the Party boss of Beijing), and the smuggling in Xiamen in which about 160 officials were entangled in a US$10 billion scandal, not only show the involvement of high ranking officials, but also the astronomical amount of money involved.[18] As a result of the capitalization of power, wealth is controlled by only a small number of people, mainly corrupt officials. Not much is left in the state coffers. Corruption has become such a serious problem that China's top leaders have depicted corruption as a "cancer within" and a "life and death" issue for the Chinese Communist Party and the state.

A main source of corruption since the late 1980s has involved children of high-ranking officials ("princelings," or *taizidang* in Chinese). These princelings wanted to seize both the opportunity available during the early stage of market reform in which rules and regulations were not well implemented, and the opportunity to advance their bureaucratic careers while their veteran parents were still powerful. Deng's three sons-in-law, for example, held the "three most lucrative businesses in the country" in the mid-1990s: One was responsible for China's weaponry business, the second was in charge of China's gold trade in the world market, and the third handled matters concerning China's high technology (He and Gao 1999, 515).

According to a survey of the children of more than 1,700 PRC central and provincial leaders conducted in the early 1990s, about 3,100 hold official positions above the government bureau or military division level. Another 900 are the principal leaders of large- and middle-sized state enterprises (He and Gao 1992, 51). During the 1980s, a large number of *taizidang* seized the medium-level leadership posts (both civilian and military) in China as part of the compensation for the retirement of their parents. Many were involved in large business corporations newly established by the state.

Some princelings later quit their official posts and engaged in private business. But more often, many high-ranking official families have created an "internal division of labor" for *taizidang* within the family—one member pursues a political or military career while others serve as CEOs or general managers of large corporate firms, including joint ventures and private enterprises (see Table 8.7). This has become a common practice after Bo Yibo, a Long March veteran who was in charge of the personnel affairs of the Fourteenth Party Congress, proposed that each senior-ranking revolutionary veteran (e.g. Politburo members, state leaders, and PLA marshals) could have one child promoted to a high-ranking official post (vice provincial governor, vice minister level or above; see Xiao 1998, 337–339).

The CCP Organization Department may have set a quota for the "family representation of *taizidang*" in political and military leadership, but high-ranking official families are not limited as to the number of *taizidang* who participate in corporate firms. Actually, in the late 1980s, three children of Bo Yibo served as governmental officials. Following Bo Yibo's "one high-ranking official family, one official seat for its offspring" proposal, two of Bo's sons, Bo Xiyong (vice president of China's Association of the Auto Industry) and Bo Xicheng (director of the Tourism Bureau of the Beijing municipal government) quit their government posts and began their business careers. Only Bo Xilai (vice mayor of Dalian) has become the sole candidate for political power from the Bo family.

Probably the best example in terms of *taizidang*'s active involvement in business is the Kanghua Development Corporation, which was founded by Deng Pufang, Deng Xiaoping's son, in 1984. Many members of *taizidang* joined the Kanghua, which was supposed to be a business firm run by and for China's disabled people. During its peak, the Kanghua was believed to have as many as over 200 members of *taizidang* as its managers and representatives.[19] Various provincial branches of the Kanghua were often headed by the princelings of provincial top leaders. The high profile of the Kanghua could also be seen in the composition of its management team. In 1987, Tang Ke (former Minister of Petroleum Industry), Gao Yangwen (former Minister of Coal Industry), and Han Boping (former executive vice mayor of Beijing) served on the board of directors of the Kanghua. The appointments of these high profile cadres to the management team suggest the powerful political connections of this particular corporation. Deng Pufang also recruited Yu Zhengsheng (whose brother was Deng Pufang's elementary school classmate) to administer daily affairs of both the Kanghua and the China Welfare Fund for Handicapped. Yu is now Minister of Construction and a member of the Central Committee of the CCP. During the 1980s, when China accelerated its market reform by adopting some new economic incentives such as the establishment of joint ventures, a stock market, and land lease to foreigners, many members of *taizidang* rushed to the business sector in order to make huge personal gains (He 1998, 120–

Table 8.7

The "Internal Division of Labor" among Children of High-Ranking Cadres

Name	Current position	Family background
Party and government		
Deng Pufang	CC alternate, president, Chinese Federation for the Disabled	Father: Deng Xiaoping, fmr. secretary general CCP
Deng Nan	Vice minister, Science and Technology	Father: Deng Xiaoping (see above)
Chen Yuan	President, State Development Bank	Father: Chen Yun, fmr Politburo standing member
Bo Xilai	Mayor of Dalian	Father: Bo Yibo, fmr. Politburo member
Fu Rui	Vice president, China National Nuclear Corporation	Father: Peng Zhen, fmr. chair of NPC
Li Xiaolin	Vice president, China Friendship Association	Father: Li Xiannian, fmr. president of the PRC
Chen Haosu	Vice president, China Friendship Association	Father: Chen Yi, marshal, fmr. Politburo member
Military		
He Pengfei	Vice admiral, vice commander, Navy	Father: He Long, marshal, fmr. Politburo member
Dong Liangju	Lt. general, director, General Office Central Military Commission	Father: Dong Biwu, fmr. vice president of PRC
Ye Xuanning	Lt. general, director, the Liaison Department of the PLA General Political Department	Father: Ye Jianying, fmr. PLA marshal
He Ping	Major general, director, Armament Dept. Hydropower Control Department, PLA	Father-in-law: Deng Xiaoping, (see above)
Corporate		
Wang Jun	China International Trust & Investment Co.	Father: Wang Zhen, fmr. vice president of PRC
Deng Zhifang	CEO, Shifang Group, Ltd.	Father: Deng Xiaoping, (see above)
Chen Weili	CEO, China Venturetech Investment Corp.	Father: Chen Yun, (see above)
Bo Xicheng	Chair, board of directors, Beijing Liuhe Hotel	Father: Bo Yibo, (see above)
Fu Yan	Chair, board of directors, Beijing Fuli Ltd.	Father: Peng Zhen, (see above)
Wang Xiaochao	General manager, the Poly Group, Ltd.	Father-in-law: Yang Shangkun, fmr. PRC president

Source: Liao Gailong and Fan Yuan, comp., *Zhongguo renming da cidian xiandai dangzhengjun lingdaorenwujuan* (Who's who in China, volume on current party, government, and military leaders), 1994 edition. Beijing: Foreign Languages Press, 1994; Shen Xueming, ed., *Zhonggong di shiwujie zhongyang weiyuanhui minglu.* Beijing: Zhongyang wenxian chubanshe, 1999; He Pin and Gao Xin, *Zhonggong "Taizidang"* (China's Communist "princelings") (newly revised edition) Taibei: Shibao chuban gongsi, 1999; He Pin and Gao Xin, *Zhonggong "Taizidang"* (China's Communist "princelings") Taibei: Shibao chuban gongsi, 1992; and *China Directory* 1999. Tokyo: Radiopress Inc., 1999. The data were tabulated by the author.

124). It was certainly not a surprise that in 1988 the State Council ultimately had to issue an order to dismantle the Kanghua Development Corporation because of its rampant corruption and other illegal business activities.

The Kanghua was, of course, not the only business firm through which *taizi* made huge fortunes and/or advanced their political careers. A large corporation in the country, the China International Trust and Investment Corporation (CITIC), has also been headed by *taizidang*. For example, Wang Jun, son of Wang Zhen, controls CITIC while his two brothers run two other large state-backed business firms. With the political power of their families and the economic resources that they now control, informal political networks of princelings, such as the ones based in the Wang family, the Bo family, and the Deng family, have become a new formidable force of bureaucratic capitalists in the country.[20] Yet, these bureaucratic entrepreneurs have increasingly been faced with new restraints. They have become less effective because there are now more regulations and rules to restrain illegal activities, and because there is not much left in the State coffers.

Technical Entrepreneurs: The Impact of the Telecommunications Revolution

The third group of entrepreneurs emerged in the late 1990s, largely as a result of the Internet and the rapid development of the computer industry. New Chinese terms, *zibenjia* or *zhishi ziben jia* (knowledge capitalist), have been created to refer to these technical entrepreneurs.[21] They have become rich mainly because of their technological innovations in the era of the telecommunications revolution. By the end of 1999, there were about nine million Internet accounts in China, in contrast to 17 million in Japan and 35 million in the United States. However, it is estimated that the number of China's Internet accounts will surpass that of the United States in 2005.[22] Similarly, China now has 50 million mobile phones, but the number will increase to 200 million within ten years.[23]

In 1999, the number of technology-intensive private enterprises increased rapidly in China. In Shanghai, for example, over 5,800 private enterprises specialized in information technology and scientific consultant business. There were 1,245 private firms that specialized in computers in 1999, an increase of 139 percent over those in 1998.[24] Similarly, in Guangdong Province, the number of technology-intensive private firms that have over ten million yuan in output increased from 25 in 1993 to 106 in 1995, and the number of these firms whose output surpassed 100 million yuan increased from seven in 1993 to 26 in 1995 (Chen 1997, 4).

Just as Bill Gates' Microsoft fostered tens of thousands of millionaires, the telecommunications revolution has also brought fortunes to those Chinese who are engaged in technology-intensive industries. The relationship between technical entrepreneurs and the Chinese government, however, is more cooperative than the relationship between Microsoft and the American government right now. For example, the assets of the Legend Company (*Lianxiang*), which is 61 percent owned by the state and the rest by private investors, increased in value from 200,000 yuan in 1988 to two billion yuan in 1998 (Shi 1999, 6). In the third quarter of 1999, Legend's market share in China surged from 17.3 percent to 23 percent. Legend's revenue was up 46 percent in fiscal 1999, and its net profit jumped 34 percent.[25] Meanwhile, Legend's stock on the Hong Kong Stock Exchange soared in 1999. Ma Xuezhen, the woman vice president of Legend, personally owns shares worth 158 million Hong Kong dollars.[26] As a result of this meteoric prosperity, several hundred employees of Legend became millionaires overnight. Their average age is below 30, and most of them hold college and postgraduate degrees.[27] About 60 percent of middle- and high-level managers in the company are under 35 years old (Xiao 1999, 172).

Legend's case is not unique. The Fangzheng Company, which is affiliated with Beijing University, increased its assets from 400,000 yuan in 1984 to three billion yuan in 1999, an approximate 7,000–fold growth in fifteen years.[28] Wang Xuan, professor-turned-entrepreneur and the CEO of the Fangzheng Company, claims that his company will "foster" 100 young millionaires in the year 2000 alone.[29] The Chinese language software that the Fangzheng Company invented now has a market share of 80 percent. At present, Fangzheng is determined to dominate the new information technology system in China's television networks.[30]

Both the Legend and Fangzheng companies are located in Beijing's Zhongguancun Science and Technology Park (hereafter Zhongguancun), the so-called "silicon valley of China." Zhongguancun is the district in which 68 colleges and 213 research institutions are located, including Beijing University, Qinghua University, and China's Academy of Sciences. Approximately 360,000 college graduates (most of these are engineers) work in this district.[31] Since the establishment in 1981 of its first technology-intensive company, the Huaxia Silicon Valley Company,

Zhongguancun has existed almost for two decades. Zhongguancun now has over 5,000 registered enterprises. Since the late 1990s, Zhongguancun has also become known for its wealth. The district had an annual growth rate of 30 percent throughout the 1990s.[32] In 1999, residents in this area paid 590 million yuan in income tax, an amount much higher than in any other district in Beijing.[33] One individual technical entrepreneur alone paid four million yuan in income tax.[34] Zhongguancun also has more private cars than any other district in the city.

Workers in Zhongguancun have not only included graduates and professors of nearby schools such as Beijing and Qinghua universities, but also many Chinese who recently received Ph.Ds or post-doctoral training in the United States and other advanced industrial countries.[35] In 1998, Bill Gates' Microsoft invested 80 million US dollars in the Microsoft China Research Institute in Zhongguancun. Bai Chunli, vice president of China's Academy of Sciences, recently predicted that, in the coming five to ten years, many top-notch Chinese scholars and students who have studied or worked abroad will return to China, especially to places like Zhongguancun.[36] Bai's prediction is based on several factors: the improved political and economic conditions in the country, the government's aggressive program to recruit talented people, and China-bashing in the United States, especially the recent espionage charge. In the 1998–99 academic year, about 51,000 students from China were enrolled in colleges in the United States, accounting for 10 percent of the total number of foreign students, the largest representation from any single country. A majority of them studied engineering, computer science, and business administration.[37]

In Guangdong, the Giant Company, a technology-intensive private firm, has over 1,000 employees, 90 percent of whom are college graduates (Chen 1997, 1). According to a 1996 study of 350 intellectuals who worked in private enterprises in Guangdoing Province, almost half of them were under 30 years of age (see Table 8.8). Young recent college graduates constitute the larger portion of technical entrepreneurs. About 63 percent are migrants to Guangdong from other regions.[38] According to a sample study conducted in Wuhan in 1997, 94 percent of technical entrepreneurs were less than 45 years old. Among them, 52 percent were between 26 and 35 years old, and one-third were just under 25 (Zhou 1997, 33).

In the beginning of 2000, five undergraduate students at Qinghua University established an Internet service company. These students were

Table 8.8

A Survey of Intellectuals in Private Enterprises in Guangdong Province
(1996) (N=350)

	Percentage
Age group	
30 and below	48.8
31–45	34.6
46–60	12.6
60 and above	4.0
Total	100.0
Educational attainment	
Technical school	10.4
2-year college	40.0
4-year college	44.6
Post-graduate	5.0
Total	100.0
Origins	
From Guangdong	36.6
From other regions	63.1
Unknown	0.3
Total	100.0

Source: Chen Shengdong, "Guanyu Guangdong siying qiye zhishi fenzi qingkuang de diaocha" (A survey of intellectuals who work in private firms in Guangdong), *Guangdong shehui kexue* (Social sciences in Guangdong), no. 1 (1997): 1.

not only granted two-year leaves of absence from the university, but also received a risk fund worth six million yuan from the government.[39] Similarly, six students at China's University of Science and Technology received stocks worth 6,688,500 yuan in light of their innovations in the field of computer voice recognition.[40] A 26–year-old Ph.D student in Shanghai recently received a risk fund worth 20 million yuan for his research on a Chinese language on-line search program.[41] Several recent studies show that "a young age, an advanced education, and the willingness to take risks" are three main characteristics of this new group of entrepreneurs.[42]

In 1999, the Chinese Academy of Social Sciences conducted a survey of occupational prestige among 2,599 people above 16 years of age who live in China's 63 cities. The age group between 16 and 30 ranked "computer engineer" as the first choice, although the whole study pool ranked this occupation fourth, after "mayor," "government minister," and "college professor."[43] The differentiation among age groups regarding occupational prestige suggests the new trend and the rapid social mobility in the country. This also echoes the fact that about 75 percent of Internet users in China are between 18 and 30 years old.[44] The rapid development of the Internet and telecommunications has brought about this young and well-educated entrepreneur group, contributing to both the expansion and the diversity of the Chinese entrepreneurial class.

Furthermore, the rise of technical entrepreneurs has significantly changed the income structure in reform China. During the first decade of the reform, China's "knowledge elites" or intellectuals—those who have graduated from college—seemed to be particularly resentful of the private entrepreneurs with peasant origins and poor educational backgrounds. They often used the term "misplacing the body above the brain" (*naoti daogua*) to express their dissatisfaction. For them, it was "abnormal" and unfair that these "country bumpkins" should have become rich. From their viewpoint, it would be "normal" and "balanced" if those who work with their brains had incomes several times more than those who work with their hands (Hu 1993, 8). Many academics, teachers, and engineers have to supplement their low income through moonlighting. In the late 1980s and early 1990s, applications for graduate schools declined because there was no correlation between personal income and educational attainment.

This situation has changed in recent years. For example, in January 2000, about 392,000 people took the national exam for post-graduate studies. In Hebei Province, there were 13,000 applicants for Masters programs in 2000, an increase of 25 percent compared to 1999.[45] College professors, researchers, and engineers now receive a much higher salary than they did just a few years ago. The Ministry of Education, for example, recently granted 1.8 billion yuan each to Beijing University and Qinghua University. One-third of the funding will be used to increase faculty salaries.[46] In these two schools, the highest ranking professors can receive 50,000 yuan as an annual allowance.[47] Similarly, Shanghai's Fudan University and Jiaotong University both received about 1.2 billion yuan. According to a proposal made by the Ministry of Education, by 2005 the income of college faculty members will be higher than most other professions receiving state salaries.[48]

In November 1999, the Shanghai municipal government conducted a survey of income distribution of 10,000 firms. The study showed that the higher level of education one attended, the higher the income one receives (see Table 8.9). In general, these technical entrepreneurs own many times more personal possessions than other workers in the same

Table 8.9

**A Survey of Monthly Income of Technical Personnel in 10,000
Enterprises in Shanghai, 1999** (yuan)

	Average	Highest	Lowest
Education Level			
Ph.D.	3,000	8,000	2,000
Masters Degree	2,500	7,000	1,200
4-Year College	1,900	4,000	800
2-Year College	1,400	3,000	800
Technical School	1,100	2,000	600
Titles/positions			
Chief engineer	6,000	17,000	2,900
Software engineer	4,100	9,500	1,500
Internet manager	3,200	7,300	1,000
Homepage designer	2,800	5,500	1,000
Marketing chief	5,500	12,000	1,800
Project manager	3,500	8,000	1,500
Sales manager	3,800	8,000	1,800
Ownership			
(Executive managers)			
Foreign-owned enterprise	7,000	na	na
Joint venture	6,500	na	na
Private firm	3,300	na	na

Source and notes: Zhongguo qingnian bao (China youth news), January 4, 2000, 1.
All the incomes are income after tax. They include salary and bonuses but not other benefits and subsidies.

city. It was reported that in Shanghai, a large number of young college graduates with skills and knowledge in information technology have recently become millionaires.[49]

The three major groups of entrepreneurs discussed above are all very active in today's China. They will likely co-exist and share the country's wealth for many years to come, although the weight of each group may vary from time to time. The demographic characteristics, including age distribution, of these three groups may change as China's industrialization and urbanization continues. A small number of entrepreneurs may have already crossed the boundaries of these three distinct groups. An increasing number of bureaucratic entrepreneurs, especially princelings, have recently been involved in telecommunications, especially in Internet-related businesses. For example, in 1998 Jiang Xiaoming (Simon Jiang), son of Qiao Shi, former chair of the National People's Congress, moved from New York, where he managed a United Nations pension fund, to Shenzhen. Jiang has established an Internet investment firm called Cyber City Holdings, and he alone now owns shares worth millions of US dollars.[50] Another example is Ren Kelei, the CEO of the Jiakang Company, the largest technology-intensive firm in Shenzhen. His father, Ren Zhongyi, used to serve as Party secretary of Guangdong Province.

Nevertheless, the majority of both self-made entrepreneurs and technical entrepreneurs are not officials or children of officials by origin. Corrupt officials and their relatives certainly constitute a significant part of China's nouveaux riches. But reform has also opened the door for poor, less-educated, and underprivileged people to pursue upward social mobility. Some of its members might have been rural officers before, but many did not have official backgrounds or political connections. More recently, the technological revolution and privatization have given more opportunities to people with advanced education and skills, especially those trained in science and technology, to reap more financial rewards.

Toward Cultural and Ideological Pluralism

The occupational and demographic differences among these three groups of entrepreneurs have already added to the diversity of cultural values and political ideologies in Chinese society. To a certain extent, each group of entrepreneurs holds a distinctive worldview. Self-made entrepreneurs, for example, usually adhere to a strong sense of entrepreneurship, which is fundamentally incompatible with Confucian meritocracy and technocrats' credentialism. The latter has served as an ideological justification for technocratic rule in reform China (Li 1999, 86–111). Although both self-made entrepreneurs and technical entrepreneurs may have used political connections and *guanxi*, they are resentful of unfair business competition they have experienced as a result of bureaucratic entrepreneurs' "capitalization of power."

More importantly, the rapid rise of self-made entrepreneurs and technical entrepreneurs in China during the reform signifies a historical change in Chinese society. According to the late Joseph Needham, the great British scholar who wrote a multivolume history of Chinese technology, a primary reason for the decline of China in the middle of the last millennium was that the country "lost its edge by suppressing entrepreneurs whose power posed a threat to the Emperor."[51] Echoing this view, Paul Bracken, a professor of management at Yale, recently argued that the conditions in the Middle Kingdom that Needham described are now ending. As a result of this, Bracken believes that Chinese capitalism may be especially dynamic.[52]

In addition, market reform, especially the rapid development of TVEs during the 1980s, created an income gap between peasants-turned-entrepreneurs and professionals. But self-made entrepreneurs have little sympathy for the intellectuals' resentment. "If they're so smart, why ain't they rich?" was a common response of entrepreneurs to the criticism of professionals in the 1980s. Self-made entrepreneurs claim that the market economy is primarily a "capable people's economy (*nengren jingji*)."[53] The principle of entrepreneurship is the belief that those who are capable will be successful in a competitive market. In a market economy there is no law that says school teachers should earn more than street vendors.

Meanwhile, bureaucratic entrepreneurs have also tried to justify their prominence and wealth, which are often derived from corruption and other illegal activities. They argue that the nature of the reform is the transfer and redistribution of property. Prior to the reform, there were no market forces in China, only political power. For them, there were two ways to transform the planned economy: one was the collapse of power (often through revolutionary means), and the other was a gradual process of creating a market through use of power. China took the latter path. It is not surprising that the Communist leaders who controlled resources under the planned economy took advantage of their political power and converted the wealth of the state into their own wealth during the reform. Bureaucratic entrepreneurs argue that this process of "marketization of power" is not unique to China's reform. A similar phenomenon occurred during the Industrial Revolution in Great Britain and the Meiji Restoration in Japan. During the economic transition of the former Soviet Union, some Communist officials gave up their political and legal privileges, but they became new entrepreneurs and legislators. In all these cases, the transformation of the economic structure was accompanied by a continuation of the elite strata. In their view, corruption in a transitional economy is inevitable. To a certain extent, corruption can be seen as the "lubricating oil of the economy."[54]

For technical entrepreneurs, their growing prominence in today's China parallels the heated discussion about the so-called "knowledge economy" (*zhishi jingji*). The term *zhishi jingji* did not exist in the Chinese language before 1998 (Wu 1998, iii). But since 1998, it has become one of the most frequently used catch phrases in the Chinese media. A Chinese news magazine listed it as one of the top ten most popular terms in China in the final years of the 1990s.[55] Several dozen books on the knowledge economy have been published in the past two years.[56]

Yang Fujia, a nuclear physicist and president of Fudan University in Shanghai, identifies the "knowledge economy" as the third form of economy after "labor economy" (*laoli jingji*) and "natural resource economy" (*ziran ziyuan jingji*) (Yang Fujia 1998, 58–59). A labor economy, which is also called an agricultural economy, is based on land and labor. A natural resource economy, also called an industrial economy, depends on natural resources from which people develop industries. In contrast, a knowledge economy relies on intellect and information. It is therefore also called an intellect economy or an information economy. According to Yang, as a result of rapid technological development, the world is moving toward "an era in which knowledge can be used as capital for promoting economic growth."[57] According to some technical entrepreneurs, there is a fundamental difference between an industry economy and a knowledge economy: in the former, knowledge serves only as an additional input, which may increase productivity, while in the latter, knowledge becomes an asset and a product (Zhao 1998, 8). In today's world, the linkage between knowledge (especially innovative knowledge in telecommunications) and wealth is closer than ever before.

In summary, these three groups have contributed to the diversity within the Chinese entrepreneurial class, to the dynamics of social mobility, and to the diffusion of political power, economic wealth, and social prestige. Although these three entrepreneurial groups have some shared interests, their worldviews are by no means identical. If economic and technological development serves as the "engine of change" in Chinese society, the transforming cultural norms and ideological values, especially their pluralistic nature, may determine the "direction of change." This suggests that a truly pluralistic socio-political system is looming large in China as a new century begins.

Notes

1. Yang (1994, 259). Tu Weiming's original quote is from *Zhongwai wenhua bijiao yanjiu* (Comparative studies of Chinese and foreign cultures) (Beijing: Sanlian chubanshe, 1989), 75.
2. For a similar argument, see *Far Eastern Economic Review*, November 26, 1998, 50; and Dirlik and Zhang, 1997, 8.

3. Arthur Miller, "In China," *The Atlantic Monthly*, March 1979, 90.

4. Vaclav Havel, "The Post-Communist Nightmare," *The New York Review of Books*, May 27, 1993, 8.

5. Dorothy Solinger, for instance, argues that migrant laborers constitute a form of civil society because this social group "stands apart and against the state." See Solinger (1993, 97–98) and Solinger (1999).

6. *China News Analysis*, no. 1501, January 1, 1994, 2.

7. *Encyclopedia Americana* (International edition) (Danbury, Connecticut: Grolier Inc. 1992), 10: 477.

8. Zhongguo siying jingji yanjiuhui (1994, 75).

9. According to China's 1982 census, only 0.87 percent of the total labor force had a college education; 10.54 percent, a senior high school education; and 26 percent, a junior middle school education; while 34.38 percent had only a primary school education and 28.2 percent were illiterates or semi-illiterates. See China Financial & Economic Publishing House, *New China's Population* (New York: Macmillan Publishing Company, 1988), 173.

10. *China Daily*, November 11, 1994, 4.

11. *China Daily*, July 13, 1994, 4.

12. According to a statistical study conducted by China's Association of Industry and Commerce in November 1999, there were 31,749,000 registered *getihu*, employing 62,257,900 workers. See *Shijie ribao*, February 9, 2000, A9.

13. *Renmin ribao*, September 24, 1998, 1.

14. *Renmin ribao*, September 24, 1998, 1.

15. For more discussion of informal political networks and corruption, see He 1998 and Li (2000, 123–157).

16. The data in this discussion are from Yang Fan (1998) and He (1997).

17. *Beijing qingnian bao* (Beijing youth news), February 12, 2000, 1.

18. *Jingji ribao* (Economics daily) (Hong Kong), January 25, 2000, 1.

19. For a detailed discussion of *taizi* at Kanghua, see He and Gao (1999, 520–549).

20. For a further discussion of networks of *taizidang*, see Li (2001).

21. Zhao (1998) and *Shijie ribao* (Weekly edition), December 26, 1999, 2.

22. "Zhongguo wuniannei jiancheng quanqiu zuida wangluo shichang" (China will become the largest Internet market in five years), February 13, 2000, http://www.chinesenewsnet.com.

23. "Zhongguo wuniannei jiancheng quanqiu zuida wangluo shichang." See n. 22.

24. *Jiefang ribao*, February 1, 2000, 1.

25. Julie Schmit, "PC Legend in the making," *USA Today*, December 6, 1999, 1.

26. *Beijing wanbao* (Beijing evening news), February 25, 2000, 1.

27. *Beijing qingnian bao*, December 1, 1999, 1.

28. *Wenhui ribao*, December 12, 1999, 1.

29. *Renmin ribao*, January 19, 2000, 1.

30. *Wenhui ribao*, December 12, 1999, 1.

31. *Shijie ribao* (Weekly edition), January 2, 2000, 1.

32. "Beijing Zhongguancun kejiyuanqu huo jinrong zhichi" (Zhongguancun Science and Technology Park receives support from the financial institutions), February 20, 2000, http://www.chinesenewsnet.com.

33. "Zhongguancun kejiyuanqu naoti daogua xianxiang jianshao" (The decline of the phenomenon of "misplacing the body above the brain" in Zhongguancun Science and Technology Park), February 19, 2000, http://www.chinesenewsnet.com.

34. "Zhongguancun dagong huangdi nianshui sibaiwan" (The largest taxpayer in Zhongguancun paid 4 million yuan tax), February 20, 2000, http://www.chinesenewsnet.com.

35. *Wenhui ribao*, December 12, 1999, 1.

36. *Renmin ribao* (Overseas edition), November 23, 1999, 1.

37. "Liuxue Meiguo Zhongguo pai diyi" (China is ranked first in foreign students in the United States), December 6, 1999, http://www.chinesenewsnet.com.

38. In recent years, many cities have adopted measures to attract technical experts to their cities. The municipal government of Shanghai, for example, has adopted a policy that grants permanent residence permits to those college graduates from other regions who are under 35 and want to be employed in Shanghai. In addition, nationwide, more than half of the private firms established by those students who have recently returned from overseas have been established in Shanghai. See *Shijie ribao*, February 5, 2000, A10.

39. *Renmin ribao* (Overseas edition), January 18, 2000, 1.

40. *Guangming ribao*, November 12, 1999, 1.

41. *Shijie ribao*, December 20, 1999, A11.

42. *Shijie ribao*, December 20, 1999, A11.

43. *Shijie ribao*, December 23, 1999, A7.

44. *Shijie ribao*, January 19, 2000, A9.

45. *Renmin ribao*, January 28, 2000, 1.

46. *Renmin ribao*, January 19, 2000, 1.

47. *Shijie ribao* (weekly edition), January 23, 2000, 1.

48. *Shijie ribao*, November 25, 1999, A9.

49. "Shanghai chuxian pingjie keji shili faming zhifu yizhu" (The emergence of the newly rich through technical expertise in Shanghai), December 20, 1999, http://www.chinesenewsnet.com.

50. Lin Sen, "Zhongguo taizidang kaishi wangshang taojin" (Chinese princelings' "Gold Rush" on the Internet), January 29, 2000, http://www.chinesenewsnet.com.

51. Quoted from Paul Bracken, "Will China be Number 1?" *Time*, May 22, 2000,

55. For a detailed discussion of Joseph Needham's argument, see Needham (1954).

52. For a detailed discussion of Paul Bracken's argument, see Bracken (1999).

53. *Lilun dongtai* (Theoretical news), June 25, 1993, 4.

54. For a critique of this view, see Yang Fan (1998).

55. The other terms included *Y2K* and *sexual harassment* (in the case of Bill Clinton). *Kua shiji* (Cross-century), no. 3 (March 1999): 19.

56. *Kua shiji*, no. 3 (March 1999): 19. For example, Wu (1998), Zhao (1998), and Jiang and Tan (1998).

57. *Kua shiji*, no. 3 (March 1999): 19.

Bibliography

Bracken, Paul (1999) *Fire in the East : The Rise of Asian Military Power and the Second Nuclear Age.* New York: Harper Collins.

Chamberlain, Heath B. (1994) "Coming to Terms with Civil Society." *Australian Journal of Chinese Affairs,* no. 31 (January):113–117.

Chen Baorong (1994) "Jiushi niandai Shanghai geti siying jingji fazhan yanjiu" (Study of the development of the private economy in Shanghai during the 1990s), working paper, Shanghai Academy of Social Sciences.

Chen Shengdong (1997) "Guanyu Guangdong siying qiye zhishi fenzi qingkuang de diaocha" (A survey of intellectuals who work in private firms in Guangdong). *Guangdong shehui kexue* (Social sciences in Guangdong), no. 1.

China Financial & Economic Publishing House (1988) *New China's Population.* New York: Macmillan.

Dirlik, Arif, and Zhang Xudong (1997) "Postmodernism and China." *Boundary 2,* no. 24 (fall): 1–18.

Fairbank, John King (1983) *The United States and China.* 4th edition. Cambridge, MA: Harvard University Press.

He Pin, and Gao Xin (1999). *Zhonggong "Taizidang"* (China's Communist "princelings"). Newly revised edition. Taibei: Shibao chuban gongsi.

——— (1992) "Taizidang jieban de shishi yu kenengxing" (The succession of the "party of princes": reality and possibility). *Dangdai* (Contemporary monthly), April.

He Qinglian (1997). "Zhongguo dangdai de ziben yuanshi jilei" (Private capital accumulation in contemporary China). *Zhongguo yu shijie,* December.

——— (1998) *Xiandaihua de xianjing: Dangdai Zhongguo de jingji shehui wenti* (The pitfall of modernization: Economic and social problems of contemporary China). Beijing: Jinri Zhongguo chubanshe.

Hu Xianzhong (1993) "Naoti daogua xintan" (Further exploration of the problem of inequitable payments for intellectuals and workers). *Jilin daxue xuebao* (Jilin University journal), no. 5 (1993).

Jiang Yuncai, and Tan Jianfeng (1998) *Shiji tiaozhan: Zhongguo fuxing qidai zhishi jingji* (The challenge of the century: China's rejuvenation calls for a knowledge economy). Beijing: Lantian chubanshe.

Li Cheng (1997) *Rediscovering China: Dynamics and Dilemmas of Reform.* Lanham, Maryland: Rowman & Littlefield Publishers.

———. (1999) "'Credentialism' Versus 'Entrepreneurism': The Interplay and Tensions between Technocrats and Entrepreneurs in the Reform Era." In *Chinese Business Network: State, Economy and Culture,* edited by Chan Kwok Bun. New York: Prentice Hall, pp. 86–111.

———. (2000) "Promises and Pitfalls of Reform: New Thinking in Post-Deng China." In *China Briefing,* edited by Tyrene White. Armonk, NY: M.E. Sharpe, pp. 123–157.

——— (2001) *China's Leaders: The New Generation.* Lanham, Maryland: Rowman & Littlefield Publishers.

Lu Xiaobo, and Elizabeth J. Perry, eds. (1997) *Danwei: The Changing Chinese Workplace in Historical and Comparative Perspectives.* Armonk: NY: M.E. Sharpe.

Lu Xieyi, ed. (1992) *Gaige zhong de nongcun yu nongmin* (Countryside and peasants in the age of reform). Beijing: Central Party School Press.

Needham, Joseph (1954) *Science and Civilization in China.* Vol. 1. Oxford: Cambridge University Press.

Perry, Elizabeth J. (1999) "Partners at Fifty: American China Studies and the PRC." Unpublished paper prepared for conference titled "Trends in China Watching." George Washington University, October 8–9.

Project Group for Research on Private Entrepreneurs in Contemporary China (1995) "The Group Characteristics of the Owners of Private Businesses in China." *Social Sciences in China* 16, no. 2: 61–69.

Schumpeter, Joseph A. (1975) *Capitalism, Socialism and Democracy*. New York: Harper Torchbooks.

Shi Qingqi (1999) "Ershiyi shiji gaojishu chanyu fazhan zhong de renli ziben" (Human capital in the development of high-tech industry in the 21st century). *Zhongguo renli ziyuan kaifa* (Human resource development of China), August.

Solinger, J. Dorothy (1993) "China's Transients and the State: A Form of Civil Society?" *Politics & Society* 21, no. 1 (March):91–122.

—— (1999) *Contesting Citizenship in Urban China: Peasant Migrants, the State, and the Logic of the Market*. Berkeley, CA: University of California Press.

Wang Hansheng (1994) "Gaige yilai Zhongguo nongcun de gongyehua yu nongcun jingying goucheng de bianhua" (Changes in China's rural industrialization and the formation of a rural elite since the reform). *Chinese Social Sciences Quarterly* 15, no. 4.

Wu Jisong (1998) *Zhishi jingji: Ershiyi shiji shehui de xin qushi* (Knowledge economy: The new social trend of the twenty-first century). Beijing: Beijing kexue jishu chubanshe.

Xiao Chong (1998) *Zhonggong disidai mingren* (The fourth generation of leaders of the Chinese Communist Party). Hong Kong: Xiafeier guoji chuban gongsi.

Xiao Yandeng (1999) *Zhongguo meiyou qiyejia: Zhongguo disidai qiyejia quexian fenxi* (China has no entrepreneurs: An analysis of the deficiencies of the fourth generation of entrepreneurs). Nanchang: Jiangxi renmin chubanshe.

Yang Dongping (1994) *Chengshi jifeng: Beijing he Shanghai de wenhua jingshen* (City monsoon: The cultural spirit of Beijing and Shanghai). Beijing: Dongfang Press.

Yang Fan (1998) "Zhongguo de weiji: quanli ziben exing pengzhang" (China's crisis: The vicious expansion of political capital." *Zhongguo yu shijie* (China and the world), on-line electronic magazine.

Yang Fujia (1998) "Zhishi jingji chujian dunani" (The coming of a knowledge economy). *Xin shiji lingdao zhe* (The leaders of a new century) no. 11 (November).

Zhang Houyi (1995) "The Position of the Private Entrepreneur Stratum in China's Social Structure." *Social Sciences in China* 16, no. 4: 29–36.

Zhao Yunxi (1998) *Zhishi zibenjia: Zhongguo zhishifenzi miandui zhishi jingji de jueze* (Knowledge capitalists: Chinese intellectuals' choices in the era of a knowledge economy). Beijing: Zhonghua gongshang lianhe chubanshe.

Zhongguo siying jingji yanjiuhui (Research association of Chinese private economy) (1994) *Zhongguo siying jingji yanjiu wenji* (Collection of studies of Chinese private economy). Beijing: Sanlian Publishers.

Zhou Zhangcheng (1997) "Wuhan shi keji shiying qiyezhu diaocha" (A survey of technical entrepreneurs in Wuhan). *Shehui kexue dongtai* (Social sciences information), no. 2.

Zhu Guanglei (1998) *Dangdai Zhongguo shehui gejieceng fenxi* (Analysis of social strata in China). Tianjin: Renmin chubanshe.

9

Provincial Identities and Political Cultures: Modernism, Traditionalism, Parochialism, and Separatism

Alan P.L. Liu

Provincial sentiments are rising rapidly in China. Chinese cultural historians are busy at work, turning out more and more works on local, provincial, and regional histories. The number of titles of local histories in *Quanguo Zongshumu* (National Bibliography) increased from 33 in 1980 to 305 in 1991 (*Quanguo* 1980, 1991). So far, scholars and journalists have offered widely divergent political interpretations of the rise of provincial consciousness in China. Damned and redeemed scenarios coexist. China is becoming another Yugoslavia exemplifies the first, and China is evolving toward federalism, the second school of thought. What is needed is fact finding. We need to know whether there are variations in provincial sentiments and, if there are, to identify their possible social, economic, or historical reasons. We need to know whether there are explicit or implicit political agendas in the recent provincial sentiments. If so, what accounts for the different political thoughts? These specific facts must be determined before one can indulge in generalizations. The chief aim of this chapter is to ascertain facts about the rise of provincial identities in post-Mao China.

To put the present provincial consciousness in perspective, we shall first review briefly the time-honored Chinese notion about the alleged North-South cultural and political divisions. After that, the analysis turns to the late nineteenth century, when explicitly divergent political identities and cultures emerged among Chinese provinces. The next phase of Chinese provincialism represents a serious reversal under Mao's centralist policy. The impact of Mao's rule in Chinese provincial identity construction is deep and long lasting. No analysis of current provincialism in China can proceed without first examining the effects of centralism under Mao. These historical influences enable us to suggest a preliminary typology of Chinese provincial identities and political cultures. In the conclusion, I discuss the long-term political consequences of rising provincial consciousness in the post-Mao period, particularly with respect to the nature of the Chinese state system.

The North-South Division

Regional or provincial cultural differences have fascinated Chinese scholars since ancient times. Most works on regional cultures, however, dealt with general or anthropological, not political, cultures (Cheng M. 1995; Dai Y. 1991; Han Y. 1991; Lu Y. 1990; Tan J. 1986). Dynastic rulers had deliberately deterred any possible rise of provincial political identities. Thus Chinese provinces have been given locational names, though most had ancient state names (these have been revived in recent historical works): *Hebei* means "north of the river (Yellow River)"; *Henan*, "south of the river"; *Shandong*, "east of the mountain"; *Shanxi*, "west of the mountain"; and so on. The national administration, the civil service examination, and Confucianism all tended to dampen the growth of divergent provincial political cultures. One exception to this overall centralism is the alleged North-South cultural and political differences, which are openly referred to in historical works. But this may be due to the fact that the Chinese state originated in the Yellow River region and subsequently colonized the rest of the country. Given the different anthropological cultures of the North and the South (the Yangtze River region), it is natural to presume that there would be divergent political cultures. For example, the early Qing scholar Wang Fu-chi maintained that northerners were "good" at forming cliques and causing internecine conflicts in the inner sanctum of the central government, while southerners were generally base and not above committing regicide and national treason (Chen H. 1976). Facts from history cast doubt on Wang's proposition. Chen K'uan-ch'iang's study of violent purges of high court officials in different dynasties shows that the Ming dynasty (1368–1644),

Figure 9.1 **Political Purges and Southern Premierships in Traditional China**

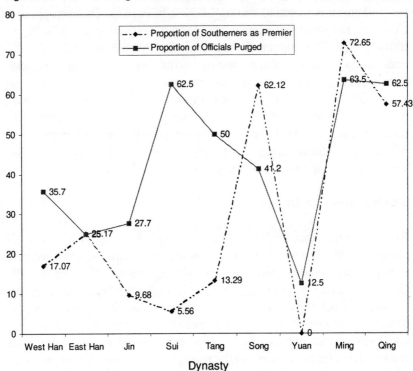

which had the highest proportion of southerners among its premiers, also had the highest proportion of senior officials purged (Chen K. 1972; Lu S. and Lu M. 1991). Furthermore, the Ming dynasty also had the highest frequency of violent clashes among cliques and parties (Zhu Z. and Chen S. 1992). At least so far as political incivility is concerned, the only significant difference between the dynasties seems to be national, not regional. In Figure 9.1, I compare proportions of southerners as premiers and that of high officials purged (based on Chen K'uan-ch'iang). The Mongolian Yuan dynasty (1279–1368) had no high official killed or banished, which is a striking contrast with other dynasties, particularly the Qing, which was non-Han but was highly Sinicized.[1] Mao's regime also provided facts contrary to Wang's thesis. There is more evidence that in traditional times regional identity served as the basis of clique formation and colonization of parts of the state administration, thus limiting mobility chances of other provincials (Skinner 1976). There is also evidence that beginning with the Tang dynasty (618–906), court reformers tended to hail from the South. According to Chinese historian Ren Shuang, southerners entered high politics later than northerners and brought with them a degree of dynamism (Ren S. 1987). But there has not yet been any evidence of correlations between provincial political cultures and distinct provincial political systems from Chinese history, such as those among the city-states of ancient Greece. If there were distinct provincial political cultures then, they lay dormant, waiting for the right channels and opportunities to make them explicit.

But the coming of the West changed all that. The West brought to China both the concepts and institutions of political participation. As the entire country was forced to adapt to Western civilization, the provinces showed marked differences in their receptivity to Western ways, especially new political ways. As a result, modern political cultures emerged in those provinces more intensely exposed to Western influences. One might call the late nineteenth century the axial period of China's social, political, and economic developments, in the same sense that Jaspers (1953) referred to the Spring-Autumn dynasty and Warring States (722–221 B.C.) as the intellectual axial period of China. The basic political and socio-economic divisions that were bared then among the provinces have persisted to this day. Anthropologist David Sopher (1972) suggested that a community might show a cultural response surface which exhibits a gradient of receptivity to cultural changes. In the late Qing period, such a cultural response surface came to the fore in Mainland China.

The Late Nineteenth Century

What the West had done in China was to separate, culturally and institutionally, a handful of southeastern provinces from the rest of the country. New political cultures emerged in Jiangsu (including Shanghai), Zhejiang, Guangdong, and, to a lesser extent, Fujian. The West brought novel political theories, but more importantly, knowledge about institutions of participation, such as political parties, a modern press, and parliament. The general cultures of these provinces were already different from the rest of the country, as shown in their emphasis on commerce, achievements in Confucian scholarship, and general receptivity to innovation. The people, particularly the elites, of these provinces adapted quickly to Western ways. Various scholars and commentators, Chinese or westerners, have taken note of the exceptionalism of the southeastern

Figure 9.2 **Career Patterns of Provincial Elites, 1912–1930**

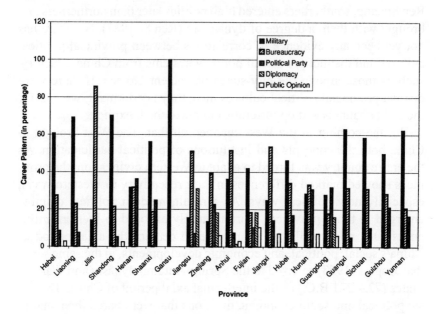

seaboard of China. Liang Qichao (1955), perhaps modern China's greatest political writer, maintained that the future of China lay in the area between the Yangtze and the Xi rivers (in Guangdong). Tawney (1966) suggested that the eastern coastal areas south of the Yellow River had the resources and cultures to serve as the base for a modern Chinese state.

Japanese scholar Kazuki Sonoda's study of the career patterns of 677 Chinese provincial elites from 1912 to 1930 threw into relief the cultural transformations that had occurred in the southeastern provinces. I have presented Sonoda's statistical compilations of the career patterns of these provincial elites in a schematic way in Figure 9.2. Sonoda divided the occupations of these provincial leaders into five types: military, bureaucracy, party politics, diplomacy, and leadership in public opinion (scholars with notable impact on public opinion). Figure 9.2 shows that Jiangsu, Zhejiang, Fujian, and Guangdong stood out in having a sizable portion of their elites specializing in diplomacy—an entirely new and West-inspired profession in China. The only hinterland province that had a small presence of diplomats among its elites was Hubei, a major commerical city on the Yangtze River. In contrast, the elites in the hinterland chose mainly traditional occupations, such as the military and bureaucracy.[2] That diplomats tended to concentrate in these four coastal provinces is symptomatic of their overall outward orientations and receptiveness to culturally novel things.

The national political schism between the Kuomintang and the Communist Party was at least partially a reflection of the cultural divisions between the southeast coast and the hinterland. For instance, North and Pool's study of the elites of these two parties (up to 1945) concluded that the Kuomintang elite came more extensively from the coastal areas, while the Communist leaders were mainly from Central China. They further made the point that modern Chinese history showed South China as a revolutionary incubator while the North had been more conservative (North and Pool 1966). These cultural divergencies between the regions probably foreshadowed not only developmental disparities between the provinces in the post-Mao period but also the political and economic contradistinctions between China and Taiwan today.

The Mao Interlude

Growing provincial political differences were cut short by civil wars, Japan's invasion, and, most important of all, Mao's extreme centralism from 1949 to 1976. The Mao administration built a strong Party-state institution and launched one national project after another. Failures or not, these projects and the state institution have had a deep impact on provincial identities. In general, according to Putnam, the state "affects the identities, power, and strategies of political actors" (Putnam 1993, 8). The late Joseph Levenson (1967) likened Mao's treatment of provincialism to a stage play, in which the Party, being the director, assigned roles for the provinces to play. Genuine provincial identities were not allowed in Mao's theatre. But Levenson did not inquire into whether and/or which Chinese provinces in 1949 still had genuine identities. A century of wars and social and economic disintegration in China, in the interior in particular, had significantly damaged the traditional identities of many of the provinces. Moreover, the provinces in the Northeast had been ruled by the Manchu royalty under the Japanese from 1931 to 1945 and thus experienced identity fluidity. Furthermore, underneath war destruction and social disorder was the basic fact that much of China had not successfully adapted to the challenge of modernization. Into this cultural and identity flux, rose Maoism. Mao had great hopes of building socialism in the interior provinces that had suffered from identity crises, which he thought would make it easier for his projects to work (Domenach 1995). As Jonathan Friedman points out, for communities that have failed in modernization, their answer to identity crisis might be to engage in a larger project "in which identity is concrete and fixed, irrespective of mobility, success and other external changes in social conditions" (Friedman 1993, 361). Mao had provided the lesser-developed provinces in the interior a number of large projects for rejuvenation and the basis for new, albeit ideological, identities. Furthermore, socialism being so novel in China, no province had a head start on its development. Before socialism, every Chinese province was equal, so to speak. The provinces in the southeast that were comparatively successful in modernization, such as Jiangsu, Zhejiang, and Guangdong, had to suppress their pre-Communist identities, while the North and the interior lived off state-created identities. The Maoist period was, in some sense, a diversion. Much of China was diverted from searching for realistic answers to their socio-economic impoverishments by following Mao's grand projects. Mao left behind two legacies. First, the traditional identities of those provinces that were relatively successful in modernization were undermined and even corrupted, as exemplified by the case of Shanghai. Almost thirty years of socialism significantly eroded Shanghai's traditional commercial tradition. Second, those provinces less successful in socio-economic development grew dependent on Mao's grand projects at the expense of constructing genuine identities for the benefit of mobilizing the people's local pride in development.

The Deng administration declared that Mao had led China "into a blind alley" and then granted the provinces a high degree of autonomy to deal with their problems (Li, P. 1997, 106). Those that used to depend on Mao's projects for identity were left to face the harsh and retroactive reality. For the first time since the founding of the People's Republic, many Chinese provinces, the interior ones in particular, had to take their fates into their own hands and confront the daunting tasks of constructing their own identities for development. They were forced to be free.

Chinese provinces thus began their identity construction in the post-Mao period on an unequal footing. Some provinces mobilized quickly, while others did less so. Provincial variations in identity-building may be seen in the degrees of provincial activism in local gazette (*fangzhi* or *difangzhi*) publications. The gazettes have been Chinese provinces' identity-maintaining institution for centuries and are an important com-

Figure 9.3 **Provincial Gazette Publications in Qing and PRC**
(titles; percentage in national total)

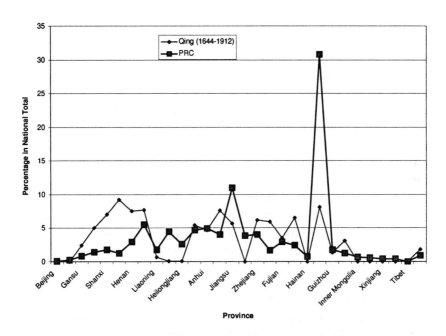

ponent of traditional Chinese scholarship. The fortunes of local gazettes reflect the fate of the whole nation. According to historian Chu Shih-chia, during the two decades of the Republican period (from 1911 to 1930), the provinces of China published a total of 193 titles and 3,123 copies of local gazettes, as compared with 393 tiles and 8,803 copies in the 23–year period from the reign of Xianfeng to that of Tongzhi (from 1851 to 1874) during the last dynasty (Chu, S. 1932). In other words, a precipitous decline in gazette compilations had taken place from the Qing to the Republic, presumably due to wars and turmoil throughout the country. During Mao's reign, gazette publications were neglected at first and then banned totally from the start of the Cultural Revolution to Mao's death in 1976. In the case of Zhejiang, for example, not a single gazette was published from 1949 to 1979 (Wei Q. 1988). The same was true in Fujian (Lee K. 1996). After the Deng administration's policy on provincial autonomy took effect in the 1980s, provinces resumed compilations of local gazettes.

To examine the possible impacts of wars and Mao's repression on

provincial identities, Figure 9.3 compares proportions of provincial gazettes in the national totals between the Qing dynasty and the post-Mao
period up to 1992 (*Zhongguo Xinfangzhi* 1993).[3] To the extent that gazette publishing signifies varying strengths of provincial consciousness,
the data in Figure 9.3 suggest that provincial consciousness in China
depends on complex interactions of cultural, historical, political, and
strategic factors. Chinese provincial identities are not monocausal.

First, local gazettes being a distinct Chinese or Confucian institution,
the ethnic minorities in China (Inner Mongolia, Ningxia, Xinjiang,
Qinghai, Tibet, and Guangxi) showed little or no interest in compiling
them from the time of the Qing to the People's Republic. A partial exception is Guangxi, which had been significantly Sinicized and was not
even treated as an ethnic minority area during the Republican period.
That is why Guangxi has shown some interest in publishing local gazettes. Second, six provinces have been more active than others in re-
suming gazette compilations from the 1980s—Liaoning, Jilin,
Heilongjiang, Jiangsu, Shanghai, and Sichuan. The first three provinces
are commonly referred to as a single group, the Northeast. The Northeast and the rest of the provinces form a sharp contrast in history and
culture. The northeastern region is, so to speak, "without a history,"
while Jiangsu, Shanghai, and Sichuan are rich in history. The Manchus,
Russians, and Japanese separated the Northeast from the rest of China
until the end of the Second World War. That Liaoning, Jilin, and
Heilongjiang have been actively compiling their provincial histories may
be due to several reasons, such as strengthening their Chinese cultural
credentials, expressing their pride in being the heartland of Chinese defense industries, and, most importantly, safeguarding their status in
Deng's era. We shall have more to say about the identity crises of these
northeastern provinces in the post-Mao period. Strong cultural pride
and identity apparently account for the vigorous interest in Sichuan,
Jiangsu, and Shanghai in publishing local gazettes. Sichuan's geographic
isolation, immense population, and long tradition made the province the
first one to advocate nationwide resumptions of studies of local history
in the early 1980s ("Historical Studies" 1981). Third, Figure 9.3 shows
that the majority of Chinese provinces have not kept up gazette publications. The provinces in the North (Shaanxi, Shanxi, Hebei, Henan, and
Shandong) have suffered a significant decline in gazette compilations
since their heyday during the Qing dynasty. The same is true in the southern provinces of Jiangxi, Zhejiang, Hunan, and Guangdong. Political

discrimination under Mao probably accounted more for the decline of gazette publications in Zhejiang, Guangdong, and Fujian than socio-economic causes. Deng's decentralization liberated Zhejiang, Fujian, and Guangdong from Maoism economically, but the cautious spirit in politics and ideology that these provinces had cultivated during the time of Mao persisted in the post-Mao period. In contrast, the important roles that Jiangxi and Hunan played in Mao's revolution in the early stage probably made them less willing to indulge in such a "feudalistic" activity as publishing local gazettes. Similarly, the less-than-active records of publishing gazettes of the northern provinces after 1949 may be, as stated earlier, due to their new Maoist ideological identities.

Provincial Identity Constructions

Today, after the experience in the late nineteenth century, the civil war between the Nationalists and the Communists, and Mao's intensely politicizing rule, distinct provincial identities (or identity crises) and political cultures among Chinese provinces are more discernable than before, but by no means totally identifiable. Those whose identities and political cultures have become more explicit tend to form into five clusters, due to common cultures and/or political or strategic reasons.[4] The first cluster may be called the modernist group, which is composed of the politically and culturally distinct southeastern provinces of Jiangsu, Shanghai, Zhejiang, Fujian, and Guangdong. This group of provinces shares similarities in history, socio-economic structure, and a long-term interest in reforms. They evince a strong modernist identity. Deng had coopted this group of winner provinces and assigned them to the "getting rich earlier" category. The second cluster is the traditionalist group, which is composed of the northern and northeastern provinces (Shanxi, Hebei, Henan, Liaoning, Jilin, and Heilongjiang). Being the chief beneficiaries of Mao's big projects, these provinces have experienced serious difficulties in making the transition from Mao to Deng, economically, socially, and culturally. Not having Mao as their patron, and being relegated by Deng's administration to the "getting rich later" category, the northern and northeastern provinces are suffering from acute identity crises. They have become the militant defenders of the CCP revolutionary tradition. The third cluster consists of the southern interior provinces—Sichuan, Hunan, and Jiangxi—whose identities and cultures are in flux. They may be described as the transitional group. Their socioeconomic structures are still pre-industrial but their political identities waver between modernism and traditionalism. The fourth cluster, for deep social, economic, cultural, and political reasons, has been dominated by parochialism. These provinces are mostly on the border regions of China—Gansu and Shaanxi in the North, and Guizhou and Guangxi in the South. The fifth cluster includes the major minority nationalities of China. They exhibit varying degrees of separatism in their identities. Their political cultures range from open rebellion to peaceful pursuit of cultural autonomy. What follows is an analysis of each of these groups. My focus is on each group's strategy of identity construction and the political culture of the elite.[5]

1. The Modernist Identity and Political Culture

The modernist identity and political culture of Jiangsu, Shanghai, Zhejiang, Fujian, and Guangdong prefer the type of society in which civil society is strong and the state intervenes minimally in social and economic affairs. They value differentiation, secularization, and pluralism. The political cultures of these five southeastern provinces resemble what Elazar (1966) calls the individualistic political culture of the Middle Atlantic States in the United States (Massachusetts, Rhode Island, New York, Pennsylvania, New Jersey, Ohio, Illinois, and Indiana). Elazar (1966, 86) describes the individualistic political culture as follows:

> In its view, a government is instituted for strictly utilitarian reasons, to handle those functions demanded by the people it is created to serve. A government need not have any direct concern with questions of the "good society" except insofar as it may be used to advance some common conception of the good society formulated outside the political arena just as it serves other functions.

The modernist identity of the southeastern provinces is first and foremost manifested in their cultural elites' recollections of their histories in the late nineteenth century. As Putnam (1993, 174) writes, "Faced with new problems requiring collective resolution, men and women everywhere look to their past for solutions." According to recent historical works published in and for the southeast region, in contrast to stagnancy, disintegration, and war destruction in the hinterland of China, the southeastern seaboard thrived (less so in Fujian) in urbanization, commercialization, and intellectual growth as a result of Western influences. Modern business groups, unions, and associations strengthened civil society, especially in the southern Yangtze region. These provided the basis for modern political movements at the turn of the century, such as the constitutional monarchy movement in the last years of the Qing dynasty and the party politics and federalist movement of the early Republican period (Chen J. 1992; Fan S. 1990; Fei Z. 1995; Geng Y. 1980; Gu H. and Xu Y. 1997; Hou Y. 1993; Peng Z. 1988; Tang W. 1986; Xu D. 1986; Xu M. 1989; Yang L. 1993). It is this historical legacy of the Southeast that has resulted in the contrasting fates of the region under Mao and Deng; the former suppressed it, while the latter legitimized it.

Against this general cultural background, it is no wonder that the elites of the southeastern provinces have espoused political decentralization, revision, and secularization of the Marxist ideology, transforming the unitary Party into a pluralistic organization to meet the needs of a market economy and maintaining above all an open-door policy toward the outside, and toward libertarian Western nations in particular.

According to this regional group, Chinese history has given ample evidence that a decentralized system was economically and intellectually more productive than a centralized system. Furthermore, centralization in Chinese history was said to be more a fiction than reality. China has been a culturally diverse nation, and there have always been North-South cultural divergences, with the North being the political center and the South the economic and cultural center. Compared with Europe, Chinese people have yet to enjoy the prerogative that the Europeans have always enjoyed—choosing their political system to suit their cultural differences (Hu A. 1996; Li P. 1987; Ma B. 1992; Ni P. 1987; Wang S. 1987). The ideologues of the Southeast strongly supported Deng's (or Hu Yaobang's) thesis on the criterion of truth ("practice is the sole criterion of truth") and strongly supported the opening of trade and cultural exchanges with the West as well. One of the first provincial broadsides in favor of Deng's line on truth hailed from Nanjing University. The media of the Southeast boldly publicized the views that Marxism, being based on European social conditions, should not have been applied mechanically to China and that capitalism as a historical stage may be skipped politically, but not economically (Ma Q. and Chen D. 1982; Qian X. 1987; Shen D. 1988).

The type of political system that the intellectual and ideological establishments of the southeastern provinces have strongly endorsed is characterized by a strict division of functions between the Communist

Party and the government, an increasing delegation of regulatory work to civil society, and a deference to expert opinions. The Communist Party, in their view, needs to be reorganized to suit a market economy. Specifically, the Party should shed its centralized and unitary structure and reorganize itself into a loosely coordinated association. The cohesion of the Party should be based on the members' common interests, not on centrally imposed discipline. A Shanghai journal even published the view that it is unconstitutional to demand all members to be loyal to the Party Center. The Party Charter calls for all members to be loyal to the Party Congress, not the Party Center. Other writers maintained that the main goal of the Party should be economic development and management and that the right of the Communist Party to govern China should be based on its economic performance. The market principles of autonomy, equality, and competition are what the Party needs to reform. It is only right and reasonable that the Party should allow members to engage in commerce and business. Furthermore, the Communist Party itself should have an open-door policy so as to have regular communications with other social groups and parties. The so-called democratic parties must boldly assume their functions of supervising and checking the Communist Party's competence in organizing and executing economic construction. Above all, the Communist Party must adapt to the fast and fundamental changes going on in the world, such as the rise of regionalism, interdependence, and information-based societies (Chen G. 1999; Gao F. 1988; Gu Y. 1994; He J. 1992; Huang Z. 1998; Jiao W. 1995; Ke R. 1988; Li Q. 1997; Liu Y. 1988; Shi P. 1983; Xia J. 1997; Yan S. 1987; Yan J. 1990; Yu J. 1997; Yu J. and Fa Y. 1994; Zhang D. 1988; Zhang Y. 1997).

The modernist political culture of the southeastern provinces has been significantly strengthened by their newly established contact with Hong Kong and Taiwan. Since the 1980s (1987 so far as Taiwan is concerned), there have been substantial transactions between the southeastern provinces and these two largely autonomous or wholly independent overseas Chinese communities, in investments, visits, mail, telephones, telegrams, telex, and state-regulated cultural exchanges. Taiwan's businessmen, for example, concentrated their investments in the southeastern provinces. In 1998, according to the Executive Yuan of the Nationalist government, the distribution of Taiwan's investments in China was as follows (in descending order of value in US dollars): Guangdong, 4.5 billion; Jiangsu, 4.1 billion; Fujian, 1.5 billion; Hebei, 822 million;

Zhejiang, 575 million; Shandong, 366 million; the Northeast region, 239 million; Sichuan, 183 million; Hubei, 156 million; Hainan, 124 million; Hunan, 115 million; Guangxi, 43 million; and Henan, 38 million (*Statistics on* 1998). Taiwan's cultural exchanges with China have also been skewed toward the southeast. For example, half of Taiwan's book exhibitions since 1984 were held in the southeast, with Canton city leading the rest in the number of such exhibitions (Liu S. 1999). Undoubtedly, Hong Kong's transactions with Guangdong and other coastal provinces in China must be even more substantial than Taiwan's.

While the Chinese in Hong Kong and Taiwan have been reaching into China, the local governments and businessmen in China's southeastern seaboard have also been actively reaching out to these two overseas Chinese societies (*Chung-kuo Shih-pao* [China times], March 23, 1994; April 6, 1994; May 5, 1996). Shanghai elites openly treated Hong Kong as their chief reference, whether in lamenting the city's decline after 1949 or planning for its rebirth after 1978 (Cai B. 1988; Chen Z. and Wang L. 1995; Jiang Z. 1987; "Rui Xingwen" 1987; Wang H. 1989). It is implausible that the influences of Hong Kong and Taiwan in the southeast provinces are restricted entirely to the economic realm. For instance, in 1991, the Communist Youth League in Fujian issued a special circular expressing concern over the cultural influences of Taiwan among the youth of Fujian (*Chung-kuo shih-pao*, December 26, 1991). As a general rule, trans-societal cultural influences have more telling effects on the one whose culture is in a more advanced state of flux, such as West Germany's impact on East Germany (Jarausch 1997; Varan 1998). It is reasonable to presume that the transactions between the southeastern seaboard of China and Hong Kong and Taiwan are strengthening the modernist political culture of the southeastern provinces (*China Strategic* 1997). The peoples of southeastern China, Hong Kong, and Taiwan will increasingly share a trans-societal identity based on a common ethnicity and a global orientation. Such a "geobasic" identity will make it more difficult for Beijing to employ a conventional and narrowly based nationalism in the southeast region (Belay 1996; for more on this, see Friedman's contribution to this volume).

2. The Traditionalist Political Culture

While the southeastern provinces (re)collect their modern histories with pride and hope, the elites of Shanxi, Hebei, Henan, Liaoning, Jilin, and

Heilongjiang remember the nineteenth century as a period rife with natural disasters, warlordism, social disintegration, and foreign exploitation. From the vantage point of northern and northeastern elites, the Communist revolution and Mao's socialist construction gave them new identities and a ray of hope. As a result, their political views accentuate the role of the Party-state in social reconstruction and laud the virtues of collectivism. The elite political culture of this provincial cluster resembles Elazar's (1966, 92–93) "traditionalistic political culture." As he explains it:

> The *traditionalist political culture* is rooted in an ambivalent attitude toward the marketplace coupled with a paternalistic and elitist conception of the commonwealth. It reflects an older, pre-commercial attitude that accepts a substantially hierarchical society, as part of the ordered nature of things, authorizing and expecting those at the top of the social structure to take a special and dominant role in government. Like its moralistic counterpart, the traditionalistic political culture accepts government as an actor with a positive role in the community.

The traditionalist political culture of the North and Northeast is embedded in their general social, economic, and historical conditions. The northern provinces of Shanxi, Hebei, and Henan have been the birthplaces of traditional Chinese high culture, including the long enduring state institution. They have also borne the brunt of repeated invasions by nomads from outside of the Great Wall. Their cultures are similar to that of historical Eastern Europe, which was originally a frontier region. Consequently, as Parsons explains it, the culture of Eastern Europe stressed military skills, a hierarchical social order, political authority, and centralization (Parsons 1971). These are the same characterizations that one finds in the recent cultural histories of the northern provinces of China. For example, Henan is proud of its heritage as the cradle of the central state institution; Shanxi of its role as the arsenal of ancient China; and Hebei of its alleged "self-sacrifices" in bearing the brunt of barbarians' attacks so the rest of the nation might enjoy peace and development (Feng B. 1995; Zhang J. 1995; Zhang Z. 1995). For the cultural elites of the northern provinces, politics and statism form the core of their identities.

In the nineteenth century, the northern provinces, being predominantly agricultural, had not been penetrated significantly by the commercial cultures of the West. Nothing like the prosperous southeastern towns ever developed in the North. Though Shanxi and Shaanxi had once fostered traditional bankers and merchants, they relied too much on state patronage and nepotism that fatally undermined their adaptation to a modern competitive economy. In sum, the North was marginalized by capitalism (Huang J. 1992; Ma Y. 1992; Qiao R. 1992; Qiao Z. and Gong G. 1993; Wei G. 1992; Zhang H. 1995; Zhao R. 1987). After the founding of the PRC, the North experienced a degree of rebirth, due to Mao's concentration of major industrial projects in the interior. Under Mao, writes Murphey, "the big news stories are reserved for the rapid transformation into industrial centers of places like Changchun [in the Northeast], Loyang [Henan], Kunming [Yunnan], Chungking [Sichuan], or Chengchow [Henan], or the creation out of the wilderness of manu-facturing towns such as Paotow [Inner Mongolia] or Ta-ch'ing [Heilongjiang]" (Murphey 1974, 69). In the vast countryside of the North, as sociologist Fei Xiaotong discovered even in the 1990s, the old traditions of making a living either out of subsistence farming or joining the revolution have persisted (Fei X. 1994a, 1994b, 1994c, 1994d). In the eyes of the northern elites, both their ancient and recent histories point to politics, in ideological or institutional terms, as their pathway from the periphery. The deputy chancellor of the Shanxi Party School put it well: "Since Shanxi is an interior province, its developmental strat-egy should play up the role of politics and the people's spirit, not eco-nomics" (Cai X. 1997, 3:106). This is essentially a reaffirmation of Mao's perspective.

The northern provinces have found a natural ally in the Northeast. In contrast to the North, the Northeast's Chinese cultural and political iden-tity is problematic. While the North at least could claim to be the ances-tral home of Chinese high culture, the Northeast was not even a Chinese territory until 1907, when the Manchus finally allowed legal Chinese immigrants into the area. Before long, the Northeast became the prey of Chinese warlords and Russian and Japanese imperialists. It has been a region of maximal cultural flux. The Chinese identity of the Northeast has a certain Cinderella quality to it, and Mao was its prince. The Mao administration, with massive Soviet aid, turned the Northeast into the heartland of the Chinese defense industry. In China, the Northeast is virtually synonymous with central planning and state-owned enterprises.

The North's and the Northeast's elite political cultures and identities have thus put a premium on statism. Their worldview is totalitarian, in which the boundaries between the Party, the state, and society cease to exist. For this reason, the ideological elites of the northern and north-

eastern provinces seem to have never tired of repeating the revolutionary history of the Communist Party and Mao's leadership. Henan ideologues have been the most militant of all. In 1978, the Henan Party
establishment mobilized like-minded ideologues in the hinterland to
compile a 55–volume history of important figures in the history of the
Chinese Communist Party. Its editorial board was composed almost
entirely of persons from the interior. Furthermore, the publishing house
was from the northern province of Shaanxi (*Dangshi* 1991). Zhengzhou
(Chengchow), the capital of Henan, also hosted the first meeting of the
"ultra-Left" faction of the CCP, which in 1994 voiced fundamental opposition to Deng's reforms ("Leading Conservatives" 1994). Since the
early 1980s, the core journals of the North and the Northeast have persisted in calling on the country to return to Maoism, with socialism and
collectivism as the national goal, Party-state totalitarianism the norm,
selfless dedication to revolution the duty of every member of the Party,
and uncompromising struggle against class enemies both at home and
abroad a constant national priority. The Party elites of these two regions
have painted a dark picture of the impact of a market economy on the
Party, including corroding the will of Party members, undermining the
Party spirit, confusing the thinking of Party members, and corrupting
their morality. The ideal economy of the northern and northeastern elites
is moral or political economy as exemplified in Mao's communes, with
the state acting as the sole guardian of the welfare of the people. To this
day, Henan maintains a Mao-type commune in one of its communities
(Dong W. 1990; Guan L. 1998; Guo Q. 1987; Li Y. 1987; Liao T. 1995;
Liu E. 1982; Liu G. 1987; Liu Y. 1995; Nan J. and Wang Y. 1997; Shen
Z. 1987; Tang X. 1997; Wang J. 1987; Wang R. 1987; Wang L. 1993;
Wu Z. 1995; Yang C. 1982; Yang M. 1982; Yao H. 1992; Yao Y. 1996;
Yue D. 1997; Zhonggong Henan 1991; Zhang X. 1992; Zhou L. 1987).
In all this, the northern and northeastern provinces capitalize on the Deng
administration's political ambivalence, the so-called "political left, economic right" dualism. While the southeastern provinces have constructed
their identities around Deng's economics, the North and the Northeast
have made Deng's political conservatism the vortex of their identity constructions. It is no wonder that whenever Beijing saw the need to whip up
xenophobic nationalism among the people, it could always count on these
northern and northeastern provinces for support (see Friedman's essay in
this volume for a discussion of this matter).

The Southeast, North, and Northeast have discernable political cultures, but we now enter into regions with various degrees of opaqueness in political identities and cultures. The three cosmopolitan value systems in Chinese history—Confucianism, capitalism, and socialism—have a relatively weaker impact in the following provinces.

3. The Transitionals

The three central-southern provinces of Sichuan, Hunan, and Jiangxi share two common cultural and historical characteristics. First, Confucianism has had more impact in this group of provinces than has capitalism or socialism. Western commercial influences in the nineteenth century did not reach far into this region. Mao's socialist projects did not put this region high on its priority. In other words, their histories have shown mainly impressive Confucian scholarship that is of little relevance to their present tasks. Second, they were the battlegrounds of the Chinese civil wars from the 1930s to 1949. War and poverty have undermined their provincial identities. Historically, sovereigns as well as rebels had used Sichuan and Jiangxi as temporary refuges in times of invasions and rebellions. Once the emergency situations were over, these high or low-class residents abandoned Sichuan and Jiangxi like used tools. Sichuan, for example, provided shelter for Tang dynasty (618–906) emperors and, during the Second World War, for Chiang Kai-shek of the Republic. In the 1960s, fearing a possible attack by the Soviet Union, Mao built his so-called Third Front of defense in Sichuan and other southwest provinces. Jiangxi once was a haven for the southern Song royalty (1126–1279) escaping from the Mongolian onslaught, and in modern times Mao established his first guerrilla base in Jiangxi. Sichuan and Jiangxi were valuable to the state in times of need precisely because of their peripheral status. Even more significantly, Sichuan's impressive achievements in local gazette publications do not signify a strong *provincial* identity. According to a recent book on Sichuan's cultural history, a sizeable number of Sichuan residents do not think of themselves as Sichuanese. Rather, they identify themselves as immigrants from other provinces, particularly Hunan and Guangdong. Mass genocide and destruction of property during the Mongol invasion in the thirteenth century and the civil wars in the later years of the Ming dynasty (1368–1644) had left vast vacant areas in Sichuan (Yuan T. 1991). Immigrants from neighboring provinces subsequently filled the spaces. Thus, Sichuan is a province with rich *local* identities but a weak *provin-*

cial identity. Although Hunan was famed for its generals and politicians in the nineteenth century, one is never certain whether that was due to some peculiar provincial qualities or the time-honored Chinese nepotism in the bureaucracy. In any case, the so-called Hunanese character is time-bound. It was constructed in a bygone era, as Maoism was.

As a result of all the foregoing, the elite cultures of Sichuan, Hunan, and Jiangxi are affected by a sense of marginality. The political cultures of these three provinces waver between traditionalism and modernism. The political views in the core journals of these provinces follow no consistent line or identity. Sichuan was where former Party General Secretary Zhao Ziyang first experimented with decollectivization. Sichuan elite opinions seemed to be in favor of reform in the early 1980s. When the reformists began their industrial restructuring, however, the Sichuan climate of opinion became more reserved. One possible reason for this change is that Sichuan, being the war capital of China during the Second World War and one of the bases of Mao's Third Front strategy in the 1960s, has acquired more state-owned heavy industries than either Jiangxi or Hunan. Because of their vested interests in these socialist industries, Sichuan elites have expressed political preferences close to the stands taken by the elites of the North and the Northeast. As for Jiangxi and Hunan, their interior locations and agricultural economies make it expedient for them to take a traditionalist or centrist line whenever the Party Center calls on them to do so. At the same time, there is clearly a continuous reformist spirit among a part of their cultural elites (Cao D. 1991; Chen P. 1990; Fu B. 1996; Guo X. 1996; Huang J. 1995; Jiang L. and Cheng X. 1990; Li X. 1995; Liu Y. 1993; Liu X. 1997; Lo Z. 1992; "Propaganda Outline" 1987; Song B. 1995; Tai Q. 1986; Xue Q. 1987; Yang B. 1982; Yao Q. 1997; Zhong J. 1990; Zhonggong Jiangxi 1991).

4. The Parochial Political Culture

The provinces with a parochial political culture form an arc from the northern province of Shaanxi, westward to Gansu, and southward to Guizhou and, finally, Guangxi. Generally speaking, these provinces withdraw into their own worlds. Their elites seem to be indifferent to the national mainstream and quite content with locally rooted identities. The key Chinese phrase describing these provinces is *bise*, or inaccessibility and uniformity. Historically, these provinces were weakly influenced by all three cosmopolitan value systems: Confucianism, capitalism, and socialism.

The dynamic entrepreneurial spirit so common in the Southeast is relatively absent in the parochial cultures. In this group of provinces, outsiders initiate most important changes, economic or otherwise. In a recent book on Guizhou culture, for example, there is a reference to "the resist-Japan war culture" (*kangzhan wenhua*). That is to say, the only high culture that Guizhou had come into contact with in the modern period consisted of the schools and literary activities brought there from other provinces by people escaping Japan's invasion during the Second World War (Huang D. 1998). After the establishment of the PRC, these parochial provinces became heavily dependent on the central government for relief. In the case of Guangxi, "the livelihood of the province relies on annual state subsidies," and has done so ever since 1949 (Zhang Z. and Lu J. 1989, 102). Illiteracy, poverty, isolation, and strong local identities are what distinguish these provinces. Strictly speaking, there is not any provincialism in the sense of pride in provincial cultural distinctness. Instead, local identities prevail. In Gansu, as one account goes, "every village is a world onto itself" (Wu W. 1987, 143).

Atomistic social structures tend to be receptive to authoritarianism. The central characteristics of parochial political culture are dependency and statism. It is not surprising that when occasions arose for the leaders of these parochial provinces to make political pronouncements in the past, their views were not very different from those of the North and the Northeast (Li Q. 1990; Song F. 1989).

5. The Separatist Political Culture

The ethnic minorities of Inner Mongolia, Ningxia, Xinjiang, and Tibet display varying degrees of alienation and separatism, Tibet being the most extreme case. More recently, the separatist movements in Xinjiang have turned violent. As mentioned earlier in connection with local gazette publications, these minorities have never been receptive to Chinese civilization. Their political cultures are embedded in their own religions and are diffuse in nature. As long as their desires for separation from China are not realized or accommodated by the existing state system in some fundamental ways, the minorities will remain the most significantly alienated political culture in China.

Conclusion

This brief review has made it quite clear that not every Chinese province is capable of constructing a meaningful identity. Values, traditions, wars, and Mao's enervating centralization have hampered provincial identity searches. Moreover, in the post-Mao period, provincial identity-building is for mobilization for development. Quite a number of provinces in the interior are ill equipped to plan, manage, and execute their economic development. A significant number of these provincial leaders are more interested in restoring Mao's centralist ways than in taking the advantages offered by Deng's policy of local autonomy and marketization. Only a handful of southeastern provinces have viable identities and are sufficiently self-confident to make full use of Deng's decentralist strategy.

Against this background, the fears on the part of some people that provincial autonomy in post-Mao China might cause the country to repeat the tragic fate of Yugoslavia are unwarranted. This essay shows that dependency, not disintegration, is the real problem for the post-Mao regime. Except for the few ethnic minorities whose desires for independence prevail over those for economic growth, a large number of Chinese provinces must depend on the central state for making their ends meet, let alone development. Their provincial identities are weak and their political cultures are either explicitly or implicitly traditionalist. Their elites have not yet shed the mentality of *apparatchiki*.

As a result of the foregoing, the central state is confronted with a paradox. On the one hand, the diverse provincial identities in China constitute what Horowitz characterizes as a horizontal ethnic system. In other words, each province maintains its own social structure and stratification, and the relations between the provinces are marked by a degree of "mutual repulsion and disdain." The central state has some flexibility, for "[t]he plurality of groups ordinarily enables the center to deal with one conflict at a time," and "when the center intervenes it may do so as a neutral arbiter" (Horowitz 1971, 232–33, 238). Beijing has not only flexibility but also the advantage to obtain different resources from different provinces. In the political crises of 1986–87 and 1989–90, the center received open endorsements of "anti-bourgeois liberalism" from provinces with traditionalist political cultures. On the other hand, the kind of economic and social dynamism that Deng's administration hoped to tap for China's modernization is not forthcoming from those provinces with uncertain identities. Despite massive state assistance, the North and Northeast remain China's most notable rust belt, plagued by low social morale and rising social disorganization.

The uneven rate of provincial identity-building and the divergent provincial political cultures also dim the hopes of those who are excited by the prospect of federalism in China (Montinola, Qian, and Weingast 1995). Whether one can federate units such as the provinces of China, with widely divergent political cultures and strength of identities, is highly questionable. "You cannot federate hopelessly incompatible units," writes Sawyer (1969). For the federal bargain to take place among elites, says Riker, the first condition is that "all parties are willing to make them" (1987, 13). The evidence as presented in this essay is not reassuring, for it suggests that no such general will among Chinese provincial elites for a fundamental change of the state system exists at present.

The foregoing is not meant to suggest that the political cultures of the provinces outside of the southeastern coast will stay the same indefinitely. As one province after another followed the examples of the Southeast by opening communications with the outside, cultural change will take place, varying in speed and extent among the provinces. Though it may be difficult to transform old centers of the socialist economy (Shanghai being an example of that, despite its long commercial tradition before 1949), new centers in each province might rise to exploit the opportunities of the reform era. Take, for example, the Northeast, the heartland of socialist industry. The three provinces in the region—Heilongjiang, Jilin, and Liaoning—have been more active recently in reaching out to Taiwan's investors. Provoked by the successes of the Southeast, the northeastern provinces have been exploring the possibility of establishing a "northeastern Asian economic cooperation zone" that will link them with the Russian maritime province, Japan, and the two Koreas (Yu W. 1994). Meanwhile, new developmental centers are emerging gradually that might radiate their influences to the rest of the provinces. One such example is the city of Haicheng in Liaoning province. Being a county town, Haicheng was marginal to the state-owned industries around the city. But Haicheng people took to heart the new opportunities from the legalization of private business and long-distance trade in the era of reform. They engaged in private business and trade. The prosperity of Haicheng contrasts with the demoralization and decline in nearby old centers of socialist industry. In Haicheng, a popular saying goes: "There are no Communists in Haicheng" (*Haicheng meiyou gongchandang*), as the city's economy has been dominated by private businesses (*Shih-chieh* 1998). The example of Haicheng seems to conform to the historical lesson of the Southeast. That is, the motive force for a fundamental change in China's political culture must come from below.

To tap into popular forces for development, there have been discussions among Chinese scholars that the provinces might have to be reconstituted. There are significant intra-province cultural, social, and economic divisions, such as those between northern and southern Jiangsu. In the early years of the Republican period, there were suggestions that the provinces were too large to govern effectively. As China then was confronted with warlordism, the debates about provincial jurisdictions were geared toward effective governing. The present debates about the sizes of the provinces, however, revolve around developmental needs (Huang R. 1995; Jiang M. 1992; Shen Y. 1971; Tian S. 1987; Zhou Z. 1989). Undoubtedly, part of the problem of identity-building in some provinces is due to their large size. Rationalization of provincial jurisdictions is likely to enhance people's geographically based identities and their energy for development. Herein also lies the key to a revolution in Chinese political culture.

Notes

1. Figure 9.1 is meant to provoke more discussions on this subject. The data and interpretations herein are suggestive only.

2. That Fujian had a substantial number of military men among its leaders is due to the construction there of China's first naval academy. Similarly, the large number of military men among the Guangdong elite is due to the Nationalist Party's Whampoa Military Academy in Canton. In other words, extraneous reasons account for the prominence of the military in these two coastal provinces.

3. The dates of the post-1949 gazettes are from *Zhongguo Xinfangzhi Mulu*. But this publication contains a large number of histories of industries. Figure 9.3 includes only those pertaining to communities, the total number being 2,129.

4. Not all the provinces are included in my discussions. I lack sufficient data on some provinces to allow analysis.

5. My source on provincial elite views is *Zhongguo Gongchandang*, which reprints articles from core provincial press and journals on ideology and Party affairs. *Zhongguo Gongchandang* (*ZGD* hereafter) is published by the Center of Reprinted Press and Journals, China People's University. The writers of the articles that I have cited include heads of provincial Party committees, Party propaganda directors, and faculty and graduate students at Party schools and major provincial universities. In other words, these are provincial opinion leaders.

Bibliography

Belay, Gentinet. "The (Re)construction and Negotiation of Cultural Identities in the Age of Globalization." In Harmut B. Mokros, ed. *Interaction & Identity*. New Brunswick: Transaction Publishers, 1996.

Cai Beihua. "The Transition and Outlook of the Economic Relations between China's Interior and Hongkong." *Shehui Kexue*, no. 7 (1988).

Cai Xinmin. "Seriously Carrying Out the 'Resolution' of the Sixth Plenum of the Fourteenth Central Committee to Enable the Party School to Play an Important Role in Building Socialist Spiritual Ethics." *Lilun Tansuo*, no. 2 (1997). In *Zhongguo Gongchandang* [Chinese Communist Party; *ZGD* hereafter], no. 3 (1997).

Cao Deqi. "On Problems of Implementing Party Construction." *Sichuan Shelian Tongxun*, no. 5 (1990). In *ZGD*, no. 1 (1991).

Chen Guoquan. "On Supervision of the CCP." *Shehui Kexue*, no. 1 (1999).

Chen Hsu-ching. *Chung-kuo Nan-pei Wen-hua-kuan*. Taipei: Mu-tung Chu-pan-she, 1976.

Chen Jianhua. *Zhongguo Jiangzhe Diqu Shisizhi Shiqi Shiji Shehui Yishi yu Wenxue*. Shanghai: Xuelin Chubanshe, 1992.

Chen K'uan-ch'iang. *Li-tai K'ai-kuo Kung-chen Tsao-yu*. Taipei: Chia-hsin Shui-ni Kung-shih, 1972.

Chen Peijun. "Strengthen Party Construction in the Process of Developing a Socialist Commodity Economy." *Jiangxi Daxue Xuebao*, no. 4 (1989). In *ZGD*, no. 1 (1990).

Chen Zhaoshun and Wang Lingyi. "On Economic and Trade Relations among Shanghai, Hong Kong, and Macao and Their Influence upon the 'Chinese Economic Zone.'" *Shehui Kexue*, no. 2 (1995).

Cheng Minsheng. "An Outline of Regional Cultures in the Song Dynasty." *Lishi Yanjiu*, no. 1 (1995).

China Strategic Review 2, no. 3 (May/June 1997).

Chu Shi-chia. "Compilations of Chinese Local Gazettes." *Shih-hsueh Nien-pao* 1, no. 4 (June 30, 1932).

Chung-kuo Shih-pao (China Times) (Taipei), December 26, 1991; March 23, 1994; April 6, 1994; and May 5, 1996.

Dai Yi. "Promote Regional Cultural Studies: In Memory of Professor Chen Yuan." *Lishi Yanjiu*, no. 5 (1991).

Dangshi Renwuzhuan. 50 volumes. Xian: Shaanxi Renmin Chubanshe, 1991.

Domenach, Jean-Luc. *The Origins of the Great Leap Forward: The Case of One Chinese Province*. Translated by A.M. Berrett. Boulder: Westview Press, 1995.

Dong Wanmin et al. "Party Construction Must Start from the Basics." *Xuexi Luntan*, no. 7 (1990). In *ZGD*, no. 7 (1990).

Elazar, Daniel J. *American Federalism: A View from the States*. New York: Thomas Y. Crowell, 1966.

Fan Shuzi. "A Comprehensive Study of Urban Culture South of the Lower Reaches of the Changjiang River." *Fudan Xuebao* (Social Science edition), no. 4 (1990).

Fei Xiaotong "A Trip to Xinyang (1)." *Liaowang*, no. 35 (1994a).

———. "A Trip to Xinyang (2)." *Liaowang*, no. 36 (1994b).

———. "A Trip to Jiaozuo (1)." *Liaowang*, no. 48 (1994c).
———. "A Trip to Jiaozuo (2)." *Liaowang*, no. 49 (1994d).
Fei Zhengzhong. *Jiangnan Shifeng Yu Jiangsu Wenxue*. Changsha: Hunan Jiaoyu Chubanshe, 1995.
Feng Baozhi. *Sanjin Wenhua*. Shenyang: Liaoning Jiaoyu Chubanshe, 1995.
Friedman, Jonathan. "Narcissism, Roots and Postmodernity: The Constitution of Selfhood in the Global Crisis." In Scott Lash and Jonathan Friedman, eds. *Modernity and Identity*. Oxford, U.K.: Blackwell, 1993.
Fu Boyan et al. "Work Creatively—Upholding Central Authority Consciously." *Dangjian Yanjiu*, no. 7 (1996). In *ZGD*, no. 9 (1996).
Gao Fang. "A Micro-Probe into Some Traditional Stipulations in the Party Constitution." *Shehui Kexue*, no. 2 (1988).
Geng Yunzhi. "On the Constitutionalists' Agitation for Parliamentary Democracy toward the End of the Qing Dynasty." *Zhongguo Shehui Kexue*, no. 5 (1980).
Gu Hongliang and Xu Yi. *Shuangfeng bingzhidi Zheshang*. Hangzhou: Zhejiang Renmin Chubanshe, 1997.
Gu Yaochang. "Six Changes of Party Construction." *Xinhua Ribao* (Nanjing), August 19, 1994. In *ZGD*, no. 10 (1994).
Gu Yongpin. "No Modernization without a Modern Ruling Party." *Dangzheng Luntan*, no. 3 (1989). In *ZGD*, no. 5 (1989).
Guan Lianzhu. "Thoughts on the Relations between Party Construction and Economic Work." *Changbai Xuekan*, no. 4 (1998). In *ZGD*, no. 9 (1998).
Guo Qiang. "Adhering to the Four Cardinal Principles Is a Concentrated Expression of a Party Member's Party Spirit." *Xue Lilun*, no. 3 (1987). In *ZGD*, no. 3 (1987).
Guo Xuegao. "Thoughts on the Admissibility of Private Businessmen into the CCP." *Qiushi*, no. 4 (1996). In *ZGD*, no. 6 (1996).
Han Yangmin. "Customs and Cultures in China: Overview and Regional Survey." *Lishi Yanjiu*, no. 5 (1991).
He Jun. "On Lenin's Big Changes in Thoughts on Party Construction during his Old Age." *Jianghai Xuekan*, no. 1 (1992). In *ZGD*, no. 2 (1992).
"Historical Studies in China." *Lishi Yanjiu*, no. 2 (1981).
Horowitz, Donald L. "Three Dimensions of Ethnic Politics." *World Politics*, no. 23 (January 1971).
Hou Yijie. *Ershi Sijie Chu Zhongguo Zhengzhi Gaige Fengchao*. Beijing: Renmin Chubanshe, 1993.
Hu Anquan. "Problems of Regional Development during the Spring-Autumn Period." *Shehui Kexue*, no. 2 (1996).
Hu Jingzhou and Xue Qingchao. "Persist in Regarding the Leadership of the CCP As Historically Determined." *Henan Caijingxueyuan Xuebao*, no. 3 (1987). In *ZGD*, no. 8 (1987).
Huang Dimin. *Qiangui Wenhua*. Shenyang: Liaoning Jiaoyu Chubanshe, 1998.
Huang, Jianhui. *Shanxi Piaohaoshi*. Taiyuan: Shanxi Jingji Chubanshe, 1992.
Huang Jingzheng. "On Party Construction and the Market Economy." *Mao Zedong Sixiang Yanjiu*, no. 4 (1994). In *ZGD*, no. 1 (1995).
Huang Renwei. "On Regional Economy and the 'Feudal Princes Economy.'" *Shehui Kexue*, no. 8 (1995).
Huang Zhong. "On Changes of Party Leadership Practices at the Present Phase." *Tansuo Yu Zhengming*, no. 9 (1998). In *ZGD*, no. 11 (1998).

Jarausch, Konrad H., ed. *After Unity: Reconfiguring German Identities*. Oxford: Berghahn Books, 1997.
Jaspers, Karl. *The Origin and Goal of History*. London: Routledge & Kegan Paul, 1953.
Jiang Lin and Cheng Xianyu. "Persist in CCP Leadership, Opposition to 'Political Pluralism.'" *Dangjian Yanjiu*, no. 7 (1990). In *ZGD*, no. 7 (1990).
Jiang Meiqiu. "Administrative Divisions of Federal China." *Papers of the Center for Modern China* 3, no. 11 (November 1992).
Jiang Zemin. "Shanghai's Development Must Adhere to the Socialist Road." *Hongqi*, no. 11 (1987).
Jiao Wenfeng. "On the State-Society Relationship in China." *Zhongguo Zhengzhi*, no. 8 (1995).
Ke Ruan. "On Some Problems of Party Construction in a New Situation." *Shehui Kexue*, no. 7 (1988). In *ZGD*, no. 8 (1988).
"Leading Conservatives Reportedly Discuss Reversing Reforms." *Daily Report*, FBIS-CHI-94–172 (6 September 1994).
Lee Kam Keung. *Qingdai Fujian Shilun*. Hong Kong: Hong Kong Educational Publishing, 1996.
Levenson, Joseph. "The Province, the Nation and the World: The Problem of Chinese Identity." In Albert Feuerwerker, Rhoads Murphey, and Mary C. Wright, eds. *Approaches to Modern Chinese History*. Berkeley: University of California Press, 1967.
Li Peidong. "Reflections on the Centralized System of State Power in China's History." *Shehui Kexue*, no. 12 (1987).
Li Pin, ed. *Jiedong Niandai*. Beijing: Jingji Ribao Chubanshe, 1997.
Li Qiang. "On the Culture of Poverty." *Shehuixue*, no. 1 (1990).
Li Qing et al. "Improve the System of Leading Cadres' Making Connections with the Masses." *Dangzheng Luntan*, no. 4 (1997). In *ZGD*, no. 5 (1997).
Li Xishi. "On Objectives of Party Construction in a New Age." *Tansuo*, no. 6 (1994). In *ZGD*, no. 2 (1995).
Li Youhuai. "Persist in Regarding CCP Leadership as Historically Determined." *Harbin Shizhuan Xuebao*, no. 1 (1987). In *ZGD*, no. 9 (1987).
Li Yongjun and Wang Junqing. "New Problems in Recruiting Party Members." *Dangjian Yanjiu*, no. 12 (1994). In *ZGD*, no. 1 (1995).
Liang Qichao. *Yin-ping-she Wen-chi* II. Taipei: Hsin Hsin Shu-chu, 1955.
Liao Tuan. "A Collection of Theories on Party Construction." *Dangzheng Ganbu Xuekan*, no. 1 (1995). In *ZGD*, no. 3 (1995).
Liu Enge. "Only Socialism Can Save China." *Qiqihar Shifan Xueyuan Xuebao*, no. 4 (1981). In *ZGD*, no. 1 (1982).
Liu Guoen. "A Party Member Must Be One with the Center Intellectually and Politically." *Lilun Tantou*, no. 2 (1987). In *ZGD*, no. 4 (1987).
Liu Sun-chi. "Cross-Strait Book Exchanges." *Chung-kuo Ta-lu Yen-chiu* (Mainland China studies) 42, no. 11 (November 1999).
Liu Xuemin. "Problems and Solutions of Party Construction in Private Businesses." *Jianghan Luntan*, no. 7 (1997). In *ZGD*, no. 10 (1997).
Liu Yefei. "Errors in the Practice of Establishing the Party System." *Dangxiao Luntan*, no. 3 (1993). In *ZGD*, no. 3 (1993).
Liu Yifei. "Ideological Emancipation and Construction of the CCP at the Turn of Centuries." *Shehui Kexue*, no. 11 (1988).

Liu Yongzhe. "Collections of Views on a Socialist Market Economy and Party Construction." *Gansu Lilun Xuekan*, no. 5 (1994). In *ZGD*, no. 1 (1995).

Lo Zhengyu. "Party Construction Must Serve the Economy." *Lilun Yu Gaige*, no. 4 (1992). In *ZGD*, no. 8 (1992).

Lu Shaogang and Lu Meiquan. *Zhongguo Lida Zaixiang Zhi*. Changchun: Jilin Wenshi Chubanshe, 1991.

Lu Yun. "Chinese Intelligentsia's Regional Traits and Political Conflicts." *Fudan Xuebao* (Social Science edition), no. 3 (1990).

Ma Bohuang. "The Unbalanced Development of the Geographical Economic History in China." *Shehui Kexue*, no. 1 (1992).

Ma Qibin and Chen Dengcai. "The Thought of Mao Zedong Is the Treasured Spiritual Asset of our Party." *ZGD*, no. 8 (1982).

Ma Yushan. "Municipality and Township Economy in Shanxi Province in the Ming and Qing Dynasties." *Shanxi Daxuexuebao* (Philosophy and Social Science edition), no. 4 (1992).

Montinola, Gabriella, Yingyi Qian, and Barry R. Weingast. "Federalism, Chinese Style: The Political Basis for Economic Success in China." *World Politics* 48 (October 1995).

Murphey, Rhoads. "The Treaty Posts and China's Modernization." In Mark Elvin and G. William Skinner, eds. *The Chinese City between Two Worlds*. Stanford, California: Stanford University Press, 1974.

Nan Junyin and Wang Youlo. "The Party Is the Key to Building a Socialist Spiritual Civilization." *Zhongzhou Xuekan*, no. 1 (1997). In *ZGD*, no. 3 (1997).

Ni Peihua. "On the Problem of Centralization in the Process of Modernization." *Shehui Kexue*, no. 8 (1987).

North, Robert C. and Ithiel de Sola Pool. "Kuomintang and Chinese Communist Elites." In Harold D. Lasswell and Daniel Lerner, eds. *World Revolutionary Elites: Studies in Coercive Ideological Movements*. Cambridge, Mass.: M.I.T. Press, 1966.

Parsons, Talcott. *The System of Modern Societies*. Englewood Cliffs, N.J.: Prentice-Hall, 1971.

Peng Zeyi. "Some Questions Concerning Studies of the History of Guilds (*hanghui*) in China." *Lishi Yanjiu*, no. 6 (1988).

"Propaganda Outline of 'Resolution of the Central Committee of the CCP on Guidance of Construction of Socialist Ethics.'" *Qiushi*, no. 6 (1986). In *ZGD*, no. 1 (1987).

Putnam, Robert D. *Making Democracy Work: Civic Transitions in Modern Italy*. Princeton, N.J.: Princeton University Press, 1993.

Qian Xiaoqian. "Re-study and Re-assess Socialism from the Concrete Course of the Socialist Revolution." *Shehui Kexue*, no. 8 (1987).

Qiao Renlin. "Traditional Customs and Regional Characteristics of Shanxi Society." *Shanxi Daxuexuebao* (Philosophy and Social Science edition), no. 4 (1992).

Qiao Zhiqiang and Gong Guan. "About Country Fairs in Modern North China." *Shanxi Daxuexuebao* (Philosophy and Social Science edition), no. 4 (1993).

Quanguo Zongshumu. Beijing: Xinhua Shudian, 1980, 1991.

Ren Shuang. "The Regional Colors Reflected in the Strife within the Ruling Cliques of the Late Tang and Early Song Dynasties." *Lishi Yanjiu*, no. 2 (1987).

Riker, William H. *The Development of American Federalism*. Boston: Kluwer Academic, 1987.

"Rui Xingwen on Instituting Shanghai Reforms." *Daily Report* FBIS-CHI-87–203 (21 October 1987).

Sawyer, Geoffrey. *Modern Federalism.* London: C.A. Watte, 1969.

Shen Dade et al. "Marxism Needs a New Momentous Development." *Shehui Kexue,* no. 2 (1988).

Shen Yun-lung, ed. *Ming-kuo Ching-shih Wen-pien.* Vol. 5. Taipei: Wen-hai Chu-pan-she, 1971.

Shen Zhichen. "A Historical Investigation into the Guideline 'Self-reliance and Independence.'" *Henan Daxuexuebao* (Philosophy and Social Science edition), no. 1 (1987). In *ZGD,* no. 3 (1987).

Shi Jun and Jing Guozheng. *Zongheng yu Neidi Sushang.* Hangzhou: Zhejiang Renmin Chubanshe, 1997.

Shi Pin. "On Some Theoretical Points Regarding Intellectuals." *Zhongguo Zhengzhi,* no. 8 (1983).

Shih-chieh Jih-pao (Los Angeles), August 20, 1998.

Skinner, G. William. "Mobility Strategies in Late Imperial China: A Regional System Analysis." In Carol A. Smith, ed. *Regional Analysis.* Vol. 1. New York: Academic Press, 1976.

Song Baorui. "Understand Accurately about the Current Situation, Strengthen Study, and Improve the Quality of the Leadership in a Comprehensive Way." *Lilun Yu Gaige,* no. 4 (1995). In *ZGD,* no. 6 (1995).

Song Fuquan. "On the Economic Cultural Characteristics underneath the Poverty Line." *Shehuixue,* no. 2 (1989).

Sopher, David E. "Place and Location: Notes on the Spatial Patterning of Culture." *Social Science Quarterly,* no. 53 (September 1972).

Statistics on Overseas Chinese & Foreign Investment. Taipei: Investment Commission, Ministry of Economic Affairs, December 31, 1998.

Tai Qingliang. "Study the Policy Thoughts of Mao Zedong." *Mao Zedong Sixiang Yanjiu,* no. 2 (1986). In *ZGD,* no. 7 (1986).

Tan Jixiang. "Differences of Chinese Culture in Times and Regions." *Fudan Xuebao,* no. 2 (1986).

Tang Wenquan. "The Rise and Fall of Suzhou's Industrial and Commercial Guilds." *Lishi Yanjiu,* no. 3 (1986).

Tang Xiaoqing et al. "A Basic Assessment of and Thoughts on the Current Conditions of Party Construction." *Dangzheng Ganbu Xuekan,* no. 7 (1997). In *ZGD,* no. 8 (1997).

Tawney, R.H. *Land and Labor in China.* Boston: Beacon Press, 1966.

Tian Shuishen. "Thoughts on the System of Provinces." *Zhongguo Zhengzhi,* no. 5 (1987).

Varan, Duane. "The Cultural Erosion Metaphor and the Transcultural Impact of the Media System." *Journal of Communication* (Spring 1998).

Wang Huizhen et al. "A Comparison between the Finances of Shanghai and Hong Kong." *Shehui Kexue,* no. 10 (1989).

Wang Jiyuan. "It is Necessary to Persist in the Party's Leadership of Socialist Modernization." *Zhonggong Changchun Shiweidangxiao Xuebao,* no. 1 (1987). In *ZGD,* no. 5 (1987).

Wang Lei. "The Party Faces Ten New Problems in Transition to a Socialist Market Economic System." *Dangde Ganbu Xuekan,* no. 7 (1993). In *ZGD,* no. 10 (1993).

Wang Renshen. "Cadres with Party Membership Must Seriously Obey the Party's Political Discipline." *Xuelilun*, no. 4 (1987). In *ZGD*, no. 4 (1987).

Wang Shida et al. "A Regional View of Contemporary Chinese Culture." *Shehui Kexue*, no. 8 (1987).

Wei Guanglai. "A Study of Shanxi Handicraft Industry in the Ming Dynasty." *Shanxi Daxuexuebao* (Philosophy and Social Science edition), no. 4 (1992).

Wei Qiao et al. *Zhejiang Fangzhi Yuanliu*. Hangzhou: Zhejiang Renmin Chubanshe, 1988.

Wu Wenjun. "The Manifestation of Uncouthness among Gansu Cadres and Its Causes." *Lanzhou Xuekan*, no. 5 (1986). In *ZGD*, no. 2 (1987).

Wu Zhengtian. "Adapting to the New Situation of a Socialist Market Economy and Exploring New Topics on Party Construction." *Lilun Tantou*, no. 1 (1995). In *ZGD*, no. 3 (1995).

Xia Jun. "Taking Stock of Drastic Changes in the World and Learning Marxism from Practice." *Dangzheng Luntan*, no. 8 (1997). In *ZGD*, no. 11 (1997).

Xu Dingxin. "A Summary of Research on the Chinese Chamber of Commerce." *Lishi Yanjiu*, no. 6 (1986).

Xu Mao. "Fifty Years of Exploration of Federalism by the Chinese Bourgeoisie." *Fudan Xuebao* (Social Science edition), no. 2 (1989).

Xue Qiliang. "Grasping Important Points: Deepen Understanding of the Spirit of the 'Resolution.'" *Xuexi Zazhi*, no. 12 (1986). In *ZGD*, no. 1 (1987).

Yan Jiadong. "Unify Thinking: Strengthen Party Construction." *Dangzheng Luntan*, no. 7 (1990). In *ZGD*, no. 8 (1990).

Yan Shi. "Persist and Improve Party Leadership: Push for the Development of Society's Productive Forces." *Shehui Kexue*, no. 7 (1987). In *ZGD*, no. 9 (1987).

Yang Boan. "Economic Construction Is the Party and the State's Central Task." *Sichuan Shiyuan Xuebao*, no. 4 (1981). In *ZGD*, no. 1 (1982).

Yang Chunzhang. "On 'Self-reliance and Independence.'" *Hebei Xuekan*, no. 1 (1982). In *ZGD*, no. 9 (1982).

Yang Liqiang. "On the Political Parties, Party Struggle, and Society in the Early Years of the Republic of China." *Fudan Xuebao* (Social Science edition), no. 2 (1993).

Yang Mulin et al. "A Model of Searching for Truth from Facts." *Shanxi Shiyuan Xuebao*, no. 4 (1981). In *ZGD*, no. 2 (1982).

Yao Heng. "New Conclusions from Recent Studies of Party Construction." *Dangjian Wenhui*, no. 1 (1992). In *ZGD*, no. 1 (1992).

Yao Qingan. "On the Unity between Party Leadership and Using Law to Govern the Country." *Lilun Daobao*, no. 6 (1997). In *ZGD*, no. 8 (1997).

Yao Yumin. "On the Negative Effects of a Market Economy and Party Construction." *Xinyang Shifan Xueyuan Xuebao* (Philosophy and Social Science edition), no. 2 (1995). In *ZGD*, no. 2 (1996).

Yu Juan and Fa Yang. "On the Dual Effects of a Market Economy on Party Construction." *Weishi*, no. 12 (1993). In *ZGD*, no. 1 (1994).

Yu Junyi. "On the Watchdog Functions of Parties Taking Part in the Political Process." *Shehui Kexue*, no. 10 (1997). In *ZGD*, no. 11 (1997).

Yu Wenshen. "The Present Condition and the Developmental Model of the Northeastern Asian Economic Cooperation Subzone." *Shehui Kexue Zhanxian*, no. 3 (1994).

Yuan Tingdong. *Basu Wenhua*. Shenyang: Liaoning Jiaoyu Chubanshe, 1991.
Yue Dezhang. "On the Functions of Party Construction in the Process of Social Control." *Henan Shehui Kexue*, no. 6 (1996). In *ZGD*, no. 2 (1997).
Zhang Dinghong. "The Most Important Subject Matter of Party Construction in a New Age." *Dangzheng Luntan*, no. 1 (1988). In *ZGD*, no. 2 (1988).
Zhang Haiyin et al. *Shanxi Shangbang*. Hong Kong: Chung-hua Shu-chu, 1995.
Zhang Jinghua. *Yanchao Wenhua*. Shenyang: Liaoning Jiaoyu Chubanshe, 1995.
Zhang Xiuyin. "The *Communist Party* Monthly's Contributions to the Theory of Party Construction." *Henan Daxuexuebao* (Social Science edition), no. 1 (1992). In *ZGD*, no. 5 (1992).
Zhang Yongqian. "A Brief Commentary on Political Participation in Political Structural Reforms." *Zhongguo Zhengzhi*, no. 4 (1997).
Zhang Zhenggui and Lu Jiaxiang. "Fully Understand the Poverty and Ignorance of Guangxi during the Primary Stage of Socialism." *Shehuixue*, no. 3 (1989).
Zhang Zhifu. *Zhongzhou Wenhua*. Shenyang: Liaoning Jiaoyu Chubanshe, 1995.
Zhao Ruyou. "Why Did So Many Distinguished Talents in Shanxi in the Ming and Qing Dynasties Abandon Their Official Careers to Go into Commerce?" *Shanxi Daxuexuebao* (Philosophy and Social Science edition), no. 4 (1987).
Zhong Jiyan. "Some Problems in Recent Studies on Party Construction." *Lilun Daobao*, no. 6 (1990). In *ZGD*, no. 8 (1990).
Zhonggong Henanshengwei Zuzhibu Zhengceyanjiushi. "Eleven Problems in Strengthening Party Construction." *Lingdao Kexue*, no. 12 (1990). In *ZGD*, no. 1 (1991).
Zhonggong Jiangxishengwei Zuzhibu Ketizu. "On the Situation and Tasks of Party Construction in the 1990s." *Zhengming*, no. 4 (1991). In *ZGD*, no. 9 (1991).
Zhongguo Xinfangzhi Mulu, 1949–1992. Beijing: Shumu Wenxian Chubanshe, 1993.
Zhou Luanshu. "Improve Understanding and Bear Heavy Responsibility." *Zhengming*, no. 1 (1987). In *ZGD*, no. 2 (1987).
Zhou Zhenhe. "Some Ideas about Reforming the Administrative Divisions of China." *Shehui Kexue*, no. 8 (1989).
Zhu Ziyan and Chen Shengmin. *Peng Dang Zheng Zhi Yan Jiu*. Shanghai: Xinhua Shudian, 1992.

10

Political Culture of Election in Taiwanese and Chinese Minority Areas

Chih-yu Shih

Interpreting Elections

Although democracy and election are not interchangeable concepts, many political observers expediently refer to the holding of elections as an indicator of democratization. At least they consider elections to be a necessary condition for democracy.[1] This is especially true if marketization occurs simultaneously with them. Marketization and elections are similar in their common emphasis on the idea that individualized motivation lies behind each political and economic behavior. This individualism is what allows democracy to thrive. While the conditionality of elections as related to democratization may be reasonable, elections can also be a useful instrument in sustaining social forces irrelevant, if not hostile, to democratization. If one overlooks the various meanings of elections that do not lead to the rise of liberal culture familiar to political scientists, one would not appreciate the possibility that there might be different kinds of democracy. These kinds are the ones that do not treat individual rights seriously in either politics or the marketplace.

To observe democratization today means nonetheless focusing on elections in terms of procedural fairness and acceptability of results. Procedures are matters of institutional technicality, while acceptance is a matter of political culture. The former receives more attention both because technical matters can be improved relatively easily over time and because frequent application of fair electoral procedures is believed to be conducive to the breeding of democratic culture. The interest of political scientists in elections implies that elections can create, if not just reflect, the knowledge of individual citizens/voters as well as their willingness to participate in politics for the purpose of protecting their personal stakes.

The same line of reasoning may explain the rising interest among political scientists in the installation of electoral mechanisms in most Chinese villages. Outside observers cannot but wonder if the nascent practices of ballot casting may bring a more democratic China.[2] I argue against this observation elsewhere based upon my findings that Chinese peasants take part in voting for reasons irrelevant to either individualism or liberalism. On the contrary, my past interviewees were concerned with maintaining some sort of identification with kinship, not just religious but political as well. People care more about expressing trust for a leader who should know their interests best than about imposing their own concept of interest upon candidates. Despite the rhetoric concerning democratic checks of politics that has been promoted in the official media, the quest for benevolent leadership rather than for political checks is clear in these elections.[3] In the interviewed areas, nevertheless, it is often the ability to improve the economic welfare of the village as a whole that attests to the existence of benevolent leadership.

If one argues that this quest for benevolent leadership is destined to die out eventually with the development of a market economy, one carries the burden of proof that, first, collective ownership systems in villages will dwindle and, second, that collective identity will concomitantly perish. If either of these two processes fails, the holding of elections may simply represent a new form of collectivism rather than one of liberal democracy. Whether or not democracy is part of this new form turns into a matter of semantics. Past experiences in Taiwan seem to suggest that existing human relational culture constrains the range of political changes caused by the holding of elections.[4]

Human relational culture refers to affective tendency as well as cognitive necessity to always interpret one's own action and role in accordance with one's relationship to a larger social network, so that there is the little self as oneself and the great self as society at different levels. The expression of one's own interest is legitimate only if it involves some selfless positioning which from time to time requires theatrical sacrifice of the interests that presumably prompt one's action in the first place. The human relational culture survives through child rearing, school education, and socialization. A growing person learns to relate his or her role in any given event from the situational context, which may be family, work unit, community, state, nation, or race. The acquiring of one's own material interest should come as a byproduct rather than a direct goal. Consequently, for people in the higher socio-political ladder, private interests and public interests are often difficult to distinguish. "Elections" as a measure of leaders' characters, not voters' interests, would be useful to the consolidation of a collective spirit since the ruled have the right to determine whether or not leaders have confused the "public" with the "private."

Compared with typical villages in Han areas, minority villages should show this collective tendency more clearly. In theory, elections in these areas individualize minority members such that they leave behind their sense of duty to the ethnic groups of which they are members and create a stronger sense of loyalty to the Chinese state. Although democratization is not the same as sinification, democratization that carries civilizing discourses cannot avoid triggering sinification. If ethnic identity is important to people, their responses to the introduction of electoral procedures to their villages should be even more mixed than in Han villages. In other words, human relational culture in minority areas should be richer. This is why one can expect that the meaning of elections other than in terms of individualism is relatively very apparent in minority areas.

Little research has been done in this area. Democratization of minority villages is not conceptually distinguishable from that of Han villages, probably because democratization is conceived of as universal progress regardless of the country or ethnic origin of the areas under study. In this paper, I will report on a number of interviews with local minority scholars and cadres at the township and village levels. They include three minority areas in China and one in Taiwan. The paper will draw a comparison among these ethnic groups. Both China and Taiwan possess "human relational" culture, while the latter is institutionally the more democratic in politics and the more liberal in economics.

I conducted the interviews in China in 1996 and 1997 with Bai people in Dali, Yunnan; Naxi people in Lijiang, Yunnan; and Tujia people in Yongshun, Hunan. These interviews lasted from roughly an hour to four hours. In Yunnan, a university professor accompanied me throughout and made the arrangements to meet local scholars as well as officials. In Hunan, officials of the Taiwan Office helped me greatly with establishing contacts with village cadres as well as factory managers. In Taiwan, the research subjects were Zou people in Shanmei Village, Ali Mountain County. (For the personal backgrounds of interviewees, please refer to the Appendix.) Dr. Chaochi Shan was in charge of the interviews. Each interview lasted over an hour, and most took place in the interviewees' offices, with only one in the house of the interviewee and another in a Yunnan University guesthouse. Typically, interviews start with questions concerning the interviewees' personal background. I developed later questions from their answers to the previous questions. Election was never a major issue during interviews anywhere in China, but I would mention it casually at a proper time and wait for the response. Only when there was a response did I pursue the matter further. I simply dropped the issue otherwise.

I do not pretend that my interviewees totally represent the ethnic group of which they are members, but their views are useful because they teach us how elections can have different meanings. It is perfectly all right for readers of this article to interpret my quotes according to their own needs. The purpose of my exercise is not to pin down a law-like relation between elections and democracy. Rather, what I want to do is to see how elections change the strategy of the interviewees in their identity politics.

A Zou Village in Ali Mountain County

The Zou people live in Ali Mountain County, Jiayi Prefecture, Taiwan.[5] For the purpose of this paper, I use interviews mainly with the Zou people in Shanmei Village. Unlike in China, where elections in ethnic areas are a politically sensitive issue usually not to be discussed with outside researchers, elections are a common-sense activity for the Zou people. Shanmei villagers are basically concerned with two types of elections: elections for village director and county director, and elections for the board members of the Association of Community Development.

Three factors stick out of the interviews as relatively important in determining voter choice in the villages: the position of the elderly in the family or the kinship group, the position of Han dwellers living in the nearby plain, and the position of the ruling Kuomintang's local division. The sense of unity among villagers at the time of elections affects how well all these factors can mutually adapt. To achieve unity, villagers stress the role of mutual consultation. The presumption seems to be that all Shanmei villagers should have only one position. The discussion is typically about unity or lack of unity, not about the freedom of choice by individual villagers.

In the last decade, the village's community development centered on tourism and environmentalism. The issue of Zou identity was first sensitized by the upsurge of identity politics in Taiwan since the mid-1980s. Shanmei villagers have been able to settle on their Zou identity only with some struggle. In the end, fortunately, villagers successfully adopted Shanmei's environmental resources, personified as Gufish, for Shanmei's mascot. The protection of Gufish against Han stealers and the growth of it for Han tourists together serve villagers' quest for a meaningful identity perfectly.[6]

Villagers have established the Association of Community Development to manage tourism and environmental protection. Election for the board members has always been a big issue in the village. There was once the worry that election results might challenge the existing "social ethics," or relational balance among kinship groups. It turns out that every election reflects the balance well. The interviewees stress the contrast between the elections for village and county directors, where such a balance has never been attained. The contrast suggests not just that villagers are more independent voters in the elections for directors but also that, for the villagers, the Association is more important than village or county offices. Mr. Wen Ying-chie cannot be more satisfied with "the balance." He comments:

> The distribution of seats reflect[s] our long-standing tribal ethics. This is not a negotiated result but a spontaneous one. In the case of Shanmei, the An family and the Chuang family are the largest two. . . . You will find that An and Chuang took most seats in the last election. Other families have their shares, too. The only family left out was the Tu family yet the Tu family and the Yang family are related and the Yang family won a seat. In brief, the Association incorporates different positions, be they political, familial, or religious. . . . In contrast, the composition of village cadres does not incorporate different positions. I think this organized balance was formed under the previous system of the Commission of Tourist Development. I realized this only at a later stage. In that previous system, every family had seats. This is why the subsequent Association is able to shelve the village officials. (Interview scripts)

The village directorship cannot be shared. This explains why villagers generally do not feel close to that position, as they do to the Association. One former Chief Commissioner of Tourist Development, who later became General Secretary of the Association of Community Development, and is now village director, never treats the Association as subordinate to his governmental office. On the contrary, he accepts his secondary role and uses the patriarchal metaphor that the man handles the outside world and the woman handles the domestic world to describe the relationship between the board and the village office:

> When the election for the Association's board took place, Ying-feng won. Ying-feng has strong leadership. He has been very active and able to raise a lot of funds. The village director loses his focus in comparison. He did not know what to do in the beginning. He wanted to contribute but had no place for him. His relationships with villagers were not as close as Ying-feng's. . . . Later, he may have realized his vulnerability and said that Ying-feng took care of the outside world while I took care of the domestic world. . . . Whether or not there will be harmony between the board and the village depends on the attitude of these two. (Interview scripts)

In these remarks, we see that elections should produce leaders who are not there to promote specific interests. They must demonstrate that they have no personal interests to serve. Wen Ying-chie, the interviewee, is a brother of Ying-feng, and it is natural that he stresses harmony and balance among families, especially when the largest family, the Chuang, seems to be a little cynical about its underdeveloped leadership in the village office. Wen tells us that the Chuangs have most seats in the Association so every development is ethical (*lunli*). One should note that "to be ethical" is to be selfless. Moreover, for his brother to lead the Association and the village legitimately, Wen needs to stress the fact that the Tu family was not left out in actuality. If not because of this ethical balance—Wen points to the neighboring village for the possible consequence—the "suppression of Western religion on aboriginal people" will take place in Shanmei.[7]

In the age of elections, it is interesting to hear how Shanmei villagers emphasize unity and harmony. Indeed before every election, Shanmei cadres work hard on "integrating" (*zhenghe*) different ideas. Cadres and villagers come together, and everybody is allowed to express their opinion. As Yang Ching-shi observes:

We aboriginal people are minorities in the first place and if we spread thin our votes, the result would be very negative. We always work hard on integration, but we do not say you must vote so and so. We respect everyone's own choice. I mean, cadres will tell their ideas and analyze pros and cons for the villagers to know. Most of the time, after listening to our promotion, the villagers can understand better and cooperate. This is true for elections of county director as well as for the head of Jiayi prefecture. (Interview scripts)

Shanmei is special among all Zou villages in the sense that villagers are allowed time to question cadres or candidates after listening to their speeches. Mr. Kao Cheng-sheng, the current village director, finds this kind of participation a unique feature in Shanmei unity.

Other Zou villages cherish unity, too. Even though when younger generations have their own ideas and indeed decide not to cooperate with the elderly in the village, villagers still believe that the village as a whole should have a consensus with respect to its position vis-à-vis the public. The public appearance of consensus is an affective need because the image of unity is essential to the sense of belonging, which is dying out in the age of development. One cadre in Tabang Village comments:

We belong to the Wang family, for example. There are many divisions in our kinship network and we always have a strong sense of belonging. We used to have the elderly family head come out to enlist votes. This is a relatively out-of-date mode of mobilization today because the younger generation has better education and has stronger self-consciousness. We now depend on human relational networks, just like the relationship between you and me. For the sake of harmony, we continue to rely on mutual consultation, hopefully we can always come out with someone acceptable to everybody. . . . Remember, we are an underdeveloped village; if anyone remains selfish, our development would be even slower. (Interview scripts)

Tabang villagers feel that Shanmei villagers have a strong sense of unity, perhaps too strong, for even Shanmei cadres acknowledge that before every election for county director, they should hold an elderly meeting and send the decision of the meeting to the local KMT office. In fact, it is not just the Zou people who demonstrate unity; the Han people living in the lowland areas are also unified during elections. For example, the Han-inhabited Ali Third Village and Fengshan Village always vote together. One Shanmei cadre reveals his feeling of being threatened and questions "how the two villages which are apart from each other by such a long distance can coordinate between them so well?" This breeds the conspiracy theory that the Han people want to split the aboriginal people. Some Zou cadres are even in awe about the unity demonstrated by the Han in the lowlands. This implies that unity is a virtue for the commentators, too. The following is a typical expression of their admiration or envy:

> In the past, whenever the government arranged social activities, the Han in the plains never showed up. It is different now, they are everywhere. For example, they are the key in determining the results of county director elections. . . . The unity among them is impressive. Anything they promise you during election time they can get it done. . . . My husband asked for their support in the last elections, they apologized: you're too late, we have promised another candidate, they said. Another Zou candidate from a different village requested our support earlier. They said [to my husband], why didn't you come earlier? We are old friends, if you had said it earlier, there would have been no problem. Then they said, well, let's see, how about this, I will give you six votes. He meant it, for after the election there were exactly six votes for my husband coming out of his booth. He said it and he made sure you would get the votes. I really admired them for this. (Interview scripts)

One Shanmei cadre is worried that the unity in his village perceived by the Tabang observers is breaking down. He thinks that the old social ethic is gone forever due to Japan's colonial ruling and the subsequent KMT reign. He feels that the choice of village director is no longer made by the elderly. I find it difficult to substantiate his analysis. To compare the power of the elderly and the political regime is to compare apples with oranges. The elderly want to make sure that elections become an occasion to readdress the issue of unity, while the KMT uses them to gain legitimacy. In any case, the notion of unity continues to be a reference point when villagers judge events, as this anxious cadre comments:

> Under the system of the elderly, the elderly from each Kuba [i.e., the rule of the elder] will stand out to resolve the competition. But, the Kuba system broke down long ago during Japanese rule. The KMT was even more destructive. There is no core in the village today. The core gave in to the county office. In the past, it was the KMT that appointed the county

director. Indeed, we have elections now, but most of the time they designate you to vote so and so and the villagers all vote so and so. The KMT's will dominates the county director's. As a result, the sense of community of our tribe is close to total destruction. Unless the party decides to let it open, there is no way the elderly can still coordinate. (Interview scripts)

Recent elections are more competitive as people realize that they can take advantage of elections by articulating their need for the superior KMT division to be heard. Facing competition, the KMT often makes the first move to inform the villagers of the party's choice. One county cadre who prefers to remain anonymous comments:

In the past, when we urged people to become a candidate or to be our representative, nobody wanted to. . . . People's concept has gradually changed. People now understand that we can take advantage of elections to promote and procure our community interests or needs. . . . This is different from passive waiting which is what we did before. . . . That is why there are many people jumping out to run in elections for county director in recent years. When we try to coordinate, I feel the party has more influence. They will pick up one of the willing candidates from our tribe and tell us to support him. (Interview scripts)

The local KMT also actively intervenes in the election for the chair of the county assembly. In the past, the KMT preferred a Han chair as a balance to a Zou director. The party is more open to elections today, and the Han in the plains use a lot of tricks, one of the more popular being to get all the assemblymen out for sightseeing a few days before elections so that the Zou people are unable to find and lobby them. If the election is totally open to competition, the majority of Zou assemblymen would definitely elect a Zou, as happened when the KMT held open elections for the first time.

In that year, the assembly under the Zou chairmanship moved quickly to change the name of the county from Wu Feng County to Ali Mountain County. Wu Feng is a folk hero constructed by the Japanese colonial rulers. It is said that Wu, a Han widely respected by the Zou people, offered his life for human sacrifice as the Zou people pleaded for rain. Wu did this because, according to the story, he failed to persuade the Zou people to forego their barbarian ritual and hoped instead to offer his life in the interest of changing Zou practice. It is said that the Zou people were so sorry after discovering their beloved dead that they gave up the barbaric custom.

There is no doubt that the story is a construction reflecting the superiority complex of the Japanese rulers.[8] The KMT took it over after Japan left and included it in primary-school textbooks. The Zou people have for generations felt degraded by it, and the move to change the name of the county was a triumph. However, the change of name irritated those Han dwellers in the plains who used to ask for fortune in the local temple of Wu Feng. Partially as a result of this incident, the Han in the plains have felt it necessary to compete more effectively in the subsequent elections.

The Zou people are not used to the change of electoral style. The Han candidates have begun to buy votes. Some have developed good human relational networking skills among the Zou villagers. All have learned to use negative campaigning which discloses a lot of behind-door exchanges and is detrimental to social harmony. With Han leaders reassuming power in the assembly, the county office and the assembly boycott each other. The KMT has lost control in recent years. One Zou assemblyman recalls what he once witnessed:

> Here in front of us are all kinds of accusations from both sides. Staff and supporters on each side almost burst into fist fighting. The conflict in the past was at most . . . well, they did not reach the level of fist fighting before. During the meeting, they continued the boycotting, delaying, and fault-finding. The county office then imparts its plan to do such and such if the assembly dares to do this or that. (Interview scripts)

Neither the Zou nor the Han in Ali Mountain County are ready for electoral politics that rest upon individual differences on issues. Differences are considered challenges to the harmony of all the people involved. For political scientists the electoral system is premised upon differences, while people in Ali Mountain County care more about human relational harmony.[9] Competition and difference necessarily push the game into one of mutual negation.

Elections used to mean little to the Zou people. Once elections become part of political life, one needs those coordinating elderly and some community development body like the Association in Shanmei to avoid the vicious competition seen in county politics. The KMT intervention and the solidarity of the Han voters in the plains contribute to the Zou sense of unity. On the whole, values that Zou cadres care about, such as balance, ethics, unity, community development, etc., relate more to the tribe or the village than to individual interests. One needs to wait a few more decades to judge if the sense of community will diminish as the more worrying Zou cadres predict. More likely the election-related thinking will continue to spring from a collective perspective. From my interviews, the best indication is that the Zou's understanding of elections reproduces (albeit in a rather peculiar way) rather than distracts from the Zou's sense of belonging.

Democratic Autonomy in Some Mainland Ethnic Areas

The Chinese Communist Party Center has the policy of promoting democracy at the village level. Ethnic cadres in villages respond accordingly. However, the installation of electoral mechanisms at the village level does not necessarily promise real politico-cultural change. Not only is it that local ethnic cadres elected through village democracy may not appreciate the meaning of democracy as we political scientists understand it, but also that the rationale behind the village democratic system in China is not familiar to us.[10] From the perspective of the Ministry of Civil Affairs, which plans the new democratizing project, democracy is useful because it relieves the party of the duty of executing policies such as those regulating birth control, grain extractions, fee levies, and so forth. Village cadres thus elected do not have much room of their own here. They have to be held responsible by the township government and at the same time cope with villagers' democratic participation during election time.

   Institutionally speaking, village cadres have been left alone to deal with peasants after the introduction of the electoral system. They should not expect the same level of political support from the township government as before when encountering resistance in villages. If they cannot handle matters, the party will look for someone else to take over in the next elections. The party in the village would like to stay behind the scenes now, although it is still actively involved in the daily operation of many villages. Except for a few sporadic cases, village cadres are in no position to challenge the township government. Nonetheless, the electoral system seems effective in compelling most elected directors and their village councils to find ways acceptable to villagers in fulfilling policy requirements. Despite the rising responsibility, village directors generally appear willing to continue their work. Monetary incentives explain part of this willingness. In Dashi Township of Beining County, Liaoning, for example, the Manchurian directors in villages lose their salaries if the township investigation team decides that their performance fails to meet the expectations established at the beginning of the year.

The party leaders at the top of the provincial and central governments are invariably Han or Han-coopted, and their policies are naturally not ethnically based. If policies are ethnically based—as for example, exemptions for birth control policies—they are made by Han officials. Ethnic cadres at the village level would have to be responsible for Han-made policies, being minority-regarded or not. Electoral systems successfully camouflage the non-ethnic nature of government policies by holding ethnic cadres directly responsible for their implementation.

In the above discussion, a generally overlooked assumption of the village democracy shows itself, that being that the villagers care more about fair implementation than the substance of a policy. If the villagers cared about the substance, they would use democratic processes to articulate their own interests and compel whomever was interested in taking the position of village director to promote their interests. Indeed, villagers usually care more about the candidates for director as persons than they do about the concrete policy, if any, the candidates advocate. Since the government mainly wants to resolve the problem of policy implementation and believes that finding the right director will do that, the government must have similarly assumed, first, that it knows villagers' interests better than the villagers themselves do and, second, that the villagers think so, too. The widespread assumption that the villagers use elections only for choosing a person and not to promote their specific interests is incompatible with the popular wisdom that, in a democracy, each person knows and promotes their own interests.

The Chinese assumption about elections at the village level thus explains why it is required that ethnic villages should have ethnic directors. Although this requirement may not be universally followed, it is to a large extent followed. Obviously ethnic directors are better off in implementing policies in ethnic villages. Once directors are members of local minorities and elected by ethnic villagers, the Han-centered government will not face any ethnically based challenge to its policies.

There could be a risk, though, if, one day, policies are so bad that ethnic cadres in an autonomous area, be it a district or a prefecture, decide to mobilize their villagers to resist the policies. The loyalty of these ethnic cadres is therefore a politically highly sensitive condition that the government wants to assure. Most of the time, ethnic villages are supervised by an ethnic township, which is under an ethnic county or prefecture. When villagers are popularly elected, this can put the village director and the township director against each other. Strong county leadership can often control the situation, rendering village elections sheer formality. Since directors at the county level are also minorities, the government can avoid the risk of appearing to witness ethnic resistance to Han policy. In any case, whichever level (village or township) provides the locus for the real power, ethnic cadres at that level are always concerned with the implementation issue instead of the substance issue.

The process of nomination of candidates for village director makes sure of both the participation of villagers and the control by the township. According to Mr. Peng, a Tujia general manager of Yongshun Tobacco and previously a township director with much experience with elections at the village level:

> We have elections. Villages are the most democratic places in China. We go through a prolonged and repeated process of consultation. The township level would gather all the information, evaluate it, and nominate a list for the villagers to vote. We don't have the problem of vote buying. To be a village director in Yongshun is very tiring. They have the thought of wanting to serve people. The township director here must be a minority. The Han is a minority here in actuality and should receive special protection. (Interview scripts)

What is interesting about this comment is its revelation that although nominees must go through a consultation process among villagers, the township level determines the final candidates. In this particular case, villagers are economically underdeveloped and rely heavily on the township subsidy. There is little benefit to gain by becoming a director other than some feeble allowance provided by the township. The township hereby gets the power to interfere in village elections to the extent that consultation is little more than promotion of the official candidates. However, the township government strives to avoid weak directors who will not help very much in executing government policies.

That is why the township wants to find directors capable of developing village economies. The ability to boost the local economy is the most important source of power. Mr. He Pinzheng, a Naxi scholar in Lijiang, Yunnan, comments that, when villagers vote, "primarily they look at the economic management despite other obvious problems the candidates have. The good old man can no longer win votes. A good old man listens to the superior, having no skills of his own." Even in villages where ethnically unique religion continues to thrive, candidates during elections must promise to develop the economy, according to Professor Gao at Yunnan University. In other words, the government needs someone to help develop the economy so that the person can have the reverence of the villagers necessary for effective execution of government policy.

The thinking here is quite different from the modernization theory familiar to political scientists in the outside world. According to modernization theory, economic growth brings the rise of plural, civil society.[11] Citizens participate in the policy-making process with the idea of protecting their interests against governmental intervention.[12] The government's power should be limited by law and supervised by the elected legislature. The Chinese assumption is that villagers will have more trust in cadres that bring in growth and willingly cooperate with them on policies. Economic growth helps to integrate a community at the brink of a breakdown caused by the weakness of collective business in the village.[13] Integration is achieved through the rise of a trustworthy and revered leader in these Chinese ethnic villages, whereas in Western individualist societies it is achieved through the consolidation of personal rights.

In reality, however, most ethnic villages have yet to achieve a level of economic growth that is strong enough to support village leadership. The extant social organizations, such as family, surname faction, religious sect, and so on, continue to dominate. Electoral mechanisms usually strengthen the existing organization, not weaken it. According to Professor Gao:

> Anyone who relies on kinship and patriarchal structures can play with elections in places where there are closed geography, a sense of community unity, and weak government control. When the village director is old and should be replaced, whom to vote for? Everybody knows whom to vote for. The process of holding elections is required nevertheless. The process legitimates the succession. The successor still comes from the same family. (Interview scripts)

The government officials face a dilemma between stepping in and letting go. On the one hand, villagers apparently support the family, not the policy, and this bias would weaken the government's leverage in the village should the policy some day contradict the ruling family's interests as determined by the presumed benevolent leadership in the family rather than by the individual family members. On the other hand, as long as the village director keeps in mind the work of policy implementation, the township government, which is not influential in the village anyway, should not complain. In fact, village cadres, through facile social networking, often abuse their power or government policy. This problem may be more serious at the township level than at the village level in some areas.

Together with various old conventions, elections may reproduce local dictatorship. This happens even in relatively advanced ethnic areas such as the Bai areas. Professor Li Donghong comments:

> Election is a sheer matter of formality. Most people don't care too much. People winning elections are those who do not work. Those elected are whom villagers fear, not those who do the real work. They can be very oppressive. During elections villagers only know those who come to mind most quickly. These are perhaps leaders of productive teams, the economically better-off villagers, those who villagers fear most, and the more eloquent. The result often defeats the purpose of having elections in the first place. (Interview scripts)

Thus, at high levels government has a tendency to intervene in local dictatorships, especially if the government is conscious of the potential stake of aborting democratization. Professor Gao argues as follows:

> The township government goes down to investigate and intervene. . . . The key is how to handle the forces of family and kinship. If village councils and these forces combine, the consequence could be beyond imagination. If they do not combine, it is still possible for the government to influence the village councils. Nonetheless, the stability of the central political regime could run into problems. This is the situation where each village has a different minority and there is another new minority community every two to three kilometers. All issues in villages are resolved through private means. (Interview scripts)

Private means exist both inside and between ethnic villages. Under these circumstances, few people would develop loyalty to an abstract state. In Yunnan, the primary function of elections is thus to produce village cadres who will cooperate with the township government willingly. In fact, the government's intervention may disapprove the result of elections.

It sometimes happens that those directors winning the elections may be willing to cooperate but are unable to mobilize the support of the villagers. Over time, experienced villagers adapt and vote for only those whom they know the township government can accept. He Pingzheng recalls what happened in his Naxi village:

> In the past, the party appointed village directors and village council members. All productive team divisions had their own team leaders, succumbing to the control of the party secretary. Election has become a built-in mechanism in choosing directors toward the end of the 1980s. The masses voted first, but the party would judge the result afterwards. If the party was not satisfied with the result, it held another election. The party was not concerned about the loyalty problem, but purely about its liking or disliking the elected. The masses like those who have economic ability. The party accepts them as long as they are not bad people. Election by the masses is only the first step. The township is the one who finalizes it. When casting votes, the masses sometimes take into account the possibility of getting the superior approval. (Interview scripts)

In Yongshun, the seat of a prefecture-level government of the Tujia and Miao Autonomous District in western Hunan province, the government's intervention is more sophisticated. Director Tian of Lingxi Township, a Tujia cadre, was appointed by the prefecture government to Lingxi a year before elections. In Yongshun, the township director is elected by a township people's congress, but the nomination is made by the masses or mass organizations. This is to assure that the township government has some popular support. A year of work acquainted Mr. Tian with his constituency, and this contributed to his acceptance by the local people a year later. Yongshun's Bureau of Civil Affairs is similarly sophisticated in managing village elections. According to Bureau Chief Wang, who hails from Tujia, an average of one-third of village directors failed in the reelection last time: "Those who cannot even run public welfare or take care of public interest cannot get reelected" (Interview scripts).

It appears that in these ethnic villages the township government plays a critical role in arranging candidates for village cadre positions. The right candidates are those who, once elected, can effectively implement government policies, mobilize support for reform, and feed information concerning social mood back to the government. The function of elections, as the party envisions them, is ultimately to keep villagers in harmony among themselves, with the government, and, most importantly, with the party leadership so as to facilitate the policy implementation process.

It is worth noting that ethnic villages and Han villages are not necessarily different in terms of the function of elections envisioned by the party. Ethnic villages are relatively poor economically, remote geographically, and unique religiously. The felt sensitivity of electoral politics in ethnic villages clearly does not result from these characteristics. It has to do with the fear that the impression of a Han-ethnic split may ruin the political unity of the whole country. As a result, the intervention by the party often carries with it some policy privileges or exemptions. In addition, demands regarding the pace of reform of electoral procedure is similarly loose in ethnic villages. This is especially true in Yunnan and less true in Hunan. The government as well as the party is cautious enough to make sure that intervention is conducted by the superior cadres who often belong to the same ethnic group, with the exception of ethnically mixed Xishuangbanna, where a Han superior can appear as an arbitrator.

The meaning of elections for ethnic villagers whom I met in my sporadic stops in Yunnan and Hunan is yet to be determined. What seems obvious is that elections serve functions other than that of protecting individual interests. There is also little expression that elections have a base in liberal individualism. Furthermore, while the notion of democratic control is alien to the ethnic villages, it is not necessarily so to the Han villages. Yet, indeed, many a minority cadre—for example, Mr. Wang, Mr. Peng, or Mr. Tian—stresses that there is no difference between the ethnic and the Han villages in terms of village reform. None in the Han areas ever mentioned the comparison to me.

The villagers' wanting to be no different from the Han seems relevant for understanding the relatively slow pace of political reform in ethnic villages. Not only do the ethnic superiors at the township and county levels, to avoid embarrassment, ignore the sheer formality of elections in many villages under their jurisdiction, but also village-dwelling ethnic cadres I met never seemed interested in resisting the party or the government whatever the latter's policies were. The government's problem with them is not resistance, but that they are not capable of implementing policies, which often means little to them. Birth control is one example. From this perspective, electoral mechanisms are themselves forms of intervention.

Conclusion

Democratization occurred in Ali Mountain County and in various Yunnan sites and Yongshun roughly at the same time in the early 1980s.[14] Its most conspicuous feature is that ethnic villagers now elect their cadres. The fact that ethnic villagers vote individually does not mean that they think individualistically when they evaluate candidates. Political regimes at the higher level in all these areas typically require the elected administrators to be ethnic. Coordination and mutual consultation are necessary parts of electoral politics and put all villagers under pressure to adapt and to accept their status of belonging to a larger community. For Chinese ethnic areas, coordination takes place more in the nomination process, while for Shanmei Village, it also occurs in the process of distributing ballots.

There are differences among Zou in Ali Mountain County, Bai and Naxi in Yunnan, and Tujia in Yongshun. First of all, policy implementation is a less prominent concern in Ali Mountain County than in its mainland counterparts. Secondly, ethnic villagers in the Yunnan sites are not mixed with Han dwellers as the Zou and Tujia are. Tujia feels no intrusion because the level of development of Tujia and Han is roughly the same, while Zou fares much worse than the Han in the plains. This explains the expression of a stronger sense of unity in Zou villages. Finally, the KMT's control in Ali Mountain is weaker than that of the Communist Party in China, and the former is not as politically sensitive to the ethnic issue. However, for the more remote mountain villages in Yunnan, the Communist Party's reach can be even weaker than the KMT's is in Shanmei village.

The similarities among the sites are significant. First of all, electoral competition is not highly valued in any of these ethnic villages. Integration and unity are the major concerns. Competing on the human relational front is more typical than intra-system campaigning. Anxiety over loss of social control is a built-in element of democracy, not a constraint of it. Family and kinship organizations are by far the most influential factors in election-related discourse. Even though people no longer blindly follow the family position, the repeated reference by the interviewees to "unity" or "consensus" implies a worldview where the meaning of life begins in the family, the tribe, and the kinship instead of with the individual. Electoral politics have not yet changed the fundamental thinking about the priority of the collective over the individual.

The practice of electoral politics and the result of elections do not solely depend on this collectivistic worldview, though. The extent of the party's intervention, the degree of mix of the ethnic people and the Han people, and the difference in the levels of development between the ethnic and the Han people, together with the continuing importance of mutual consultation among the elderly as well as between local cadres and the party, are elements determining election results. Due to the combination of these factors, no ethnic villages in the interviewed areas resembled, nor are comparable with, the rise of individualism in cases popular in political science literature.[15]

The sense of unity differs depending on the local situations and the history of the ethnic identity. In other words, one should not expect that electoral mechanisms unilaterally transform ethnic villages. The responses from the ethnic villages are active and creative, if not always straightforward or conscious. Elections actually strengthen and further sensitize the Zou identity as opposed to the Han identities. Elections can legitimize the existing ruling structures as, for example, in some Bai villages in Yunnan. Some Naxi villagers cleverly elect those people the township can accept in exchange for minimal support of their preference for economic leadership. With relatively little felt need for ethnic solidarity, the Tujia superiors maintain stability in Yongshun County by engineering the change of a good proportion of incompetent village directors. The burden of fixing the Tujia identity shifts to the Han regime, which responds with its policy privileges and exemptions. None of these responses is related to, or less important than, the emergence, if any, of individualistic thinking.

Perhaps, in the more democratic Han villages, similar responses in social relational activities are overlooked. If we incorporate social relational perspectives in our study of village democracy in Han villages, we may be able to provide a much richer reading of the meaning of democratization in those areas. We may also have misinterpreted the meaning of democratization in those villages.

Appendix: Interviewees Relevant to this Chapter

Shanmei Village, Ali Mountain

Name* (Gender)	Position	Year of Birth
Wen Lichen (F)	Secretary of ACD Community Chorus	1967
Chuang Yuemei (F)	Accountant of ACD	1951
Wen Yingchie (M)	Head of ACD Cultural Education	1962
Wen Yingfeng (M)	Head of ACD Board	1960
Yang Chinghsi (M)	ACD Board member	1950
Kao Chengsheng (M)	ACD Board member	1943
An Shenchi (M)	ACD Standing Supervisory member	1954
An Pingyao (M)	ACD Supervisory member	1953

ACD: Association of Community Development, Shanmei
* Some of the names remain anonymous in the text

Chinese Ethnic Interviewees

Name (ethnicity)	Position
Mr. Peng (Tujia)	General Manager of Yongshun Tobacco
He Pingzheng (Naxi)	Scholar, Yunnan Social Science Academy, Lijiang Division
Mr. He (Naxi)	Scholar, Yunnan Social Science Academy, Lijiang Division
Mr. Gao (Han)	Professor of Political Science, Yunnan University
Mr. Li (Bai)	Professor of Anthropology, Yunnan University
Mr. Tian (Tujia)	Township Director, Lingxi, Yongshun
Mr. Wang (Tujia)	Director of Yongshun County Bureau of Civil Affairs

Notes

1. Minxin Pei, "Creeping Democratization in China," *Journal of Democracy* 6, no. 4 (October 1995): 76; Larry Diamond, "Beyond Authoritarianism and Totalitarianism," in Brad Roberts, ed., *The New Democracies* (Cambridge: MIT Press, 1990), 227–249.

2. "People's Republic of China," International Republican Institute, n.p., n.d. Mimeographed.

3. Chih-yu Shih, "Public Citizens, Private Voters," in Chong-pin Lin, ed., *PRC Tomorrow* (Kaohsiung: National Sun Yat-Sen University, 1996), 145–168.

4. On authoritarian culture and democratization in Taiwan, see Fu Hu and Yun-han Chu, "Electoral Competition and Political Democratization in Taiwan" (paper presented at the Conference on Democratization in Taiwan, Institute of International Relations, National Chengchi University, Taipei, January 8–10, 1989).

5. For a more detailed account of the background of this study, see Tang Hongchong, "The Legends of Shanmei" (Jiayi: Tang Hongchong, 1999) (mimeo). Tang was the acting township director for Ali Mountain Township for three years between 1996 and 1998 and is currently a staff member of the Jiayi County government.

6. About Shanmei's history, see Chih-yu Shih, "Ethnic Economy of Citizenship in China" (paper presented at the Conference on Chinese Citizenship, Harvard University, Cambridge, Massachusetts,October 30, 1999).

7. By suppression, I think he meant that different churches split the villagers into confrontational groups.

8. Wu Feng was pursued and killed in 1769 for being suspected of poisoning Zou people, kidnapping Zou girls, and cheating Zou traders. It was the Japanese colonial government that rewrote the Wu Feng incident into its modern version, which was conveniently adopted by the KMT government when it took over in 1945. The rationale of the rewriting was to mobilize and civilize the Zou through the construction of an inferior Zou identity. See Hsu Chiyi, "Exploring Ancient Sites in Chiayi," *Chiayi Literature (Jiayi wenxian)* 28 (1998): 23.

9. For various interpretations of Chinese elections in general, see James A. Robinson, comp., *Villager Committee Elections in China: A Selected Collection of Essays* (Atlanta: The Carter Center, n.d.).

10. For dissenting views, see, for example, Chih-yu Shih, *Collective Democracy* (Hong Kong: Chinese University Press of Hong Kong, 1999); Kevin O'Brien, "Implementing Political Reform in China's Villages," *Australian Journal of Chinese Affairs* 32 (1994).

11. See, for example, Gordon White, *Riding the Tiger: The Politics of Economic Reform in Post-Mao China* (Stanford: Stanford University Press, 1993).

12. See, for example, Merle Goldman, Perry Link, and Su Wei, "China's Intellectuals in the Deng Era: Loss of Identity with the State," in L. Dittmer and S. Kim, eds., *China's Quest for National Identity* (Ithaca: Cornell University Press, 1993), 125–153.

13. Government intervention as well as economic growth may create various seemingly incompatible results that do not allow any generalized conclusion. See the discussion in Mette Halskov Hansen, *Lessons in Being Chinese: Minority Education and Ethnic Identity in Southwest China* (Seattle: University of Washington Press, 1999).

14. For Shanmei, the Association of Community Development was established in 1982. This was the point when elections became a relevant factor in Shanmei's life.

15. Recent ethnic studies confirm that each ethnic area has its own feature and is not characterized by general descriptions. See, for example, Gerald A. Postiglione, ed., *China's National Minority Education: Culture, Schooling and Development* (London: Flamer, 1999).

References

Diamond, Larry. 1990. "Beyond Authoritarianism and Totalitarianism." In *The New Democracies*. Brad Roberts, ed. Cambridge: MIT Press. 227–249.
Goldman, Merle, Perry Link, and Su Wei. 1993. "China's Intellectuals in the Deng Era: Loss of Identity with the State." In *China's Quest for National Identity*. L. Dittmer and S. Kim, eds. Ithaca: Cornell University Press. 125–153.
Hansen, Mette Halskov. 1999. *Lessons in Being Chinese: Minority Education and Ethnic Identity in Southwest China*. Seattle: University of Washington Press.

Hsu, Chiyi. 1998. "Exploring Ancient Sites in Chiayi." *Chiayi Literature (Jiayi wenxian)*, vol. 28.

Hu, Fu and Yun-han Chu. 1989. "Electoral Competition and Political Democratization in Taiwan." Paper presented at the Conference on Democratization in Taiwan, Institute of International Relations, National Chengchi University, Taipei, January 8–10.

O'Brien, Kevin. 1994. "Implementing Political Reform in China's Villages." *Australian Journal of Chinese Affairs,* no. 32.

Pei, Minxin. 1995. "Creeping Democratization in China." *Journal of Democracy* 6, no. 4 (October).

"People's Republic of China." n.d. International Republican Institute, n.p. Mimeographed.

Postiglione, Gerald A., ed. 1999. *China's National Minority Education: Culture, Schooling and Development.* London: Flamer.

Robinson, James A., comp. n.d. *Villager Committee Elections in China: A Selected Collection of Essays.* Atlanta: The Carter Center.

Shih, Chih-yu. 1996. "Public Citizens, Private Voters." In *PRC Tomorrow.* Chongpin Lin, ed. Kaohsiung: National Sun Yat-Sen University. 145–168.

———. 1999. *Collective Democracy.* Hong Kong: Chinese University Press of Hong Kong.

———. Forthcoming. "Ethnic Economy of Citizenship in China" In *The View of Chinese Citizenship.* M. Goldman and E. Perry, eds. Cambridge: Harvard University Press.

Tang, Hongchong. 1999. "The Legends of Shanmei." Jiayi: Tang Hongchong. (mimeo).

White, Gordon. 1993. *Riding the Tiger: The Politics of Economic Reform in Post-Mao China.* Stanford: Stanford University Press.

11

Religion and Society in China and Taiwan

Wenfang Tang

This chapter addresses two questions. The first concerns religiosity in China and Taiwan; that is, who believes in what religion. The second concerns the manner in which religion affects one's political and economic attitudes. To answer the first question, I will examine the number of followers of each religion, the religious values associated with each religion, and the geographic, social, and economic characteristics of the followers of each religion. For the second question, I will discuss the impact of religion and religious values on political obedience, economic efficacy, and attitudes toward money. By comparing China and Taiwan, one can gain insights into the development of religions and their role under different political and economic systems with a common cultural tradition.

Data

I will use survey questions from both Taiwan and the mainland in this study. Questions for Taiwan are from the 1990 Taiwan Social Change Survey, conducted by Professor Chiu Hei-yuan at the Institute of Ethnology, Academia Sinica.[1] This was a probability sample of the whole society drawn from household registers, both urban and rural, but dominated by the largely urban population of Taiwan. The survey includes

2,531 respondents and over 240 questions. It was managed by social scientists with Ph.D.s from leading universities in Taiwan and the U.S. The interviewers were social science students with formal training in social science and research methods.

Questions for the mainland are from the 1992 China Urban Social Survey, conducted by Yang Guansan of the Economic System Reform Institute of China (ESRIC). This survey was based on a probability sample of 2,395 respondents in 44 cities, ranging in population from a low of 93,800 (Zhangshu) to a high of seven million for Shanghai. Within cities, there was random selection first of neighborhood districts and then, within neighborhoods, of individual respondents as drawn from the household registration system. To assure accurate comparison, this survey repeated all the key questions and background questions used in the above-mentioned 1990 Taiwan survey. The survey methods utilized by ESRIC helped insure response validity. In the self-administered questionnaires (in the presence of an interviewer), respondents were asked not to give their names and were assured that their answers would not be identified. After Deng Xiaoping's southern tour advocating further reform, the generally open political atmosphere on the mainland in 1992 encouraged the respondents to speak out even on the more sensitive political questions.

In addition to detailed information on the respondent's background (education, age, party identification, gender, income, occupation, etc.), both surveys included questions on the respondent's religion, attitudes toward various religious values, the role of religion in society, and religious activities. They also included questions on political compliance, economic efficacy, and attitudes toward money. These parallel questions provide an excellent opportunity to compare the role of religion in the two societies.

One possible source of sample bias is that the mainland survey addresses the urban population only while the Taiwan sample takes in both urban and rural populations. This difference leads to a higher level of education and higher percentages of professionals and administrators on the mainland than in Taiwan. Another possible source of sample bias is that essential information for the mainland study was drawn from the household registration system, which did not include the large urban "floating" population, consisting mostly of rural surplus laborers of less education and in lower occupational groups. A comparison of education levels between the sample and the population indicates the upward bias of the sample in both surveys, although the problem is worse for the mainland sample. To correct this problem, I have weighted both samples by education of the population as reported in the 1990 population census of China and the 1990 Labor Force Survey of Taiwan for descriptive statistics (see Appendix 1). In multivariate analyses, which typically include the education variable, I assume that the inclusion of the education variable resolves most of the representation issues.

Research Questions

Religiosity

The first question is religiosity, i.e., how religious people are and in what religion and religious values they believe. Several factors are related to religiosity in a society, including modernization, culture, and class theory. For the modernizationist, there are three stages in the intellectual development of humanity: theological, metaphysical, and positive. In the theological stage, the understanding of reality is essentially religious in nature. The metaphysical stage is a transitional stage from the theological. The positive stage represents the development of modern scientific thought along with the decline of religious ideas (Hamilton 1995). Weber argued that religion helps people feel more confident when faced with uncertainties, difficulties, injustices, and misfortunes of life (Weber 1970a). Education creates a belief in one's ability to predict change, master one's fate, and reduce one's reliance on religion for dealing with uncertainty. Other factors, such as higher occupational status, increased income, the fact of being male, and urbanization, may also be related to a stronger sense of controlling one's fate and may, therefore, lead to less religiosity (Hamilton 1995, 169). In the 1970s, industrialized nations experienced a secularization movement. In China, winners of economic reform were less likely to join religious cults than losers (Tang 1999). Furthermore, religiosity should also follow the regional economic development imbalance, with more developed areas (Taiwan and more developed regions of China) being less religious than the less developed areas. Finally, since modernization is associated with Christianity, Christian religions may be more popular than folk religions among the "modernized."

A variation of the modernization argument is the return of religion in post-industrial societies, as reflected in the New Religious Movements

(Stark and Bainbridge 1980, 1985, 1987). According to this view, the desecularization in contemporary Western Christian societies is essentially an attempt to cope with the unbalanced development between the abundance of material goods, on the one hand, and the alienation, isolation, and psychological stress caused by the highly regulated and mobile lifestyle with declined community solidarity and deteriorating interpersonal relations on the other. Religion serves the function of strengthening social solidarity (Durkheim 1915, 225). Accordingly, post-materialist attitudes, which should be more obvious among social elites and in the more developed regions, may lead to an increase of religiosity.

The culturalist would argue that religion is closely related to cultural tradition (family and community). Even under modernization, religious values and practices persist. According to this view, ethnic origin and old age (thus, more traditional influences) should be related to a higher level of religiosity. In regions under the influence of a particular culture or religion, religiosity should also be strong.

A variation of the culturalist view is the emphasis on the emotional aspect of religion. Freud thought that religion was an attempt to humanize as gods the threats and limitations imposed by nature. As in a small child's relations to its father, the father is feared but also looked to for protection (Freud 1961, 29–30). For Marett (1914), education and other factors related to one's social and economic status should not make a difference, since religion is a suspension of normal rationality.

The class model advanced by Marx and Engels holds that religion is a result of alienation of the ruled. In the meantime, it is also an instrument, or spiritual opium, if you will, used by the ruling class for manipulation and oppression (Marx and Engels 1957, 63). To liberate the ruled from alienation and resignation, the socialist state should discourage or transform religious belief and practices. The Communist government in China permitted the existence of religions only if their practitioners agreed to support the government. During the Cultural Revolution, religious practices were banned. Thus, one would expect less religiosity in China than in capitalist Taiwan. Due to the effort to restrict and transform the content of religions, one may expect differences in the values and attitudes related to a religion in China as compared with that in Taiwan. Furthermore, one would also expect less religiosity among the generations in China which experienced their political socialization during the radical years.

Religion, Capitalism, and Democracy

The second question concerns the impact of religion on attitudes related to democracy and capitalism. Different religions may have different impacts. Weber (1970b) argued that the Protestant ethic is inner-worldly ascetic. Salvation is achieved through hard work and the constant pursuit of wealth. The other extreme is represented by Buddhism, where salvation is achieved through the rejection of all worldly desires, pursuits, responsibilities, and involvement. The inner-worldly mystical Taoism values earthly existence and seeks longevity and material immortality, but only in order to pursue and to continue in contemplation of mystical truth and union with the divine. The other-worldly ascetic Catholic achieves salvation through complete mastery and the overcoming of all worldly desires. According to Weber, then, one should expect the Protestant and, to a lesser degree, the Taoist to have stronger economic efficacy and materialistic attitudes than the Buddhist and the Catholic.

Similarly, the civic culture that democracy is based upon is closely related to Christianity, which encourages the development of individualism, the idea of human rights, the rule of law, and the spirit of compromise. Other religions, such as Islam and Taoism, do not result in such civic culture and democracy (Huntington 1991). Therefore, one would expect Christianity, particularly Protestantism, to positively impact democratic and capitalist values and attitudes.

Measures

Denominations. In the mainland survey, people were asked about their religious beliefs: Buddhism, Catholicism, Protestant Christianity, Taoism, Islam, other religions, and no belief. Other religions were mostly folk religions. In later analyses, sometimes "other religions" was combined with Taoism to assure an adequate number of cases. In the Taiwan survey, religions included Buddhism, Taoism, folk religions, *yiguandao* (the unity sect, which emerged in the early Qing period and was a combination of folk religions), *xuanyuanjiao* (created in Taiwan in 1957, worshipped the Yellow Emperor), Islam, Catholicism, Protestant Christianity, other, and no belief. In the analysis, folk religions will be combined with *yiguandao* and *xuanyuanjiao*, since these are Chinese in origin. To make results more comparable, only the urban portion of the Taiwan sample will be compared with the mainland sample in univariate and bivariate analyses. In a multivariate analysis, the use of an urbanity variable will allow me to include both rural and urban populations in the Taiwan sample.

Beliefs. Religious beliefs were measured by six parallel questions in the two surveys: (1) there is life after death, (2) pick auspicious dates for important events, (3) ancestor worship, (4) religion is good for social stability, (5) geomancy is important in house building, and 6) one should have religious belief. The respondent was given a four-point scale, from strongly agree, agree, disagree, to strongly disagree. Similarly, I will compare the urban portion of the Taiwan sample to the mainland in univariate and bivariate analyses. In a multivariate analysis, I will include an urbanity variable in both samples. The six items were also combined into a single scale of religious belief through a factor analysis.

Political Compliance. This was based on four similar questions in both surveys: (1) government should decide state affairs, no matter how big or small, (2) a society will become chaotic if people's ideas are not uniform, (3) government should decide whether an idea or an opinion becomes popular in society, and (4) not supporting the government is unpatriotic. The scale had a similar four-point range: strongly agree, agree, disagree, and strongly disagree. To simplify the analysis, the four questions were combined with a factor analysis. For each society, this produced an index of political compliance with a mean of zero and a range from about −2.5 to 2.5. This similar five-point range and similar standard deviation (.75) means that the size of later regression coefficients can generally be assumed to have similar significance across the two societies.

Economic Efficacy. This was a measure of the role of individual effort in economic success. For China, it was based on two items: "One only needs to be willing to exert oneself and then one will surely succeed" (the first verbal phrase was, literally, "be willing to eat bitterness") and "If one wants to become successful, then one must have a very good family background." The implication of the second was that, to succeed, one must be born of a high status family with good connections. This item was combined with the first in a factor analysis in a reverse direction. In Taiwan, the two items had little correlation and thus only the first question was used. These questions also had a four-point answer from strongly agree to strongly disagree.

Money Good, or "money mindedness" or "money crassness," included seven items, with the first five having a possible response of strongly agree, agree, disagree, strongly disagree, and don't know or "not clear." After giving the "not clear" response the mean (average) score for that item (also the factor scores of beliefs, political compliance, and economic efficacy), all items were combined. The individual items (with their original variable numbers) were as follows:

1. "As long as one doesn't steal or kill, any means of making money is fine."
2. "Work is merely for earning money to get by."
3. "One only needs to have money to gain respect from others, and it makes no difference how one got the money."
4. "Generally speaking, tranquility alone is wealth. One needn't be too concerned with fortune, fame, and success."
5. "An individual's earning of money is always beneficial to society" (in short, does one believe in Adam Smith?).
6. "Two people, A and B, are looking for work. A is looking for a job with prestige that is not so highly paid. B is looking for a job lacking in prestige but with pay twice as high. If it were you, what kind of work would you choose?"
7. "There are three people, A, B, and C. A says the more money one has the better. Moreover if he got a lot of money, he wouldn't work again. B says money is not a good thing. Having a lot is pointless. C says one can't get by without money. One just needs a little to get by. With which manner of speaking do you most agree?"

As should be obvious from the wording, items 2, 4, and 7 entered the summary money mindedness scale with weighting inverse of the other items.

Background Variables. There were several individual background characteristics that needed to be taken into account. These included the respondent's education in year, age, gender, and occupational status ranging in two spectra as follows: from (1) student, (2) no work, (3) private, (4) manual, (5) sales and services, (6) clerical, (7) managerial, (8) administrative, to (9) professional in the mainland; and from (1) no work (including student), (2) unskilled manual, (3) lower level manual, (4) higher level manual, (5) farmer, (6) services, (7) sales, (8) clerical, (9) administrative and managerial, to (10) professional in Taiwan. Income was the total monthly family income in yuan in China, and a 1–7 scale in Taiwan. Both occupational scales were used as continuous variables, with a high value representing a high occupational status. The respondent's membership in the Communist Party was included in China. For Taiwan, the respondent's party preference was either KMT (the ruling Kuomintang party), DPP (the opposing Democratic Progressive Party), or no preference. Urbanity was the administrative level of the respondent's residence: Taipei, Kaohsiung, provincial city, county, and so on in Taiwan; and the 1991 non-agricultural population in a city in China. In both cases, a high value reflects a high level of urbanity.

Urbanization could serve as a measure of modernization, but may not be a measure of regional cultural differences. Then, regional effect in Taiwan was measured by the respondent's geographic origin: Minnan, Hakka, mainlander, aborigine, and other. The first two groups were earlier immigrants from southern China. In China, besides the population of each city, the forty-four mainland cities were grouped by region on inductive and historical grounds as follows: Beijing, Shanghai, Tianjin, North Central (Hebei, Shandong, Shanxi, Inner Mongolia, Shaanxi, Gansu), Northeast (Heilongjiang, Jilin, Liaoning), Central (Henan, Hubei, Hunan, Anhui, Jiangxi), Yangzi Delta (Jiangsu, Zhejiang), South (Guangdong, Guangxi, Hainan, Fujian), and Southwest (Guizhou, Yunnan). If cultural diffusion occurred, the areas first to show a difference as compared with other regions should be those near Hong Kong and Taiwan and those in areas subject to considerable foreign investment and foreign media contact, followed by places such as Lingnan and Fujian. The summary statistics for the above variables are presented in Appendix 2.

Religiosity in China and Taiwan

Believers

One question concerns the matter of how many people are believers. In China, religious practices came back rapidly after the radical anti-religion policy during the Cultural Revolution. Catholics and Protestants together reached ten million in 1992, about one percent of China's total population (top of Table 11.1). Though the number for believers in Buddhism is missing, Buddhist monks totaled 82,000, as compared with only about 4,600 Christian priests. Folk religions were also popular. Among Taoists, there were 72,000 known monks in 1992.

Table 11.1

Religions in China and Taiwan

Religion	Temples	Priests	Followers	Year
China				
Han Buddhism	5,000	40,000	unknown	1992
Tibetan Buddhism	1,400	34,000	unknown	1992
Yunnan Buddhism	1,000	8,000	1,000,000+	1992
Taoism	600	72,000	unknown	1992
Islam	unknown	unknown	unknown	—
Catholicism	3,600	900+	3,500,000	1992
Protestantism	15,400	3,700	6,500,000	1992
Taiwan				
Buddhism	4,020	10,942	4,900,000	1990
Taoism	6,777	31,640	990,436	1991
Islam	5	unknown	50,000	1990
Catholicism	unknown	740	295,686	1991
Protestantism	1,867	12,893	519,731	1991
Xuanyuan	unknown	unknown	4,507	1991
Yiguandao	28,068	unknown	833,000	1990

Source: Zhu (1994).

Similarly, in Taiwan in the early 1990s, the largest group was Buddhists, followed by Taoists and other folk religions (*xuanyuanjiao* and *yiguandao*), Protestants and Catholics, and a small group of Muslims (bottom of Table 11.1).

Although the ranking of different religious groups is similar in the two societies, urban China was much less religious than urban Taiwan. In the Chinese urban sample (panel A, Table 11.2), 86 percent were non-believers. In the urban portion of the Taiwan sample (panel B, Table 11.2), non-believers were much less, only 19 percent. The numbers of Protestants and Taoists were only a few percentage points higher than in China. The real difference came from the much higher percentages of Buddhists and folk religion believers in Taiwan than in China. Compared with a few years ago, the 19 percent figure for non-believers in Taiwan in 1990 represents a trend of secularization. In a 1985 Taiwan social change survey, non-believers represented only 9 percent of the sample (Chiu 1988, 243).[2]

In spite of the secularization trend in Taiwan, the overall picture was of an atheist China and a religious Taiwan where Buddhism, Taoism, and other folk religions were dominant. I will discuss later the question of whether this difference was due to government policy toward religion in the two societies or to other reasons.

Religious Values

Besides self-claimed believers, we also wanted to know how many people believed in different religious values, and how these values were related to different religions. For all the six items of religious beliefs (see descriptions above), again, Taiwan was significantly more religious than China (column under "total," Table 11.2). For each religion, the Taiwanese believer seemed to be more involved than the Chinese counterpart (rows in panels A and B next to "mean score").

One contrast is that while, in China, religion was more important for oneself than for society, it was more important for social stability than for self in Taiwan. The Taiwan independence movement might have been a concern for some respondents who desired more political and social stability in Taiwan.

The Catholics and Protestants in China were more likely to believe in ancestor worship, choosing dates for important life events, and geomancy (*fengshui*), but less likely to believe in life after death, than the Catholics and Protestants in Taiwan. This suggests that these two religions in China were given more of a Chinese flavor than in Taiwan.

In both societies, one is struck by the religious values held by non-believers (column under "atheist," Table 11.2). In Taiwan, over half of the non-believer respondents believed in ancestor worship and choosing dates for life events. Over a third of the Taiwanese non-believers believed in life after death. Even in the less religious China, almost half of the non-believers believed in ancestor worship and choosing dates for life events. The actual practice of religious activities among the Chinese and Taiwanese non-believers was also common.[3] The relatively high percentage of non-believers who thought religion was good for oneself (comparing with for society) suggests that the number of believers in China would grow faster than in Taiwan.

Characteristics of Believers

After examining how many people believed in each religion, in various religious values, and the relationship between religion and religious values, we wanted to know the other background factors that were associated with each religion. These included geographic regions in China, geographic origins in Taiwan, education, age, gender, occupational status, political affiliation, income, and urbanization in both places.

Table 11.2

Religion and Values in China and Taiwan (weighted, urban only)

	Atheist	Buddhist	Catholic	Protestant	Islamic	Taoist	Folk	Total N
A. China								
Base %	86	5	1	1	1	6	100	2336
Ancestor	49.55	61.15	72.30	41.14	51.26	58.54	50.71	2325
Luckyday	42.18	69.13	54.32	41.36	21.34	68.43	44.89	2323
Geomancy	12.30	44.39	45.22	32.87	32.22	12.96	14.77	2311
After life	7.01	25.30	47.67	31.10	6.27	13.02	8.88	2321
Relig-society	8.02	9.61	53.79	49.35	6.27	8.86	8.97	2316
Relig-self	22.23	48.35	55.70	79.15	92.34	33.86	26.23	2317
Mean score (0–6)	1.41	2.62	3.29	2.75	2.10	1.93	1.54	2287
B. Taiwan								
Base %	19	36	1	5	7	31	98	1614
Ancestor	59.42	79.33	77.46	26.09	76.18	80.13	73.11	1614
Luckyday	55.24	80.76	33.40	30.49	86.14	82.76	74.35	1614
Geomancy	38.92	58.92	41.57	21.72	65.57	52.66	51.84	1614
After life	38.63	50.41	81.49	61.73	53.98	46.39	48.12	1614
Relig-society	33.03	47.01	55.38	65.54	52.54	51.36	47.10	1614
Relig-self	9.93	42.99	60.55	70.30	38.59	34.72	35.09	1614
Mean score (0–6)	2.31	3.59	3.76	3.46	2.72	3.44	3.26	1621

Sources: 1992 China Urban Survey and 1990 Taiwan Social Change Survey.
Notes:
Taiwan base % does not include the 2% "other" religious denominations.
Ancestor: belief in ancestor worship.
Luckyday: belief in picking auspicious dates for important events.
Geomancy: belief in geomancy as important in house building.
After life: belief in life after death.
Relig-society: religion is good for social stability.
Relig-self: one should have religious belief.
Mean score is an additive index of the six items in the left column.

Figure 11.1 **Religion by Region, China 1992**

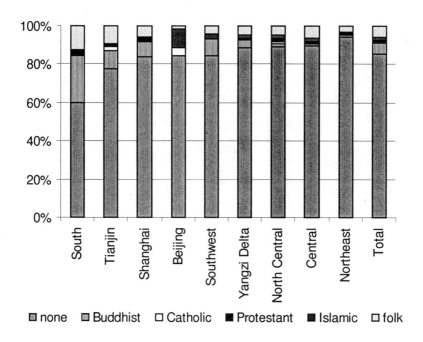

□ none   ▦ Buddhist   □ Catholic   ■ Protestant   ▧ Islamic   □ folk

Sources: 1992 China Urban Survey and 1990 Taiwan Social Change Survey.

First, let us look at the regional variation of different religions in China. One interesting characteristic is the uneven geographic distribution of religions, particularly in the South (Fujian, Guangdong, Guangxi and Hainan), where there were only 60 percent non-believers as compared with the 86 percent in the national average (Figure 11.1). Buddhism and folk religions were more popular than other religions in these regions. The Northeast seems to be the least religious. One possibile reason for the stronger religious influence in the South is its closeness to capitalist Hong Kong and Taiwan. Another possibility is that southern regions are traditionally more religious than the North, regardless of reform and opening to outside influence.

Second, let us look at the effect of one's geographic origin on different religions in Taiwan (Figure 11.2). The number of non-believers was

Figure 11.2 **Religion by Origin, Taiwan 1990**

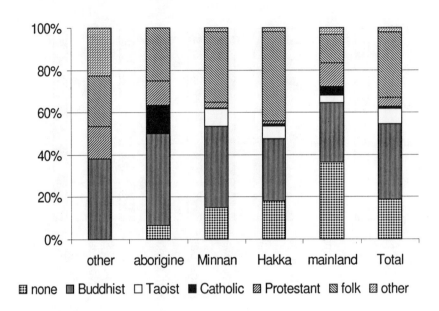

Sources: 1992 China Urban Survey and 1990 Taiwan Social Change Survey.

the highest among the mainlanders, being almost twice of the urban Taiwan average. The fact that the mainlanders were less religious than those with Minnan and Hakka origins seems to confirm the above second possible explanation for why the southerners in China were more religious than the northerners, that is, that local culture had a stronger influence on religiosity than reform and opening. One manifestation of the local religious tradition in Fujian and among the Fujian immigrants in Taiwan (Minnan) is their worship of the popular goddess Mazu (mother goddess).

Similar to the case of southern China, among the Minnans and the Hakkas folk religions were more popular. Catholicism and Protestantism were popular among both the native Taiwanese and the mainlanders.

To examine the multiple sources of religious beliefs, the respondent's education, age, gender, occupational status, political affiliation, income, and urbanity were included in a multinomial logit analysis (Table 11.3) that included controls for region in China and origin in Taiwan. This analysis shows the characteristics associated with each religion as compared with non-believers. The reported coefficients are relative risk ratios. They seem to suggest that the odds of a particular outcome change with a one-unit increase in the size of each independent variable. A coefficient of 1.00 indicates a neutral relationship. The odds of a given outcome are neither increased nor decreased by a given background condition. A coefficient of 2.00 indicates the odds are doubled, and a coefficient of .50 indicates that the odds are cut in half (further details for the variables in Table 11.3 are in Appendix 2).

Education reduced the tendency of an individual to be Buddhist, Taoist, or folk-religions in orientation but seemed to increase one's chances of being Catholic or Protestant. This was particularly clear in Taiwan. In China, the young were more likely to be Buddhist than the old. In Taiwan, in contrast, the old were more likely to believe in either Buddhism, Catholicism, or folk religions than the youth. In all these categories, however, the middle-aged group (45–55, results not shown) in both societies was more religious than either the young or the old. As expected, the Communist Party members in China were less religious than non-members. The Democratic Progressive Party in Taiwan seemed to favor Catholicism. Income led to less belief in folk religions in both places. In China, high income was also related to more belief in Buddhism, but less Catholicism. With geographic regions controlled for China (not shown in Table 11.3), urbanization did not have significant impact but did have a negative impact on belief in folk religions in Taiwan.

In short, the distinction between the two societies in religiosity was quite obvious: urban China was much less religious than urban Taiwan, even though the latter was more modernized. Modernization did seem to play a small but noticeable role in reducing religiosity in traditional belief over time in Taiwan. The much wider gap between the two societies could only be explained by the Communist Party's policy discouraging religious belief and practices in China. To a lesser extent, geographic origin also played a role in increasing religiosity in southern China.

Religion and Other Values

As mentioned at the beginning of this chapter, the purpose of this study was to examine not only religiosity but also the impact of religion on one's political and economic attitudes. To do so, a multiple regression

Table 11.3

Religious Belief by Selected Characteristics in China 1992 and Taiwan 1991 (multinomial logit regression, relative risk ratios)

	Buddhist	Taoist	Catholic	Protestant	Folk	Islamic
China						
Education	0.893**	1.060	1.078	0.939	0.966	0.932
Age	0.907*	1.416	1.147	0.916	1.003	1.037
Age (squared)	1.001*	0.996	0.999	1.001	1.000	1.000
Male	0.680	2.970	0.786	0.492	1.064	2.390#
Occupational status	0.964	0.509*	0.951	0.900	1.089	0.782#
Party membership	0.116**	0.000	0.000	0.000	0.481**	1.257
1991 family income (log)	1.588#	1.237	0.367#	0.603	0.663*	0.899
1991 urban population	1.000	1.001	1.000	1.000	1.000	0.999
$R^2 = .14$						
Cases = 2251						

	Buddhist	Taoist	Catholic	Protestant	Folk	Other
Taiwan						
Education	0.954*	0.975	1.198*	1.148**	0.911**	1.057
Age	1.181**	1.081	1.310*	1.079	1.140**	1.128
Age (squared)	0.998**	0.999	0.997*	1.000	0.998**	0.999
Male	0.911	1.208	0.537	0.450*	1.167	1.064

Occupational status	1.021	1.040	0.923	1.085#	1.014	0.994
KMT	1.168	1.223	1.949	0.857	1.026	0.963
DPP	1.056	0.663	5.406#	1.240	0.871	1.150
(no party preference as comparison)						
1990 Family income	0.963	0.953	0.853	1.103	0.958#	0.93
Urbanity	0.994	0.959	0.837	1.102	0.935**	0.975
R^2 = .06						
Cases = 2525						

Sources: 1992 China Urban Survey and 1990 Taiwan Social Change Survey.
Notes:
Non-believer is the base group.
Regions in China and origins in Taiwan are included in the equations but not shown.
# P<.10, * P<.05, ** P<.01.

Table 11.4

Religion and Attitudes (OLS, unstandardized regression coefficients)

	Political obedience	Economic efficacy	Cash-minded
China			
Catholic	−0.249	0.062	−0.123
Protestant	0.000	0.111#	−0.189
Buddhist	0.157#	0.014	0.047
Taoist/folk	0.150*	0.026	0.212**
Muslim	0.164	−0.035	−0.112
Non-believer as comparison			
_cons	0.252	0.110	0.487*
R²	0.092	0.094	0.130
Cases	2,185	2,082	2,160
Taiwan			
Catholic	−0.242#	0.227#	−0.158#
Protestant	−0.079	−0.107	−0.070
Buddhist	0.111**	−0.153**	−0.036
Taoist	0.061	0.007	0.016
Folk	−0.000	−0.076#	−0.031
Other	0.056	−0.154#	−0.117*
Non-believer as comparison			
_cons	0.655*	2.021**	0.531**
R²	0.166	0.049	0.119
Cases	2,525	2,525	2,523

Sources: 1992 China Urban Survey and *1990 Taiwan Social Change Survey.*
Notes:
Religious beliefs (a factor index of the six items in Table 11.2), education, age, age 2, male, occupation, party id and preference (CCP, KMT, DPP), income, urbanization are controlled. Geographic origin is controlled for Taiwan.
 # P<.10, * P<.05, ** P<.01.

analysis is necessary. With political obedience, economic efficacy, and cash-mindedness as dependent variables (see above descriptions for definitions), one can examine what religion is associated with what attitude, while controlling for religious beliefs, education, age, being male, occupational status, political affiliation, urbanity, and geographic origin (Taiwan only). The reported regression coefficients (Table 11.4) show each religion's likelihood of supporting each attitude. For example, the coefficient of Buddhist on political obedience is .157, indicating that a Buddhist's political obedience is about 16 percent higher than that of a non-believer; and nine out of ten times this finding is true (significant at .10).

In both societies, the difference seemed to be between Western religions and Eastern religions. Although the results were not uniform, both Catholicism and Protestantism showed strong political and economic individualism, but were less cash-minded. Catholics in Taiwan showed significant political disobedience, economic efficacy, and anti-cash attitudes. These attitudes were the ripe conditions for the development of a civil culture upon which liberal democracy could be based.

On the other hand, Eastern religions, particularly Buddhism, Taoism, and folk religions, showed more political obedience and less individual economic efficacy (but perhaps more family-based or group economic efficacy) in both China and Taiwan. Taoism and folk religions in China were also related to the pro-cash attitude. From the ruler's point of view, these were the ideal citizens to rule—obedient and greedy.

In short, the small group of followers of Western religions was more inclined to hold political and economic values associated with democracy and capitalism than the much larger group of followers of Eastern religions. One interesting exception was that the latter was more cash-minded than the former. Characterized by obedience and greed, the popular Eastern religions may be part of the explanation for the crony capitalism in Taiwan and, increasingly, in China.

Conclusion

Now let us return to the conditions of religiosity discussed at the beginning of this chapter. These are, in a reversed order, (1) government policy based on class theory, (2) culture, and (3) modernization. We saw that mainland China was much less religious than Taiwan, and that Communist Party members and the older generations who experienced longer influence of the communist leadership were also less religious. It seemed that the Chinese government's effort to reduce religiosity was quite effective. This was only part of the picture, however. Mainlanders were less religious anywhere, including in Taiwan. The higher level of religiosity in southern China, where the Minnans and the Hakkas in Taiwan were originally from, indicated that religiosity was also influenced by a strong local culture. If we subtract the nearly 40 percent non-believer mainlanders in Taiwan (who would not be believers under any society or policy) from the 86 percent non-believers in China, the government policy succeeded in turning only a little over half of them into non-believers. Therefore, government policy alone, although quite effective, does not explain the entire difference between the two societies. The weak tradition of organized religion in the mainland before the communist government was also a factor.

To a more limited extent, modernization, as reflected in education, occupational status, and urbanity, tended to reduce religiosity. The trend of secularization in Taiwan between 1985 and 1990 was a possible consequence of economic development, urbanization, and modernization. One exception was the positive role of education in promoting Western religions in Taiwan. This was not surprising, since these religions were associated with more individualistic values that the educated find more appealing. On the other hand, the trend among the educated and the social elite to turn to foreign culture and religions seems to be universal. In recent years in the West, there has been a trend toward Eastern religions.

One has to remember that Catholics and Protestants in both societies were only a small percentage. The largest numbers of believers were those in non-Christian religions. These religions created a political and economic culture that emphasized political authority and group social identity. When such a culture was dominant, the role of modernization in promoting a civil culture became limited. However, in Taiwan, democratic institutions developed without a full-grown civil culture.

Appendix 1

Sample Biases and Weighting

	Mainland		Taiwan	
Education	Sample	1990 Census (urban)[a]	Sample	1990 Labor survey[b]
Illiterate	2	10	7	6
Primary school	10	23	1	2
Junior high	29	36	26	32
Senior high	24	18	17	18
Tech. school	13	5	28	27
Junior college	13	5	13	9
College	9	4	10	8
Total:	100%	100%	100%	100%

Notes:
[a]1990 Chinese census data for cities, 16–64, see Census Office, 1993.
[b]Raw data from DGBAS, 1990 Taiwan Labor Force Survey.

Appendix 2

Characteristics of Variables in Tables 11.3 and 11.4

Variable	Observations	Mean	Standard deviation	Minimum	Maximum
China					
Attitudes					
Political compliance	2,344	0.0759256	0.7582622	−2.22926	2.305185
Economic efficacy	2,243	−1.53e-10	0.3059331	−0.7324793	0.5421084
"Money good"	2,317	−6.82e-09	0.7567702	−1.702401	2.254946
Religion					
Atheist	2,310	0.8744589	0.3314032	0	1
Buddhist	2,310	0.04329	0.2035533	0	1
Catholic	2,310	0.0051948	0.0719031	0	1
Protestant	2,310	0.0103896	0.1014205	0	1
Islamic	2,310	0.0095238	0.0971452	0	1
Other religion	2,310	0.0571429	0.2321656	0	1
Belief index	2,395	1.802036	0.7386824	−0.7847055	2.586741
Region					
Beijing	2,395	0.0425887	0.2019702	0	1
Tianjin	2,395	0.0425887	0.2019702	0	1
Shanghai	2,395	0.0425887	0.2019702	0	1
North central	2,395	0.2141962	0.4103493	0	1
Northeast	2,395	0.2020877	0.4016411	0	1
Central	2,395	0.2125261	0.4091805	0	1
Yangzi Delta	2,395	−0.0680585	0.2518988	0	1
South	2,395	0.1114823	0.3147941	0	1
Southwest	2,395	0.0638831	0.2445956	0	1
Education (year)	2,387	10.89862	3.195073	0	18
Age	2,389	40.81415	15.02892	16	82
Age squared	2,389	1,891.568	1,331.534	256	6724
Male	2,393	0.5106561	0.4999909	0	1
Occupational status	2,384	5.205956	2.127875	1	9

(continued)

Appendix 2 *(continued)*

Variable	Observations	Mean	Standard deviation	Minimum	Maximum
Party membership	2,387	0.294093	0.4557294	0	1
1991 per capita Family income (logged)	2,359	4.624885	0.5098205	2.445686	7.090077
1991 City non—agricultural Population (1000)	2,395	1,647.029	1,882.388	93	7,528.2
Taiwan					
Attitudes					
Political compliance	2,531	-4.21e-09	0.7455831	-2.637917	2.851057
Economic efficacy	2,531	3.134729	0.6843991	1	4
"Money good"	2,529	-1.76e-08	0.4697509	-1.049894	1.740227
Religion					
Atheist	2,531	0.17661	0.3814137	0	1
Buddhist	2,531	0.3148953	0.4645659	0	1
Catholic	2,531	0.011853	0.1082458	0	1
Protestant	2,531	0.0205452	0.1418841	0	1
Folk	2,531	0.4460687	0.4971811	0	1
Other religion	2,531	0.0300277	0.1706971	0	1
Belief index	2,531	0.2964107	0.1065988	-0.1798605	0.4605764
Education (year)	2,531	9.789016	4.23347	0	16
Age	2,531	37.53062	11.52636	20	64
Age squared	2,531	1541.352	953.2641	400	4,096
Male	2,531	0.4907151	0.5000126	0	1
Occupational status	2,531	4.498222	3.149298	1	10
Party preference					
KMT	2,531	0.3393915	0.4735964	0	1
DPP	2,531	0.0525484	0.2231742	0	1
1990 Family income level	2,525	3.915644	2.388814	1	9
Geographic origin					
Minnan	2,531	0.7340972	0.4419001	0	1
Hakka	2,531	0.1363098	0.343185	0	1
Mainland	2,531	0.1201106	0.3251551	0	1
Aborigine	2,531	0.0063216	0.0792725	0	1
Other	2,531	0.0031608	0.0561432	0	1
Urbanity	2,531	4.891742	1.994492	1	8

Notes

I am grateful to Lisa Weaver and Yu Nan for their valuable help in revising this article.

1. I am grateful to Professor Chiu for setting a precedent in East Asia of providing data sets for public use.

2. Admittedly, the 19 percent non-believers in 1990 were only among urbanites in Taiwan. The entire 1991 sample (including both urban and rural population) has 17 percent non-believers, only slightly lower than that in the urban population. The secularization trend in Taiwan from 1985 to 1991 was still real.

3. In the urban Chinese sample, for example, 28 percent experienced fortune-telling, and 57 percent worshipped ancestors (weighted raw data). In urban Taiwan, non-believers involved in fortune-telling, geomancy, burning incense, and other religious activities were 29, 27, 19, and 38 percent, respectively (weighted raw data).

References

Census Office, State Council (and State Statistical Bureau, Department of Population Statistics). 1993. *Tabulation on the 1990 Population Census of the People's Republic of China.* Beijing: China Statistics Press (in Chinese and English).

Chiu, Hei-yuan. 1988. "Taiwan diqu minzhong de zongjiao xinyang ji zongjiao taidu," *Taiwanese Society in Transition.* Kuo-shu Yang and Hei-yuan Chiu, eds. Vol. 1. Institute of Ethnology Monograph Series B, no. 20. Taipei: Academia Sinica.

DGBAS (Directorate-General of Budget, Accounting and Statistics). 1990. *Taiwan Labor Force Survey, 1990.* Taipei: Executive Yuan, Republic of China.

Durkheim, Emile. 1915. *The Elementary Forms of the Religious Life.* London: Allen and Unwin.

Freud, Sigmund. 1961. *Complete Works.* London: Hogarth Press.

Hamilton, Malcolm. 1995. *The Sociology of Religion: Theoretical and Comparative Perspectives.* London: Routledge.

Huntington, Samuel P. 1991. *The Third Wave.* Norman: University of Oklahoma Press.

Marett, R. R. 1914. *The Threshold of Religion.* London: Methuen.

Marx, Karl, and Frederick Engels. 1957. *On Religion.* Moscow: Progress Publishers.

Stark, R., and W. S. Bainbridge. 1980. "Towards a Theory of Religion: Religious Commitment." *Journal for the Scientific Study of Religion* 19 (2): 114–28.

———. 1985. *The Future of Religion.* Berkeley: University of California Press.

———. 1987. *A Theory of Religion.* New York: Lang.

Tang, Wenfang. 1999. "'Forum: How to Keep China Stable' (The Falun Gong Religious Movement and the Changing Social Contract in China)." *The Pittsburgh Post-Gazette,* December 12.

Tang, Wenfang, and William L. Parish. 2000. *Chinese Urban Life under Reform: The Changing Social Contract.* New York: Cambridge University Press.

Weber, Max. 1970a. "The Protestant Sects and the Spirit of Capitalism." In *From Max Weber: Essays in Social Theory.* H. Gerth and C. W. Mills, eds. London: Routledge.

———. 1970b. "The Social Psychology of the World Religions." In *From Max Weber: Essays in Social Theory.* H. Gerth and C. W. Mills, eds. London: Routledge.

Zhu, Yueli, ed. 1994. *Jinri Zhongguo Zongjiao* (Religion in Contemporary China). Beijing: Jinri Zhongguo Chubanshe.

12

Culture Shift and Regime Legitimacy: Comparing Mainland China, Taiwan, and Hong Kong

Yun-han Chu and Yu-tzung Chang

Introduction

The third wave of democratization has prompted a paradigmatic shift in the study of political culture since the second half of the 1980s (Almond 1990; Eckstein 1988; Pye 1990). From its inception, third-wave democratization was understood in terms of socioeconomic structure, strategic interaction of elites, and institutional design, while changes in mass politics and belief systems and in the way political culture influences the process of democratization have not been the focus of discussion (Klesner 1998, 478; Shin 1994, 154). A growing number of scholars have pointed out that mass politics and cultural shifts are very important factors in consolidating democratic regimes. Thus, political scientists now talk of "bringing the people back in."[1]

Our paper examines the nature of cultural shifts and explores their sources and effects in three Chinese societies—mainland China, Taiwan, and Hong Kong—tracing the contours of political culture in terms of state-value orientation, democratic versus authoritarian-value orientation, and moral state-value orientation. We compare the socioeconomic and institutional sources for differences in political beliefs and attitudes.

Furthermore, we evaluate the implications of political culture for regime legitimacy. The empirical analysis is based on three comparable surveys conducted respectively in mainland China, Taiwan, and Hong Kong during 1993 and 1994 under the auspices of the Political Participation and Political Culture in Mainland China, Taiwan, and Hong Kong Project.[2]

Over the last fifteen years, we and our collaborators have respectively explored the impact of socioeconomic modernization on mass political behavior and political culture. We have also provided empirical analyses of the reciprocal interaction among political predisposition, political participation, and collective actions, on the one hand, and the strategies of elites and macro-political processes, on the other, all in their given political settings (Hu and Chu 1992; Chu 1992; Hu and Chu 1996; Lau and Kuan 1988; Nathan and Shi 1993; Shi 1997). This paper represents our latest effort to expand the analytical loci and to develop new research parameters within a comparative framework.

Re-conceptualizing Political Culture

The notion of political culture swept the field of political science in the late 1950s and early 1960s. Despite its popular appeal, the concept has engendered a certain amount of controversy (Elkins and Simeon 1979, 127). In order to meet quantitative research requirements, its definition has often carried a psychologically or individually subjective meaning. For example, Gabriel A. Almond and Sidney Verba defined political culture as "the particular distribution of patterns of orientation toward political objects among the members of the nation." These psychological orientations consist of three parts: cognitive, affective, and evaluational (Almond and Verba 1963, 13015). Glenda M. Patricks described this as a combination of fundamental beliefs, values, and attitudes that give the political system its characteristics and guide interactions between its members (Patricks 1984, 297). However, some academics argued that Almond committed the "individualistic fallacy," since data at the individual level fail to establish collective cultural characteristics (Dittmer 1977, 555). And others charged he neglected individual behavioral patterns (Fagen 1969, 5). Thus, despite years of academic discourse, political culture still lacks a concrete, commonly accepted definition (Gibbins 1989, 15; Lane 1992, 363).

Nevertheless, a new trend in the study of political culture has emerged in the last few years, encompassing a number of new issues. Early research emphasized the participation and efficiency of the political process, but neglected general political attitudes. The present understanding of political culture includes "mass culture" as well as "civic culture" (Street 1993). For Aaron Wildavsky and others who view political culture as ways of life and interpersonal relations, observations of social behavior have become important areas of inquiry (Thompson et al. 1990, 1). Robert Putnam, one of the field's premier scholars, recently described political culture as a combination of civic participation, interest in political matters, political equality, tolerance, and trust (Putnam 1993, 86–91).

Although this chapter does not attempt to resolve the dispute over definitions, we do adopt some basic assumptions. Firstly, we do not believe that political culture is simply a mixture of concrete behavioral patterns. Instead, we see political culture as a body of internal norms and values developed from normative principles and political rules embodying a particular worldview. These values and beliefs help determine the acceptability of an idea or a way of behaving by society (Elkins and Simeon 1979, 129). When the public holds a general consensus on a matter, individual members become bound by these norms, regardless of their own personal views. Deviants risk punishment and ostracism.

Secondly, we argue that political culture maintains a certain degree of autonomy and continuity. Contemporary developments in cultural studies converge in their emphasis on the separation of culture from social structure. Instead, it must be studied as a pattern in and of itself (Alexander 1990, 25). Whenever culture faces some kind of environmental pressure, it changes the "micro-political culture" immediately and the "meso-political culture" afterward. But the "macro-political culture" is rarely challenged (Girvin 1989, 34–6).

Finally, despite varying levels of socioeconomic modernization and democratic development, all countries are made up of competing cultures. A single, uniform political culture and policy culture simply does not exist (Thompson et al. 1990, 215–6). Almond divided political culture into three categories: system culture, process culture, and policy culture. The system culture incorporates attitudes toward the national community, the regime, and the political authorities. The process culture includes beliefs about the self in politics and other political actors. The policy culture consists of the distribution of preferences regarding the outputs and outcomes of politics and the rank ordering by different population groups of political values such as welfare, security, and liberty (Almond 1980, 28). Although Almond and Verba examined political processes in a comparative study of the United States, the United Kingdom, Germany, Italy, and Mexico, they neither developed an instrument for measuring system culture, nor engaged in any empirical research on the subject (Almond and Verba 1963).

Within this paper we would like to introduce new indicators for the measurement of system culture. Most Western scholars have neglected system culture because they concentrate their study on advanced democratic countries, where the theoretical agenda is democratic stability, not regime crisis (Almond 1990, 144). When the loci of our research shifts from stable democracies to emerging democracies as well as transitional authoritarian regimes, we need to adjust (or actually restore) our focus from process culture to system culture.

The Measurement of System Culture

If culture consists of a set of principal norms and values that are widely held, what are the principal norms and values in politics? We believe that in non-Western states, values and principles concerning national community, the organization of the state, and structure of governance are the most important cultural components of a modern political system.

There are three sets of issues a modern nation-state has to address. First, there are questions about how to construct and maintain a political community and about what kinds of rights and obligations a modern state and its citizens can claim on each other. The second set of questions refers to the principles upon which the government is founded: are they democratic ones or non-democratic? The third set consists of questions regarding the legitimate realm and purpose of public authority. Is the government responsible for social morality and should the government ensure social safety and economic equity? In this article we address the first issue with a battery of indicators measuring "state-value orientation," the second with a battery measuring the "belief in democratic- versus authoritarian-value orientation or 'regime legitimacy,'" and the third with a battery measuring "moral-state orientation," which is perhaps unique to Confucian societies.

State-Value Orientation

We define *state legitimacy* as the value orientation toward the normative principles around which the modern nation-state is constituted. The organizing principles of a modern nation-state are divided into its existential rationale and its compositional rule. In the Western liberal tradition, the existential rationale of the state rests fundamentally on individualism and contractual relationships. The state exists to serve the interests of its citizens, while the composition of a modern state rests essentially on voluntarism. In addition to the principle of territorial integrity, the principle of self-determination is also respected. The power of an existing state is not absolute. It is qualified by a respect for the rights of minorities.

This liberal tradition exists in stark contrast to modern state-nationalism, which upholds sovereignty/territorial integrity as an overarching principle. This is a strongly held belief, especially in countries inheriting an anti-imperialist past. Societies that emphasize communitarian/nationalistic values promote state interests over individual objectives. The state becomes the end in and of itself. Individuals are expected to sacrifice their personal interests for the sake of the collective whole.

In a nutshell, for the existential rationale of the state, we have constructed a communitarianism-cum-collectivism versus contractarianism-cum-individualism dimension, while the compositional rule of the state is measured by an expansionism versus separatism dimension. For legitimacy orientations of the individual toward state structure, we have developed a scale originally incorporating ten indicators. In our trilateral surveys, the following two items are employed: belief in state priority (don't ask what the country can do for you, ask what you can do for the country) and belief in national unity (a country is a big family and minorities should not demand separation).

Regime Legitimacy

We are certainly not alone in asserting the imperative of bringing back the legitimacy dimension. Almond, in "The Civic Culture Revisited," observed: "The system culture of a nation would consist of the distributions of attitude toward the national community, the regime and the authorities. . . . These would include the sense of national identity, attitude toward the legitimacy of the regime and its various institutions, and attitudes toward the legitimacy and effectiveness of incumbents of various political roles" (Almond 1980, 28). Ronald Inglehart regarded "legitimacy" as the long-term attribute of political support (Inglehart 1990,

16). Stephen M. Weatherford argued that political legitimacy is a key concept in both macro- and micro-politics (Weatherford 1992, 149). The difference is that our study develops the conceptual framework for cross-cultural comparison.

We view *regime legitimacy* as the value orientation toward the normative principles that govern the organization of political power and authority. These commitments lay the groundwork for the formation of attitudes toward legitimacy and incumbent support. The legitimacy orientation incorporates two components—desirability and feasibility. To regard a set of norms as legitimate requires them to be not only preferable but also achievable. The organizing principle of a modern political regime consists of three basic dimensions:

1. relationships among members of the political community
2. relationships between authorities and citizens
3. horizontal relationships among the government authorities themselves

The value orientation toward political equality corresponds to the first dimension. It states that all citizens should be entitled to equality under the law, regardless of race, gender, education, religion, class, political affiliation, and so forth. In contrast, in some societies the majority may believe in a hierarchical and/or exclusionary order rather than an egalitarian/inclusionary political order. It is widely accepted as legitimate that certain groups are privileged and others should and can be disenfranchised or discriminated against.

The second dimension encompasses the value orientation toward political liberty, pluralism, and popular accountability. Correspondingly, we developed the following three subdimensions: (a) the value orientation toward political liberty holds that there are certain legitimate realms of individual liberty which should be free from state intrusion and regulation; (b) the value orientation toward pluralism holds that there should be a realm of civil society in which the civic organizations can freely assemble themselves for public expression and for the advancement of their interests without state interference; and lastly, (c) the value orientation toward popular accountability refers to the belief that the government should be accountable to the people, with an effective means of conveying popular will and obtaining public consent. On the other hand, some societies believe that the realm of individual liberty should be minimized, that civil society must be subject to state guidance, and that the assertion of popular control over authority is unacceptable and even dangerous.

The value orientation toward separation of powers (or horizontal accountability) corresponds to the third dimension. It holds that government power should be divided among various branches of government and that a good-order polity is achieved through a design of horizontal accountability (checks and balances). On the contrary, some societies believe in the necessity and desirability of the supremacy of executive power or the fusion of legislative, executive, and judicial authority.

Thus, we build our measures of regime legitimacy around five essential elements of democracy:[3]

1. Political equality
2. Popular accountability
3. Political liberty
4. Political pluralism
5. Separation of powers

Unlike others (Booth and Seligson 1986; Dalton 1991), we do not believe it best to study these principles in an abstract manner. Such indicators are not as discriminating and tend to result in uniformly positive answers. Legitimacy orientation is not a set of political ideals, and belief in democratic legitimacy is separable from support for democratic beliefs.

We recognize that most modern authoritarian regimes do not challenge (or repudiate) these democratic norms in principle. Rather, the lines of defense for an authoritarian arrangement (or the lines of subtle offense against democratic norms) typically fall into one of two camps:

1. The Desirability Argument: The country should develop a different form of democracy (people's democracy, Chinese democracy, socialist democracy, guided democracy) that provides a better fit than Western democracy.
2. The Feasibility Argument: The country is not ready for a full democracy (because of lacking civic culture, low levels of socioeconomic modernization, conflicts with national development priorities, and/or an imminent external threat). The country would pay a high price in terms of inefficiency, insecurity, and disorder if it acquires Western democracy immediately.

To construct a valid scale, we essentially combine two analytical tasks into one. This enables us not only to measure the popular commitment to democratic norms but also to identify clusters of beliefs and attitudes that are typically nurtured under authoritarian or anti-democratic regimes and are inimical to the development of democratic values and institutions. In short, it serves as a multi-dimensional scale for the measurement of authoritarian orientations and, conversely, democratic values.

This formulation provides a coherent framework for cross-system and cross-time comparisons of legitimacy orientation toward the political regime. For example, we can build a simple three-fold typology to epitomize the differences in the structure of political culture in the three societies. The first one can be called "traditional authoritarianism," in which a majority of the population acquires a pro-authoritarian legitimacy orientation on all five dimensions (or all negatives toward a democratic legitimacy orientation). The other extreme is a stable liberal democracy in which a majority of the population acquires a democratic legitimacy orientation on all five dimensions (or are all negatives toward a pro-authoritarian legitimacy orientation). The configuration of the system culture in most developing nations, we believe, lies in between these two polar opposites, with a dominant democratic orientation in some power dimensions, typically those of political equality and popular accountability, and a dominant pro-authoritarian orientation in others. This configuration may be termed as a *modern*, or *transitional, authoritarian* political culture.

For an empirical observation of an individual's legitimacy orientation, we have developed a scale consisting of twenty-three indicators. In our comparative surveys, the following five items are employed in all three regions:

- Political Equality—better educated people should have more say in politics.
- Popular Accountability—top government officials are like the heads of a big family. We should follow all their decisions on national issues.
- Political Liberty—the government should have the power to decide which opinions (perspectives) are to be circulated in a society and which are not.
- Political Pluralism—if there are several political groups, peace and harmony will be disrupted.
- Horizontal Accountability—if a government is often constrained by an assembly, it will not be able to achieve great accomplishments.

Moral-State Orientation

In Confucian culture, authoritarianism is linked with the idea that human nature is good (Pye 1985, 326–336). Politics is a moral realm where "goodness" is taken into account and tested. This represents the consummate, non-instrumental view of politics that politics is supposed to make men morally upright. Also implied is the idea that government is judged by results rather than by procedures. The fruition of positive outcomes represents good government. This category incorporates at least three aspects: who should be chosen as a political leader; what political leaders can be expected to achieve; and what is within the government's span of control. In all three areas, the distinctively Chinese answer has a "moral" quality. A political leader should be chosen primarily because of his/her virtue, not competence. The most important task for the leader is not to be led or managed but to set a moral example for the rest of society. Thus, public morality falls within the legitimate scope of government responsibility.

For an empirical observation of an individual's moral-state orientation, we have developed a scale that originally consisted of four indicators. In our comparative surveys, the following two items are employed:

- Government Responsibility—the profusion of moral problems in the society is the government's fault.
- Trust in Virtuous Leaders—we can leave everything to morally upright leaders.

The Comparative Settings

Our study compares three distinctively different political systems. The socialist regime in mainland China is characterized by a single-party system and a transitional economy with substantial collective ownership of the means of production. Taiwan is a relatively open, increasingly competitive polity operating under an outward-looking market economy. Hong Kong was both a colony and a major financial center. Before 1997, it maintained a bureaucracy with allegiance to the British government. The state was largely separate from society and exercised minimum control over the citizenry and its economy. Because the three systems differ so greatly, we will be able to see how system types affect the relationship between socioeconomic variables and political culture.

Another important difference at the systemic level is socioeconomic development. The three systems form a scale ranging from an underde-veloped hinterland in mainland China, to middle-income coastal prov-inces, to a newly industrialized Taiwan, and, finally, to a highly developed Hong Kong. Purchasing Power Parity (PPP) GNP per capita ranges from US$1,745 to US$15,920 as of 1993 (World Bank 1994). Urbanization and education rates also illustrate significant disparities. Since each of our three surveys sample the entire national population in each system, we can break the development scale down to sub-regional or sectional levels, comparing, for example, Taiwan and Hong Kong to urban China. In addition, both regime type and pace of regime transition affect cul-ture. Politically, mainland China can be described as having shifted from a mobilization to a post-mobilization phase; Taiwan has recently com-pleted its democratic transition; and Hong Kong is undergoing limited democratic reform. Each of these system-change variables can be ex-pected to influence political culture. Our analysis seeks to separate these effects to the fullest extent possible.

Our Hong Kong survey yields 892 valid cases, the Taiwan survey 1,402 cases, and the mainland survey 3,296 cases. All three samples are reasonably large in relation to their respective degree of demographic heterogeneity. The number of samples in mainland China is sufficiently large for statistically meaningful analysis of its sub-samples. Through-out our analysis, we single out respondents with urban household regis-trations to create an "urban China" sub-sample (N = 704). It is assumed that this sub-sample represents the most modernized segment of the Chinese population.[4]

The Convergence and Divergence of Political Culture in Hong Kong, Taiwan, and Mainland China

State-Value Orientation

Table 12.1 displays the distribution of state-value orientation in the three localities employed in this survey. We present the data from mainland China in two categories—one reflecting urban China and the other re-flecting all of China. This procedure helps uncover the influence of modernization. Belief in state priority seems to be the highest in the urban China sample, with 93.7 percent of respondents agreeing, com-pared to the overall support of 86.2 percent in the mainland. The levels for Hong Kong and Taiwan are 60.7 percent and 57.5 percent, respec-

Table 12.1

State-Value Orientation

Indicator	Alternatives	Hong Kong %	Taiwan %	Urban China %	All China %
Belief in state priority					
	Strongly disagree	1.0	1.3	0.0	0.1
	Disagree	22.0	17.4	3.8	4.7
	Agree	51.7	50.9	78.3	75.6
	Strongly agree	5.8	9.8	15.4	10.6
	Don't know or no answer	19.5	20.6	2.5	9.0
Belief in national unity					
	Strongly disagree	0.9	1.1	0.2	0.4
	Disagree	18.3	14.3	3.5	6.5
	Agree	61.5	53.6	74.4	74.2
	Strongly agree	6.8	10.4	18.8	10.2
	Don't know or no answer	12.5	20.6	3.1	8.7
Total cases		892	1,402	705	3,296

tively. Table 12.1 also shows the distribution of belief in national unity among the four groups. The strongest belief in national unity is again found in the urban China sample, with 93.2 percent of respondents sharing this orientation, while China is second overall with 84.4 percent. The figures for Hong Kong and Taiwan are 68.3 percent and 64.0 percent, respectively.

Overall, it can be said that in all three locations majorities share a more than modest belief in state priority and national unity, with more than 80 percent support in mainland China and around 60 percent agreement in Taiwan and Hong Kong. As the figures show, differences in political systems do have an influence, but system differences did not fundamentally change culturally Chinese beliefs in state priority and national unity. Both principles are still accepted by the majority of people in all three societies despite huge differences in system-level attributes. In the case of a national crisis, it appears relatively easy to mobilize the masses on the basis of state-nationalism. Moreover, we can clearly observe the impact of modernization on the belief in state priority and national unity. If we temporarily neglect the urban China samples, we then can observe that belief in state priority and national unity shrinks as modernization increases. Comparing the urban China data with the overall China data, however, this relationship appears to work in reverse. In other words, modernization promotes individualist and contractarian values in Taiwan and Hong Kong but not in mainland China, at least at the current stage of regime evolution.

Regime Legitimacy

Table 12.2 displays the distribution of the five indicators we used as measures of regime legitimacy orientation in the three societies. With respect to support for political equality, the four samples show that in Taiwan 55.7 percent and in Hong Kong 49.2 percent of respondents hold this principle, while approval seems to be lowest in mainland China, with 37.0 percent of the urban and 19.7 percent of the overall sample expressing concurrence. With 69.2 percent agreeing that the government should be accountable to the people, Hong Kong shows the highest level of support, followed by Taiwan with 55.8 percent of the respondents agreeing to popular accountability. The lowest levels are again found in both urban and overall China, with 33.2 percent and 18.2 percent support, respectively. Table 12.2 also indicates Hong Kong as having the strongest belief in political liberty, with 63.2 percent support, followed by Taiwan with 49.3 percent, urban mainland China with 43.6 percent, and overall China with 21.8 percent. The next element employed to measure regime legitimacy is that of support for political pluralism. Hong Kong, with 48.8 percent, exhibits the highest level of support, while urban China comes in second with 37.9 percent of respondents expressing agreement. The lowest levels are found in the overall China sample, with 29.2 percent, and in Taiwan, with 26.5 percent. The reluctance toward political pluralism in Taiwan may be explained by the experience of occasionally violent clashes among political groups as well as between demonstrators and riot police during the tumultuous years of regime transition. For the principle of horizontal accountability (also labeled as "separation of power") urban China's support ranks the highest with 46.7 percent of the respondents agreeing, followed by Hong Kong with 39.1 percent. Taiwan and the overall China sample indicate the lowest show of support, with 32.4 percent and 31.8 percent, respectively.

We can see that Hong Kong maintains a relatively high level of convergence with respect to political equality, popular accountability, and

Table 12.2

Regime Legitimacy

Indicator	Alternatives	Hong Kong %	Taiwan %	Urban China %	All China %
Political equality					
	Strongly disagree	5.0	8.0	0.5	0.3
	Disagree	44.2	47.7	36.5	19.4
	Agree	40.8	27.0	55.5	64.8
	Strongly agree	3.7	4.3	1.0	2.4
	Don't know or no answer	6.3	13.0	6.5	13.1
Popular accountability					
	Strongly disagree	8.9	7.9	0.8	0.7
	Disagree	60.3	47.9	32.4	17.5
	Agree	23.1	27.2	59.6	69.5
	Strongly agree	0.9	2.9	3.5	3.8
	Don't know or no answer	6.8	14.1	3.7	8.5
Political liberty					
	Strongly disagree	6.5	7.1	1.2	0.4
	Disagree	56.7	42.2	42.4	21.4
	Agree	24.8	25.4	41.3	53.2
	Strongly agree	0.8	1.6	2.6	2.4
	Don't know or no answer	11.2	23.7	12.5	22.6
Political pluralism					
	Strongly disagree	2.2	2.6	2.1	1.3
	Disagree	46.6	23.9	35.8	27.9
	Agree	39.6	48.2	43.7	42.3
	Strongly agree	2.0	6.1	2.3	1.5
	Don't know or no answer	9.6	19.2	16.1	27.0
Separation of powers					
	Strongly disagree	2.0	2.5	3.0	1.2
	Disagree	37.1	29.9	43.7	30.6
	Agree	41.6	38.2	29.1	33.0
	Strongly agree	2.4	3.1	0.5	0.5
	Don't know or no answer	16.9	26.3	23.7	34.7
Total cases		892	1,402	705	3,296

Table 12.3

Moral-State Orientation

Indicator	Alternatives	Hong Kong %	Taiwan %	Urban China %	All China %
Trust in virtuous leaders					
	Strongly disagree	4.5	2.2	3.2	1.2
	Disagree	59.5	34.5	34.2	22.0
	Agree	26.0	42.9	57.6	66.3
	Strongly agree	1.2	5.1	2.1	3.4
	Don't know or no answer	8.8	15.3	2.9	7.1
Government responsibility					
	Strongly disagree	2.1	1.8	0.2	0.3
	Disagree	63.8	30.5	16.9	11.2
	Agree	23.3	41.9	71.2	73.1
	Strongly agree	0.6	10.8	9.3	8.1
	Don't know or no answer	10.2	15.0	2.4	7.3
Total cases		892	1,402	705	3,296

political liberty, but offers a polarized picture regarding political plural-ism and horizontal accountability. Taiwan exhibits strong support for political equality, popular accountability, and political liberty, but a majority of respondents do not support the principles of political plural-ism and separation of powers. Urban China failed to show convergence on any measure of democratic-value orientation, and most respondents disagree with all the measures aside from horizontal accountability. A majority in China rejected every indicator, with a lower level of support than in the urban sample.

Based upon these observations, we can infer that system differences seem to have a sizeable impact on democratic-value orientation. Hong Kong, although being long governed by Great Britain, has enjoyed a high degree of political freedom, while Taiwan has recently completed its democratic transition. That both societies show a stronger democratic-value orientation than mainland China is to be expected. Furthermore, we can see that the level of socioeconomic development is positively correlated with demand for democratic principles, suggesting that mod-ernization generally facilitates the growth in democratic-value orienta-tion even when societies have followed different trajectories of regime evolution.

Moral-State Orientation

Table 12.3 presents the two items that we used to measure moral-state orientation. The first measure is "trust in virtuous leaders." The overall China sample shows the highest level of trust with 69.7 percent and it is nearly matched by urban China respondents at 59.7 percent. Concerning Taiwan and Hong Kong, the level of trust in virtuous leaders is somewhat lower, with 48.0 percent in Taiwan and 27.2 percent in Hong Kong.

The second measure quantifying moral-state orientation is the question of government responsibility. As Table 12.3 indicates, 81.2 percent of the overall China sample's respondents agree that social immorality is the government's fault. This is virtually indistinguishable from the urban China sample's 80.5 percent. In Taiwan and Hong Kong, 52.7 percent and 23.9 percent, respectively, say the government is accountable.

The differences in the moral-state orientation are fairly significant among the three culturally Chinese societies. Hong Kong and mainland China are almost on the two polar ends of the spectrum, while the Taiwan sample is somewhat in between. It is safe to infer from the data that government actions, as much as the political system itself, have an impact on the moral-state orientation. The British administration's secular and non-interventionist approach to state-society relations has thoroughly transformed the popular expectation for public authority. The level of socio-economic development is negatively associated with levels of trust in virtuous leaders and government responsibility, suggesting that a more liberal and secular worldview came with modernization.

Culture Shift and Political Stability

Given that system cultures in all three regions are under profound transformation, it is important to ask what the implications of these changes for regime transition and regime stability are.

In recent years, several distinguished scholars attempted to address this issue. Larry Diamond suggested that a state with a flourishing democratic political culture will not suffer any setback in democratization, even when suffering economic or political crisis (Diamond 1993, 422–26). In a comparative study involving over forty nations, Ronald Inglehart found that the level of trust in others and the vitality of voluntary associations are positively correlated with the degree of political stability in that country (Inglehart 1997, 189–205). Another example is Robert

Putnam's analysis of local government in Italy. In his study he attributed contrasts in performance between local governments in northern and southern Italy to be the result of differences between regional cultures. Society in North Italy tended to be more pluralistic and participatory, and the level of trust in others was higher. The operation of local government followed a "classical democratic pattern." On the other hand, South Italy offered a completely different picture. The allocation of resources through society followed the lines of relationships on the personal level, and the general level of participation tended to be low as was the degree of trust in others. These differences in social capital had a direct impact on the operation of local government in Italy (Putnam 1993, 7–12).

Changes in political culture play an active role on the political system as a whole. An earlier study done by Gabriel A. Almond and Sidney Verba cites "civic culture" as the most important factor in producing a stable and effective democratic system (Almond and Verba 1963, 74). But this approach has become subject to criticism as other scholars have found the reverse, stating that a political culture is a result of a stable democracy (Pateman 1980, 66–67; Barry 1970, 51–52). In recent years, most scholars picture the relationship between political culture and political system from a modernization perspective. Within this theoretical framework, the relationship between culture and system is seen as a reciprocal rather than a "one-way" causality. Cultural shifts are then variables that we cannot ignore in research on democratic consolidation (Diamond 1993, 422–26; Inglehart 1997, 10; Lijphart 1980, 47). Thus, an analysis of political stability will have to treat political culture as a significant and endogenous factor (Chazan 1993, 67).

To examine the impact of a changing political culture on regime support we used a multiple regression to analyze possible causal relationships between the two variables. Within these models we treat regime legitimacy as the dependent variable, which we designate by using different measures of political support. We believe that there is an intimate relationship between regime support and political stability, meaning that a system is stable when there is a high level of political support and unstable if the level of political support is low.

In this study we included three items to gauge political support. For government support, we queried respondents as to the central government's ability to make the right decisions. For regime support, we asked people if they believed that the current political system was suitable for the current situation in the country. In the third item, measuring political change, we asked respondents to state whether or not they believed further democratization would negatively influence public security and social stability.

We imposed three primary considerations regarding independent variables. First, we looked for differences that might stem from different socioeconomic backgrounds. Items reflecting this are age, education, and gender. Second, we asked if differences might be the result of rational choice. As a rational (materialistic) consideration, we employed the basic assumption that people only view short-term benefits. Therefore, we inferred that people trust and support the regime and government if it is able to improve their socioeconomic condition in the present or foreseeable future. Third, we assumed that a country with low levels of democratic political culture would show strong support for an incumbent authoritarian regime, while a country with a high level of democratic culture would show strong support for a democratic political system. Therefore, we include items for measuring political culture such as those discussed in the above paragraphs.

In order to tell which independent variable has the strongest effect we included socioeconomic status and future economic expectation in a first model to quantify their individual ability to explain. In a second model, we included political culture to test the ability of these factors to explain changes in the dependent variables after controlling for the variables in the first model.

The results of the multiple regression, shown in Table 12.4, illustrate how changes in the level of support for the government can be attributed to socioeconomic and political culture variables. Applying Model I, socioeconomic background variables and economic expectation explain about 10 percent of all changes. The exact adjusted R Square for the four samples are Hong Kong .085, Taiwan .107, urban China .099, and overall China .104. Education alone has the greatest impact across all four samples (beta = .232, .189, .254, .295, respectively). In all three regions the level of trust in government declines when level of education rises, and vice versa. The factor with the second highest ability to explain is age, with older people tending to show higher levels of trust in government than younger respondents. This association is especially strong in the Taiwan sample, with a beta of −.205. Gender, social status, and economic condition remained without measurable impact.

In Model II, variables of political culture are included to explain

Table 12.4

Socioeconomic Backgrounds, Political Culture, and Government Support : Multiple Regression Analysis

Government support	HK		Taiwan		Urban China		All China	
Independent variable	Beta Model I	Beta Model II	Beta Model I	Beta Model II	Beta Model I	Beta Model II	Beta Model I	Beta Model II
Gender (male)	0.034	-0.014	0.004	0.006	0.089*	51	-0.003	0.000
Age	-0.089	-0.039	-0.205***	-0.166***	-0.092*	-0.061	-0.061**	-0.038*
Education	0.232***	0.102*	0.189***	0.069	0.254***	0.105*	0.295***	0.183***
Social status	0.017	0.023	-0.002	-0.003	-0.017	-0.009	0.017	-0.002
Present life	-0.005	-0.009	-0.045	-0.011	-0.021	-0.027	-0.012	-0.003
Future life	0.041	0.034	-0.068*	-0.059	-0.069	-0.040	-0.038*	-0.022
State priority	—	0.000	—	0.047	—	0.052	—	0.010
National unity	—	-0.017	—	0.039	—	-0.069	—	-0.006
Political equality	—	0.082*	—	0.074*	—	0.146***	—	088***
Accountability	—	0.108**	—	0.181***	—	0.215***	—	0.228***
Political liberty	—	0.119**	—	0.147***	—	0.130***	—	0.075***
Pluralism	—	-0.068	—	-0.018	—	-0.038	—	0.009
Separation	—	0.058*	—	-0.012	—	0.059	—	0.028
Virtuous leaders	—	0.123**	—	0.060	—	0.154***	—	0.208***
Responsibility	—	0.021	—	-0.039	—	-0.084*	—	-0.048**
Regime support	—	0.192***	—	0.092**	—	0.141***	—	0.079***
Political Change	—	0.043	—	0.048	—	-0.019	—	-0.003
Adj. R square	0.085	0.194	0.107	0.225	0.099	0.290	0.104	0.271
N	672	672	920	920	615	615	2,904	2,904

* Signif. LE 0.05, ** Signif. LE 0.01, *** Signif. LE 0.001.

Note 1: Sex is a dummy variable.

Note 2: All independent variables pass the Multicollinearity Test.

changes in government support. One clearly sees that the inclusion of the political culture variable contributes to an increase in the overall confidence level by 10 to 20 percent. The exact improvements for Hong Kong, Taiwan, urban China, and overall China are reflected in the following adjusted R Squares: .194, .225, .290, and .271, respectively. Our models best explain change in the urban China sample, followed by overall China, Taiwan, and Hong Kong. In Hong Kong, the most significant political culture variables are support for the political system, trust in virtuous leaders, and political liberty (beta = .192, .123, .119). In other words, low support for the political system, low trust in virtuous leaders, and little belief in political liberty will all lead to lower support for government. A different picture emerges in Taiwan, with popular accountability, age, and political liberty being the strongest independents (beta = .181, .166, .147). High levels of belief in popular accountability, youth, and emphasis on political liberty are all factors leading toward low levels of government support. With respect to the urban China sample, popular accountability, trust in virtuous leaders, and belief in political equality proved to be the strongest factors (beta = .215, .154, .146). The strength of these independents appears to result in lower levels of trust in government. For the whole of China, support for popular accountability, trust in virtuous leaders, and education had the greatest power to explain changes in government support (beta = .228, .208, .183). Accordingly, stronger belief in popular accountability, trust in virtuous leaders, and years of education are likely to lead to lower levels of government support.

Table 12.5 displays the multiple regression of socioeconomic background and measures of political culture, with support for the political system being the dependent variable. Using Model I and only incorporating socioeconomic background, social position, economic situation, and expectation, we find that all factors combined are able to explain less than 10 percent of the changes in level of support for the political system (adjusted R Square = Hong Kong .006, Taiwan .018, urban China .012, overall China .043). Of all single independent variables, education offers the strongest correlation, particularly in the overall China sample (beta = −.156). The second most significant factor is gender, especially in Hong Kong and overall China among male respondents (beta = Hong Kong −.088, mainland China −.053).

In Model II, we include the variables of political culture in the multiple regression. The overall ability to explain the dependent variable

Table 12.5

Socioeconomic Backgrounds, Political Culture, and Regime Support : Multiple Regression Analysis

Government support	HK		Taiwan		Urban China		All China	
Independent variable	Beta Model I	Beta Model II	Beta Model I	Beta Model II	Beta Model I	Beta Model II	Beta Model I	Beta Model II
Gender (male)	−0.088*	−0.074	−0.039	−0.050	0.014	0.003	−0.053**	−0.043*
Age	0.025	0.048	−0.003	0.037	0.027	0.038	−0.006	0.020
Education	0.080	0.014	−0.087	−0.125**	−0.034	−0.099*	−0.156***	−0.191***
Social status	−0.004	0.000	−0.040	−0.048	−0.103*	−0.110**	−0.036	−0.035
Present life	−0.050	−0.048	−0.084*	−0.051	−0.016	−0.017	−0.057**	−0.053**
Future life	0.074	0.062	−0.003	0.013	−0.043	−0.019	−0.050*	−0.038*
State priority	—	0.045	—	0.114**	—	0.160***	—	0.133***
National unity	—	0.043	—	0.126**	—	0.127**	—	0.084***
Political equality	—	0.007	—	0.000	—	−0.077	—	0.003
Accountability	—	0.017	—	0.072	—	0.132**	—	0.096***
Political liberty	—	−0.012	—	−0.007	—	−0.015	—	0.069***
Pluralism	—	−0.013	—	0.085*	—	−0.057	—	0.015
Separation	—	0.031	—	0.067*	—	−0.068	—	0.051**
Virtuous leaders	—	0.022	—	0.055	—	−0.004	—	0.021
Responsibility	—	−0.035	—	−0.013	—	0.071	—	0.044*
Gov. Support	—	0.223***	—	0.104*	—	0.173***	—	0.095***
Political Change	—	0.023	—	0.009	—	0.056	—	0.010
Adj. R square	0.006	0.050	0.018	0.123	0.012	0.134	0.043	0.128
N	672	672	920	920	615	615	2,904	2,904

* Signif. LE0.05, ** Signif. LE0.01, *** Signif. LE0.001.

Note 1: Sex is a dummy variable.

Note 2: All independent variables pass the Multicollinearity Test.

increases by 10 percent (adjusted R Square = Hong Kong .050, Taiwan .123, urban China .134, overall China .128). Urban China increases the most, followed by China overall, Taiwan, and Hong Kong. Taking a closer look at the Hong Kong sample, we find that our overall ability to explain is rather low, and we only find one individual factor moderately capable of explaining changes in the level of support for the current political system. This factor is trust in government, where low levels of trust tend to bring about a low level of support for the current political system (beta = .223). For the Taiwan sample we isolated three independents that show a higher ability to explain: state priority, education, and national unity (beta = .114, –.125, .126). In other words, a lower level of belief in state priority, fewer years of schooling, and lower level of belief in national unity are all likely to bring about a lower level of support for the current political system. For urban China, trust in government, belief in the priority of the state, and popular accountability are the three factors with the highest ability to explain (beta = .173, .160, .132). For overall China, the years of education received and belief in the priority of the state are the two factors with the highest ability to explain (beta = –.191, .133).

Table 12.6 depicts the results of the multiple regression between the same independent variables—socioeconomic background, social status, and political culture—as used in Tables 12.4 and 12.5, with belief in the feasibility of democratic reforms without worry about social unrest as the dependent variable. Following the same procedures as before, we only incorporate socioeconomic, social status, actual economic situation, and economic expectation in the first step, to explain changes in the belief in the necessity of further democratic reforms. In all four samples, we are only able to explain 5 percent of change from these factors (adjusted R Square = Hong Kong .049, Taiwan .071, urban China .066, overall China .063). We find education to be the most capable of the single independents in explaining changes. An increase in years of education brings about a clearly stronger belief in democratic reforms without worrying about social unrest (beta = Hong Kong .187, Taiwan .270, urban China .192, overall China .250).

If we include items of political culture as independent variables in the second step, we find that the overall ability of Model II in explaining changes regarding the level in belief in democratic reforms increases nearly 10 percent (adjusted R Square = Hong Kong .125, Taiwan .129, urban China .166, overall China .137). With respect to the Hong Kong

Table 12.6

Socioeconomic Backgrounds, Political Culture, and Political Change : Multiple Regression Analysis

Government support Independent variable	HK		Taiwan		Urban China		All China	
	Beta Model I	Beta Model II	Beta Model I	Beta Model II	Beta Model I	Beta Model II	Beta Model I	Beta Model II
Gender (male)	0.021	0.019	0.076*	0.070*	0.057	0.026	0.027	0.026
Age	-.051	-0.005	0.007	0.052	-0.081	-0.033	0.033	0.041
Education	0.187***	0.081	0.270***	0.175***	0.192***	0.066	0.250***	0.158***
Social status	-0.075	-0.068	-0.005	-0.007	0.068	0.067	0.037*	0.034
Present life	0.081	0.065	-0.017	0.002	0.035	0.021	0.022	0.023
Future life	-0.018	-0.005	-0.037	-0.038	-0.015	-0.010	0.000	0.005
State priority	—	-0.021	—	-0.035	—	-0.055	—	-0.018
National unity	—	0.019	—	0.005	—	-0.122**	—	-0.037*
Political equality	—	0.012	—	0.066*	—	0.083*	—	0.060**
Accountability	—	-0.017	—	0.078*	—	0.053	—	0.035
Political liberty	—	0.059	—	0.125***	—	0.137***	—	0.112***
Pluralism	—	0.254***	—	0.059	—	0.034	—	0.038*
Separation	—	-0.016	—	0.059	—	0.201***	—	0.176***
Virtuous leaders	—	0.043	—	0.021	—	0.053	—	070***
Responsibility	—	0.080*	—	0.023	—	0.048	—	-0.002
Gov. support	—	0.046	—	0.054	—	-0.023	—	-0.004
Regime support	—	0.021	—	0.009	—	0.054	—	-0.010
Adj. R square	0.049	0.125	0.071	0.129	0.066	0.166	0.063	0.137
N	672	672	920	920	615	615	2,904	2,904

* Signif. LE0.05, ** Signif. LE0.01, *** Signif. LE0.001.
Note 1: Sex is a dummy variable.
Note 2: All independent variables pass the Multicollinearity Test.

sample, we find that belief in political pluralism is the strongest component (beta = .254). A strong belief in political pluralism is likely to be associated with a view in favor of further democratization. For Taiwan, the strongest measures are education and belief in political liberty (beta = .175, .125). Thus, increased years of education and strong belief in political liberty bring about a perception of democratization as not jeopardizing social harmony. For the urban China sample, separation of power (horizontal accountability), political liberty, and national unity best explain changes in the dependent variable (beta = .201, .137, −.122). Belief in separation of powers, support for political liberty, and support for national unity tend to result in the belief that democratic reforms do not cause social disorder. In the overall China sample, support for separation of power, years of education, and belief in political liberty (beta = .176, .158, .112) are most able to explain changes in the belief in democratic reforms. High levels of support for separation of power, more years of education, and strong belief in political liberty tend to support a belief that democratic reforms do not cause social unrest.

Conclusion

In this chapter, we have attempted to examine the relations between socioeconomic development, institutional differences, and changes in political culture, as well as the implications of value changes for regime stability. The results of the multiple regression analysis can be summarized as follows:

First, political stability in all three culturally Chinese societies is affected by political culture to varying degrees. It is worth noting that there is a relatively strong resemblance between the Taiwan and overall China samples. Meanwhile the level of support for government by educated elites offers evidence of polarizing tendencies. As years of schooling increases, support for government decreases while support for the current political system rises. This indicates that the well educated are likely first to cast doubt on the incumbent elite before questioning the current political system itself. Therefore, in order to advance political reforms, the educated person is more inclined to choose a path within the existing framework than to strive to reform the system itself. In other words, educated people identify themselves with the system.

Second, socioeconomic status and economic expectation for the near future are unable to explain a considerable portion of change in the level of regime support. This is in fundamental opposition to a recent study on East European countries by Stephen Whitefield and Geoffrey Evans (Whitefield and Evans 1999). Obviously, the mass of society believes that one's personal situation is related to particular circumstances that the government and/or political system cannot be blamed for. Another possible difference between the three Chinese societies and Eastern Europe is that mainland China, Taiwan, and Hong Kong have all experienced economic success over the last decade, making this variable not very discerning. Even though the above generalization holds true, we still find a weak association in mainland China, where respondents who perceive their personal economic situation improved over the past and expect it to keep on improving are more likely to support the government and the political system. Conversely, a perception of a deteriorating personal economic situation tends to be associated with a decline in government and system support. This characteristic of the mainland China sample reflects the difference of the role played by the government in the economy. In Hong Kong, with a lower level of government involvement, personal economic situation and expectation are not as linked to government and system support.

Third, in Taiwan as in mainland China, state-value orientation is the most important factor in support of the current political system. High levels of belief in state priority and in national unity tend to be associated with high levels of support for the government and the system. In both societies, political stability seems to rest on nationalism. One may ask, if in both societies political stability rests on a strong belief in state priority and belief in national unity, why is it that Taiwan can start democratic reforms and mainland China cannot? The answer is closely related to Taiwan's special historical conditions, where during the period of authoritarianism the distribution of political power was uneven, with native Taiwanese being under-represented in terms of access to power.

Fourth, we found that respondents with a stronger democratic-value orientation are likely to support the political regime but are also likely to show low levels of government support and to criticize the government. It is important to understand that high levels of democratic-value orientation do not necessarily indicate that a high potential for a democratic movement is present. The primary reason is that people are willing to accept the system as long as critical mistakes remain absent.

Finally, in respect to the moral-state orientation, we found that government responsibility and high levels of trust in virtuous leaders were related to government support; but that there is no detectable association with support of the current political regime.

In sum, we find a shift in political culture has important implications for political stability throughout all three societies. In mainland China, whether for urban or all of China, we find high levels of belief in state priority and national unity providing the authoritarian regime a basis for legitimacy. In Taiwan, the Taiwanese consciousness integrates democratization with transformation of the old ruling elite. And in Hong Kong, cultural factors have less of an impact on political stability. This is not at all surprising. Before 1997, the people in Hong Kong were inclined to think that they lived in a "borrowed time in a borrowed place." They tended to acquire a very practical and instrumental orientation toward the political system. The colonial administration was judged by its administrative efficiency and cleanness. It was not evaluated on the basis of democratic legitimacy, nor supported by a traditional sense of moralism.

Appendix: A Note on Survey Methodology

In both Taiwan and Hong Kong, territory-wide stratified random sampling based on the PPS (probability proportional to size) criterion was drawn. The survey in Hong Kong was conducted during May 1993 under the supervision of Professors Hsin-chi Kuan and Siu-kai Lau of Chinese University, Hong Kong. The survey in Taiwan was conducted during June and July of 1993 under the supervision of Professors Fu Hu, Yun-han Chu, and Ming-tong Chen of National Taiwan University and Dr. Huo-yan Shyu of Academia Sinica.

In both Taiwan and Hong Kong, scientifically reliable sampling depends on having excellent official household registration data to serve as a sampling frame. Such data did not exist in mainland China, but Professor Tianjian Shi and his colleagues at the Survey Research Center of the People's University have substantially solved the sampling problem for the mainland, providing what is, so far as we know, the first and only scientifically valid national-level sampling frame for the mainland. This "master sample" remains valid for ten years from the date of construction. It was put to use for the first time in the 1990 pilot survey. The national survey was conducted from October 1993 to March 1994 under the supervision of Professor Tianjian Shi. As a check on interviewer reliability, up to one-twentieth of all interviews were randomly selected for double-checking, with a supervisor making sure that the interview was conducted with the person indicated. In addition, each of the prospective interviewees received a letter from the central office to tell them that an interviewer would visit the family within a certain period of time and to ask for their cooperation. All three of our questionnaires are in Chinese; cross-cultural equivalency is less of a problem than it would be in a multi-language survey. Yet, due to dialectal and, especially, sociopolitical differences among the three regions, the three questionnaires are not exactly identical.

Notes

1. See Barnes and Simon, eds. (1998); Diamond (1999); Eckstein et al. (1998); Handelman and Tessler (1999); Inglehart (1990, 1997); McDonough et al. (1998); Rose et al. (1998); Schaffer (1998); Shin (1999).
2. The project is a collaborative effort among nine principal investigators. The eight other members are Andrew Nathan, James Tong, Hsin-chi Kuan, Siu-kai Lau, Tianjian Shi, Fu Hu, Ming-tong Chen, and Huo-yan Shyu. The views presented in this paper are the authors' alone.
3. The principle of majority rule is not explicitly included in our conceptual formulation. If Arend Lijphart (1999) is correct, then majoritarian rule is not a first-order principle of Western democracy, or at least it is always qualified by respect for minorities and a requirement of consensus.
4. For a non-technical note of the survey methodology, see Appendix.

References

Alexander, Jeffrey C. 1990. "Analytic Debates: Understanding the Relative Autonomy of Culture." In Jeffrey C. Alexander and Steven Seidman (eds.), *Culture and Society: Contemporary Debates*, pp. 1–27. Cambridge: Cambridge University Press.
Almond, Gabriel A. 1980. "The Intellectual History of the Civic Culture Concept." In Gabriel A. Almond and Sidney Verba (eds.), *The Civic Culture Revisited*, pp. 1–36. Boston: Little, Brown and Company.
———. 1990. "The Study of Political Culture." In Gabriel A. Almond (ed.), *A Discipline Divided: Schools and Sects in Political Science*, pp. 138–169. London: Sage Publications.
Almond, Gabriel A., and Sidney Verba. 1963. *The Civic Culture: Political Attitudes and Democracy in Five Nations*. Princeton: Princeton University Press.
Barnes, Samuel H., and Janos Simon, eds. 1998. *The Postcommunist Citizen*. Budapest: Erasmus Foundation.
Barry, Brian. 1970. *Sociologists, Economists and Democracy*. Chicago: University of Chicago Press.

Booth, John A., and Mitchell A Seligson. 1984. "The Political Culture of Authoritarianism in Mexico: A Reexamination." *Latin American Research Review* 19(1): 106–124.

Chazan, Naomi. 1993. "Between Liberalism and Statism: African Political Cultures and Democracy." In Larry Diamond (ed.), *Political Culture and Democracy in Developing Countries*, pp. 67–106. Boulder: Lynne Rienner.

Chu, Yun-han. 1992. *Crafting Democracy in Taiwan*. Taipei: Institute for National Policy Research.

Dalton, Russell J. 1991. "Communists and Democrats: Attitudes toward Democracy in the two Germanies." Paper presented at the annual meeting of the American Political Science Association, Washington, D.C.

Diamond, Larry. 1993. "Political Culture and Democracy." In Larry Diamond (ed.), *Political Culture and Democracy in Developing Countries*, pp. 1–36. Boulder: Lynne Rienner.

———. 1999. *Developing Democracy: Toward Consolidation*. Baltimore: The Johns Hopkins University Press.

Dittmer, Lowell. 1977. "Political Culture and Political Symbolism: Toward a Theoretical Synthesis." *World Politics* 29(4): 552–583.

Eckstein, Harry. 1988. "A Culturalist Theory of Political Change." *American Political Science Review* 82(3): 789–804.

Eckstein, Harry, Frederic J. Fleron Jr., Erik P. Hoffmann, and Willian M. Reisinger. 1998. *Can Democracy Take Root in Post-Soviet Russia: The Explorations in State Society Relation*. New York: Rowman and Littlefield.

Elkins, David, and Richard E. Simeon. 1979. "A Cause in Search of Its Effects, or What Does Political Culture Explain." *Comparative Politics*, 11(2): 127–145.

Fagen, Richard J. 1969. *The Transformation of Political Culture in Cuba*. Stanford: Stanford University Press.

Gibbins, John R. 1989. "Contemporary Political Culture: An Introduction." In John R. Gibbins (ed.), *Contemporary Political Culture: Politics in a Postmodern Age*, pp. 1–30. London: Sage Publications.

Girvin, Brian. 1989. "Change and Continuity in Liberal Democratic Political Culture." In John R. Gibbins (ed.), *Contemporary Political Culture*, pp. 31–51. London: Sage Publications.

Handelman, Howard, and Mark Tessler, eds. 1999. *Democracy and Its Limits: Lessons from Asia, Latin America, and the Middle East*. Notre Dame: University of Notre Dame Press.

Hu, Fu, and Yun-han Chu. 1992. "The Development of New Partisanship in Taiwan's Regime Transition." Paper presented at the 1992 annual meeting of the American Political Science Association, Chicago.

———. 1996. "Neo-Authoritarianism, Polarized Conflict and Populism in a Newly Democratizing Regime: Taiwan's Emerging Mass Politics." *Journal of Contemporary China* 5(11): 23–41.

Inglehart, Ronald. 1988. "The Renaissance of Political Culture." *American Political Science Review* 82(4):1203–1230.

———. 1990. *Culture Shift: In Advanced Industrial Society*. Princeton: Princeton University Press.

———. 1997. *Modernization and Postmodernization: Cultural, Economic and Political Change in 43 Societies*. Princeton : Princeton University Press.

Klesner, Joseph L. 1998. "An Electoral Route to Democracy?: Mexico's Transition in Comparative Perspective." *Comparative Politics* 30(4): 477–497.

Lane, Ruth. 1992. "Political Culture: Residual Category or General Theory." *Comparative Political Studies* 25(3): 362–87.

Lau, Siu-kai, and Hsin-chi Kuan. 1988. *The Ethos of the Hong Kong Chinese.* Hong Kong: The Chinese University Press.

Lijphart, Arend. 1980. "The Structure of Inference." In Gabriel A. Almond and Sidney Verba (eds.), *The Civic Culture Revisited,* pp. 37–56. Boston: Little Brown.

———. 1999. *Patterns of Democracy: Government Forms and Performance in Thirty-Six Countries.* New Haven: Yale University Press.

McDonough, Peter, Samuel H. Barnes, and Antonio Lopez Pina. 1998. *The Cultural Dynamics of Democratization in Spain.* Ithaca: Cornell University Press.

Nathan, Andrew J., and Tianjian Shi. 1993. "Cultural Requisites for Democracy in China: Findings from a Survey." *Daedalus* 122(2): 95–123.

Pateman, Carole. 1971. "Political Culture, Political Structure and Political Change." *British Journal of Political Science* 1: 291–305.

———. 1980. "The Civic Culture: A Philosophic Critique." In Gabriel A. Almond and Sidney Verba (eds.), *The Civic Culture Revisited,* pp. 265–314. Boston: Little Brown.

Patricks, Glenda M. 1984. "Political Culture." In Giovanni Sartori (ed.), *Social Science Concepts: A Systematic Analysis,* pp. 265–314. London: Sage Publications.

Putnam, Robert D. 1993. *Making Democracy Work: Civic Tradition in Modern Italy.* Princeton: Princeton University Press.

Pye, Lucian W. 1985. *Asian Power and Politics: The Cultural Dimensions of Authority.* Cambridge, MA: Harvard University Press.

———. 1990. "Political Science and the Crisis of Authoritarianism." *American Political Science Review* 84(1): 1–19.

Rose, Richard, Willian Mishler, and Christian Haerpfer. 1998. *Democracy and Its Alternatives: Understanding Post-Communist Society.* Baltimore: The Johns Hopkins University Press.

Schaffer, Frederic C. 1998. *Democracy in Translation: Understanding Politics in an Unfamiliar Culture.* Ithaca: Cornell University Press.

Shi, Tianjian. 1997. *Political Participation in Beijing.* Cambridge, MA: Harvard University Press.

Shin, Doh Chull. 1994. "On the Third Wave of Democratization: A Synthesis and Evaluation of Recent Theory and Research." *World Politics* 47(1): 135–170.

———. 1999. *Mass Politics and Culture in Democratizing Korea.* Cambridge: Cambridge University Press.

Street, John. 1993. "Review Article: Political Culture—From Civic Culture to Mass Culture." *British Journal of Political Science* 24(1): 95–114.

Thompson, Michael, Richard Ellis, and Aaron Wildavsky. 1990. *Cultural Theory.* Boulder: Westview Press.

Whitefield, Stephen, and Geoffrey Evans. 1999. "Political Culture versus Rational Choice: Explaining Responses to Transition in the Czech Republic and Slovakia." *British Journal of Political Science* 29(1): 129–154.

Contributors

Roger Ames is Professor of Philosophy and Director of the Center for Chinese Studies, University of Hawaii. His major publications include *Self and Deception: A Cross Cultural Philosophical Inquiry* (ed. with W. Dissanayke; 1996); *Sun Pin: The Art of Warfare* (with D.C. Lau; Ballantine, 1996); and *Anticipating China: Thinking through the Narratives of Chinese and Western Culture* (with David Hall; 1995). Professor Ames is the editor of *Philosophy East and West* and *China Review International*.

Yu-tzung Chang received his baccalaureate and his doctorate in political science at National Chengchi University. He is currently Senior Researcher for the East Asian Democratization and Value Changes Project at National Taiwan University. He has published articles examining democratization, voting behavior, and identity politics in Taiwan.

Godwin Chu joined the East-West Center as a Senior Fellow in 1973 and is currently Emeritus Senior Fellow. His major publications include *The Great Wall in Ruins: Communication and Cultural Change in China* (with Yanan Ju, 1993), *Rural Chinese Family in Transition* (with Wu Shengling and Yu Zhenwei, 1993), *To See Ourselves: Comparing Traditional Chinese and American Cultural Values* (with Zhongdang Pan, Steven Chaffee, and Yannan Ju, 1994).

Yun-han Chu is Professor of Political Science at National Taiwan University and serves concurrently as Director of the East Asian Democratization and Value Changes Project at National Taiwan University. He has written a number of essays on constitutional reform and is co-editor of *Consolidating the Third Wave Democracies* (1997).

Edward Friedman is the Hawkins Chair Professor of Political Science at the University of Wisconsin, Madison. His major publications include *The Politics of Democratization: Generalizing the East Asian Experience* (1994), *National Identity and Democratic Prospects in Socialist China* (1995), and *What if China Doesn't Democratize? Implications for War and Peace* (2000). Friedman is on the editorial board of *China Perspectives, Journal of Contemporary China, The American Asian Review*, and *Pacific Affairs*.

Shiping Hua is Assistant Professor of Political Science, Eckerd College. He is the author of *Scientism and Humanism: Two Cultures in Post-Mao China* (1995). He is a member of the editorial board of *Asian Thought and Society*. His articles have appeared in *Modern China, Bulletin of Concerned Asian Scholars, Asian Thought and Society*, and other journals. His forthcoming book is titled *Utopianism in Chinese Political Culture*.

Huixin Ke is with the Survey and Statistics Institute, Beijing Broadcast Institute, Beijing, China. She received her Doctor of Science from Kyushu University in 1989. She is a professor and the director of the Survey and Statistics Institute at Beijing Broadcast Institute. Her main research interests include communication research methodology and the application of statistics in public opinion and marketing research. She has published a number of books (in Chinese) including *Statistical Analysis in Survey Research* (1992), *Practices of Public Opinion Survey* (1996), *The Techniques that Make You Smarter: Statistical Concepts and Methods in Daily Life* (1996), and *Marketing Survey and Analysis* (2000).

Cheng Li is Professor of Political Science at Hamilton College, New York, and a member of the Institute of Current World Affairs in Hanover, New Hampshire. He is the author of *Rediscovering China: Dynamics and Dilemmas of Reform* (1997) and *China's Leaders: The New Generation* (2001). He is currently writing a book on Chinese technocrats and their domestic and foreign policies as well as their interaction with entrepreneurs and public intellectuals. Li's academic writings have appeared in *World Politics, Asian Survey, The China*

Quarterly, *The China Journal*, *Modern China*, and various edited volumes. He discourses frequently on China and Sino-U.S. relations for the BBC, CNN, C-SPAN, the Voice of America, and the PBS News Hour with Jim Lehrer.

Alan P.L. Liu is Professor of Political Science, University of California, Santa Barbara. His major publications include *How China is Ruled* (1986), *Phoenix and the Lame Lion: Modernization in Taiwan and Mainland China, 1950–80* (1987), and *Mass Politics in the People's Republic* (1996). His articles have appeared in *The American Political Science Review*, *Asian Survey*, *Journal of International Affairs*, *Journalism Quarterly*, and *Political Psychology*. He is an Associate Editor and a member of the editorial board of *Asian Thought and Society*.

Kam Louie is Director of the Asian Studies Centre at the University of Queensland. He is the author and co-author of a number of books on Chinese philosophy, literature, language, and culture, including *The Literature of China in the Twentieth Century* (1997), *The Politics of Chinese Language and Culture* (1998), and *Theorizing Chinese Masculinity* (forthcoming). He is an editorial board member of *The China Journal* and the editor of *Asian Studies Review*.

Kalpalna Misra is an Associate Professor of Political Science at the University of Tulsa. Her areas of specialization are Chinese politics, international relations, and the women's movements of Asia. She is the author of *From Post-Maoism to Post-Marxism: The Erosion of Official Ideology in Deng's China* (1998), and co-author of *Advanced Political Theory* (1987). Her articles have appeared in *Strategic Analysis*, *China Report*, *Women in Politics*, and *Contemporary South Asia*. She currently directs the International Studies Certificate Program at the University of Tulsa and also serves on the governing board of the Certificate in Women's Studies.

Peter Moody, Jr. is Professor of Government and International Studies at the University of Notre Dame. He specializes in the study of Chinese politics and in Asian politics and international affairs generally. His books include *Tradition and Modernization in China and Japan* (1994), *Political Change in Taiwan* (1991), and *Political Op-*

position in Post-Confucian Society (1988). He is the book review editor of the *Review of Politics.*

Andrew Nathan is Professor of Political Science, Columbia University. Nathan's recent publications include *China's Crisis* (1990), *The Great Wall and the Empty Fortress* (with Robert S. Ross; 1997), and *China's Transition* (1997). He is chairman of the Advisory Committee of Human Rights Watch/Asia and serves on the editorial boards of *The China Quarterly, Journal of Contemporary China,* and *China Information,* among others.

Chih-yu Shih is Professor of Political Science, National Taiwan University. Shih teaches political psychology, international politics, and Chinese Studies at National Taiwan University. He writes on postcolonial feminism and is a Miao descendent acculturated to Han. Most of his publications, including *The Spirit of Chinese Foreign Policy* (1990), *State and Society in China's Political Economy* (1995), *Collective Democracy,* and *Postmodern National Identity,* draw lessons from Chinese historical literature as well as from field interviews in China. Outside of the academic curriculum, he coaches intramural basketball and has accumulated eight national titles, which he seriously considers intrinsic to his epistemology of China studies.

Wenfang Tang is Associate Professor of Political Science, University of Pittsburgh. His major publications include *Chinese Urban Life under Reform: The Changing Social Contract* (with William L. Parish; 2000) and *Who Should Rule? Enterprise Decision Making in Contemporary China* (1996). His articles have appeared in *Journal of Contemporary China, Journal of Public Policy, American Journal of Political Science,* and *Mid-American Journal of Political Science.*

Jonathan J.H. Zhu, Associate Professor, English Department, City University of Hong Kong, received his Ph.D. in Mass Communications from Indiana University in 1990. He was an assistant/associate professor of communication sciences at the University of Connecticut and is currently an associate professor of communication and new media at the City University of Hong Kong. His research interests include media agenda-setting, presidential elections, journalistic professionalism, the diffusion of new media technologies, and survey methodology in the Chinese context. He has published in *Journal of Communication, Human Communication Research, Public Opinion Quarterly, International Public Opinion Quarterly, Journalism and Mass Communication Quarterly, Journalism Monographs, Gazette, Asian Survey, Asian Journal of Communication, The Journal of Contemporary China,* and elsewhere.

Index

F

Fa Yang, 258
Fagen, Richard J., 321
Fairbank, John King, 221
Falun Gong, 4, 13, 64, 181–182
Family
  in electoral politics, 289–290,
    293
  impact of economic reform,
    52
  traditional values of, 44, 45
Fan Liqin, 143
Fan Shuzi, 257
Fang Lizhi, 151
Fangzheng Company, 234
Farewell, My Concubine, 10
Fei Xiaotong, 261
Fei Zhengzhong, 257
Feng Baozhi, 260
Feng Chen, 140
Feng Youlan, 28
Filial piety (*xiao*), 45
Fitzgerald, John, 162
Five-Anti movement, 52–53
Folk religions, 302, 305,
    306, 309, 311, 314, 315,
    318
Four Clean-Ups movement, 58
"Four Olds," 4
Freud, Sigmund, 301
Friedman, Edward, 14, 103–132,
    154
Friedrich, Carl J., 161
Frieman, Jonathan, 252
Fu Boyan, 264
Fu Rui, 232
Fu Yan, 232
Fudan University, 237
Fujian, 255, 256–259

G

Gamson, William A., 188
Gang of Four, 32, 34, 55, 56–57
Gansu, 264–265
Gao, Professor, 289, 290
Gao Fang, 258
Gao Xin, 230
Gao Yangwen, 231
Geertz, Clifford, 7
Gender
  and Confucianism, 25–29
  and nationalism, 107–108
Geng Yunzhi, 257
Gerbner, George, 190
Giant Company, 235
Girvin, Brian, 322
Gold, Thomas, 166
Goldman, Merle, 179
Gong Guan, 261
Great Leap Forward, 4, 137
Great Wall, 83
Gross, Larry, 190
Gu Hongliang, 257
Gu Xin, 85
Gu Yaochang, 258
Guan Lianzhu, 262
Guan Yu (god), 23, 25, 26
Guangdong, 255, 256–259
Guangmin daily, 30
Guangxi, 264–265
Guizhou, 264–265
Guo Qiang, 262
Guo Xuegao, 264

H

Haicheng, 267–268
Half of Man Is Woman (Zhang
    Xianliang), 32

Hall, David L., 23, 87
Hamilton, Malcolm, 300
Han Boping, 231
Han Yangmin, 247
Hartshorne, Charles, 91
Hauss, Charles, 13
He Jun, 258
He Long, 232
He Pengfei, 232
He Pin, 230
He Ping, 232
He Qinglian, 231
He Shang, 12
He Zhou, 190
Hebei, 247, 255, 259–263
Heilongjiang, 255, 260–263, 267
Henan, 247, 255, 259–263
Hershock, Peter, 75, 76
Hiroshima, 108–109
Hodge, Bob, 23
Hofstede, Geert, 34
Hong Kong
  investments in China, 259
  political culture in, 328, 329–345
Hong Kong, mainland attitudes
    toward, 14, 189–190
  cognitive base for, 190, 193–194,
    197–200, 208
  on handover of 1997, 191,
    194–195, 202–208
  media effects in, 191, 195–197,
    203, 204, 206–208, 209,
    210–211
  methodology and measurement of
    study, 192–197, 211–214
  objectives of study, 190–192
  perceived images in, 190–191,
    194, 200–202, 208
Hong Ying, 105
Horne, Gerald, 118

Horowitz, Donald L., 266
Hoston, Germaine, 162
Hou Dejian, 104
Hou Yijie, 257
Hoynes, William, 188
Hu Angang, 149
Hu Anquan, 257
Hu Dongyuan, 36
Hu Fu, 321, 344
Hu Jingzhou, 262
Hu Jiwei, 146, 151
Hu Ping, 104
Hu Qiaomu, 135, 141, 144
Hu Shi, 4, 70
Hu Yaobang, 55, 164
Hua Mulan, 26
Hua Shiping, 3–17, 7, 10, 12, 13
Huang Dimin, 265
Huang Jianhui, 261
Huang Jingzheng, 264
Huang Renwei, 268
Huang Zhong, 258
Huixin Ke, 188–215
Human relational culture, 277–278
Human rights, 125–126
Hunan, 255–256, 263–264
Hundred Flowers Movement, 4, 30,
    53, 61
Hungarian Revolution of 1956, 53
Huntington, 302
Hussein, Saddam, 113, 124

I

Ideological trends, 133–134
  demotion of Marxism, 138
  in Jiang Zemin era, 154–156
  neo-Conservatism, 146–153
  neo-Maoism, 14, 134–145, 155
  See also Antipolitics; Nationalism

Provincial identity *(continued)*
and North-South division,
247–249
parochial, 264–265
separatist, 265
traditionalist, 255, 259–263
transitional, 255–256, 263–264
Public opinion surveys
in China *vs* West, 12
deficiences of, 7
on Hong Kong, mainland attitudes
toward, 189–214
on Hong Kong/Taiwan/mainland
political culture, 329–345
on religiosity/religious values,
298–318
on submission to authority,
55–57
Public-Private Joint Management
campaign, 53
Purges, 58–59
Putnam, Robert D., 251, 256, 322,
334–335
Pye, Lucian W., 5, 11, 12, 320

Q

Qian Xiaoqian, 257
Qian Yingyi, 267
Qiao Renlin, 261
Qiao Shi, 238
Qiao Zhiqiang, 261
Qinghua University, 234, 237

R

Red Flag, 165
Red Guards, 11, 62
Regime legitimacy, 324–327,
331–333, 343

Regional cultures. *See* Provincial
identity
Religion
class model of, 301
conditions of religiosity,
305–311, 312–313,
315–316
culturalist view of, 301
and democratic/capitalist values,
302, 311, 314–315
methodology and measurement
Provincial identity, 246–247
of study, 298–300, 302–305
modernization theory of,
300–301
Ren Kelei, 239
Ren Shuang, 249
Richards, I.A., 73–74, 77
Riker, William H., 267
Riskin, Karl, 142
Rong Jian, 147
Rosen, Stanley, 117
Rowe, Sharon, 27
Rural areas
cadre/peasant relationship, 50–51
communication channels in, 52,
63
economic inequality in, 142
under economic reform, 51–52, 59
elections in ethnic villages,
278–295
entrepreneurs from, 223–225, 237
loyalty concept in, 49–50, 58–59,
60
new political culture in, 52, 58–61,
62–63
revolutionary campaigns in, 48–49
Rural household contract
responsibility system, 229
Russia, 140

Studies on Contemporary China